IFIP Advances in Information and Communication Technology

520

Editor-in-Chief

Kai Rannenberg, Goethe University Frankfurt, Germany

IFIP – The International Federation for Information Processing

IFIP was founded in 1960 under the auspices of UNESCO, following the first World Computer Congress held in Paris the previous year. A federation for societies working in information processing, IFIP's aim is two-fold: to support information processing in the countries of its members and to encourage technology transfer to developing nations. As its mission statement clearly states:

IFIP is the global non-profit federation of societies of ICT professionals that aims at achieving a worldwide professional and socially responsible development and application of information and communication technologies.

IFIP is a non-profit-making organization, run almost solely by 2500 volunteers. It operates through a number of technical committees and working groups, which organize events and publications. IFIP's events range from large international open conferences to working conferences and local seminars.

The flagship event is the IFIP World Computer Congress, at which both invited and contributed papers are presented. Contributed papers are rigorously refereed and the rejection rate is high.

As with the Congress, participation in the open conferences is open to all and papers may be invited or submitted. Again, submitted papers are stringently refereed.

The working conferences are structured differently. They are usually run by a working group and attendance is generally smaller and occasionally by invitation only. Their purpose is to create an atmosphere conducive to innovation and development. Refereeing is also rigorous and papers are subjected to extensive group discussion.

Publications arising from IFIP events vary. The papers presented at the IFIP World Computer Congress and at open conferences are published as conference proceedings, while the results of the working conferences are often published as collections of selected and edited papers.

IFIP distinguishes three types of institutional membership: Country Representative Members, Members at Large, and Associate Members. The type of organization that can apply for membership is a wide variety and includes national or international societies of individual computer scientists/ICT professionals, associations or federations of such societies, government institutions/government related organizations, national or international research institutes or consortia, universities, academies of sciences, companies, national or international associations or federations of companies.

More information about this series at http://www.springer.com/series/6102

Lazaros Iliadis · Ilias Maglogiannis
Vassilis Plagianakos (Eds.)

Artificial Intelligence Applications and Innovations

AIAI 2018 IFIP WG 12.5 International Workshops
SEDSEAL, 5G-PINE, MHDW, and HEALTHIOT
Rhodes, Greece, May 25–27, 2018
Proceedings

 Springer

Editors
Lazaros Iliadis
School of Engineering
Democritus University of Thrace
Xanthi
Greece

Vassilis Plagianakos
University of Thessaly
Lamia
Greece

Ilias Maglogiannis
University of Piraeus
Piraeus
Greece

ISSN 1868-4238   ISSN 1868-422X (electronic)
IFIP Advances in Information and Communication Technology
ISBN 978-3-030-06348-1   ISBN 978-3-319-92016-0   (eBook)
https://doi.org/10.1007/978-3-319-92016-0

Printed on acid-free paper

This Springer imprint is published by the registered company Springer International Publishing AG part of Springer Nature
The registered company address is: Gewerbestrasse 11, 6330 Cham, Switzerland

Preface

It is a fact that the world is changing extremely fast. Technological advances in artificial intelligence (AI) are leading this change. We have already passed from theory and algorithmic approaches, to actual delivery with several real-life practical applications. We have entered the fourth "industrial revolution" era. AI will definitely rupture the human-centric status of our civilization. Many philosophical and ethical issues will arise mainly due to the challenge and fear that the machines might take over. However, the contribution of AI so far to the improvement of our quality of life is profound. The AIAI conference offers insight into all timely challenges related to intelligent systems-algorithms and their applications.

AIAI is a mature European conference, well established in the scientific area of AI. It has a very long and successful history, following and spreading the evolution of AI. The first event was organized in Toulouse, France, in 2004. Since then, it has had a continuous and dynamic presence as a major European scientific event. More specifically, it has been organized in China, Greece, Cyprus, and France.

Through the years it has always been technically supported by the International Federation for Information Processing (IFIP) and more specifically by the WG12.5.

Following a long-standing tradition, this Springer volume belongs to the IFIP AICT Springer series and it contains the papers that were accepted for oral presentation at the workshops held as parallel events of the 14th AIAI conference. An additional volume comprises the papers that were accepted and presented at the 14th AIAI main conference.

The event was held May 25–27, 2018, in the Aldemar Amilia Mare five-star Hotel in Rhodes, Greece.

Four scientific workshops on timely AI subjects were organized successfully during the 2018 event:

- The 7th Mining Humanistic Data Workshop (MHDW) supported by the Ionian University and the University of Patras, Greece. The 7th MHDW was organized by Professor Christos Makris, Department of Computer Engineering and Informatics, University of Patras, Professor Phivos Mylonas Department of Informatics, Ionian University, Dr. Andreas Kanavos, Department of Computer Engineering and Informatics, University of Patras, and Georgios Drakopoulos, Department of Informatics, Ionian University Greece. The Steering Committee of MHDW 2018 comprised Dr. Ioannis Karydis, Department of Informatics, Ionian University, Professor Katia Lida Kermanidis Department of Informatics, Ionian University, and Professor Spyros Sioutas, Department of Informatics, Ionian University. We express our sincere appreciation to the committees of MHDW 2018 for organizing this important event for the seventh consecutive time.
- The Third Workshop on 5G-Putting Intelligence to the Network Edge (5G-PINE 2018). The Third 5G-PINE was driven by the hard work of Dr. Ioannis P. Chochliouros (Hellenic Telecommunications Organization, OTE,

Greece) Dr. Alexandros Kostopoulos (OTE, Greece), Professors Oriol Sallent and Jordi Pérez-Romero (Universitat Politècnica de Catalunya UPC, Spain), Dr. Ioannis Neokosmidis (INCITES Consulting S.A.R.L, Luxembourg), Professor Fidel Liberal (Universidad del Pais Vasco/Euskal Herriko Unibertsitatea EHU, Spain), Dr. Emmanouil Kafetzakis (ORION Innovations Company, Greece), and Dr. Ioannis Giannoulakis (National Center for Scientific Research, Demokritos, Greece). We would like to thank all of these colleagues for their hard work.

- The Workshop on Semantics in the Deep: Semantic Analytics for Big Data (SEDSEAL 2018) supported by the University of Patras, Greece. The workshop was organized by Professor Spiridon D. Likothanasis, Department of Computer Engineering and Informatics, University of Patras, and Dr. Dimitrios Koutsomitropoulos, University of Patras, Greece. We wish to express our gratitude to these colleagues for their invaluable contribution.
- The Intelligent Cloud and IOT Paradigms in EHealth (HEALTHIOT). This scientific event was organized by Professor Ilias Maglogiannis, Department of Digital Systems, University of Piraeus, Greece, Dimosthenis Kyriazis, Department of Digital Systems, University of Piraeus, Greece, and Vassilios Plagianakos, Department of Computer Science and Biomedical Informatics, University of Thessaly, Greece. We are very happy for the important contribution of this workshop to the success of AIAI 2018.

The diverse nature of papers presented at the AIAI 2018 workshops demonstrates the vitality of neural computing and related soft computing approaches.

The Organizing Committee was delighted by the overwhelming response to the call for papers. All workshops papers went through a peer review process by at least two independent academic referees. Where needed, a third reviewer was consulted to resolve any conflicts.

Full accepted papers were presented orally for 20 minutes each and were included in the AIAI 2018 workshops proceedings with 12 pages maximum. Owing to the high quality of the submissions, the Program Committees of the workshops decided to additionally accept short papers that were given 15 minutes for oral presentation and 10 pages each in the proceedings. The workshops followed the same rules as the main event. More specifically, 5G-PINE accepted six full papers (42.85%) and one short one out of 14 submissions, whereas MHDW accepted seven full (46.6%) and four short papers out of 15 submissions. HealthIOT accepted four full papers (44.5%) out of nine contributions, and SEDSEAL accepted two full papers out of five submissions (40%).

The accepted papers of the AIAI 2018 workshops are related to the following thematic topics:

- AI in 5G and telecommunications
- AI and e-health services
- AI in 5G networks
- Incremental learning
- Clustering
- AI in text mining
- Visual data analytics
- AI in molecular biology, DNA, RNA, proteins

- Big data analytics
- Internet of Things and recommender systems
- AI in biomedical applications

The authors of the 14th AIAI workshops came from 13 different countries from all over the globe, namely: Europe (Austria, France, Germany, Greece, Ireland, Italy, Luxembourg, Poland, Spain, UK), America (Brazil, USA), and Asia (India).

We hope that these proceedings will help researchers worldwide to understand and to be aware of novel AI aspects. We do believe that they will be of major interest for scientists over the globe and that they will stimulate further research in the domain of AI in general.

May 2018

Lazaros Iliadis
Ilias Maglogiannis
Vassilis Plagianakos

Preface to SEDSEAL 2018

During the past decade, the field of artificial intelligence (AI) has been experiencing an outburst of applications and innovations, having many facets: on the one hand, there are strong symbolic representations to underpin the next generation of the Web, and the advent of the Semantic Web has a major role in giving everyday browsing tasks a blend of intelligence; and on the other hand, deep learning techniques and achievements have been proven to tackle problems that would seem intractable some time ago. The wide availability of information on the Internet, storage space, and Web-generated content add more impetus to devising applications that would take advantage of such unprecedented resources but would also stand up to the challenges posed by processing and value extraction out of big data.

The SEDSEAL 2018 workshop's particular aim was exactly to put emphasis on big data analysis and more specifically on how semantics-aware applications can contribute in this field. Still, there are often issues that need to be dealt with. These range from efficient ontological processing of big data ontologies to knowledge graph maintenance to ontology evolvement with machine-learning techniques.

Semantic interoperability inside data lakes composed of vast IoT networks is addressed by Kalamaras et al. The authors propose an architecture for big data analytics in the context of large-scale IoT systems consisting of multiple IoT platforms. The efficient management of the spectrum crunch in the field of wireless communication necessitates processing of a large volume of information and requires knowledge-based decision-making upon ever-changing circumstances. Nagpure et al. explain how semantic models can be employed to analyze complex spectrum data. Semantic ambiguity in natural language has been a problem that traditionally hampers Semantic Web applications. To resolve this ambiguity, Gadag and Sagar describe a deep learning architecture, trained to compute semantic similarity between words.

Indeed, the interplay between the logical formalisms of the Semantic Web and machine- and deep-learning techniques is currently a hot research topic for both technologies to reach their next step and forms the state of the art in this area. We believe that the overall outcome of the SEDSEAL 2018 workshop can offer a valuable and timely snapshot, bringing together a multidisciplinary audience under the general AI and data science framework, of current advances, practices, and lessons learned.

We were honored to have Prof. Panos Kalnis as the SEDSEAL keynote speaker, to whom we express our gratitude for kindly accepting our invitation. There could be no better way than his motivating lecture on scalable querying of big RDF data to open this workshop. We are grateful to the number of people who served in the SEDSEAL 2018 Program Committee. Their eager participation and thoughtful remarks have been invaluable. We would also like to thank the AIAI 2018 chair, Prof. Lazaros Iliadis, and the workshop co-chairs, Profs. Christos Makris and Spiros Sioutas, for their help and support for a successful SEDSEAL 2018.

Dimitrios A. Koutsomitropoulos
Spiridon D. Likothanassis

Organization

Program Chairs

Dimitrios A.   University of Patras, Greece
   Koutsomitropoulos
Spiridon D. Likothanassis   University of Patras, Greece

Program Committee

Christos Alexakos   University of Patras, Greece
Andreas Andreou   Cyprus University of Technology, Cyprus
Efstratios Georgopoulos   Technological Institute of Kalamata, Greece
Dimitrios   University of Patras, Greece
   Koutsomitropoulos
Spiridon Likothanassis   University of Patras, Greece
Vassilis Plagianakos   University of Thessaly, Greece
Filipe Portela   University of Minho, Spain
Miguel-Angel Sicilia   University of Alcala, Spain
Dimitrios Tsolis   University of Patras, Greece
Jouni Tuominen   University of Helsinki, Finland
Dimitrios Tzovaras   CERTH/ITI, Greece
Konstantinos Votis   CERTH/ITI, Greece
Minjuan Wang   San Diego State University, USA

Preface to 5G-PINE 2018

The Third 5G-PINE Workshop has been established to disseminate knowledge obtained from actual EU projects as well as from any other action of EU-funded research, in the wider thematic area of "5G Innovative Activities – Putting Intelligence to the Network Edge" and with the aim of focusing upon artifical intelligence (AI) in modern 5G telecommunications infrastructures.

The Third 5G-PINE Workshop had a strong impact in the broader context of the AIAI 2018 Conference. The preparatory work was mainly driven by the hard effort of Dr. Ioannis P. Chochliouros (Hellenic Telecommunications Organization, OTE, Greece) also coordinator of the relevant EU-funded 5G-PPP projects "SESAME" and "5G-ESSENCE," with the support of Dr. Alexandros Kostopoulos (Hellenic Telecommunications Organization, OTE, Greece), Profs. Oriol Sallent and Jordi Pérez-Romero (Universitat Politècnica de Catalunya, UPC, Spain), Dr. Ioannis Giannoulakis (National Center for Scientific Research Demokritos, NCSRD, Greece), Prof. Fidel Liberal (Universidad del Pais Vasco/Euskal Herriko Unibertsitatea, EHU, Spain), Dr. Emmanouil Kafetzakis (ORION Innovations Private Company, Greece), and Dr. Ioannis Neokosmidis (INCITES Consulting S.A.R.L., Luxembourg). Apart from these members of the Workshop Organizing Committee, the entire effort was also supported by more than 30 European experts (mainly from the relevant EU-funded 5G-PPP projects "SESAME" and "5G-ESSENCE"). Among the originally submitted 14 proposals, six were finally accepted as full papers (acceptance ratio of 42.85%) and one as a short paper.

The Third 5G-PINE Workshop promoted the context of modern 5G network infrastructures and of related innovative services in a complex and highly heterogeneous underlying radio access network (RAN) ecosystem, strongly enhanced by the inclusion of cognitive capabilities and intelligence features with the aim of improving network management. Based upon the well-known self-organizing network (SON) functionalities, the Third 5G-PINE Workshop promoted network planning and optimization processes through AI-based tools, able to smartly process input data from the environment and come up with knowledge that can be formalized in terms of models and/or structured metrics, able to "represent" the network behavior. This allows us to gain in-depth and detailed knowledge about the whole 5G ecosystem, understanding hidden patterns, data structures, and relationships, and using them for a more efficient network management.

The 5G-PINE Workshop supports delivery of intelligence directly to the network's edge, by exploiting the emerging paradigms of network functions virtualization (NFV) and edge cloud computing. Moreover, it supports promotion of rich virtualization and multi-tenant capabilities, optimally deployed close to the user. Interalia, it emphasizes the small cell (SC) concept, so as to support improved cellular coverage, capacity, and applications in a fully dynamic and flexible manner with vertical applications.

The accepted papers focus on several innovative findings coming directly from modern European research in the area, mainly from the 5G-PPP projects 5G-ESSENCE and 5GCIty as well as from the Spanish RAMSES and SONAR 5G Grants, covering a wide variety of technical and business aspects and promoting options for growth and development. One additional work focusing on vertical markets and within cloud environments comes from the H2020 VICINITY European project.

Organization

Program Chairs

Ioannis P. Chochliouros   Hellenic Telecommunications Organization S.A.,
      Greece

Ioannis Giannoulakis   National Center for Scientific Research "Demokritos",
      Greece

Emmanouil Kafetzakis   ORION Innovations Private Company, Greece

Alexandros Kostopoulos   Hellenic Telecommunications Organization S.A.,
      Greece

Fidel Liberal   Universidad del Pais Vasco/Euskal Herriko
      Unibertsitatea, Spain

Ioannis Neokosmidis   NCITES Consulting S.A.R.L., Luxembourg

Jordi Pérez-Romero   Universitat Politècnica de Catalunya (UPC), Spain

Oriol Sallent   Universitat Politècnica de Catalunya (UPC), Spain

Program Committee

Babangida Abubakar   University of Brighton, UK

George Agapiou   OTE, Greece

Antonino Albanese   Italtel, SpA, Italy

Nancy Alonistioti   National and Kapodistrian University of Athens,
      Greece

Maria Belesioti   OTE, Greece

August Betzler   Fundació Privada i2CAT, Internet i Innovació Digital a
      Catalunya, Spain

Begoña Blanco   Universidad del Pais Vasco/Euskal Herriko
      Unibertsitatea, Spain

Pavel Blitznakov   VOSYS Open Systems SAS, France

Nikolaos Bompetsis   National and Kapodistrian University of Athens,
      Greece

Marcello Coppola   STMicroelectronics Grenoble 2 SAS, France

Luis Cordeiro   CTO, OneSource Consultoria Informatica, LDA,
      Portugal

Paolo-Secondo Crosta   Italtel, SpA, Italy

Tilemachos Doukoglou   OTE, Greece

Andy Edmonds   Zürcher Hochschule für Angewandte Wissenschaften,
      Switzerland

Jose-Oscar Fajardo	Universidad del Pais Vasco/Euskal Herriko Unibertsitatea, Spain
Kelly Georgiadou	OTE, Greece
Konstantinos Helidonis	OTE, Greece
George Heliotis	OTE, Greece
Nick Johnson	IP.Access Ltd., UK
Pouria Sayyad Khodashenas	Fundació Privada i2CAT, Internet i Innovació Digital a Catalunya, Spain
Anastasios Kourtis	National Centre for Research and Development Demokritos, Greece
Latif Ladid	IPv6 Forum and SnT/University of Luxembourg
Javier Garcia Lloreda	ATOS Spain S.A., Spain
George Lyberopoulos	COSMOTE – Mobile Telecommunications S.A., Greece
Josep Martrat	ATOS Spain S.A., Spain
Nina Mitsopoulou	OTE, Greece
Christos Mizikakis	OTE, Greece
Klaus Moessner	University of Surrey, UK
Donal Morris	CEO, RedZinc Services, Ireland
Haris Mouratidis	University of Brighton, UK
Daniele Munaretto	Athonet SRL, Italy
Karim Nasr	University of Surrey, UK
Margherita Onofrio	Fondazione Bruno Kessler, Italy
Pietro Paglierani	Italtel, SpA, Italy
Manos Panaousis	University of Brighton, UK
Michele Paolino	VOSYS Open Systems SAS, France
Ioanna Papafili	OTE, Greece
Neil Piercy	IP.Access Ltd., UK
Vincenzo Pii	Zurcher Hochschule für Angewandte Wissenschaften, Switzerland
Roberto Riggio	Fondazione Bruno Kessler, Italy
Theodoros Rokkas	INCITES Consulting S.A.R.L., Luxembourg
Evangelos Sfakianakis	OTE, Greece
Anastasia Spiliopoulou	OTE, Greece
Makis Stamatelatos	National and Kapodistrian University of Athens, Greece
Irena Trajkovska	Zürcher Hochschule für Angewandte Wissenschaften, Switzerland
Charles Turyagyenda	Fujitsu Laboratories of Europe, Ltd., UK
Seiamak Vahid	University of Surrey, UK
Eirini Vasilaki	OTE, Greece
Vassilios Vassilakis	University of West London, UK
Gianluca Verrin	Athonet SRL, Italy
Vishanth Weerakkody	Brunel University, UK
Alan Whitehead	IP.Access Ltd., UK
Mick Wilson	Fujitsu Laboratories of Europe, Ltd., UK

Preface to MHD 2018

The abundance of available data retrieved from or related to the area of the humanities and the human condition challenges the research community in processing and analyzing it. The aim is two fold: on the one hand, to extract knowledge that will help us understand human behavior, creativity, ways of thinking, reasoning, learning, decision-making, socializing, and even biological processes; on the other hand, to exploit the extracted knowledge by incorporating it into intelligent systems that will support humans in their everyday activities.

The nature of humanistic data can be multimodal, semantically heterogeneous, dynamic, time and space-dependent, and highly complicated. Translating humanistic information, e.g., behavior, state of mind, artistic creation, linguistic utterance, learning, and genomic information into numerical or categorical low-level data is a significant challenge on its own. New techniques, appropriate for dealing with this type of data, need to be proposed and existing ones adapted to its special characteristics.

The workshop aims to bring together interdisciplinary approaches that focus on the application of innovative as well as existing data matching, fusion, and mining and knowledge discovery and management techniques (e.g., decision rules, decision trees, association rules, ontologies and alignments, clustering, filtering, learning, classifier systems, neural networks, support vector machines, preprocessing, postprocessing, feature selection, visualization techniques) to data derived from all areas of the humanities, e.g., linguistic, historical, behavioral, psychological, artistic, musical, educational, social etc.

Ubiquitous computing applications (aka pervasive computing, mobile computing, ambient intelligence, etc.) collect large volumes of usually heterogeneous data in order to effect adaptation, learning, and in general context awareness. Data matching, fusion, and mining techniques are necessary to ensure human-centered application functionality.

An important aspect of humanistic studies centers around managing, processing, and computationally analyzing biological and biomedical data. Hence, one of the aims of this workshop was to also attract researchers interested in designing, developing, and applying efficient data and text mining techniques for discovering the underlying knowledge existing in biomedical data, such as sequences, gene expressions, and pathways.

The topics of interest can be found at https://conferences.cwa.gr/mhdw2018/workshop-aim/.

Organization

Program Chairs

Georgios Drakopoulos   Ionian University, Greece
Andreas Kanavos   University of Patras, Greece
Christos Makris   University of Patras, Greece
Phivos Mylonas   Ionian University, Greece

Program Committee

Ioannis Karydis   Ionian University, Greece
Katia Lida Kermanidis   Ionian University, Greece
Spyros Sioutas   Ionian University, Greece

Preface to HealthIoT 2018

It is our pleasure to welcome you to the proceedings of the Intelligent Cloud and IoT Paradigms in eHealth (HealthIoT) Workshop held as part of the AIAI 2018 conference during May 25–27, 2018, in Rhodes, Greece. Evolving from a network of interconnected computers and networking devices, the Internet is increasingly being approached as the Internet of Everything capturing the interconnections of devices with diverse characteristics, service offerings, and data flows (e.g., smart phones and tablets, wearable devices, sensor networks, cameras, vehicles, etc.). In this context, the Internet of Things (IoT) is evolving into a platform of platforms, consisting of a plethora of networked devices, infrastructures, and supporting systems of systems, addressing various application domains, with electronic health care being one of them. This workshop offers the opportunity to present recent results concerning the design, development, implementation, and deployment of big data analytics and cloud infrastructures and IoT in different areas relating to electronic health care. The workshop aims to support research and innovation on IoT-based eHealth systems and especially in: wearable systems, medical and sensor data processing, machine learning in eHealth, emerging eHealth IoT applications, network communications for health care applications, quantified self technologies and applications, intelligent data processing and predictive algorithms in eHealth, smart homes and assistive environments, data mining of health data on the cloud, security, safety and privacy in eHealth and IoT, interoperability and standardization issues in IoT and eHealth. The workshop received nine submissions of which were accepted (44% acceptance ratio). We express our special thanks to all who contributed to the organization and scientific contents of this workshop — first to the authors of the papers, to the AIAI 2018 conference organizers, and finally to the reviewers and members of the Program and Organizing Committees.

Organization

Program Chairs

Dimosthenis Kyriazis	University of Piraeus, Greece
Ilias Maglogiannis	University of Piraeus, Greece
Vassilis Plagianakos	University of Thessaly, Greece

Program Committee

Kostas Delibasis	University of Thessaly, Greece
Vasiliki Iconomidou	University of Athens Greece
George Kousiouris	National Technical University of Athens, Greece
Dimosthenis Kyriazis	University of Piraeus
Ilias Maglogiannis	University of Piraeus, Greece
Andreas Menychtas	University of Piraeus, Greece
Kostas Moutselos	University of Piraeus, Greece
Vassilis Plagianakos	University of Thessaly, Greece

Contents

HEALTHIOT

SEDSEAL

Semantic Models for Labeling Spectrum Data

Vaishali Nagpure$^{(\boxtimes)}$, Cynthia Hood , and Stephanie Vaccaro

Illinois Institute of Technology, Chicago, IL 60616, USA
{vnagpure,svaccaro}@hawk.iit.edu, hood@iit.edu

Abstract. With the increasing importance and demand for wireless communications, there is a spectrum crunch and there is no easy way to meet this increasing demand. Spectrum monitoring is a key enabler for understanding how the spectrum is currently used and identifying opportunities for spectrum sharing. This paper focuses on analysis of a large volume of complex spectrum measurements in the public safety band and involves modeling spectrum sensors, public safety domain knowledge and events involving public safety. The information models developed can be used to create labels for the complex spectrum data and facilitate the analysis of the data needed for spectrum sharing.

1 Introduction

Wireless communication plays an increasingly important role across a variety of domains. With the growing demand for new and expanded wireless services, one of the key challenges is the scarcity of spectrum. Spectrum is a finite resource and in the United States (as in most parts of the world) the spectrum has been fully allocated. This means that there is no "free" spectrum that can be utilized to meet the growing demands, thereby making spectrum sharing necessary.

An important step to determine the feasibility of sharing is to learn how the spectrum is currently being used. This involves understanding the occupancy of the spectrum in space, time and frequency and identifying where opportunities exist for sharing. Characterizing the details of how the spectrum is used – e.g., the time-frequency utilization patterns is fundamental to the design of dynamic spectrum access (DSA) systems as it can significantly increase the opportunity for spectrum sharing by leveraging signal periodicity. Obtaining detailed spectrum utilization patterns is challenging, particularly when analyzing multiple bands.

Multiband spectrum measurements are highly complex spatio-temporal data sets that require very specialized domain knowledge to collect, analyze and interpret. [1] The entire process is extremely time consuming. To analyze and interpret the measurements, a variety of contextual information ranging from the specific configuration of the spectrum sensor and potential emitters to drivers of spectrum use is needed. Current analysis is largely manual, and typically limited to one or a few bands. Multiband analysis is usually based on visual interpretation of waterfall charts or spectrograms. Although context is sometimes used anecdotally to interpret the dynamics of spectrum usage, it has not been integrated into the characterization. Deciding what is normal or abnormal

© IFIP International Federation for Information Processing 2018
Published by Springer International Publishing AG 2018. All Rights Reserved
L. Iliadis et al. (Eds.): AIAI 2018, IFIP AICT 520, pp. 3–12, 2018.
https://doi.org/10.1007/978-3-319-92016-0_1

for each band requires domain expertise. These factors limit the amount of analysis that is done on spectrum measurements and thus limit the understanding of existing spectrum use.

This work focuses on the analysis of spectrum measurements in the Land Mobile Radio (LMR) bands that include the spectrum used for public safety in Chicago. Given the nature of public safety communication, it is important to be able to meet communication demands whenever emergencies or other large-scale events occur. Therefore it is critical to understand how the public safety spectrum is used in dynamic situations, especially as these events are unfolding. More specifically, how do the communication demands evolve over time and what triggers the demands. To understand the triggers, it is necessary to understand the context of the demands.

Figure 1 was generated from two weeks of observation of Land Mobile Radio (LMR) band data in 2009 and shows the difference in spectrum occupancy on weekdays and weekends. Figure 2 shows the increase in call rate in the 406 MHz LMR band during the NATO Summit held in Chicago in May 2012. Both of these figures show that there is a relationship between spectrum use and human activity.

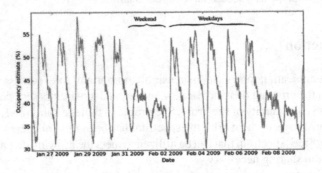

Fig. 1. Two week plot of spectrum occupancy in the 450 MHz LMR Band

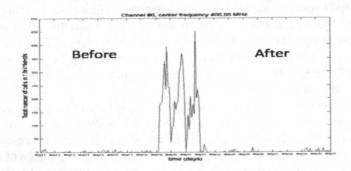

Fig. 2. Call rate in 406 MHz band

As illustrated above, context is necessary to fully understand the significance of the patterns and anomalies in the spectrum measurements. More importantly, these patterns and events need to be identified so they can be incorporated into demand models. In an urban environment like Chicago, events drive a significant portion of public safety communication. These events may be planned (i.e. sporting or entertainment events) or unplanned emergency events of different scales and at different locations.

The importance and role of human activity has been recognized in context-aware services and networks. Context enhances understanding of spectral usage through improvement in the process of spectrum data analysis as well as interpretation of the results. One of the challenges with wideband monitoring efforts is identifying events or time intervals of interest to analyze. Context may be utilized to identify potential events of interest for near-term or offline analysis. As a first step toward automation of spectrum analysis, this paper proposes to model configuration, domain knowledge and other potentially relevant information with the use of semantic modeling in a way that it can be fused with measurements for analysis and in particular can provide labels for the spectrum data.

The rest of the paper is organized as follows. Section 2 describes the challenges of measuring the spectrum and provides details on the measurements utilized in this work and typical analysis techniques. Public safety communication and related work is described in Sect. 3. Our approach and a case study during the Chicago Marathon is described in Sect. 4. Finally, conclusions and future work is discussed in Sect. 5.

2 Spectrum Measurements

The spectrum is organized into bands where a band is a contiguous range of frequencies that are used for the same general purpose. Bands may be further subdivided into channels. The frequency resolution is the sampling interval in the frequency domain whereas the resolution bandwidth (RBW) is the bandwidth of a single spectrum measurement obtained during a specific sampling interval in time at a specific location in the spatial domain. If the RBW is too large, part of the adjacent channel power is measured during the measurement of a certain channel leading to incorrect results. This is an enormously challenging constraint and may lead to the use of multiple detectors, each covering a specific portion of the spectrum to provide a small enough RBW to ensure that all channels are correctly registered and at the same time the revisit time is positioned at a level where no signals are missed.

The band plan is also a critical part that is basically a division of the particular range of radio frequencies of interest into bands with common parameter settings such as resolution bandwidth. Typically band plans are relatively static, but if you need to capture details with higher resolution measurements on a particular day for an event, the band plan can be dynamic instead of static. For example, if we are aware of an event such as a sporting event or protest, the band plan can be changed to gather higher resolution measurements in bands that might be impacted (e.g. public safety).

The IIT Spectrum Observatory has been monitoring the 30–6000 MHz radio spectrum of the city of Chicago since mid-2007 from its location on top of the 22 story Tower on IIT's Main campus on the south side of Chicago. [2] Energy detection sensing is used in our measurement system and the resolution bandwidth is kept at 3 kHz for all bands. This results in around 93 MB of data per day.

6   V. Nagpure et al.

In the case of the public safety bands where channel bandwidths are narrow (<30 kHz), due to the high sweep time, short transmissions cannot be detected. To address these issues, a new measurement system utilizing a Tektronix RSA 306 spectrum analyzer was added. This allows us to obtain higher time and frequency resolution data with a focus on the LMR bands which include the public safety bands in Chicago. After conducting experiments, resolution bandwidth of 1 kHz for the Chicago Police Department (CPD) frequencies is configured as CPD is a case study for this research. This results in around 16 GB of data per day. The measurements are transmitted to a local storage system daily.

2.1 Analysis with Spectrograms

The data files produced are transmitted from the data capture PC to a high performance workstation. The data is processed to produce a variety of plots and usage statistics. Spectrograms or waterfall charts are used to present much of the spectrum occupancy data. For these charts, time is represented on the y-axis (days or hours), frequency on the x-axis (MHz) and power (dBm) as color level, with the indicated mapping. Higher power indicates higher occupancy. Several waterfall charts derived shown below in Figs. 3, 4 and 5.

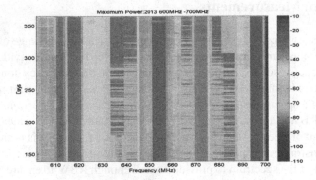

Fig. 3. 600 MHz television bands during 2013

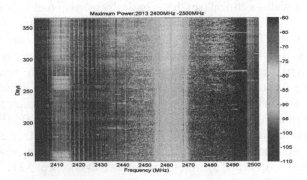

Fig. 4. 2.4 GHz Band during 2013

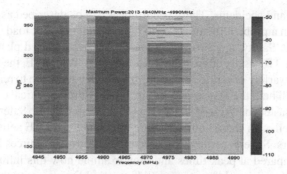

Fig. 5. 4.945–4.99 GHz Broadband Public Safety during 2013

The spectral occupancy was estimated based on the threshold method and different thresholds were selected for each band by estimating the noise floor of the system. The utilization of different bands can be found to range from highly utilized through sporadically used to not used at all. A good example of highly utilized bands is the TV bands shown in Fig. 3 with their consistently high power. The obvious reason for the high occupancy is that TV channels in a metropolitan market like Chicago are always broadcasting and are well occupied. The interpretation of Fig. 3 is quite straightforward once you know how the band has been allocated. Notice that Figs. 4 and 5 look different and explaining the visualizations shown in these figures is more challenging. It is clear that one must be familiar with the band allocations, the measurement system location and configuration, as well as usage behavior within the band to accurately interpret the measurements.

3 Public Safety Background and Related Work

Public safety communication networks are typically designed with enough capacity to handle "worst case" scenarios, with some channels largely unused under typical day-to-day activity [3]. Studies [4] have noted this to be the case with occupancy figures generally being fairly low, however during atypical periods of high activity – most notably during disasters and other emergencies – channel capacities may approach or even meet their limits.

There have been many studies of public safety traffic such as [5–8] and including [9] utilizing the SDR-based spectrum monitoring system mentioned above to collect measurements. These studies are focused on traffic in the deployed LMR systems. They generally consider typical traffic along with traffic during large-scale disaster or emergency events and generally separate these into two classes. Part of the challenge with having richer models is the lack of events to study [10].

Patterns of communication are identified [6] and models of heterogeneous networks are developed [11] and mobility on disaster sites is considered. [12] Accurate traffic models are necessary for a service provider of emergency communications to properly maintain the capacity planning of the network. To do so, good traffic models need to be developed that can capture characteristics including occurrences of few and large random incidents and accidents. These occurrences can be described as unusual spikes and/or long tails in a probability model term of an actual network load.

Today's Public Safety agencies and organizations have started planning to evolve their networks to LTE based public safety solutions [13]. With LTE, the first responders can access a wide variety of services, starting from high bandwidth to real time communications. This will help the first responders in case of mission critical communications such as natural disasters or terrorist attacks. In [14], a virtual Public Safety (PS) operator is proposed that relies on shared infrastructure of commercial LTE networks to deliver services to its users. Several methods of allocating spectrum resources between virtual operators are compared at peak times and they examine how this influences differing traffic services. They showed that it is possible to provide services to the Public Safety users reliably during both normal and emergency operation. The authors of [12] focused on the performance evaluation of the communication systems in disaster scenarios.

4   Approach and Case Study

One of the challenges with wideband spectrum measurements, particularly long-term measurements, is finding data of interest. For example, the IIT Spectrum Observatory collects wideband measurements between 30–6000 MHz. This covers many different frequency bands and channels over a wide variety of uses. There is a wealth of data over many years, so how to choose a frequency band and time period to study? In the context of dynamic spectrum sharing, the focus is on frequency bands that are not fully utilized and we are generally interested in understanding the usage and how the usage changes over various time periods. But it is not enough to understand changes in the energy from a signal processing perspective, it is also important to understand why the usage is changing. This is relatively straightforward for major events like the NATO Summit shown in Fig. 2, because you can identify the days of interest and then visualize the data. This can be quite challenging for many other types of events though given the manual nature of visualization. Patterns can also be identified manually through visualization, but for the same reasons can be challenging to capture without time-consuming visualization. This can be effective for small datasets but does not scale well. To address this issue, this paper proposes to combine different types of information from several different sources using both statistical and semantic modeling techniques.

4.1   Case Study

A large city like Chicago has many different types of events occurring almost on a daily basis providing a good opportunity to model spectrum use over a variety of different scenarios. This case study focuses on the channels used by the Chicago Police Department (CPD). The goal of this case study is to step through the analysis of an event that results in noticeable changes to identify the information and steps needed for automation. The event we studied was the Chicago Marathon on October 8, 2017. The Chicago Marathon has a 26.2 mile course that covers 22 neighborhoods in Chicago. Approximately 45,000 runners participate in the marathon and there are many fans along the way. Public safety works to secure the course as well as to do traffic management around the city. In this case study, as in the past, we traversed backwards from events of interest to see if the impact on spectrum could be detected. The first question was what frequencies to analyze. The frequencies used by CPD are shown in Fig. 7. CPD has organized the city into zones that cover one or more districts as shown in Fig. 6. [15] The Chicago neighborhood and district map is shown in Fig. 7. [15].

Fig. 6. Frequencies used by the Chicago Police Department [15]

Fig. 7. Chicago Police Department Radio Zone Map [15]

As shown in Fig. 6, there are both citywide channels for specific types of communication as well as location-specific zone channels. To determine the communication channel and frequency for a given public safety event, it is necessary to determine the type of event and also the location. Each location must be translated into the appropriate district and corresponding zone to determine the channel and corresponding frequency of communication related to the event.

The relationship between neighborhoods, districts and zones shown in Fig. 7 along with the CPD radio communication information was encoded using SWI-Prolog. Events from various City of Chicago event calendars were also encoded. For each event, the neighborhood was included. The result of a query to the resulting knowledge base for the date "October 8, 2017" is shown in Fig. 8. The marathon goes through several neighborhoods so the corresponding zones are listed. In addition, since the marathon is considered an "event" and citywide channels 1,5 and 6 are used for events, they are also listed.

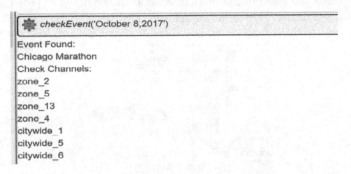

Fig. 8. Result of the query to knowledge database.

We analyzed the bands corresponding to the zone and citywide channels in the query result. Citywide channel 6 showed unusual occupancy. The waterfall charts for citywide channel 6 are shown in Figs. 9 and 10. Figure 9 shows a sweep time from 11 pm on October 7, 2017 to 11 pm on October 8, 2017. Figure 10 shows from 11 pm on October 8, 2017 to 11 pm on October 9, 2017. These waterfall charts plot the energy detected in the band on each sweep. The x-axis gives the frequency and the y-axis gives the sweep number. There is one sweep approximately every 2 s. The channel beginning at 460.25 MHz is clearly evident from the waterfall chart. The yellow color indicates a higher level of power in the band. It is clear from Fig. 9 that there is activity in the band starting very early in the morning of October 8th and continuing through 11 pm. Looking at Fig. 10, one can see the activity continuing until the early hours of October 9th. This appears to be consistent with expected CPD activity during the marathon.

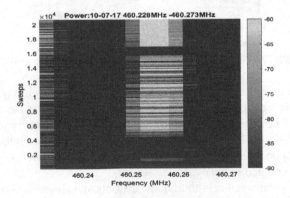

Fig. 9. Waterfall chart for Chicago Police Citywide channel 6 (460.25 MHz)

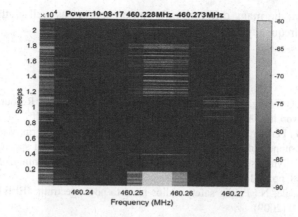

Fig. 10. Waterfall chart for Chicago Police Citywide channel 6 (460.25 MHz)

It is clear that a significant amount of information is needed to put together this simple analysis. One of the reasons we chose to study the public safety spectrum is that there are many publicly available sources of information that are relevant. This information and the relationships between various pieces of information can be modeled using semantics. These models can be used to reason about potential explanations for increased activity given unusual spectral activity. It can also be used to trigger analysis of specific frequency bands due to a certain type of event.

5 Conclusion and Future Work

This paper describes the challenges of spectrum measurement analysis and motivates the need for more in-depth analysis and fine-grained modeling for the purpose of spectrum sharing. The necessary analysis is limited by the complexity of the measurement, analysis and interpretation of the data. Analysis requires a substantial amount of domain knowledge along with contextual information. Contextual information can be derived from a variety of different information sources including events.

This paper focuses on the public safety spectrum in the LMR band in Chicago. More specifically, we study the CPD spectrum. Semantic models were developed and coded in SWI-Prolog to describe the organization and use of the CPD allocated spectrum along with planned events in Chicago. The models were used to help identify relevant channels used during the Chicago marathon. These models can be used to label periods of unusual activity. Our case study uses visualization of the waterfall charts to determine unusual activity. The contribution of this work is the use of semantic models for labeling. Our long-term goal is to automate the analysis of spectrum data across frequency and time.

Ongoing work aims to create statistical models of typical activity and identify periods of unusual activity automatically. These periods of unusual activity can then be correlated with events or vice versa. Public Safety spectrum behavior is challenging to interpret and prediction of usage is driven by many factors such as planned and unplanned events, weather and human protocols. Further development of the semantic models is needed to capture the many different information sources as well as the correlations across time and frequency bands.

References

1. Ding, G., Wu, Q. Wang, J., Yao, Y.-D.: Big Spectrum Data: The New Resource for Cognitive Wireless Networking, April 2014. http://arxiv.org/pdf/1404.6508.pdf
2. Bacchus, R.B., Fertner, A.J., Hood, C.S., Roberson, D.A.: Long-term, wide-band spectral monitoring in support of dynamic spectrum access networks at the IIT spectrum observatory. In: 3rd IEEE Symposium on New Frontiers in Dynamic Spectrum Access Networks, DySPAN 2008, pp. 1–10. IEEE (2008)
3. Lehr, W., Jesuale, N.: Public safety radios need to pool spectrum. IEEE Commun. Mag. **47**(3), 103–109 (2009)
4. Bacchus, R., Taher, T., Zdunek, K., Roberson, D.: Spectrum utilization study in support of dynamic spectrum access for public safety. In: 2010 IEEE Symposium on New Frontiers in Dynamic Spectrum, pp. 1–11. IEEE (2010)
5. Aschenbruck, N., Gerharz, M., Frank, M., Martini, P.: Modelling voice communication in disaster area scenarios. In: Proceedings of IEEE Conference on Local Computer Networks (LCN2006), pp. 211–220 (2006)
6. Aschenbruck, N., Gerharz, M., Martini, P.: How to assign traffic sources to nodes in disaster area scenarios. In: Proceedings of the 26th IEEE International Performance Computing and Communications Conference (IPCCC) (2007)
7. Sharp, D.S., Cackov, N., Lasković, N., Shao, Q., Trajković, L.: Analysis of public safety traffic on trunked land mobile radio systems. IEEE J.-SAC **22**(7), 1197–1205 (2004)
8. Vujicić, B., Cackov, N., Vujicić, S., Trajković, L.: Modeling and characterization of traffic in public safety wireless networks. In: Proceedings of SPECTS, pp. 214–223 (2005)
9. Taher, T.M., Bacchus, R.B., Zdunek, K.J., Roberson, D.A.: Empirical modeling of public safety voice traffic in the land mobile radio band. In: 2012 7th International ICST Conference on Cognitive Radio Oriented Wireless Networks and Communications (CROWNCOM), pp. 230–235. IEEE (2012)
10. Chen, C., Pomalaza-Raez, C., Colone, M., Martin, R., Isaacs, J.: Modeling of a public safety communication system for emergency response. In: 2009 IEEE International Conference on Communications, Dresden, pp. 1–5 (2009)
11. Badarch, T., Bataa, O.: Incoming traffic modeling of heterogeneous public safety network. In: 2013 15th Asia-Pacific Network Operations and Management Symposium (APNOMS), Hiroshima, Japan, pp. 1–6 (2013)
12. Aschenbruck, N., Martini, P.: Modeling public safety scenarios to evaluate wireless communication systems. In: 2009 1st International Conference on Wireless Communication, Vehicular Technology, Information Theory and Aerospace & Electronic Systems Technology, Aalborg, pp. 510–514 (2009)
13. LTE networks for Public Safety Services, Nokia Networks, White Paper
14. van de Belt, J., Ahmadi, H., Doyle, L.E., Sallent, O.: A prioritized traffic embedding mechanism enabling a public safety virtual operator. In: Proceedings of IEEE 82nd Vehicular Technology Conference (VTC2015-Fall) (2015)
15. https://www.radioreference.com. Accessed 15 Mar 2018

Towards Big Data Analytics in Large-Scale Federations of Semantically Heterogeneous IoT Platforms

Ilias Kalamaras[✉], Nikolaos Kaklanis, Kostantinos Votis, and Dimitrios Tzovaras

Information Technologies Institute, Centre for Research and Technology Hellas, Thessaloniki, Greece
{kalamar,nkak,kvotis,tzovaras}@iti.gr

Abstract. The technological advances in the Internet-of-Things (IoT) have led to the generation of large amounts of data and the production of a large number of IoT platforms for their management. The abundance of raw data necessitates the use of data analytics in order to extract useful patterns for decision making. Current architectures for big data analytics in the IoT domain address the large volume and velocity of the produced data. However, they do not address the semantic heterogeneity in the data models used by diverse IoT platforms, which emerges when large scale deployments, spanning across multiple deployment sites, are considered. This paper proposes an architecture for big data analytics in the context of large-scale IoT systems consisting of multiple IoT platforms. A Semantic Interoperability Layer (SIL) handles the interoperability among the data models of the individual platforms, using semantic mappings between them and a unified ontology. Data queries to the SIL and result collection is handled by a cloud-based data management layer, namely the Data Lake, along with storage of metadata needed by data analytics methods. Based on this infrastructure, web-based data analytics and visual analytics methods are used to analyze the collected data, while being agnostic of platform-specific details. The proposed architecture is developed in the context of healthcare provision for older people, although it can be applied to any IoT domain.

Keywords: Internet-of-Things · Big data analytics
Semantic interoperability · Healthy ageing

1 Introduction

The technological advances of the Internet-of-Things (IoT) have led to the development of human-centric IoT applications, such as e-Health and intelligent transportation systems. Such applications allow the collection of valuable domain information, assisting human operators and decision makers in providing services

L. Iliadis et al. (Eds.): AIAI 2018, IFIP AICT 520, pp. 13–23, 2018.
https://doi.org/10.1007/978-3-319-92016-0_2

for the well-being of individuals and communities. In the context of e-Health, for example, IoT systems can be used to collect data from a large number of patients, allowing a close monitoring of their health and the provision of (automatic or not) interventions, or the formation of health management policies. Currently running European research projects, such as ACTIVAGE [1] and FrailSafe [2], in an attempt to address the healthcare needs of the increasing number of ageing population, provide promising solutions towards the use of IoT technologies for older people monitoring and assistance.

The extensive use of IoT technologies has led to two outcomes. First, there is a very large volume of data (collected by a wide variety of sensors, such as wearables, environmental sensors, appliance usage monitors, etc.), which exceeds the storage and processing power limits of stand-alone applications (big data). Second, there is a growing number of developed IoT platforms providing off-the-self solutions for the development and deployment of IoT applications, without the need for extensive programming. However, in large-scale applications, spanning a large number of different installations, maybe across different countries, each installation may use a different IoT platform, having its own data model for describing the IoT devices and collected data. These models are often incompatible with each other in terms of semantics, making the necessity of semantic interoperability apparent. There is a need to have a common semantic model for describing the concepts of all IoT platforms, in order for large-scale data analytics methods to perform.

This paper proposes an architecture that allows big data analytics methods to perform on large-scale IoT deployments, spanning multiple diverse IoT platforms. Interoperability among the IoT platforms is handled by the introduced *Semantic Interoperability Layer (SIL)*, providing a unified data model and semantic mappings. Data analytics methods are supported by the introduced *Data Lake*, which is based on the SIL and maintains its own cloud storage for extracted features, trained models and any metadata that are needed by analytics methods. The architecture is developed in the context of the ACTIVAGE project [1], whose goal is to support large-scale IoT applications in deployment sites across European countries, in order to exploit the large volume of collected data. Towards this goal, existing IoT platforms already deployed in different sites are used, as well as various sensing systems, such as the behavioural monitoring systems developed in the FrailSafe project [2]. Providing an infrastructure for combining the diverse platforms and data models can provide large-scale data analytics for assisting older people, clinicians and researchers.

The rest of this paper is organized as follows. Section 2 presents background, work regarding big data analytics and semantic interoperability. Section 3 describes the proposed architecture, covering the Semantic Interoperability Layer, the Data Lake, and the data analytics and visualization components. Section 4 describes scenarios for the preliminary evaluation of the proposed architecture, while Sect. 5 concludes the paper, providing information about the next steps.

2   Background

2.1   Big Data Analytics

Data analytics aim at analyzing raw data, in order to extract information that is more meaningful and valuable to the human operator in order to understand the data and make decisions. In the context of IoT, data analytics are mostly concerned with classification, clustering and high-level data representation [3]. *Classification* methods assign an observation to one of multiple classes, after being trained using data with known classes. Common classification methods currently used include Support Vector Machines (SVM) [4], and Random Forests [5]. *Anomaly detection* methods detect unusual circumstances by classifying observations as normal or abnormal, e.g. Local Outlier Factor (LOF) [6] and Bayesian Robust PCA (BRPCA) [7]. *Clustering* methods split observations in groups of similar characteristics, without using training information [8]. Hierarchical clustering proceeds by recursively joining or separating observations, until a tree-like structure is formed, while partitioning clustering, such as k-means and k-medoids, considers an arbitrary starting split, iteratively updating it to best represent the data. Methods to construct *high-level representations* for raw data can remove unnecessary or redundant dimensions. Principal Component Analysis (PCA) [9], Multi-Dimensional Scaling (MDS) [10] and graph embedding methods [11], attempt to find subspaces (manifolds) of maximum information and minimum dimension inside the raw data space. In the context of time series analysis, ARMA models [12] and variants are used to extract high-level information, such as trends and periodicities, from the raw data.

Several architectures for big data analytics in IoT applications have been proposed. The authors of [3] provide a related review and propose an architecture where the data collected by sensors are stored in cloud databases, allowing large-scale data analytics methods to operate on them, using cluster computing frameworks, such as Apache Spark [13] and Hadoop [14]. The authors of [15] propose a framework for off-line and on-line analysis of IoT data of large volume and velocity, by computing model parameters off-line and using them for real-time analysis. The authors of [16] propose a 4-tier architecture, covering data generation by sensors, communication between sensors and gateways, data analysis using cluster computing, and finally data interpretation by human operators. Most big data analytics architectures in the IoT domain are concerned with handling the large volume and velocity of the produced data, without addressing the variety and heterogeneity in their semantics.

2.2   Semantic Interoperability

There is a large number of IoT platforms for managing devices and data, each using a different ontology to describe its semantics [17]. The SSN (Semantic Sensor Network) ontology [18] describes sensors in terms of their functionalities, measurements and deployments, although it has limitations regarding real-time data collection. The oneM2M ontology [19] has been supported by IoT standardization bodies, although it also has limitations in terms of contextual data annotation. The IoTivity platform [20] is based on the models of the Open Connectivity Foundation (OCF) [21], which aims at providing a common framework for communication among IoT devices and gateways. The OpenIoT ontology [22], utilized by the OPENIoT platform [23], is based on the SSN ontology and adds concepts related to IoT applications and testbeds. The IoT-Lite ontology [24], used by the FIWARE platform [25], is a recent attempt to collect existing concepts of the IoT domain in a common ontology. Ad-hoc data models have also been built for the purposes of various existing open-source IoT platforms, including sensiNact [26], universAAL [27], Sofia2 [28] and SENIORSome [29].

This abundance of IoT ontologies creates interoperability issues in large-scale applications, where IoT platforms with different ontologies must cooperate. *Semantic interoperability* ensures that all components have a common understanding of the meaning of the information being exchanged [30]. Attempts have been made to promote semantic interoperability by unifying existing ontologies. The SAREF (Smart Appliance REFerence) ontology [31] is such an attempt, unifying concepts from several ontologies in the smart appliances domain, in order to cover larger applications. The authors of [32] use the ontology interconnection methodology of [33], in order to unify existing ontologies in the IoT domain, within the context of the FIESTA-IoT European project [34].

The above review suggests that architectures for big data analytics in IoT systems do exist, but they focus on handling the large data volume and velocity, without addressing the heterogeneity of the available data models. Attempts to address heterogeneity are being made, but they are not targeted to providing a basis for large-scale data analytics methods. The current paper aims to contribute to this direction, by proposing an architecture for large-scale IoT data analytics, based on semantic interoperability across diverse IoT platforms.

3   The ACTIVAGE Data Analytics Architecture

The proposed architecture for large-scale data analytics is depicted in Fig. 1b. It is based on the structure of existing IoT frameworks, as depicted in Fig. 1a, forming a stack of layers ranging from the IoT devices at the bottom, towards data analytics and visualization at the top. However, instead of a single IoT platform to handle the devices at the bottom, there are now many platforms, each operating separately, with its own devices, data storage and component semantics. The following IoT platforms are considered in ACTIVAGE, although any number of platforms is supported: FIWARE [25], sensiNact [26], universAAL [27], IoTivity [20], Sofia2 [28], SENIORSome [29] and OPENIoT [23]. The next layer is the *Semantic Interoperability Layer (SIL)*, which unifies the ontologies of the IoT platforms and offers common semantics for their components. The presence of the SIL eliminates any issues of compatibility between inter-platform hardware and software, as each platform manages its own hardware and software, in order to collect data. Interoperability in ACTIVAGE happens in a conceptual

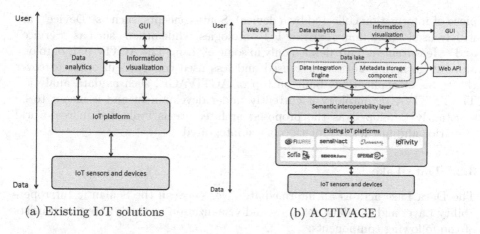

(a) Existing IoT solutions   (b) ACTIVAGE

Fig. 1. The proposed ACTIVAGE architecture (b) extends existing IoT solutions (a), by adding layers regarding platform interoperability and data management.

level, by ensuring the compatibility between different data representations, using the SIL semantic mappings. Above the SIL is the *Data Lake*, which, through its Data Integration Engine, directs the queries coming from the upper layers towards the SIL and collects the data retrieved from the IoT platforms. The Data Lake also contains a Metadata Storage component, for storing metadata (models, etc.) produced and needed by the data analytics methods. The Data Lake components are cloud-based, offering Web APIs for their usage. Based on the infrastructure of the SIL and the Data Lake, the top layers, data analytics and information visualization, can operate, extracting patterns and producing visualizations through Web APIs and graphical interfaces.

3.1   Semantic Interoperability Layer

The Semantic Interoperability Layer (SIL) is responsible for providing an abstraction for the representation of devices, attributes and data, that is agnostic of any IoT platform-specific details and naming conventions. In order to provide interoperability, the SIL maintains a common ontology describing the components of an IoT platform, namely the *ACTIVAGE ontology*. This ontology unifies the ontologies of the participating IoT platforms, so that common names are given for concepts with the same semantics. Platform-specific data representations may be both structured (schema-based databases), or unstructured (schema-less databases). The SIL provides semantic mappings between the common unified model and these individual data models of the IoT platforms.

The ACTIVAGE ontology is based on existing IoT ontologies, such as SSN [18], SAREF [31], oneM2M [19], IoT-Lite [24] and OpenIoT [22], and aims to combine and extend them. It defines basic concepts of IoT platforms, such as *Device* (a physical object able to communicate with its environment), *Service* (a software component able to perform some functionality) and *Measurement* (a piece of information collected by a device). Some concepts, such as "Device", are widely used across many existing IoT ontologies, while others, such as "Service" and "Measurement", are defined only in some of them. The ACTIVAGE ontology aims at gathering both widely used and less used concepts, in order to cover the types of applications built on top of ACTIVAGE, such as data analytics. The ACTIVAGE ontology is currently under development and is meant to be constantly developed as the proposed architecture is evaluated in real-world scenarios and further IoT platforms are integrated.

3.2 Data Lake

The Data Lake acts as an intermediate layer between the Semantic Interoperability Layer and the data analytics and visualization methods above. It consists of the following components:

- The **Data Integration Engine**, which directs queries from data analytics methods towards the SIL and collects the results from the IoT platforms.
- The **Metadata Storage Component**, a database of metadata produced by the data analytics algorithms, which are necessary for their on-line operation.

In ACTIVAGE, the data collected by the IoT sensors and used for data analytics are stored in the storage facilities of each separate IoT platform. This facilitates the registration of new platforms, since it avoids switching to a different database and duplicating data. It also promotes data security and privacy, since the sensitive raw data remain in the deployment site's premises and under any site-specific privacy-related restrictions. However, the Data Lake does offer additional central storage, dedicated to metadata necessary for the operation of data analytics. These include produced features and analysis results, e.g. trained classification models, anomaly detection thresholds, etc., which may be necessary for their operation. Metadata are usually produced off-line, at regular intervals, using historical data, in order to be later used for real-time analytics.

The operation of the Data Lake and it connection to the SIL is described in Fig. 2. Data analytics methods (e.g. anomaly detection) need raw data stored in the distributed storages of the IoT platforms (e.g. the most recent sensor measurements), as well as specific metadata (e.g. pre-computed anomaly detection thresholds). The raw data are requested from the Data Integration Engine, while the metadata from the Metadata Storage Component. In order to collect the raw data, the Data Integration Engine submits a query to the SIL, written with the naming conventions of the unified ACTIVAGE ontology. The SIL translates the query to the platform-specific data models. The IoT platforms retrieve the requested data from their storage and return them to the SIL, which translates them to the ACTIVAGE ontology and sends them back to the Data Integration Engine. The latter combines the multiple sets of returned results and sends them to the data analytics component. At the same time, the Metadata Storage Component retrieves the requested metadata and sends them to the data analytics component as well. The data analytics method now has all the necessary information to produce the requested output (e.g. the detected anomalies).

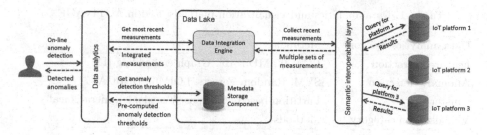

Fig. 2. Operation of the ACTIVAGE Data Lake.

3.3 Data Analytics and Information Visualization

The top layers in the ACTIVAGE architecture are the data analytics and information visualization layers, which provide meaningful representations of the raw data to the human operator. IoT applications are usually targeted at monitoring an environment, e.g. a person, a house, a city, etc, in order to facilitate decision making. In the context of e-health for older people, which is the primary target of the ACTIVAGE project, the purpose is to facilitate clinicians in monitoring an individual's health and taking proper actions, or to facilitate researchers in monitoring large sets of individuals and discover correlations. The focus of data analytics is thus on methods that extract representative features, find correlations, detect anomalies in usual behavior (e.g. to trigger alarms), and cluster objects (patients, devices, etc.) in groups of similar characteristics.

Existing data analytics methods are used in ACTIVAGE, covering the tasks outlined in Sect. 2: feature extraction, dimensionality reduction, anomaly detection and clustering. Table 1 summarizes the data analytics methods used in ACTIVAGE. This is not an exhaustive list, since other methods may be included as needed by IoT applications. Information visualization aims to produce descriptive graphical summaries of the raw data, allowing the operator to have a comprehensive overview of the data and explore them in order to detect interesting patterns. Table 1 summarizes the visualization methods used in ACTIVAGE. Commonly used visualization methods, such as bar charts and line plots are used, as well as more sophisticated graph-based visualizations for visualizing similarities and differences among objects.

4 Preliminary Evaluation

The proposed architecture is currently being evaluated using a smart home scenario and a smart mobility scenario. The purpose of the smart home scenario is to monitor the health status of older people as they perform activities of daily living, and assist the clinician in decision making through data analytics services. Environment and activity detection sensors are installed in the older person's home, constantly measuring temperature/humidity, CO levels, person motion and door/window opening. Two medical devices, a blood pressure monitor and a

Table 1. Data analytics and visualization methods used in ACTIVAGE.

Data analytics category	Methods
Feature extraction	PCA [9], MDS [10], Graph embedding [11]
Anomaly detection	SVM, Random Forests, LOF [6], BRPCA [7]
Clustering	Partition-based (k-means, k-medoids), hierarchical
Visualization category	Methods
Time-related visualizations	Line plot
Relative size comparison	Bar/pie/stacked bar/sunburst chart, treemap
Multi-variate comparison	Scatterplot, parallel coordinates, spider web, heatmap
Graph-based visualizations	k-partite graphs [35], multi-objective visualization [36]

blood glucose measurement device, are also used at specific times within the day. All devices are connected to the gateways via Bluetooth, ZigBee and ZWave protocols, while the universAAL [27] and IoTivity [20] platforms are used for their management. The scenario is currently being installed in testhomes, in order to be further deployed in several Greece municipalities, during the next period, with 500 scheduled participants in total. The purpose is to allow centralized management and analysis of the collected data by healthcare professionals.

In the mobility scenario, the purpose is to monitor and assist the older person while moving in a city, providing information and alerts when needed. The sensors involved include Bluetooth detectors installed at intersections for detecting bypassing devices, connected traffic signals, taxi data collectors, environmental pollutant detectors and pedestrian presence detectors. The FIWARE [25] IoT platform is being used for device and data management, with the aim to use more IoT platform types in the future, as part of a larger deployment. The scenario is currently being installed in test sites, with the purpose of being further deployed in Greece municipalities, with 500 scheduled participants. The purpose is to monitor the environment and the participants' movements, analyzing the collected data to provide notifications when certain patterns are detected.

5   Conclusion and Next Steps

This paper proposes an architecture for big data analytics in the IoT domain, in the context of large-scale federations of IoT platforms with heterogeneous data models. The semantic interoperability issue is addressed by introducing the Semantic Interoperability Layer (SIL), which maintains a common ontology describing relevant IoT concepts, as well as semantic mappings with the platform-specific ontologies. In this way, the upper layers can be agnostic of platform-specific naming conventions and semantics. The architecture also introduces the Data Lake layer, for directing external queries and results to and from the SIL, as well as for storing analysis metadata (extracted features, trained models, etc.) which are needed for real-time data analytics. The architecture is being tested in laboratory environments, and is about to start being tested in real-world deployment sites. The architecture has been developed in the context of health assistance for older people, although it is generic enough to be applied in any application domain, such as smart cities, traffic monitoring, etc.

The next steps will be focused on implementation, integration and large-scale deployment. The proof-of-concept of the proposed architecture has been demonstrated in laboratory settings with a limited part of the whole architecture functioning. In the next period, the SIL ontology will be defined and implemented in detail, the Data Lake infrastructure will be completed to provide the basis for all data analytics methods, and the implementation of data analytics and visual analytics as Web services will be performed. In the meantime, integration issues will be resolved in order for the whole data analytics workflow to perform end-to-end. Finally, as mentioned in Sect. 4, the architecture is going to be tested in large-scale deployment sites in Greece municipalities, with a large number of participants, in order to use and evaluate it in real-world conditions. During evaluation, fine-tuning of ontology entities and data/visual analytics will be performed, in order to identify those concepts and methods that best fit in large-scale applications.

Acknowledgments. This work is supported by the EU funded projects ACTIVAGE (H2020-IOT-2016, grant agreement no. 732679) and FrailSafe (H2020-PHC-2015-single-stage, grant agreement no. 690140).

References

1. European project ACTIVAGE. http://www.activageproject.eu/
2. European project FrailSafe. https://frailsafe-project.eu/
3. Marjani, M., Nasaruddin, F., Gani, A., Karim, A., Hashem, I.A.T., Siddiqa, A., Yaqoob, I.: Big IOT data analytics: architecture, opportunities, and open research challenges. IEEE Access **5**, 5247–5261 (2017)
4. Soualhi, A., Medjaher, K., Zerhouni, N.: Bearing health monitoring based on Hilbert-Huang transform, support vector machine, and regression. IEEE Trans. Instrum. Measur. **64**(1), 52–62 (2015)
5. Chen, J., Li, K., Tang, Z., Bilal, K., Yu, S., Weng, C., Li, K.: A parallel random forest algorithm for big data in a spark cloud computing environment. IEEE Trans. Parallel Distrib. Syst. **28**(4), 919–933 (2017)
6. Papadopoulos, S., Drosou, A., Dimitriou, N., Abdelrahman, O.H., Gorbil, G., Tzovaras, D.: A BRPCA based approach for anomaly detection in mobile networks. In: Abdelrahman, O.H., Gelenbe, E., Gorbil, G., Lent, R. (eds.) Information Sciences and Systems 2015. LNEE, vol. 363, pp. 115–125. Springer, Cham (2016). https://doi.org/10.1007/978-3-319-22635-4_10
7. Ding, X., He, L., Carin, L.: Bayesian robust principal component analysis. IEEE Trans. Image Process. **20**(12), 3419–3430 (2011)
8. Rokach, L., Maimon, O.: Clustering methods. In: Maimon, O., Rokach, L. (eds.) Data Mining and Knowledge Discovery Handbook, pp. 321–352. Springer, Boston (2005). https://doi.org/10.1007/0-387-25465-X_15
9. Wold, S., Esbensen, K., Geladi, P.: Principal component analysis. Chemometr. Intell. Lab. Syst. **2**(1–3), 37–52 (1987)

10. Cox, T.F., Cox, M.A.: Multidimensional Scaling. CRC Press, Boca Raton (2000)
11. Yan, S., Xu, D., Zhang, B., Zhang, H.-J., Yang, Q., Lin, S.: Graph embedding and extensions: a general framework for dimensionality reduction. IEEE Trans. Pattern Anal. Mach. Intell. **29**(1), 40–51 (2007)
12. Kalpakis, K., Gada, D., Puttagunta, V.: Distance measures for effective clustering of ARIMA time-series. In: Proceedings IEEE International Conference on Data Mining, ICDM 2001, pp. 273–280. IEEE (2001)
13. Apache Spark. https://spark.apache.org/
14. Apache Hadoop. http://hadoop.apache.org/
15. Strohbach, M., Ziekow, H., Gazis, V., Akiva, N.: Towards a big data analytics framework for IoT and smart city applications. In: Xhafa, F., Barolli, L., Barolli, A., Papajorgji, P. (eds.) Modeling and Processing for Next-Generation Big-Data Technologies. MOST, vol. 4, pp. 257–282. Springer, Cham (2015). https://doi.org/10.1007/978-3-319-09177-8_11
16. Rathore, M.M., Ahmad, A., Paul, A., Rho, S.: Urban planning and building smart cities based on the internet of things using big data analytics. Comput. Netw. **101**, 63–80 (2016)
17. Bajaj, G., Agarwal, R., Singh, P., Georgantas, N., Issarny, V.: A study of existing Ontologies in the IOT-domain. arXiv preprint arXiv:1707.00112 (2017)
18. Compton, M., Barnaghi, P., Bermudez, L., GarcíA-Castro, R., Corcho, O., Cox, S., Graybeal, J., Hauswirth, M., Henson, C., Herzog, A., et al.: The SSN ontology of the W3C semantic sensor network incubator group. Web Seman.: Sci. Serv. Agents World Wide Web **17**, 25–32 (2012)
19. Alaya, M.B., Medjiah, S., Monteil, T., Drira, K.: Toward semantic interoperability in oneM2M architecture. IEEE Commun. Mag. **53**(12), 35–41 (2015)
20. IoTivity. https://www.iotivity.org/
21. Open Connectivity Foundation. https://openconnectivity.org/
22. Soldatos, J., et al.: OpenIoT: open source internet-of-things in the cloud. In: Podnar Žarko, I., Pripužić, K., Serrano, M. (eds.) Interoperability and Open-Source Solutions for the Internet of Things. LNCS, vol. 9001, pp. 13–25. Springer, Cham (2015). https://doi.org/10.1007/978-3-319-16546-2_3
23. OPENIoT. http://www.openiot.eu/
24. Bermudez-Edo, M., Elsaleh, T., Barnaghi, P., Taylor, K.: IoT-Lite: a lightweight semantic model for the internet of things. In: 2016 International IEEE Conferences on UIC/ATC/ScalCom/CBDCom/IoP/SmartWorld, pp. 90–97. IEEE (2016)
25. FIWARE. https://www.fiware.org/
26. sensiNact. https://projects.eclipse.org/proposals/eclipse-sensinact
27. universAAL. http://www.universaal.info/
28. Sofia2. http://sofia2.com/home_en.html
29. SENIORSome. http://www.seniorsome.com/
30. Veer, H., Wiles, A.: Achieving technical interoperability-the ETSI approach, European telecommunications standards institute (2008)
31. Daniele, L., den Hartog, F., Roes, J.: Created in close interaction with the industry: the smart appliances REFerence (SAREF) ontology. In: Cuel, R., Young, R. (eds.) FOMI 2015. LNBIP, vol. 225, pp. 100–112. Springer, Cham (2015). https://doi.org/10.1007/978-3-319-21545-7_9
32. Agarwal, R., Fernandez, D.G., Elsaleh, T., Gyrard, A., Lanza, J., Sanchez, L., Georgantas, N., Issarny, V.: Unified IOT ontology to enable interoperability and federation of testbeds. In: 2016 IEEE 3rd World Forum on Internet of Things (WF-IoT), pp. 70–75. IEEE (2016)

33. Noy, N.F., McGuinness, D.L., et al.: Ontology development 101: a guide to creating your first ontology (2001)
34. European project FIESTA-IoT: Federated Interoperable Semantic IoT Testbeds and Applications. http://fiesta-iot.eu/
35. Drosou, A., Kalamaras, I., Papadopoulos, S., Tzovaras, D.: An enhanced graph analytics platform (GAP) providing insight in big network data. J. Innov. Digital Ecosyst. **3**(2), 83–97 (2016)
36. Kalamaras, I., Drosou, A., Tzovaras, D.: Multi-objective optimization for multi-modal visualization. IEEE Trans. Multimedia **16**(5), 1460–1472 (2014)

5G-PINE

On Edge Cloud Architecture and Joint Physical Virtual Resource Orchestration for SDN/NFV

Shah Nawaz Khan[(✉)] and Roberto Riggio

Wireless and Networked Systems (WiN), FBK CREATE-NET,
Via Alla Cascata 56/D, 38123 Trento, Italy
{s.khan,r.riggio}@fbk.eu

Abstract. 5G networks will incorporate virtualized network infrastructures and new technologies such as Software Defined Networking and Network Function Virtualization. The developments have predominantly been made in the core and back-haul network segments. However, the ambitious Key Performance Indicators (KPIs) set for 5G networks will necessitate a renewed focus on the network edge in view of the virtualized infrastructure and SDN/NFV adoption. Several challenges are anticipated to be addressed for cloud at the edge, prime among which is the heterogeneity that spans, among others, hardware, software, radio, networking and virtualization domains. In this paper, we investigate cloud at the edge architecture, its unique challenges and the technology enablers. We present a prototype heterogeneous edge cloud implementation with focus on joint physical and virtual resource management and orchestration while supporting multi-tenancy for edge services. A scheduling & orchestration module is presented that interfaces with Kubernetes cloud management system to support service deployment per two scheduling polices of load balancing and energy saving. We present details of the considered edge cloud platform, the scheduling & orchestration module and its functions inside the edge cloud. Finally, we present some preliminary results and comparisons of the implemented orchestration policies in the context of heterogeneous edge services.

Keywords: Edge cloud · SDN/NFV · Orchestration · Kubernetes

1 Introduction

Wireless communication is an integral part of modern day lives across the world. In the past decade, requirements on wireless networks to support increasing number of new services beyond the simple voice calls and connecting larger number of end-users have been consistently intensifying. Until recently, mobile communication networks have been addressing these requirements and challenges with continuous evolution of the radio access technologies and by incrementally increasing

© IFIP International Federation for Information Processing 2018
Published by Springer International Publishing AG 2018. All Rights Reserved
L. Iliadis et al. (Eds.): AIAI 2018, IFIP AICT 520, pp. 27–38, 2018.
https://doi.org/10.1007/978-3-319-92016-0_3

the overall network capacity. However, with the recent focus on and proliferation of social media, networking, augmented and virtual reality and Internet of Things applications, the requirements and challenges have intensified such that mere evolution of 4G networks will not fully address them. These requirements and challenges are more stringent and diverse ranging from ultra low latency, to massive machine type communications to enhanced multimedia and broadband applications. Moreover, the pace at which the new network services and applications are developing, it is difficult for network operators to keep pace with by upgrading the core infrastructure, back-haul and radio access capacities. It is anticipated that in the next few years, the annual global IP traffic volume will reach an unprecedented 3.3 ZettaBytes (1 ZB = 1000 Exabytes) [1]. These numbers and the associated network requirements have made 5G, the next big step in the mobile wireless communication networks, one of the most important areas of research and development.

Several key technologies are anticipated to play a major role in defining the 5G networks' characteristics including Cloud based virtualized network infrastructure, Software Defined Networking (SDN) and Network Function Virtualization (NFV). These technologies and their practical realization has been an area of immense interest among researchers from both academia and industry. A large number of initiatives have been taken under the 5G networks R&D umbrella developing virtualization, SDN/NFV, Management and Network Orchestration (MANO) solutions [5–7]. Most of these initiatives have targeted the core and back-haul network segments with centralized cloud infrastructures. The network edge, that is, the radio, networking and communication infrastructure closest to the end-users (Access Points, Base Stations) has not received the attention it warrants. Some of this can be attributed to the issues such as complexity, lack of standardized platforms, node heterogeneity, distributed nature of the edge infrastructure and the large number of Points of Presence (PoPs). These factors make it challenging to develop and manage cloud infrastructure for the edge and orchestrate the resources for multiple tenants as anticipated for 5G networks. Providing cloud architectural blueprints for resource constrained edge devices, technology components for virtualization and resource orchestration (both physical and virtual) will help bring the benefits of virtualization and SDN/NFV closer to the network edge. In this paper, we focus on lightweight virtualization and resource management at the network edge. We characterize the unique features of network edge, the limitations of state of the art solutions and present a prototype heterogeneous edge cloud with a joint physical and virtual resource orchestrator module. The orchestrator can pro-actively scale the physical and virtual resources available to multi-tenant services per a given policy of load-balancing or energy saving. Our implementation is based on Kubernetes [2] container orchestration system and integrates with its main control elements for placing VNFs at the edge. The prototype edge cloud consists of nodes having different hardware architectures and computing resources integrated into a unified cloud fabric supporting service deployment, multi-tenancy, resource isolation and scaling. We present details of the hardware platform, the cloud virtualization stack and the orchestrator module and evaluate its performance. The rest of the paper is organized as follows. Section 2 discusses state of the art on cloud virtualization and SDN/NFV related technologies in view of their limitations for the network edge. Section 3 details the main contribution of this paper and presents an edge cloud architecture and virtualization stack addressing key constraints and function requirements. Preliminary results from the evaluation platform are presented in Sect. 4. The paper concludes with a summary and an outlook for future work in Sect. 5.

2 State of the Art

Recently, the network edge has attracted significant interest from researchers as evident from the abundant literature available under synonymous concepts but different terminologies. Mobile Edge Computing, FoG Computing, Multi-Access Edge Computing, Cloudlets etc., are a few well-known umbrella terms which in essence, aim to realize computing and network services closer to the end-users. In spite of these parallel developments in nomenclature and predominantly theoretic research works, there is a general dearth of clarity on the platform for edge computing such as hardware, software and architecture. A common consensus from the SDN/NFV community is that the benefits of cloud and virtualization must be realized at the network edge to support 5G use-cases and features such as multi-tenancy, resource slicing and orchestration etc. However, the available virtualization and resource orchestration technologies tailored towards data-center oriented centralized clouds and Virtual Machine (VM) based VNF abstraction do not suit the constraints of the network edge. For creating the cloud abstraction, the existing commercial and open source hypervisor technologies for SDN/NFV such as VMware ESX and ESXi, Microsoft Hyper-V, Xen, KVM etc., have a large hardware resource requirements footprint [8]. Usually in order of multiple high power processing cores and Gigabytes of memory, these hypervisors are virtually impossible to deploy on dispersed and resource constrained nodes. From the 5G networks and SDN/NFV perspective, the additional management and control elements required in the ETSI MANO architecture [4] such as Virtual Infrastructure Managers (VIM), VNF Manager (VNFM) and NFV Orchestrators need to be deployed. Many realizations of these components such as Open-Daylight, OSM, OpenO, OpenBaton etc., are tied to the centralized data-center oriented cloud model. The hardware resources (storage, compute, networking) required for realizing the same cloud architecture at the network edge are literally unavailable as edge nodes are resource constrained devices and are spread out over larger geographical areas. The level of hardware abstraction realized for centralized clouds where VNFs are completely devoid of information about the underlying hardware features may also prove limiting for the edge. For certain services, it may make more sense to expose the features available at the nodes such as hardware architecture, computing resources, dedicated hardware etc., to tailor their scheduling towards those nodes. Another limiting factor for cloud at the edge using existing virtualization solutions is the VM based VNF realization. A VM adds many layers of software abstraction (e.g., guest OS, unnecessary libraries) between the physical processor and the actual software that carries out a virtual network function. This makes VM based VNF realization unsuited to the limited resources available at the edge cloud. Moreover, with large sizes of VM based VNFs and the limited memory and storage resources of individual edge nodes, the scheduling and VNF placement problem becomes extremely complicated. Another constraint that proves a hindrance is the dispersed nature of edge nodes and the variance of networking links among them (throughput, firewalls etc.). This necessitates a more distributed realization of edge cloud rather than the centralized solutions available for core SDN/NFV implementations. A federation umbrella could tie together dispersed edge clouds and provide an interface to service providers through which network services could be deployed across distributed edge cloud. Finally, a number of advances have been made in the cloud resource management and cloud-native software design domains which have not been considered in the cloud for SDN/NFV context. These developments include the micro-services based software design, DevOps, Serverless Functions etc., which place a higher emphasis on resource utilization efficiency, robust cloud-native designs and rapid deployment. These developments are more suited to the edge cloud context and call for a design where VNFs are composed of small services interfaced together to create the end-to-end network service.

3   Edge Cloud Architecture and Resource Orchestration

Considering the challenging KPIs for 5G networks addressed in Sect. 1 and the limitations of tailoring the existing virtualization solutions to the network edge addressed in Sect. 2, it can be argued that cloud at the edge must be based on lightweight virtualization technologies and must integrate heterogeneous hardware while supporting the 5G service requirements. Furthermore, the ETSI MANO stack where specific control elements such as VIM, VNFM and NFVO are responsible specific SDN/NFV management tasks should be realized, potentially in a converged form and with small resource requirements footprints. Considering these and the recent developments in the cloud and virtualization domains such as Micro-Services Architectures, DevOps and Function as a Service (FaaS) etc., where resources are utilized to their fullest, we condense the requirements of edge clouds into following list.

- Heterogeneity: Cloud at the edge must integrate hardware nodes of different architecture and resources (compute, storage, memory, networking) into a unified abstraction providing similar interfaces to the service providers as in centralized cloud infrastructures. Moreover, cloud at the edge should hide the complexity of these underlying hardware differences from the deployed services i.e., a service provider should not be forced to design the service template according to the hardware architecture of the host infrastructure. Any mapping between the requirements of a VNF and the capabilities of the underlying hardware should be done by the cloud control and management functions.

- Resource Awareness: Cloud at the edge should be several order of magnitude lighter in terms of hardware requirements compared with centralized cloud technologies. This implies that the edge cloud and MANO features should be realized using virtualization technologies that can run efficiently on hardware resource constrained devices deployed in end-user premises.
- MANO Features: MANO is an essential requirement from the SDN/NFV management and control point of view. Service providers must have a simple interface through which they can deploy an edge resident network service and manage it in isolation from other services. Therefore, the essential features of VIM, VNFM, and NFVO must be realized albeit considering the discussed resource constraints and heterogeneity of the network edge. Moreover, management polices for cloud resources (physical and virtual) and tenant-specific service orchestration must be supported.
- Services: Cloud at the edge must support the distinctive features of centralized SDN/NFV clouds such as resource slicing, multi-tenancy, service isolation, auto-scaling etc. Moreover, support for new cloud-native software design principles such as micro-services architecture should be supported to utilize the dispersed computing resources more effectively.

Considering these requirements and constraints, we focus on container based virtualization where VNFs can be realized in container images instead of VMs. Containers have a significantly low overhead not only in terms of storage, memory and processing requirements compared with VMs but they also eliminate the need for the hypervisor layer. This resource efficiency usually comes at the cost of security and service isolation but several measures can be taken to address these concerns including container specific Linux kernels and more sophisticated access policies. Beyond the container based VNF abstraction, we use Kubernetes to emulate the role of VIM and NFVM by extending it to support (a) heterogeneous hardware nodes, (b) custom scheduling and orchestration module and (c) allowing for mixed service deployment in architecture agnostic manner. The remainder of this section details the considered virtualization stack and MANO feature realization.

3.1   Physical Architecture and Virtualization Stack

Figure 1 depicts a subset of the physical architecture of edge cloud infrastructure and the virtualization stack used in this work. The hardware platform comprises five ARM architecture based Raspberry Pi 3 nodes and two Intel x64 based Laptops assembled in a cluster and local network. All nodes run platform specific Linux distribution and a container runtime daemon (Docker in our case). The selection of Docker in general and container based virtualization in particular was made considering the resource limitations and hardware heterogeneity of the nodes. To integrate the nodes into a cluster where services can be deployed at cloud abstraction level, we use Kubernetes [2]. Kubernetes is an open source container management and orchestration platform that can run on several types of physical nodes and has a considerably small resource

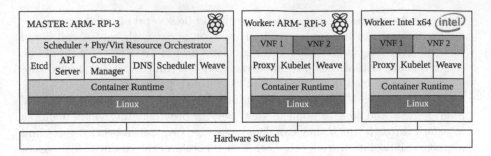

Fig. 1. Physical architecture and virtualization stack of the edge cloud

requirements footprint compared with hypervisor and VM based virtualization platforms. The core Kubernetes control elements such as Etcd, Controller Manager, API Server, DNS and default Scheduler run in Docker containers on a single Raspberry Pi node. The weave element is deployed alongside Kubernetes core control elements to provide overlay connectivity among service VNFs. The details of these control elements is beyond the scope of this work and can be found in [2]. Kubernetes uses a Master-Worker based architecture where the master node hosts all the main control plane elements while the worker nodes host a subset which enable communication with the master node. We host the master node functions on a Raspberry Pi and integrate the rest of ARM and x64 nodes as workers. However, by default, Kubernetes does not integrate nodes of different hardware architecture into a single cloud abstraction i.e., the worker nodes must be of the same architecture as the master node. This limitation arises during the Kubernetes installation where the master node downloads control plane elements container images on the worker nodes according to its own architecture. Therefore, if the master node elements are instantiated on an ARM node as in our case, Kubernetes will download ARM based images for the rest of cluster members including on the x64 nodes. To overcome this problem, we modified the configuration for master node allowing it to download architecture specific images on worker nodes. To this end, we modified the control daemon configuration for kube-proxy by duplicating it for x64 architecture and specifying the correct architecture images. This problem is expected to be natively addressed in future Kubernetes versions where control plane images are expected to be architecture specific using the Docker image manifests.

Most of the ETSI MANO control functions can be realized inside the Kubernetes cluster including VIM, VNFM and NFVO by either using the default Kubernetes control elements or by extending the cluster with new control elements. We utilize both approaches in our prototype edge cloud setup. For the VIM and NFVO functions, we have developed a dedicated scheduling and orchestration module (detailed in the next subsection). This module, depicted in yellow color in Fig. 1, takes the role of VIM by elastically scaling the infrastructure resources to the requirements of the deployed services following a scheduling policy. To this end, the available physical resources of the nodes and requirements of the deployed services are actively monitored. The same module is responsible for network service orchestration including deployment, scheduling VNFs, chaining and scaling. The VNFM role is shared between the Kubernetes control elements that actively probe the state of deployed VNFs and restart a service VNF if detected to be dysfunctional. Finally, to ensure service isolation and that tenants are allocated a specific set of resources, both physical and virtual, we use the Kubernetes namespaces feature together with labeling of the nodes. A Kubernetes namespace is a virtual container for deployed services in the edge cloud which can enforce resource restrictions on the services falling in a particular namespace. With namespaces and node labels, a service can not only be confined to specific nodes e.g., deploy on ARM or x64 nodes but also be restricted to a subset of the resources on those nodes.

3.2   Scheduler and Orchestrator Architecture

Figure 2 shows the internal architecture and functions of the scheduler and physical & virtual resource orchestrator component integrated with the kubernetes control plane elements. The orchestrator receives a policy parameter as input at start-up time and spins up two concurrent processes namely the Policy function and the Resource Monitor function. The policy parameter determines the scheduling behavior and the placement of service VNFs on the worker nodes. Currently, two options are available for policy parameter targeting energy saving and load balancing. In the energy saving mode, the orchestrator targets running the least number of worker nodes in running state in order to conserve energy expended by the cluster. Practically, this implies a single worker node is kept running for as long as the deployed service VNFs are providing the required quality of service. A new worker node is boot up only when the running services are scaled beyond the resources of the running worker nodes or when new deployments are requested that either require more physical resources or are targeting a particular node/set of nodes in the cluster with specialized hardware. A service deployment may target a specific set of nodes for several reasons such as due to assigned quota, resource constraints or performance reasons. For example, a service might request a VNF to be deployment on a node that has SSD storage or a GPU for graphic processing. The master node keeps a record of the hardware attributes of the worker nodes in the cluster. The orchestrator can map these attributes to the requirements of a service deployment. The other option for policy parameter is load balancing which keeps all the worker nodes in running state and priorities minimal delay in service deployment and scaling latency. This is achieved by compromising on the overall energy consumption of the cluster. The whole service deployment and scheduling process is executed as follows:

- Service deployment is requested by providing a service template file to the Kubernetes API Server component. To do this, a service provider needs to authenticate its access with the API Server. The service template is provided as Yaml [3] file describing the service at a high abstraction level such as

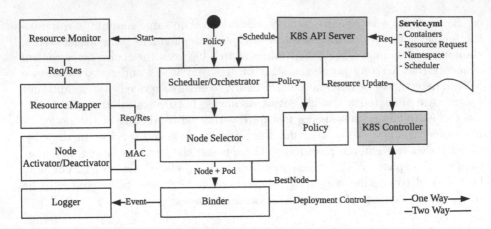

Fig. 2. Software architecture and functional diagram

the required VNFs (Docker containers to run), hardware resources required, service and target node attributes.

- The API server receives the deployment requests and pushes a scheduling request trigger to the orchestrator component. At this point, the scheduling and orchestration component has to determine the criteria of VNF placement resource scaling. These include (a) find the worker nodes in the cluster that have the required resources available to host the VNFs requested by the deployment (b) determine, for each VNF, a single node out of the possibly multiple qualified nodes as host (c) determine the state of the node which can be either ready or switched off (d) bind the VNF to the selected node if the node is in ready state (in load balancing policy) or first boot the node (in energy saving policy) and then bind the VNF to the selected node once it is in ready state.
- For task (a), a Resource Mapper function takes the requested resources of a given service deployment request and compares them to the active resource map maintained by the Resource Monitor process instantiated by the scheduler. It should be noted that the Resource Monitor keeps a real-time load of running nodes only and an indication of the physical capacity of the nodes that are offline but part of the cluster. This way, the resource mapping process considers all nodes in the cluster instead of the online ones if the scheduling policy is load balancing or the VNFs image is for a particular hardware architecture. The resource mapper will return the list of all qualified nodes that can host the service VNFs.
- For task (b), the policy function is responsible for reducing the possible list of several qualified worker nodes to a single node based on the policy used by the scheduler. It is worth pointing out here that this process is sequential i.e., a deployment may contain several VNFs (containers) and the deployment of those are carried out sequentially in order to fulfill the load balancing or energy saving policy requirements.

- For task (c), the node activator module takes care of booting up a node based on the node ID in case it is offline. It uses the Wake On Lan feature of NICs on the worker nodes.
- Finally for task (d), the binder function does the actual scheduling of the VNF on the selected node. For this, the binder interacts with the kubernetes control plane elements to download the VNF container image (if not present locally), and then boot it up with the required resources provisioned. Lastly the Binder function logs the success and failure events of the binding process.

4 Evaluation

We have carried out preliminary evaluation of the resource consumption (Storage, Memory, CPU) of the control elements in our prototype edge cloud environment and its performance in terms of service deployment and deletion latencies. Figure 3 shows the image sizes of Kubernetes core control elements and our add-on purpose-built scheduler and orchestrator (labeled as Sch+Orch). The add-on component has been implemented in Golang and compiled into a static binary. As evident from Fig. 3, the container image sizes of the core Kubernetes elements are small enough to be deployed on tiny storage resource constrained devices. Second, it is very easy to create add-on elements for specific functionality such as Sch+Orch that has our statically linked binary embedded inside a tiny sized Docker image (5.3 MB only).

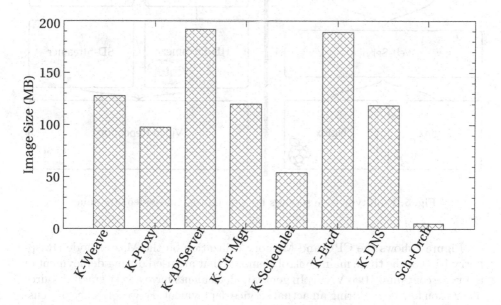

Fig. 3. Container image sizes for core control elements

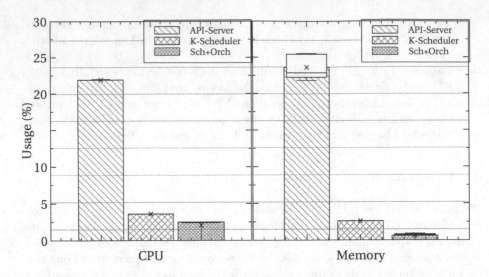

Fig. 4. CPU and Memory utilization of core control elements

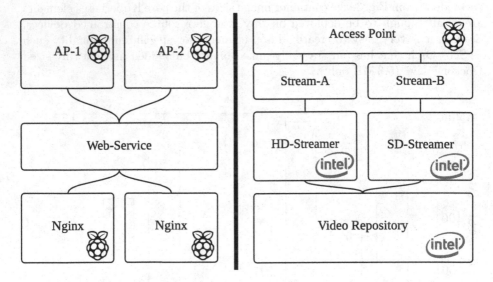

Fig. 5. Prototype edge services for web hosting and video streaming

Figure 4 shows the CPU and Memory utilization on the Master node (Raspberry Pi 3) of the three main control elements that are used during deployment of a service containing two VNFs. In general, all elements have a very small resource utilization footprint during an actual service deployment. However, since our custom Sch+Orch element takes away the scheduling and orchestration duties from the Kubernetes default scheduler, there is no observable variance in its CPU and Memory consumption during the deployment. In fact, the only significant

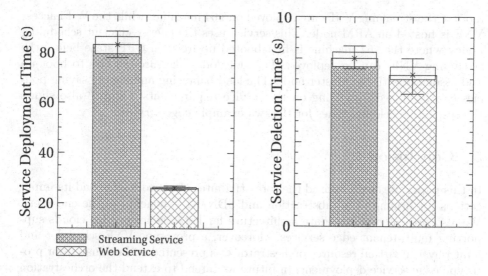

Fig. 6. Service deployment and deletion latencies

variance is in the memory footprint of the API server and the CPU utilization of our scheduler VNF. This is expected since a service deployment is an active interaction process between the Kubernetes API Server and the scheduler VNF. To evaluate the scheduling and service deployment capabilities of our platform and to analyze the effects of scheduling policies on the deployment latencies, we deployed a couple of prototype web and video streaming edge services in our evaluation platform. Figure 5 shows the two prototype services and their VNF composition. On the left side, a service that combines web services and access services is depicted presented. This service targets the ARM nodes in the cluster as the Docker images for Nginx VNF and WiFi access point VNFs have been developed for that platform. The association between VNF architecture and the nodes having that physical architecture is done by label matching between the service template (yaml file) and the labeled nodes. On the right side in Fig. 5, a mixed architecture streaming service is depicted. This service template exemplifies a video streaming scenario where users of different privileges are provisioned video streaming service of different quality. The VNFs in this service includes an access VNF (WiFi access) and two streaming VNFs that stream video files in different quality. The video files are provided to both streaming services by a back-end video store VNF. To eliminate some of the latency factors of service deployment, all the Docker images for required service VNFs were downloaded prior to the actual deployment. Figure 6 shows the service deployment and deletion time for the two services per the load-balancing and energy saving scheduling policies. The web-service is entirely hosted on ARM nodes and uses the load-balancing scheduling policy. As evident, the service takes approximately 26 s to be active in the edge cloud including providing the WiFi Access and the Nginx web-server. The video streaming service is deployed on different architecture nodes where most of the streaming VNFs are deployed on x64 machines while the WiFi access VNF is hosted on ARM node. This service uses the energy efficient scheduling policy where the x64 machine is first booted up from an OFF state before the streaming VNFs can be deployed. The x64 node takes around 50 s to boot up and associate with the Master node. The load balancing and energy saving policies can be mixed depending on the service requirements. Figure 6 also shows the respective deletion times for the two example edge services.

5   Conclusion

In this paper, we characterized the core attributes of network edge and its implications for brining cloud abstraction and SDN/NFV benefits to the end-users. We also presented a candidate architecture for heterogeneous edge clouds supporting multi-tenant edge services. Moreover, a prototype VNF scheduler and joint physical virtual resource orchestrator was presented and evaluated for prototype edge service deployment. In future we intend to extend the orchestration umbrella across multiple distributed edge-clouds by tying together a federated cloud environment. We also intend to investigate the interplay between self-organizing edge services and resource orchestration in host infrastructure using Artificial Intelligence algorithms.

References

1. CISCO: Cisco Visual Networking Index: Forecast and Methodology, 2016–2021. https://www.cisco.com/c/en/us/solutions/collateral/service-provider/visual-networking-index-vni/complete-white-paper-c11-481360.html
2. Kubernetes: Production-Grade Container Orchestration System (2018) https://www.kubernetes.io
3. YAML: Yaml ain't markup language. http://yaml.org/
4. ETSI: Network Functions Virtualisation (NFV) Management and Orchestration, Technical report (2014). http://www.etsi.org/deliver/etsi_gs/NFV-MAN/001_099/001/01.01.01_60/gs_nfv-man001v010101p.pdf
5. OSM: OpenSource Management & Network Orchestration (2018). https://osm.etsi.org/
6. OpenStack: Open source software for creating private and public clouds (2018). https://www.openstack.org/
7. CORD: Central Office Re-architected as a Datacenter (2018). https://opencord.org/
8. Blenk, A., Basta, A., Reisslein, M., Kellerer, W.: Survey on network virtualization hypervisors for software defined networking. IEEE Commun. Surv. Tutor. **18**(1), 655–685 (2016)

Use Cases for 5G Networks Using Small Cells

Alexandros Kostopoulos[1]([✉]), Ioannis P. Chochliouros[1], Daniele Munaretto[2],
Claudio Meani[3], Claus Keuker[4], Elisenda Temprado Garriga[5],
Javier Fernandez Hidalgo[6], Miguel Catalan Cid[6], Hicham Khalife[7], and Fidel Liberal[8]

[1] Hellenic Telecommunications Organization S.A. (OTE), Marousi, Greece
{alexkosto,ichochliouros}@oteresearch.gr
[2] Athonet, Bolzano, Italy
[3] Italtel, Milan, Italy
[4] Smart Mobile Labs, Munich, Germany
[5] Zodiac Inflight Innovations, Brea, USA
[6] i2CAT, Barcelona, Spain
[7] Thales, La Défense, France
[8] Universidad del Pais Vasco, Leioa, Spain

Abstract. In this paper, we discuss the main use cases and scenarios we consider in the context of 5G ESSENCE project [1]. The first use case investigates edge network acceleration at a stadium. The second use case is focused on end-to-end slicing for mission critical applications. The third scenario considers in-flight communications and entertainment system.

Keywords: Cloud-Enabled Small Cell (CESC) · Mobile edge computing (MEC) Network functions virtualization (NFV) · Radio resource management (RRM)

1 Introduction

5G ESSENCE [1] addresses the paradigms of Edge Cloud computing and Small Cell as-a-Service (SCaaS) by fuelling the drivers and removing the barriers in the Small Cell (SC) market, forecasted to grow at an impressive pace up to 2020 and beyond, and to play a "key role" in the 5G ecosystem. The 5G ESSENCE framework provides a highly flexible and scalable platform, able to support new business models and revenue streams by creating a neutral host market and reducing operational costs, by offering new opportunities for ownership, deployment, and operation.

As the telecom ecosystem moves towards the innovative 5G era, important performance factors such as end-to-end (E2E) latency critically depend on whether the mobile edge and the target applications reside in an edge cloud close to the user or not. Building upon these technological foundations [2–9], very ambitious objectives are targeted, culminating with the prototyping and demonstration of the 5G ESSENCE system in three real-life use cases associated to vertical industries, that is: (i) Edge network acceleration in a crowded event; (ii) mission critical applications for public safety (PS) communications providers, *and*; (iii) in-flight entertainment and connectivity (IFEC)

© IFIP International Federation for Information Processing 2018
Published by Springer International Publishing AG 2018. All Rights Reserved
L. Iliadis et al. (Eds.): AIAI 2018, IFIP AICT 520, pp. 39–49, 2018.
https://doi.org/10.1007/978-3-319-92016-0_4

communications. In this paper, we discuss the aforementioned use cases by considering the involved actors, *per case*, as well as the deployment topology.

2   5G Edge Network Acceleration at a Stadium

2.1   Overall Description

Broadcasters are looking for new ways to cover events, to offer exciting point-of-view perspectives to viewers *on one hand*, and to reduce production and delivery costs *on the other*. At the same time, network operators target to increase the usage of their networks and stadium owners have a strong interest in making the visitors' experience as pleasant as possible, as well as to promote sponsors increasing side-revenues apart from ticket sales. The reception of live content from cameras located in the playing field, replays, and additional contextual information on mobile devices, is a strong use case for all the above actors. The main challenges even with 4G networks are the delay in the delivery of such content in the range of milliseconds rather than seconds, and the considerable strain imposed on the backhaul network. By deploying a 5G ESSENCE-*like* network, these challenges can be efficiently addressed.

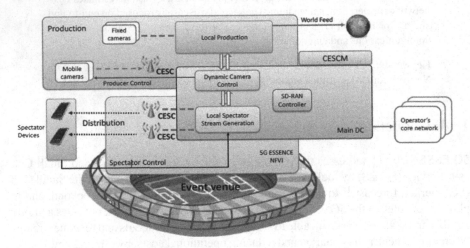

Fig. 1. 5G edge network acceleration at stadium

5G ESSENCE delivers benefits to media producers and mobile operators as it enables them to offer a highly interactive fan experience and it optimises operations by deploying "key functionalities" at the edge, i.e., evolved Multimedia Broadcast Multicast Services (eMBMS) or local network services like real-time analytics together with multitenancy support by small cells. By leveraging the benefits of small cell virtualisation and radio resource abstraction, as well as by optimising network embedded cloud, it becomes possible to ease the coverage and capacity pressure on the multimedia infrastructure, and also to increase security since content will remain locally. Furthermore, additional benefits for the operators and the venue owners arise, such as: (a) lower latency, due to shortening the data transmission path; (b) maintained backhaul capacity, due to playing out the live feeds and replays locally that puts no additional strain on the backhaul network and upstream core network components. The aforementioned use case is illustrated in Fig. 1.

2.2 Actors Involved

The actors involved in this scenario are listed below:

- **Small Cell Network Operator (SCNO):** Owner of the infrastructure deployed in the stadium.
- **Virtual Small Cell Operator (VSCNO):** Users of the infrastructure available in the stadium to provide services to the end-users.
- **End-Users (EUs):** Users of the networking services.
- **Mobile Operators (MOs):** Responsible of bringing the network and communication services to the stadium.
- **Service Provider (SPs):** Companies providing some of the Virtual Network Functions to the SCNO. Examples of key service providers for this use case could be football/sport society, live event organizer, municipality, video/content provider.
- **Spectrum Owner (SO):** In the licensed spectrum case, a stadium that leases the spectrum from an operator or a mobile operator that offers a service.
- **Mission Critical - Public Safety (MC-PS):** Public or private organizations in charge of performing, when needed, mission critical actions for the public safety (video surveillance, monitoring, autonomous local network).

2.3 Deployment Topology

5G ESSENCE will demonstrate a combined 5G-*based* video production and video distribution towards delivering benefits to both media producers and mobile operators, who will be able to offer enriched event experience to their subscribers. The production/distribution of locally generated content through the 5G ESSENCE platform, coupled with value-added services and rich user context, will enable secure, high quality and resilient transmission in real-time, thus ensuring minimal latency.

In the context of the 5G ESSENCE infrastructure sharing support, each network operator will be in position to optimise his network usage, resulting in lower OPEX. Additionally, network operators will be able to rapidly deploy new services, to deliver directly to users higher Quality of Experience (QoE), and to offer "Content as-a-Service", increased bandwidth, and storage solutions to content providers and venue owners. The content providers will also benefit from reduced latency and improved user QoE by positioning content on mobile edge and, *in addition*, they can offer augmented services by leveraging the network information. Finally, the stadium owner will obtain additional benefits by leveraging the deployed 5G ESSENCE infrastructure and its functionalities, by capitalising live contents to spectators from many cameras, etc.

The scenario provides the logic for distributing the live video feeds received from the local production room to local spectators in a highly efficient manner. Different scales facilities can be used for the validation of the deployment topology. First, a small-scale facility as the municipal open swimming pool with a capacity of 500 spectators, secondly a medium-scale facility like the municipal indoor stadium (which is used for basketball, volleyball and handball games) with a capacity of 2,000 spectators and thirdly a large-scale facility as the municipal football stadium "Stavros Mavrothalasitis" which is located at the centre of Egaleo town (in Athens, Greece) and it is an open stadium with capacity of about 8,000 spectators.

Considering a proper selection from the aforementioned facilities, the selected facility will be covered with a cluster of multitenant, eMBMS enabled as CESCs (Cloud-enabled Small Cells) and, together with the CESCM (CSC Manager) and the Main DC (Data Centre), they will be connected to the core networks of multiple telecom operators. The video content from cameras will be sent for processing locally at the Edge DC (similar to the proposed use case by ETSI MEC [13]). Then the video streams will be broadcasted locally by using the CESCs. Spectators will be able to dynamically select between different offered broadcast streams. In this and in similar big event scenarios, massive data traffic will not affect nor overload the backhaul connection, as it will be produced, processed and consumed just locally (5G MEC scenario).

3   5G E2E Slicing for Mission Critical Applications

3.1   Overall Description

Latest 3GPP releases address the key requirements expressed from the Public Safety (PS) domain for next generation broadband public safety networks [14]. Further improvements to the 3GPP standards to cope with mission critical communications requirements are being considered as a central topic in the 3GPP requirements study for 5G [15]. Regarding PS service delivery models, there is a clear trend towards different forms of network sharing models as opposed to building out dedicated PS networks. For example, the Emergency Services Network in the UK is going to use the RAN (Radio Access Network) infrastructure of a commercial provider; Blue Light Mobile service by PS operator Astrid in Belgium offers access through roaming agreements with commercial operators; FirstNet in the US, while it counts with spectrum dedicated to PS, is expected to enable secondary use by commercial applications. In this context, multitenancy becomes a cornerstone challenge at an international level.

5G ESSENCE common orchestration of radio, network and cloud resources is expected to significantly contribute to the fulfilment of the requirements of the PS sector, thus bringing new tools to share both radio and edge computing capabilities in localised/temporary network deployments between PS and commercial users. The challenge consists on allocating radio, network and cloud resources to the critical actors (e.g., the First Responders) who, *by nature*, require prioritised and high quality services.

Indeed, the public safety operators are "shifting" their business model from a completely owned infrastructure model to one playing the role of a Mobile Virtual Network Operator (MVNO) between multiple parties owning and operating mobile networks and PS end-users. From a broader perspective, such deployment can be seen as a dedicated mission critical slice spanning across multiple operators domains. In such

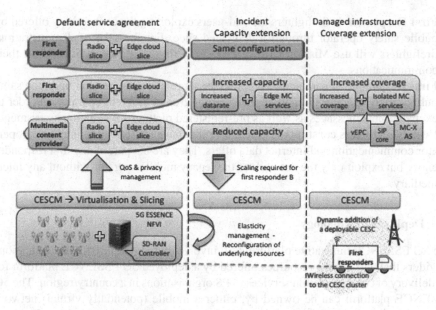

Fig. 2. Mission critical applications for public safety

configuration, the relevant public safety operator "buys" connectivity to multiple legacy mobile operators and guarantees to his public safety customers connectivity, resilience and required quality of service (QoS) for PS operations. In practice, such approach has multiple benefits to PS operators, as discussed below.

First, it reduces the costs of buying, installing and maintaining dedicated infrastructures. Note that these physical infrastructures are not exploited to their optimal capacity. Second, the flexibility offered by such solutions enables (at least theoretically) MVNOs to adapt their offers to their customers. However, this approach comes at the price of pre-negotiated contracts between the MVNOs and multiple legacy providers, in order to ensure a high availability and a "guaranteed" throughput for PS users.

For an allocation like this in order to be efficient and so to "enable" E2E network slicing, the 5G ESSENCE solution shall be applied. The aforementioned use case is schematically illustrated in Fig. 2.

3.2 Actors Involved

Demonstrating the 5G ESSENCE impact on mission critical deployments is performed with the following actors:

- **A legacy mobile operator (Platform owner)** offering its infrastructure to classical end-users as well as to Public Safety virtual operators. Note here that virtual operators can rely on multiple legacy operators for additional guarantee.
- **A public safety operator** that offers connectivity services with "strict" QoS guarantee to First Responders. Note that in our situation we can have multiple virtual operators each one offering a "separate" slice for a different First Responder agency.

- **First Responder 1:** firefighters are end-users exploiting the connectivity offered by public safety operator through a dedicated slice. For the sake of demonstration, firefighters will use Mission Critical Push-To-Talk (MCPTT) application for their communications.
- **First Responder 2:** paramedics are another set of end-users relying upon the same public safety operator or another slice coming from a different operator, in order to exchange chat messages as well as pre-registered pictures for situation assessment.
- **Legacy end-users** constitute classical user that have subscribed to the legacy operator communication and Internet data offers. They are not part of any first responder entity but exploit only the network of the legacy mobile operator without any intermediary.

3.3   Deployment Topology

The 5G ESSENCE innovative platform will involve one -or more- PS communications providers that will use the resources offered by a deployed 5G ESSENCE platform for the delivery of communication services to PS organisations in a country/region. The 5G ESSENCE platform can be owned by, either a mobile (potentially virtual) network operator or even by a venue owner, such as in the Use Case 1. In the mission critical use case, the infrastructure owner will exploit the 5G ESSENCE system's capabilities to provide the required network/cloud slicing capabilities with dedicated Service Level Agreements (SLAs) to different types of tenants, thus prioritising the PS communications providers.

The corresponding Mission Critical (MC) use case will be organised in three main stages, described as below:

Stage 1: Under normal circumstances, the 5G ESSENCE platform owner is providing the required network slices to different tenants. Each network slice is composed of an allocated data rate over a coverage area (which is mapped by the cSD-RAN (centralised Software-Defined RAN) Controller to a portion of CESC radio resources) and an allocated of cloud resources (which is mapped to processing power/storage capabilities in the Edge DC). For the service of Public Safety organisations, normal operations require a certain amount of access capacity and communications features (e.g., group communications capabilities) supported in the area of the CESC cluster. This requirement will be "mapped" to a number of radio Key Performance Indicators (KPIs) in the CESCs and the deployment of Group Communication service instances at the edge for multimedia and mission-critical Application Servers (AS) for voice with enhanced responsiveness. In addition to the QoS guarantees for each tenant, the deployment owner has to assure the required levels of isolation in the provisioning of the network slices.

Stage 2: In the case where there is an emergency in the area, the CESCM will be able to react to the new service requirements. The PS communications provider may require additional service in order to "cope with" an increased number of First Responders or additional types of services, such as mission-critical video transmissions. Based on pre-arranged or on-demand service scaling policies, the CESCM will implement new elastic resource allocation schemes, giving priority access to First Responders and taking into account both radio (for the access connections) and cloud resources (for deploying more resource-consuming edge services). The deployment of edge service instances serves a two-fold objective: first, it enables close-to-zero delay in the mission-critical services; second, it allows maintaining the operability, even when the backhaul connection is damaged.

Stage 3: In case that ICT infrastructure is damaged during a natural disaster or a terrorist attack, the first action should "address" the need for radio coverage extension. In this stage, a deployable system to mitigate the damage in the macro-base stations, will be used. In the proposed use case, the deployable system will offer 5G connectivity to the First Responders in the field, consolidating the interoperability requirements. In order to "better orchestrate" the radio transmissions, the deployable system will be considered as a new CESC that can be dynamically integrated to the small cell cluster. In this way, the enhanced 5G ESSENCE SON (Self-Organising Networks) and RRM (Radio Resources Management) features can be applied to the coverage extension unit. The interconnection of the deployable unit with the CESC cluster will be made through a wireless backhauling technology.

4   5G In-flight Communications and Entertainment System

4.1   Overall Description

Some years ago, only a single movie was available for all passengers to watch during a flight. Next, on-demand viewing options came, built onto the seats, where viewers could choose from an array of available television shows, movies and specials. Today, passengers bring their own devices on selected airlines. Thus, the wireless Inflight Entertainment (IFE) and broadband mobile connectivity increasingly have become actual commodity expectations both from airlines and passengers.

With the increasing demand for wireless IFE and passenger Bring-Your-Own-Devices (BYOD) connectivity, together with the demand for on board broadband mobile Internet connectivity, an important focus is laid on the on-board infrastructure. Current in-cabin wireless systems mainly rely on Wi-Fi technologies for the wireless IFE and broadband Internet connectivity (with backhaul connectivity offered through satellite links). Such solutions have several limitations such as prohibitive costs to the service providers, inability to support broadband cellular services, lack of flexibility for airlines operators, etc.

In order to offer cost-effective mobile broadband Internet connectivity, it is imperative to integrate on-board a neutral host solution that will allow multi-operator connectivity to the passengers, also accounting for variable service offerings. Such host-neutral services are important for European airliners, since they traverse several regional boundaries served by a large variety of mobile operators. Regarding backhauling, terrestrial direct-air-to-ground (continental airspace) and satellite (oceanic airspace) solutions can used.

The unique architecture proposed in 5G ESSENCE (as schematically depicted Fig. 3) which combines efficiently the virtualised and multi-tenant small cell networks with a multi-tier cloud edge infrastructure, is an essential and innovative step towards establishing a pioneering integrated In-Flight Entertainment and Connectivity (IFEC) system that will jointly deliver the required communication and network infrastructure for the wireless IFEC (to both the embedded IFE devices and the wireless BYODs).

Two different scenarios are envisaged in the corresponding IFEC use case. The first one consists of streaming and encoding to PErsonal Devices (PEDs) and aircraft devices (i.e., seat built-in screens). The purpose is about exploiting the Multi-Operator Core Network (MOCN) from 5G ESSENCE and LTE technologies so that to showcase multi-tenancy. That way, the Small Cell Network Operator -for instance the airline- can provide its proprietary IFEC services to the EUs (passengers) while leasing, *at the same time*, the same infrastructure to different VSCNOs, who will re-use it to give access to the same EUs to different services, such as *Netflix, Spotify*, etc., provided by themselves or by external Service Providers (SPs). For this concrete scenario, it is planned to "add" LTE to the current on-board Wi-Fi architecture, in order to provide multiple services from different operators/providers at the same time and in the same network infrastructure.

The second scenario consists upon providing efficient wireless multicast on-board. Networking speaking, the cabin of an aircraft is a super "dense" scenario. As mentioned above, all wireless communications on-board are currently done via Wi-Fi technologies, which actually "face" many limitations, in particular when many devices "share" the same medium. It becomes even more challenging, when it is planned to wirelessly multicast the same content at high-data rates to multiple PEDs and aircraft devices (for instance, video at high resolution). Thus, this specific scenario aims at dealing with and solving this problem by combining the Evolved Multimedia Broadcast Services (eMBMS) from LTE with the 5G ESSENCE architecture for on-board applications. This way, the SCNO can lease his infrastructure to VSCNOs and SPs, so that all of them can simultaneously stream their feeds (for instance, sport events, documentaries, or TV soap operas). Like that, the passengers (EUs) can watch live TV content in high resolution while, flying to a new destination.

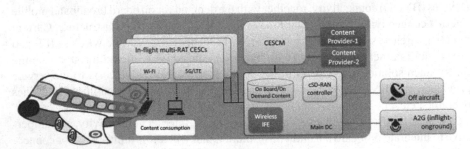

Fig. 3. Integrated in-flight connectivity and entertainment systems

4.2 Actors Involved

The actors involved in the IFEC scenario are listed below:

- **Small Cell Network Operator (SCNO):** Owner of the infrastructure deployed in the aircraft. It can be the airline flying the aircraft or a network operator/content provider, who is interested in providing its services on-board.
- **Virtual Small Cell Network Operator (VSCNO):** Users of the infrastructure available in the aircraft to provide services to the end-users.
- **End-Users (EUs):** Users of the networking services provided by the VSCNO and SCNO (a.k.a. flight passengers).
- **Mobile Operators (MOs):** Responsible of bringing the network and communication services to the aircraft.
- **Service Provider (SP):** Companies providing some of the Virtual Network Functions to the SCNO.
- **Spectrum Owner (SO):** In the licensed spectrum case, it is the airline who leases the spectrum from an operator or a mobile operator that offers a service on-board (who provides the spectrum for free or for a charge).

4.3 Deployment Topology

The 5G ESSENCE IFEC demo will test and validate the multi-tenancy enabled network solution for passenger connectivity and wireless broadband experience. The multi-RAT (Radio Access Technologies) CESCs will be implemented as a set of integrated access points to be deployed on-board. Afterwards, since IFE has to consider the explosive growth of multi-screen content consumption, the 5G ESSENCE CESCs will stream on-demand multi-screen video content (both from on-board 5G Edge DC servers and via satellite/air-to-ground links) to the wireless devices. The 5G ESSENCE CESCs will rely on broadcast links, in order to optimise the bandwidth usage.

Following the specific requirements for future IFEC solutions, as also currently outlined by various airlines and service providers, this 5G ESSENCE prototype platform will be tailored for a mock cabin deployment. The IFEC demonstration will be performed over a mock-up aircraft communications testbed installed, with core network connectivity to be incorporated both as on-board option and as a remote option steered via an emulated satellite link.

The use case will demonstrate the multitenant CESC for on-board connectivity and the Edge DC capabilities for hosting airborne applications (such as video player applications and files that can be made available for in-flight streaming) and caches (a version of the in-flight portal – gateway with which passengers can connect to).

The video encoding and packaging service will support a wide range of input file formats, allowing easy integration with existing production systems, and a comprehensive array of output formats. Output parameters will be configurable, enabling precise tuning for the desired output devices.

The topology foreseen for this use case aims at combining the current on-board topology with the one provided by the 5G ESSENCE project. Currently, an aircraft is connected to the Internet via a broadband antenna which, *at the same time*, is connected an on-board server, which is connected to the multiple access points deployed around the cabin to provide the IFEC services to the clients.

The 5G ESSENCE architecture is be added to the current cabin topology as an additional server, which is connected to the broadband access and all the other on-board servers. This new server will contain 5G ESSENCE elements, such as the MOCN, the small cell manager or the EPC (Evolved Packet Core) on-board. The current access points are going to be replaced by small cells, which will also be connected to this 5G ESSENCE server. This way, they are going to provide the different services/applications to the on-board screens and PEDs.

5   Discussion

In this paper, we have discussed the main use cases in the context of the 5G ESSENCE actual research framework. The first use case is a 5G edge network acceleration at a stadium. In particular, 5G ESSENCE will demonstrate a combined 5G-*based* video production and video distribution towards delivering benefits to both media producers and mobile operators, who will be able to offer enriched event experience to their subscribers. The second use case is 5G end-to-end slicing for mission critical applications. In particular, 5G ESSENCE will involve one or more PS communications providers that will use the resources offered by a deployed 5G ESSENCE platform for the delivery of communication services to PS organisations in a country/region. Our third scenario is focused upon in-flight communications and entertainment system. This demo will test and validate the multi-tenancy enabled network solution for passenger connectivity and wireless broadband experience.

For each use case, we investigated the involved actors, as well as the deployment topology. As a next step, we intend to focus upon the evaluation process, as well as upon the extraction of the main technical and non-technical requirements. Part of this work is already presented in [10]. Apart from the evaluation process, 5G ESSENCE will consider market and business aspects, since its architecture allows the sharing of existing and new infrastructure by many operators in a multitenant environment. Thus, it will enable new business models that will help new entrant market players to develop and analyse the perspectives of potential "win-win" strategies, based on the developed solutions [11, 12].

Acknowledgements. The paper has been based on the context of the 5G-PPP phase 2 "5G ESSENCE" ("Embedded Network Services for 5G Experiences") Project (GA No. 761592), funded by the European Commission.

References

1. 5G ESSENCE H2020 5G-PPP Project. http://www.5g-essenceh2020.eu
2. Chochliouros, I.P., et al.: A model for an innovative 5G-*oriented* architecture, based on small cells coordination for multi-tenancy and edge services. In: Iliadis, L., Maglogiannis, I. (eds.) AIAI 2016. IAICT, vol. 475, pp. 666–675. Springer, Cham (2016). https://doi.org/10.1007/978-3-319-44944-9_59

3. Goratti, L.: Network architecture and essential features for 5G: the SESAME project approach. In: Iliadis, L., Maglogiannis, I. (eds.) AIAI 2016. IAICT, vol. 475, pp. 676–685. Springer, Cham (2016). https://doi.org/10.1007/978-3-319-44944-9_60
4. SESAME 5G-PPP Project (GA No. 671596): Deliverable 2.2 ("Overall System and Architecture") (2016). http://www.sesame-h2020-5g-ppp.eu/Deliverables.aspx
5. SESAME 5G-PPP Project (GA No. 671596): Deliverable 2.3 ("Specification of the CESC Components – First Iteration") (2016)
6. SESAME 5G-PPP Project (GA No. 671596), Deliverable 3.1 ("CESC Prototype design specifications and initial studies on Self-X and virtualization aspects") (2016). http://www.sesame-h2020-5g-ppp.eu/Deliverables.aspx
7. SESAME 5G-PPP Project (GA No. 671596), Deliverable 2.4 ("Specification of the Infrastructure Virtualisation, Orchestration and Management") (2016)
8. Giannoulakis, I., Fajardo, J.O., et al.: Enabling technologies and benefits of multi-tenant multi-service 5G small cells. In: Proceedings of the EuCNC-2016, pp. 1–5 (2016)
9. Costa-Perez, X., Swetina, J., Guo, T., Mahindra, R., Rangarajan, S.: Radio access network virtualization for future mobile carrier networks. IEEE Commun. Mag. 51(7), 27–35 (2013)
10. Chochliouros, I.P., Kostopoulos, A., Giannoulakis, I., Spiliopoulou, A.S., Belesioti, M., Sfakianakis, E., Kourtis, A., Kafetzakis, E.: Using small cells from enhancing 5G networks. In: Proceedings of IEEE Conference on Network Function Virtualisation and Software-Defined Networks (NFV-SDN 2017), pp. 1–6. IEEE (2017)
11. Chochliouros, I.P., Sfakianakis, E., Belesioti, M., Spiliopoulou, A.S., Dardamanis, A.: Challenges for defining opportunities for growth in the 5G era: the SESAME conceptual model. In: Proceedings of the EuCNC-2016, pp. 1–5 (2016)
12. Khan, G.A., et al.: Network sharing in the next mobile network: TCO reduction, management flexibility, and operational independence. IEEE Commun. Mag. 49(10), 34–142 (2011)
13. European Telecommunication Standards Institute (ETSI): http://www.etsi.org/technologies-clusters/technologies/multi-access-edge-computing
14. The Third Generation Partnership Project (3GPP). http://www.3gpp.org/news-events/3gpp-news/1455-Public-Safety
15. The Critical Communications Association (TCCA): 4G and 5G for Public Safety – Technology options (White Paper), Cambridgeshire, UK (2017)

Enhancing Network Management via NFV, MEC, Cloud Computing and Cognitive Features: The "5G ESSENCE" Modern Architectural Approach

Ioannis P. Chochliouros[1]([✉]), Anastasia S. Spiliopoulou[1], Anastasios Kourtis[2],
Ioannis Giannoulakis[2], Michail-Alexandros Kourtis[2], Emmanouil Kafetzakis[3],
Eirini Vasilaki[1], Marinos Agapiou[4], and Mike Iosifidis[5]

[1] Hellenic Telecommunications Organization (OTE) S.A.,
99, Kifissias Avenue, 15124 Maroussi, Athens, Greece
{ichochliouros,evasilaki}@oteresearch.gr, aspiliopoul@ote.gr
[2] National Centre for Scientific Research "Demokritos",
Patriarchou Gregoriou Street, Aghia Paraskevi, 15310 Athens, Greece
{kourtis,giannoul,akis.kourtis}@iit.demokritos.gr
[3] ORION Innovations Private Company,
43, Ameinokleous Street, 11744 Athens, Greece
mkafetz@orioninnovations.gr
[4] National and Kapodistrian University of Athens,
6, Panepistimiopolis, 15784 Ilissia, Athens, Greece
sdi1400002@di.uoa.gr
[5] CLEMIC Services S.A., 55, Salaminos Street, 15124 Maroussi, Athens, Greece
mike@clemic.net

Abstract. The paper work presents the essential architectural approach that has been proposed in the framework of the modern "5G-ESSENCE" EU-*funded* project, intending to develop a suitable ecosystem for serving real-life use cases associated to vertical industries and built on the pillars of network functions virtualisation (NFV), mobile-edge computing (MEC) capabilities, cognitive network management and appropriate use of small cells. Apart from identifying innovative features and options for enabling service deployment, the work focuses on the fundamental 5G ESSENCE-*based* architecture with description of the corresponding modules and their capabilities. The current approach comes as a mature continuity of previous efforts and/or related findings in the 5G-PPP context (mainly from the SESAME research project), but it purely concentrates upon providing tools for a robust and agile network management.

Keywords: 5G · Cognitive management · Edge cloud computing
Mobile Edge Computing (MEC) · Network Functions Virtualisation (NFV)
Network slicing · Small Cell (SC) · Virtual Network Function (VNF)

L. Iliadis et al. (Eds.): AIAI 2018, IFIP AICT 520, pp. 50–61, 2018.
https://doi.org/10.1007/978-3-319-92016-0_5

1   Introduction: The 5G ESSENCE Context in the 5G Era

Today, Internet and communication networks are "critical" tools for most areas and sectors of our modern societies and economies as they are transforming our world; actually, these networks constitute fundamental "pillars" for any evolutionary process supporting effort for growth and development. According to recent market trends [1] as well as to actual European policy measures and/or related initiatives [2], it is assessed that the communication networks and the wider modern services/facilities environment of the year 2020 will be *"enormously richer and much more complex than that of today"*. The expected diversity of new (personal and professional) usages results in new requirements on availability, latency, reliability, trustworthiness and security. These chances are so expected to take place within the forthcoming "fifth generation" *-or 5G-* of telecoms systems, that will be the most critical building block of our "digital society" in the next decade; 5G will not only be an evolution of mobile broadband networks but will bring new unique network and service capabilities, creating a sustainable and scalable technology but also a proper ecosystem for technical and business innovation [3, 4]. Among current 5G's priorities is also to incorporate advanced automation, autonomicity and cognitive management features to advance operators' efficiency. This can also have a positive impact on the broader competitiveness of the European ICT industry. Furthermore, 5G can also support and enhance the convergence between fixed and mobile networking services with the related development of core and transport networks. 5G can "integrate networking, computing and storage resources into one programmable and unified infrastructure", which can be customized according to the interests of multiple costumers. As a consequence, the simultaneous "inclusion" of modern features (such as of virtualisation and of software-*based* network functionalities) in communications infrastructures is expected to support the corresponding transitional process via further strengthening network flexibility and reactivity [5]. Market "actors" (network operators and service providers, manufacturers, SMEs, end-users, etc.) are expected to be strongly involved in such processes; this will "redefine" existing value chains and reform roles and/or relationships between market "players", whilst creating new opportunities for novelty and investments. 5G is also expected to drastically reduce total cost of ownership of the infrastructure, *on one hand,* and the service creation and deployment times, *on the other.*

During 5G-PPP Phase-1, the ongoing SESAME project [6] evolved the small cell (SC) concept by integrating processing power (i.e., a low-cost micro-server) and by enabling the execution of applications and network services, in accordance to the Mobile Edge Computing (MEC) paradigm [7]. It also provides network intelligence and applications by leveraging the Network Function Virtualisation (NFV) concept [8]. The SESAME platform consists of one or more clusters of "Cloud – Enabled" Small Cells (CESCs), which are devices that include both the processing power platform and the small cell unit. CESCs can be deployed at low- and medium-*scale* venues and support multiple network operators (i.e.: multitenancy) and further, network services and applications at the edge of the network. In this context, SESAME has developed several small cell related functions as Virtualised Network Functions (VNFs), such as the GPRS Tunneling Protocol (GTP) en-/de-capsulation of data packets. Also SESAME has demonstrated so far that some network-*related* functions (such as content caching, firewalls and monitoring) perform adequately well when running as VNFs in the developed micro-server infrastructure (coined as "Light Data Centre" -Light DC-).

The 5G ESSENCE project [9] leverages results from the prior SESAME project, as well as from other 5G-PPP Phase-1 projects (mainly COHERENT [10], SPEED 5G [11], and SONATA [12]), in order to provide an evolution of the SESAME platform and to "meet" the 5G-PPP Phase-2 requirements, that is to cover the specific network needs of the vertical sectors and their inter-dependencies. 5G ESSENCE enhances the processing capabilities for data that have immediate value beyond locality; it also addresses the processing-intensive small cell management functions, such as Radio Resource Management (RRM)/Self Organising Network (SON) [13, 14] and, *finally*, it culminates with real life demonstrations. For all the above, 5G ESSENCE suggests clear breakthroughs in the research fields of wireless access, network virtualisation, and end-to-end (E2E) service delivery. The existing virtualised resources of small cells [15] will be exploited to their full potential and in a dynamic way, supporting extremely low-latency and the delivery of high-performance services, greater network resiliency, and substantial capacity gains at the access network for the next 5G stage.

To achieve these important goals, 5G ESSENCE will build upon the SESAME project by developing a distributed edge cloud environment (coined as ''Edge Data Centre" -Edge DC-), based on a two-tier architecture: the first tier (i.e.: Light DC), will remain distributed inside the CESCs for providing latency-sensitive services to users directly from the network's edge. The second tier will be a more centralised, "high-scale" cloud, namely the Main Data Centre (Main DC), which will provide high processing power for computing intensive network applications. It will also have a more centralised view so as to host efficient Quality of Service (QoS) - *enabled* scheduling algorithms. Both these cloud tiers will form the Edge DC in 5G ESSENCE terminology, which will be viewed as an integrated cloud infrastructure from the upper management and orchestration layers.

On the domain of hardware technologies, the processing power attached to small cells brings new capabilities to the network, as well as new challenges. In addition, the placement of low power/low cost processors to small cells, even with hardware acceleration, will be revised from the perspective of 5G ESSENCE. Although the CESC platform in SESAME is based on non-x86 architectures (ARMv8), the potential use of x86-*based*, low-cost and low-power processors will also be leveraged due to their efficiency (small form factor, low powered, passively cooled, low price) and their important share in the market.

The research domains mentioned cover only the technical aspects of the proposed 5G ESSENCE activities. However, a significant part of the project is also devoted to the actual demonstration of the outcomes in vertical industries, as they have been identified by 5G-PPP [2]. In order to showcase that 5G will be able to create a whole new ecosystem for technical and business innovation, 5G ESSENCE unifies computing and storage resources into a programmable and unified small cell infrastructure that can be provided *as-a-Service* to all related stakeholders. To that end, it provides a clear plan for real life demonstrations in the fields of: (i) multimedia/entertainment; (ii) mission critical communications at emergency events, and; (iii) in-flight connectivity and entertainment.

In addition to actual demonstrations, 5G ESSENCE is expected to accommodate a much wider range of use cases, especially in terms of ameliorated latency, resilience, coverage and bandwidth. One of its major innovations is that it provides E2E network and cloud infrastructure slices over the same physical infrastructure, in order to fulfil vertical-specific requirements as well as mobile broadband services, *in parallel*.

2   The 5G ESSENCE Ecosystem as "Enabler" for Service Deployment

Network functions are anticipated to take place over a unified operating system in a number of points of presence (PoPs), especially at the edge of the network for fulfilling specific performance targets. As a result, it will heavily rely on emerging technologies such as Software Defined Networking (SDN) [16], Network Functions Virtualisation (NFV) [15], Mobile Edge Computing (MEC) [17] and Fog Computing (FC) [18] to achieve the required performance, scalability and agility.

Entering the second phase of 5G-PPP program activities suggests that communication networks become sufficiently flexible to handle a range of applications and services originating from different domains/verticals. At the same time, a transformation towards a significant reduction in cost and the optimal allocation of available resources take the place of initial Key Performance Indicators (KPIs) for driving capacity growth, and coping with the numerous barriers on the infrastructure and management domains. On the users' side, a high-level of personalised services, along with edge mobile capabilities and innovative services are anticipated, since customers require added-value to their choices in order to accommodate specialised requirements with greater quality of both perception and experience.

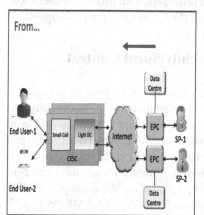 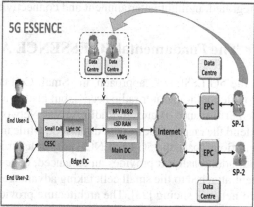

Fig. 1. 5G ESSENCE impact on service deployment.

As the telecom ecosystem moves towards the 5G era, important performance factors such as end-to-end latency critically depend on whether the mobile edge and the target applications reside in an edge cloud located close to the user or not. While the air-interface latency can be minimised independently of the service latency, having the application or service functions close to the user is also necessary to reduce the end-to-end round trip time and also the overall service creation time, which again argues for the placement of these functions in a common edge cloud. As shown in Fig. 1, the virtualisation of the small cells, as envisaged within the scope of 5G ESSENCE, supports the inclusion of enhanced mobile-edge computing capabilities that allow acceleration of content, services and applications, increasing responsiveness from the edge of the network. The 5G ESSENCE two-tier cloud resides very close to the users and performs a series of processing-intensive tasks that can neither be achieved with the traditional network infrastructure, nor with the "light" processing power introduced by SESAME which targets to virtualise mainly small cell related software. In this respect, 5G ESSENCE supports an enriched mobile users' experience, minimising service deployment time and, *at the same time*, it enables network operators and infrastructure owners to open the radio network edge to third-party partners allowing them to rapidly deploy innovative applications and services. The 5G ESSENCE effort "opens the door" to venue owners, e.g., municipalities, stadiums, site owners, and virtually anyone who manages a property and can install and run a local Small Cell network, to deploy a low cost infrastructure and to act as "neutral host network and service provider". Although probably none of such entities would offer static network coverage, many of them could foresee adequate chances for profits generated by exploiting the 5G ESSENCE concepts of multitenant small cells, able to provide wireless network coverage coupled with added-value services in close proximity to customers and visitors that belong to multiple network operators and vertical industries [20, 21]. In particular, 5G ESSENCE focuses on three real-life use cases associated to vertical industries: (i) 5G edge network acceleration for a stadium, with local video production and distribution; (ii) mission critical applications for public safety (PS) communications providers, and; (iii) next-generation, integrated, in-flight entertainment and connectivity (IFEC) services for passengers.

3   The Fundamental 5G ESSENCE Architectural Context

In the 5G ESSENCE approach, the Small Cell concept [22] is evolved as not only to provide multi-operator radio access, but also to achieve an increase in the capacity and the performance of current Radio Access Network (RAN) infrastructures as well as to extend the range of the provided services, while maintaining its agility. To achieve these ambitious goals, the 5G ESSENCE project leverages the paradigms of RAN scheduling and, additionally, it provides an enhanced, edge-*based*, virtualised execution environment attached to the small cell, taking advantage and reinforcing the concepts of MEC and network slicing [23]. The architecture provided so far by the SESAME project [7, 8] acts as a "solid reference point" for 5G ESSENCE. It combines the current 3GPP framework for network management in RAN sharing scenarios and the ETSI NFV framework for managing virtualised network functions [19]. The CESC offers virtualised computing, storage and radio resources and the CESC cluster is considered as a cloud from the upper layers. This cloud can also be "'sliced" to enable multi-tenancy.

The execution platform is used to support VNFs that implement the different features of the Small Cells as well as to support for the mobile edge applications of the end-users.

Evolving the SESAME-based high-level architecture, the technical approach of 5G ESSENCE is presented in Fig. 2, where the working architecture is illustrated with emphasis upon the functional elements and interfaces. As it is depicted, the 5G ESSENCE architecture allows multiple network operators (tenants) to provide services to their users through a set of CESCs deployed, owned and managed by a third party (i.e., the CESC provider). In this way, operators can extend the capacity of their own 5G RAN in areas where the deployment of their own infrastructure could be expensive and/or inefficient - as it would be the case of, *for example*, highly dense areas where massive numbers of SCs would be needed to provide the expected services.

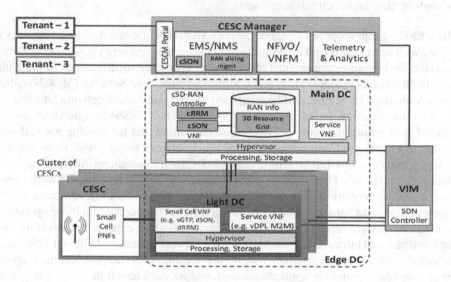

Fig. 2. 5G ESSENCE high-level architecture.

In addition to capacity extension, the 5G ESSENCE platform is equipped with a two-tier virtualised execution environment, materialised in the form of the Edge DC, which allows also the provision of MEC capabilities to the mobile operators for enhancing the user experience and the agility in the service delivery. The first tier, i.e., the Light DC hosted inside the CESCs, is used to support the execution of VNFs for carrying out the virtualisation of the Small Cell access. In this regard, network functions supporting traffic interception, GTP (GPRS Tunneling Protocol) encapsulation/decapsulation and some distributed RRM/SON functionalities are expected to be executed therein. VNFs that require low processing power, e.g., a Deep Packet Inspection (DPI), a Machine-to-Machine (M2M) Gateway, and so on, could also be hosted here. The connection between the Small Cell Physical Network Functions (PNFs) and the Small Cell VNFs can be realised through, e.g., the network Functional Application Platform Interface (nFAPI). Finally, backhaul and fronthaul transmission resources will be part of the CESC, allowing for the required connectivity. The second cloud tier, i.e., the Main DC, will be hosting more computation intensive tasks and processes that need to be centralised in order to have a global view of the underlying infrastructure. This encompasses the centralised software-defined RAN (cSD-RAN) controller which will be delivered as a VNF running in the Main DC and makes control plane decisions for all the radio elements in the geographical area of the CESC cluster, including the centralised Radio Resource Management (cRRM) over the entire CESC cluster. Other potential VNFs that could be hosted by the Main DC can also include security applications, traffic engineering, mobility management and, *in general*, any additional network end-to-end (E2E) services that can be deployed and managed on the 5G ESSENCE virtual networks, effectively and on-demand. The necessary management modules for the operation of the CESC platform and the service provisioning are also depicted in Fig. 2, within the CESCM (CESC Manager) framework. The following subsections provide a more detailed description for each of these architectural components.

The CESC: In our scope, a CESC consists of a Multi-RAT (Radio Access Technology) 5G SC with its standard backhaul interface, standard management connection (TR069 interface for remote management [24]) and with necessary modifications to the data model (TR196 data model [25]) to allow Multi-Operator Core Network (MOCN) radio resource sharing. The CESC will be composed by a physical small cell unit attached to an execution platform based on one of x86, ARMv8, MIPS64 architectures, to be decided later during the project. Edge cloud computing and networking are realised through the sharing of computation, storage and network resources of those micro-servers present in each CESC and form the Light DC for implementing different features/ capabilities of the SC. Therefore, the CESC becomes a "neutral host" for network operators or virtual network operators that want to share IT and network resources at the edge of the mobile network. The CESC is meant to accommodate multiple operators (tenants) by design, offering Platform-as-a-Service (PaaS), capable of providing the deployed physical infrastructure among multiple network operators. Different VNFs can be hosted in the CESC environment for different tenants. This also provides the support for mobile edge computing applications deployed for each tenant that, operating very near to the end-users, may significantly reduce the service delivery time and deliver composite services in an automated manner [30]. Moreover, the CESC is the termination point of the GTP-User Plane (GTP-U) tunnelling which encapsulates user IP packets from the core network entities (e.g., the Evolved Packet Core (EPC) Serving Gateway (SGW) in LTE) destined to the User Equipment (UE) and *vice versa*. The CESC exposes different views of the network resources: per-tenant small cell view, and physical small cell substrate, which is managed by the network operator, decoupling the management of the virtual small cells from the platform itself. In the CESC, rather than providing multiple S1 (or Iu-h interface) connections from the physical SC to different operators' EPC network elements such as Mobility Management Entity (MME) and SGW, such fan-out is done at the Light DC. The CESC is further the termination of multiple S1 interfaces connecting the CESC to multiple MME/SGW entities as in S1-Flex. The interconnection of many CESCs forms a "cluster" which can facilitate access to a broader geographical area with one or more operators (even virtual ones), extending the range of their provided services, while maintaining the required agility to be able to provide these extensions on demand.

The Edge DC Encompassing Main DC and Light DC: 5G ESSENCE envisages combining the MEC and NFV concepts with SC virtualisation in 5G networks and enhancing them for supporting multi-tenancy [26]. The purpose of the Edge DC will be to provide Cloud services within the network infrastructure and also to facilitate by promoting and assisting the exploitation of network resource information. To this end, all the normally hardware located modules of the Light DC and the Main DC will be delivered as resources using novel virtualisation techniques. Both networking and computing virtualisation extensions will be developed using open frameworks such as OPNFV. The combination of the proposed Edge DC architecture with the concepts of NFV and SDN will facilitate achieving higher levels of flexibility and scalability. As seen in the detailed architecture in Fig. 2, the Main DC will be able to execute different SC and Service VNFs under the control of the CESCM; in particular, the Main DC hosts the cSD-RAN controller which performs cRRM decisions for handling efficiently the heterogeneous access network environment composed of different access technologies (such as 5G RAN, LTE, and Wi-Fi). These radio access networks can be programmable and under the supervision of the centralised controller. The cSD-RAN controller updates and maintains the global network state in the form of a database called as "RAN Information", which includes, *among other* elements, an abstraction of the available radio resources in the CESC cluster. This abstraction takes the form of a "3D Resource Grid" that characterises the resources in the domains of time/space/frequency. The RAN Information will be used by the cRRM to perform the resource allocation decisions (e.g., scheduling). The cSD-RAN controller can also host centralised SON (cSON) functionalities that need to coordinate multiple small cells, so they are not appropriate for running at the Light DC (for example, this could be the case of InterCell Interference Coordination (ICIC) functions). Other distributed (dSON) functions and/or distributed RRM (dRRM) functions that are of low complexity and that do not involve the coordination of multiple small cells will run at the Light DC. For example, this could be the case of an admission control function that only takes decisions based on the current load existing at a given cell.

The CESCM: Management and orchestration of the proposed uniform virtualised environment, able to support both radio connectivity and edge services, is a challenging task by itself [27]. The management of diverse lightweight virtual resources is of primary importance, enabling a converged cloud-radio environment and efficient placement of services [28–30]. For that purpose, the CESCM shown in Fig. 2 is the central service management and orchestration component in the related architecture. Generally speaking, it integrates all the traditional network management elements and the novel recommended functional blocks to realise NFV operations. A single instance of CESCM is able to operate over several CESC clusters at different Points of Presence (PoPs), each constituting an Edge DC through the use of a dedicated VIM (Virtualised Infrastructure Manager) per cluster.

An essential component at the heart of CESCM is the Network Functions Virtualisation Orchestrator (NFVO). It will be in charge of realising network services on the virtualised infrastructure and will include interfaces to interact with the CESC provider for high-level service management (e.g., exchange of network service descriptors and

Service Level Agreements (SLAs) for each tenant). The NFVO composes service chains (constituted by two or more VNF instances located either in one or several CESCs that "jointly" realise a more complex function) and manages the deployment of VNFs over the Edge DC. The NFVO uses the services exposed by the VNF Manager, which will be in charge of the instantiation, update, query, scaling and termination of the VNFs. Moreover, the NFVO may include features to enhance the overall system performance, e.g., to improve energy efficiency. The CESCM hosts also the Element Management System (EMS), which provides a package of end-user functions for the management of both the PNFs and VNFs at the CESCs. In particular, the EMS carries out "key" management functionalities such as Fault, Configuration, Accounting, Performance, Security (FCAPS) operations. The EMS will be responsible for partitioning the single whole-cell management view into multiple virtual-cell management views, one per tenant. In this way, a virtualised SC with a set of (limited) management functionalities can be made visible to, e.g., the Network Management System (NMS) of each tenant in order to, *for example*, collect performance counters, configure neighbour lists for a proper mobility management, etc. It is worth mentioning that, based on the practical lessons learnt from SESAME, all the EMS components of the SESAME architecture (i.e., PNF-EMS, SC-EMS, Service EMS and SLA monitoring of Fig. 2), which in practice reveal to be tightly related, will be considered in the 5G ESSENCE architecture under the scope of a single EMS entity. In addition to the NMSs of each tenant, in a general situation, the CESCM can also incorporate a NMS for managing the whole set of CESCs deployed by an operator. This can be appropriate, for example in case that there exist CESCs belonging to different vendors in the same deployment, each one with its own EMS. The EMS/NMS will also host the cSON functionalities (e.g. self-planning, Coverage and Capacity Optimisation (CCO), etc.) and the functionalities for the life-cycle management of RAN slicing (i.e. for the creation, modification or termination of RAN slices). As shown in Fig. 2, the CESCM encompasses a telemetry and analytics module that captures and analyses relevant indicators of the network operation. This will provide the CESCM with accurate knowledge models that characterise the behaviour of the network and its users in relation to the utilisation of both cloud and radio resources. This will facilitate the realisation of effective optimisation approaches based on, *for example*, machine learning (ML) techniques for service placement, which can dynamically adapt to the context of the provided services and their execution environment and to enable automated enforcement of SLAs. Finally, the CESCM also incorporates the CESCM portal. It is a control panel with web Graphical User Interface (GUI) that serves as the "entry point" for the users, both the CESC provider and the tenants, to the CESCM functionalities and constitutes the main graphical frontend to access the 5G ESSENCE platform. The CESCM Portal in general provides visual monitoring information of the platform, the agreed SLAs, and the available network services/VNFs, allowing parameters' configuration.

The VIM: The CESCM functions will be built upon the services provided by the VIM for appropriately managing, monitoring and optimising the overall operation of the NFVI (NFV Infrastructure) resources (i.e.: computing, storage and network resources) at the Edge DC. The role of VIM is essential for the deployment of NFV services and to form and provide a layer of NFV resources to be made available to the CESCM functions. The NFV resources will be ultimately offered as a set of application programming interfaces (APIs) that will allow the execution of network services over the decentralised CESCs, located at the edge of the network. As seen in Fig. 2, the VIM relies on an SDN controller for interconnecting the VNFs and for offering SFC on the data-plane by establishing the path for the physical connections.

4   Overview and Concluding Remarks

The 5G ESSENCE's goal is the development and demonstration of an innovative architecture, capable of providing Small Cell coverage to multiple operators "*as-a-Service*", enriched with a two-tier architecture: a first distributed tier for providing low latency services and a second centralised tier for providing high processing power for computing-intensive network applications. To that end, 5G ESSENCE envisages to virtualise and to partition Small Cell capacity while, *at the same time*, it aims to support enhanced edge cloud services by enriching 5G ESSENCE with an edge cloud.

This paper presents a first approach to the high-level overall architecture of the 5G ESSENCE system. We have initially identified and "positioned" the 5G ESSENCE innovative framework within the modern 5G era and, furthermore, we have also examined the way how the related ecosystem can enable service deployment, in particular for service vertical-specific needs. However, the core of the present work has been to introduce a proper architectural framework, based on the pillars of network functions virtualisation, mobile-edge computing and cognitive management, to "address" the requirements of a robust and agile network management. In the context of the 5G ESSENCE approach, we have analysed and discussed the main architectural modules as well as their properties, per case, and have identified the framework for further introducing and implementing the system's high-level architecture. The work is based on findings and/or results coming from previous EU-*funded* research projects (with major contributions coming from the SESAME project) but has been extended and adapted accordingly, to be able to fulfil the requirements coming from the related use cases, associated to vertical industries.

Acknowledgments. This work has been performed in the scope of the 5G ESSENCE European Research Project and has been supported by the Commission of the European Communities (5G-PPP/H2020, Grant Agreement No. 761592).

References

1. IC Insights, Inc.: IC Market Drivers, A Study of Emerging and Major End-Use Applications Fueling Demand for Integrated Circuits. IC Insights, Inc., Scottsdale (2014)
2. European Commission and 5G-PPP: 5G Vision: The 5G-PPP Infrastructure Private Public Partnership: The Next Generation of Communication Network and Services (2015). https://ec.europa.eu/digital-single-market/en/towards-5g

3. European Commission: 5G: Challenges, Research Priorities, and Recommendations – Joint White Paper. European Commission, Strategic Research and Innovation Agenda (2014)
4. Andrews, J.G., Buzzi, S., Choi, W., Hanly, S.V., Lozano, A., Soong, A.C.K., Zhang, J.C.: What will 5G be? IEEE JSAC **32**(6), 1065–1082 (2014). Special Issue on 5G Wireless Communications Systems
5. Chochliouros, I.P., Sfakianakis, E., Belesioti, M., Spiliopoulou, A.S., Dardamanis, A.: Challenges for defining opportunities for growth in the 5G era: the SESAME conceptual model. In: Proceedings of the EuCNC-2016, pp. 1–5 (2016)
6. SESAME ("Small cEllS coordinAtion for Multitenancy and Edge services") 5G-PPP Project, Grant Agreement No. 671596. http://www.sesame-h2020-5g-ppp.eu/
7. Chochliouros, I.P., et al.: A model for an innovative 5G-*Oriented* architecture, based on small cells coordination for multi-tenancy and edge services. In: Iliadis, L., Maglogiannis, I. (eds.) AIAI 2016. IFIP AICT, vol. 475, pp. 666–675. Springer, Cham (2016). https://doi.org/10.1007/978-3-319-44944-9_59
8. Chochliouros, I.P., et al.: Putting intelligence in the network edge through NFV and cloud computing: the SESAME approach. In: Boracchi, G., Iliadis, L., Jayne, C., Likas, A. (eds.) EANN 2017. CCIS, vol. 744, pp. 704–715. Springer, Cham (2017). https://doi.org/10.1007/978-3-319-65172-9_59
9. 5G ESSENCE ("Embedded Network Services for 5G Experiences") 5G-PPP Project, Grant Agreement (GA) No. 761592. http://www.5g-essence-h2020.eu
10. COHERENT ("Coordinated Control and Spectrum Management for 5G Heterogeneous Radio Access Networks") 5G-PPP Project, GA No. 671639. http://www.ict-coherent.eu/
11. SPEED 5G ("Quality of Service Provision and Capacity Expansion through Extended-DSA for 5G") 5G-PPP Project, Grant Agreement No. 671705. https://speed-5g.eu/
12. SONATA ("Service Programming and Orchestration for Virtualised Software Networks") 5G-PPP Project, Grant Agreement No. 671517. http://www.sonata-nfv.eu/
13. Ramiro, J., Hamied, K.: Self-Organizing Networks. Self-Planning self-Optimization and self-Healing for GSM, UMTS and LTE. Wiley, Hoboken (2012)
14. Østerbø, O., Grøndalen, O.: Benefits of self-organizing networks (SON) for mobile operators. J. Comput. Netw. Commun. **2012**, 1–16 (2012)
15. Mosharaf, N.M., Chowdhury, K., Boutaba, R.: A survey of network virtualisation. Comput. Netw. **54**(5), 862–876 (2010)
16. Haleplidis, E., Salim, J.H., Denazis, S., Koufopavlou, O.: Towards a network abstraction model for SDN. J. Netw. Syst. Manag. **23**(2), 309–327 (2015)
17. Fajardo, J.O., Liberal, F., Giannoulakis, I., Kafetzakis, E., Pii, V., Trajkovska, I., Bohnert, T.M., Goratti, L., Riggio, R., et al.: Introducing mobile edge computing capabilities through distributed 5G cloud enabled small cells. Mob. Netw. Appl. (MONET) **21**(4), 564–574 (2016). Special Issues on Mobile Networks and Management
18. Vaquero, L.M., Rodero-Merino, L.: Finding your way in the fog: towards a comprehensive definition of fog computing. ACM SIGCOMM Comput. Commun. Rev. **44**(5), 27–32 (2014)
19. European Telecommunications Standards Institute (ETSI): NFV Management and Orchestration - An Overview, GS NFV-MAN 001 v1.1.1. ETSI (2014)
20. Chochliouros, I.P., Kostopoulos, A., Giannoulakis, I., Spiliopoulou, A.S., Belesioti, M., Sfakianakis, E., Kourtis, A., Kafetzakis, E.: Using small cells from enhancing 5G networks. In: Proceedings of IEEE Conference on Network Function Virtualisation and Software-Defined Networks (NFV-SDN 2017), pp. 1–6. IEEE (2017)
21. Chochliouros, I.P., Giannoulakis, I., Spiliopoulou, A.S., et al.: A novel architectural concept for enhanced 5G network facilities. In: MATEC Web of Conferences, CSCC-2017, vol. 125, no. 03012, pp. 1–7 (2017)

22. Small Cell Forum (SCF): Small Cells and 5G Evolution: A Topic Brief. (Document 055.07.01). http://scf.io/en/documents/055__Small_cells_and_5G_evolution_a_topic_brief.php
23. Sallent, O., Pérez-Romero, J., Ferrús, R., Augusti, R.: On radio access network slicing from a radio resource management perspective. IEEE Wirel. Commun. J. 24(5), 166–174 (2017)
24. Broadband Forum (BF): TR-069: CPE WAN Management Protocol (CWMP). BF (2013)
25. Broadband Forum (BF): TR-196v2: Femto Access Point Service Data Model. BF (2017)
26. Giannoulakis, I. Xylouris, G., Kafetzakis, E., Kourtis, A., Fajardo, J.O., Khodashenas, P.S., Albanese, A., Mouratidis, H., Vassilakis, V.: System architecture and deployment scenarios for SESAME: small cEllS coordinAtion for Multi-tenancy and Edge services. In: Proceedings of the IEEE NetSoft 2016 Conference and Workshops, pp. 447–452 (2016)
27. Fajardo, J.O., Taboada, Y., Liberal, F.: Improving content delivery efficiency through multi-layer mobile edge adaptation. IEEE Netw. Manag. 29(6), 40–46 (2015)
28. Blanco, B., Fajardo, J.O., Liberal, F.: Design of cognitive cycles in 5G networks. In: Iliadis, L., Maglogiannis, I. (eds.) AIAI 2016. IFIP AICT, vol. 475, pp. 697–708. Springer, Cham (2016). https://doi.org/10.1007/978-3-319-44944-9_62
29. Kostopoulos, A., Chochliouros, I.P., Kuo, F.-C., Riggio, R., Goratti, L., Nikaein, N., Giannoulakis, I., Perez-Romero, J., Chen, T., Steinert, R., and Panaiotopol, D.: Design aspects for 5G architectures. The SESAME and COHERENT approach. In: Proceedings of IEEE ICC Workshops 2017, pp. 986–992. IEEE (2017)
30. Giannoulakis, I., Kafetzakis, E., Trajkovska, I., Khodashenas, P.S., Chochliouros, I.P., Costa, C., Bliznakov, P.: The emergence of operator-neutral small cells as a strong case for cloud-like computing at the mobile edge. Trans. Emerg. Telecommun. Technol 27(9), 1152–1159 (2016)

e-Health Services in the Context of IoT: The Case of the VICINITY Project

Maria Belesioti[1], Ioannis P. Chochliouros[1(✉)], Stefan Vanya[2], Viktor Oravec[2], Natalia Theologou[3], Maria Koutli[3], Athanasios Tryferidis[3], and Dimitrios Tzovaras[3]

[1] Hellenic Telecommunications Organization (OTE) S.A., 99, Kifissias Avenue, 15124 Maroussi, Athens, Greece
{mbelesioti,ichochliouros}@oteresearch.gr
[2] bAvenir, s.r.o., Jégého 8, 82108 Bratislava, Slovakia
{stefan.vanya,viktor.oravec}@bavenir.eu
[3] CERTH/ITI - Centre for Research and Technology Hellas/Information Technologies Institute, 6th km Harilaou - Thermi, 57001 Thessaloniki, Greece
{nataliath,mkoutli,thanasic,dimitrios.tzovaras}@iti.gr

Abstract. The Internet of Things (IoT) is a new paradigm that combines aspects and technologies coming from different approaches. Ageing population and decreasing financial resources, consist one of the biggest challenges not only in Europe but also worldwide, in terms of healthcare organization complexity. At the same time, there exists an ever-growing demand for ubiquitous healthcare systems to improve human health and well-being. IoT paradigm and wearable IoT devices for home-based or mobile monitoring of vital patients' data can be a secure, reliable and cost-savvy solution to this problem. This paper analyzes the impact of Internet of Things on the design of new eHealth services and solutions in the Context of VICINITY EU-funded project.

Keywords: Internet of things (IoT) · eHealth
Mobile and portable healthcare devices · Interoperability

1 Introduction

Recently, there have been significant advances in the field of Internet of Things (IoT) in conjunction to the continuous and constantly increasing demand for support services in the emerging sector of e-health. Aged people with chronic diseases are in need for care and prevention of accidents at 24/7 basis, thus the need to define new models of healthcare that will advance existing systems is of high importance for modern electronic communications market sector. The VICINITY EU-funded project under Grant Agreement (GA) No. 688467 [http://vicinity2020.eu/vicinity/] aims to illustrate that the communication models, protocols and technologies promoted under the IoT concept have a great potential in the implementation of Internet-*based* healthcare systems. In addition, VICINITY intends to provide the owners of connected IoT infrastructures with a decentralized interoperability. The concept of "decentralism" is expressed by the fact

L. Iliadis et al. (Eds.): AIAI 2018, IFIP AICT 520, pp. 62–69, 2018.
https://doi.org/10.1007/978-3-319-92016-0_6

that the corresponding platform includes neither central operator roles nor central databases to store sensitive data about the involved users. Instead of that, it connects different smart objects into a "social network" called as *virtual neighborhood* where infrastructure owners keep under control their shared devices and data, thanks to web-*based* operator console called as the "VICINITY neighborhood manager (VNM)". When using the VNM, the user can control which of his/her IoT asset is shared with whom, and to which extent [10]. This VICINITY-*related* technology aspires to apply in its e-health scenario.

E-health comprises a novel combination of Telemedicine and IoT-*based* monitoring system and it is considered as one of "the most promising domains in the field of IoT", since it can offer effective and direct healthcare services improving the quality of existing healthcare systems by supporting reliable and efficient solutions. In order to offer and support several e-health solutions, VICINITY will build and demonstrate a device and standard agnostic platform for IoT infrastructures that will offer "*Interoperability as-a-Service*". This platform will rely upon a decentralised and user-centric approach that offer a complete transparency across vertical domains, while retaining full control of the ownership and distribution of data.

In order to realize such a network, a bridging point, the Gateway API (Application Programming Interface) facilitates an exchange of data between a connected IoT infrastructure and Value-added services. This gateway has an overall knowledge and control over both the sensor network and the data to be transmitted. More specifically, the VICINITY Gateway API utilizes a Communication Node with a set of technologies that makes the data transfer possible even in case when an IoT ecosystem resides behind the Network Address Translation – NAT [10].

2   VICINITY Concept and Approach

The ongoing digital evolution has very high impact in the healthcare system, by leading to the rapid growth of many healthcare practices supported by electronic processes and communication known as electronic Health (eHealth) applications [2]. The expected huge number of interconnected devices used in the health sector and the significant amount of data gathered by sensors and smart meters create both technical and business opportunities by introducing new services that will bring tangible benefits to the society [5]. Mobile devices, such as cellular phones, wearables and personal digital assistants (PDAs), are very popular and various IoT networks are being deployed for sensing, measuring, controlling and business process optimization purposes, while various IoT platforms are emerging on the market to manage these networks. Since these infrastructures are mostly acting as "isolated islands" in the global IoT landscape, their interconnection might bring significant value added (such as an ecosystem running on close-to-zero energy for example). Taking this into consideration, VICINITY aims to present a new approach by exploring new opportunities and addressing new challenges. For this reason, the project aims to create new ecosystems, composed by integrated platforms and smart objects which will be supported by network technologies and will make use of the evolving ICT advances.

Owners of connected IoT infrastructures could be also connected to this ecosystem, which is called "virtual neighborhood" and which represents a social network where each one will be able to keep under control their shared devices and data, thanks to a web-*based* operator console called as the "VICINITY neighborhood manager" (VNM). When using the VNM, each user can control which of his/her IoT asset is shared with whom and to which extent, just like they do in existing social networks and, *furthermore*, to manage access rules to his/her discovered smart objects through a catalogue appeared in the user's device when open the "VICINITY auto discovery device", through the "VICINITY gateway API" with sample implementations. Once user's IoT infrastructure is connected to the VICINITY platform, the IoT value chains become unlocked, thus opening the way towards seamless interoperability between IoT islands present in the current IoT landscape and this enables the exploitation of independent value-added services, including various cross-domain IoT applications (as discussed in [6]).

Figure 1, as illustrated below, depicts a generalized concept coming from the wider VICINITY approach.

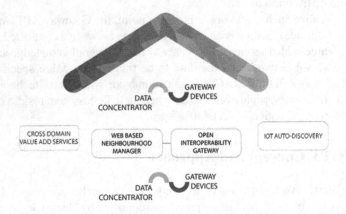

Fig. 1. Visualised VICINITY concept.

The VICINITY quality features focus mainly upon user experience, trust, privacy, security and scalability. VICINITY functions are designed around the user so as to ensure "as best as possible" user experience during installation, configuration, integration of VICINITY components in its infrastructure and usage of the VICINITY interoperability features. The high availability and performance quality measures do enable VICINITY to scale-up and scale-out to "handle" various communication loads within neighborhoods, as introduced by different applications coming from building, energy, transport and health domain requirements.

The VICINITY Cloud components such as the VICINITY Neighborhood manager (providing user interface to the VICINITY Users), Semantic discovery and dynamic configuration agent platform (providing semantic platform) and the VICINITY Communication Server (providing control of communication between integrated infrastructures) shall be deployed as high available software components being to scale in/out the

VICINITY cloud to current needs to the integrated infrastructures and value-added services. The distributed infrastructure of the VICINITY context is enhanced by an interoperability approach aiming to provide a standard way to both Discover and Access heterogeneous IoT objects, distributed among sparse IoT infrastructures based on the work being done by the W3C Web of Things (WoT) WG. Therefore, VICINITY shall rely on Thing description (TD) introduced by WoT to describe every IoT object (which can represent either physical or abstract Things) that belong to any integrated IoT infrastructure which, *in turn*, shall be described as an ecosystem of IoT objects.

The IoT Operator should manage privacy throughout the lifecycle, by using consent to process any sort of private data. These consents should be associated with value-added services and, *additionally*, confirmed consents should be part of the value-added service's profile. They should be visible only to the IoT Operator and the Service provider. The second one should also be able to create -or remove- a value-added service group and add -or remove- value-added services from this group and to perform group actions on value-added services (such as changing value-added service access rules). Each value-added service group should have a profile including at least name, avatar, description, value-added service group visibility, accessibility rules, optionally terms and conditions and/or consent to process the private data template. Finally, the device owner should be able to confirm consent so that to process private data by a value-added service -or organization-, which has access to the IoT device and to manage all confirmed consents and revoke them, *individually*. Furthermore, the device owner should be able to create -or remove- an IoT device group and add -or remove- IoT devices from this group.

The next figure (Fig. 2) depicts a schematic view of the essential VICINITY neighborhood concept.

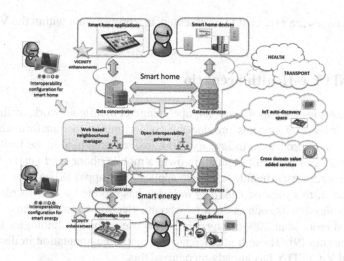

Fig. 2. Schematic view of the VICINITY neighborhood concept [10].

Integrated IoT infrastructures consist of existing IoT assets. The VICINITY Gateway Adapters translate the end-user devices' specific communication protocol into

VICINITY Interoperability Gateway API calls while, *at the same time*, the Gateway Adapter will offer a control interface towards the end-user devices by establishing bidirectional communication with the end-user devices. In most of IoT-*based* patient monitoring systems, especially at smart homes or hospitals, there exists a bridging point (i.e., a gateway) between a sensor network and the Internet, which often just performs basic functions such as translating between the protocols used in the Internet and sensor networks [1]. The VICINITY solution is expected to be based upon an open interoperability gateway, enabling different IoT networks to be connected into large ecosystems. The connections will be organised in a peer-to-per way, building social networks of smart objects (i.e., virtual neighborhoods). The operators of the particular IoT infrastructures can select which other systems they wish to connect to in a similar way as we are selecting friends in social networks, via a web-*based* neighborhood manager where they can configure the scope of the cooperation with other systems (e.g. to decide which data are visible and which controls are applicable for a particular partner entity). Facilitating the integration of smart objects built on widely adopted standards the platform will be equipped with semantic discovery and dynamic configuration features automatically integrating such assets to VICINITY. At this point, it should be mentioned that several potential barriers could occur, such as:

- Lack of IoT protocol interoperability (systems are often vendor locked by design);
- Interconnected smart objects of different owners require data sharing that raises serious privacy issues;
- IoT component vendors might be reluctant to share interface specifications (Intellectual Property problem), and;
- Large-scale integration imposes rules that are disadvantageous for particular participants.

All these issues are expected to be assessed, in a proper way, within the VICINITY framework.

3   VICINITY e-Health Scenario

Digital technologies such as 4G and the upcoming 5G mobile network, artificial intelligence and IoT-*based* systems provide new opportunities to transform the way of healthcare services provision. In January 2014, in a research held in the United States, revealed that 85% of the adult population owns a mobile phone, and nearly 46 million smartphone owners used health or fitness applications (apps) [8]. At the same time, another research, *this time on behalf of industry*, has reported a 40% increase among health care professionals such as doctors, who use electronic tools for patient communications, and more than 20% of physicians now use mobile technologies for remote patient monitoring [9]. These figures create a potential augmentation in distance care practices and VICINITY has already recognized this.

In Europe, eHealth systems are developing despite the existence of many different healthcare systems. According to the European Commission, e-health comprises the following four interrelated categories of applications [6]:

(i)   Clinical information systems;
(ii) telemedicine and home care, personalized health systems and services for remote patient monitoring, teleconsultation, telecare, telemedicine and tele-radiology;
(iii) integrated regional/national health information networks, distributed electronic health record systems and associated services such as e-prescriptions or e-referrals, *and*;
(iv) secondary usage of non-clinical systems such as specialized systems for researchers, or support systems such as billing systems.

E-health still receives a great deal of attention at the EU level, and the Commission has invested in several research programs related to this area [7]. The VICINITY ehealth scenario aims to transform healthcare delivery for elderly patients with long terms needs (such as people with dementia and obesity) and to provide a scalable and holistic approach in healthcare systems. Moreover, it shall be deployed where the term "virtual neighborhood" is referred to supporting communication of personal health status data to selected participants of the network such as family members, for example. The novelty of VICINITY project in the e-health domain is due to the fact that participants can decide with whom they wish to cooperate and to which extent. Thus, each participant can decide on the conditions for himself in his own maximal favor.

The VICINITY ehealth scenario is divided to two sub-scenarios: The first one is called ehealth & assisted living and its main purpose is to demonstrate, through constant remote monitoring, how sensors, actuators and integrated communication devices installed at home can provide assisted living to elderly people and people with long-terms needs, as previously mentioned. The second scenario is about fitness and preventive medicine with wearable IoT and aims mainly at middle-aged persons, who need to promote their health as a method of diseases' preventions. Unique identification of the user is of high importance in this use case. VICINITY platform repeatedly associates the entities within the system with an individual name, code, symbol, or number and offering interaction with the entities, or tracing and controlling their activities. This distinction is the key enabler for interoperability and global services across heterogeneous IoT systems and it is important for entities to be uniquely identifiable so that IoT systems can monitor and communicate with specific entities.

Figure 3 illustrates as schematic view of the VICINITY ehealth scenario in Greece, as proposed by the national involved partners. The entire approach is based upon the broader VICINITY context.

The sensors and wearables will be in direct communication with a call center manned with specialized staff and maybe doctors or alternatively with their relatives. The real-time combination of information, provided by the sensors, creates a unique user profile and, *therefore*, any deviation from this is characterized as "abnormal behavior" thus triggering an alarm. The target of the ehealth scenario is to assist both elderly and middle-aged people to support their everyday life by offering them a secure and independent way of living. This VICINITY service has all the potential to be a new promising vehicle able to enhance the limited abilities of the healthcare system by assisting patients with chronic disease management and monitoring and by tracking their everyday activities so as to promote a healthier lifestyle. Of course, despite these potential benefits, there

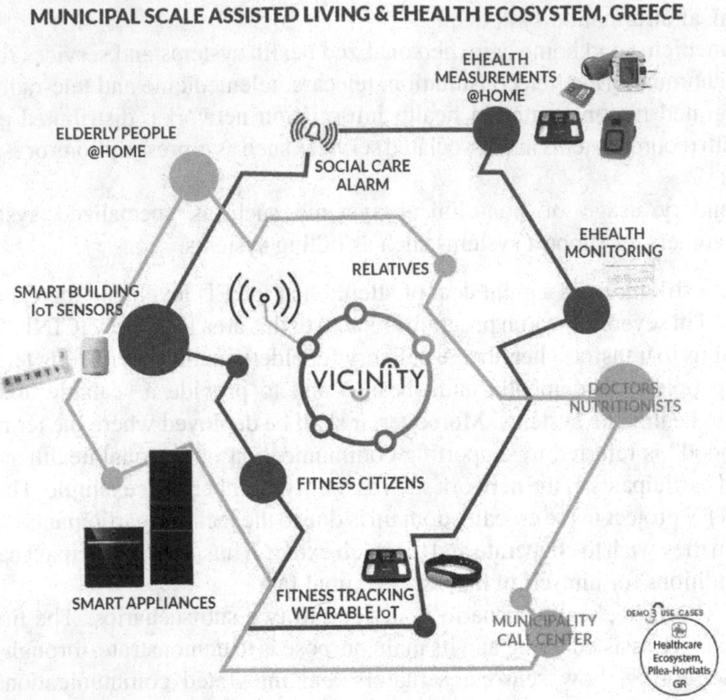

MUNICIPAL SCALE ASSISTED LIVING & EHEALTH ECOSYSTEM, GREECE

Fig. 3. Schematic view of the VICINITY e-Health scenario in Greece [11].

are several issues and barriers and limitations that should overcome and many quality measures that should be addressed ([3, 4, 12, 13]).

4 Conclusion

The importance of prevention and monitoring in the health sector becomes clear when the combined effects of the limited capacity of the existing healthcare system to support the increasing demands of the aging population, and the continuous increase of need for disease prevention and healthier way of living expand. Using information technology to monitor patient's care and if need be to assist them, may have a positive impact especially in developing countries.

The evolution of IoT has created a variety of application in several domains, including healthcare. E-Health could transform healthcare delivery by offering the potential to improve the quality, accountability, and cost-effectiveness of healthcare services. The VICINITY project through its "virtual neighborhood" and its applications aims to redesign modern healthcare services with promising technological, economic, and social prospects. The proposed services can have positive results like improved everyday life with increased quality.

Acknowledgments. This work has been performed in the scope of the VICINITY European Research Project and has been supported by the Commission of the European Communities (H2020, Grant Agreement No.688467). This paper reflects only the authors' views and the Commission is not liable for any use that may be made of the information contained therein.

References

1. Rahmani, A.M., et al.: Smart e-health gateway: bringing intelligence to internet-of-things based ubiquitous healthcare systems. In: Proceedings of the 2015 12th Annual IEEE Consumer Communications and Networking Conference (CCNC), Las Vegas, NV, pp. 826–834 (2015)
2. An Open NCP-based Secure eHealth Data Exchange System. Available at: https://www.researchgate.net/publication/322775597_KONFIDO_An_OpenNCP-based_Secure_eHealth_Data_Exchange_System. Accessed 01 Feb 2018
3. Clarke, G., Yarborough, B.J.: Evaluating the promise of health IT to enhance/expand the reach of mental health services. Gen. Hosp. Psychiatry **35**(4), 339–344 (2014)
4. Chang, B.L., Bakken, S., Brown, S.S., Houston, T.K., et al.: Bridging the digital divide: reaching vulnerable populations. J. Am. Med. Inform. Assoc. **11**(6), 448–457 (2004)
5. Borgia, E.: The internet of things vision: key features, applications and open issues. Comput. Commun. **54**(1), 1–31 (2014)
6. eHealth Taskforce: Accelerating the Development of the eHealth Market in Europe. eHealth Taskforce Report, p. 10 (2007)
7. European Commission: eHealth portfolio of projects. European Commission Information Society and Media, Brussels (2007). http://ec.europa.eu/information_society/activities/health/docs/publications/fp6upd2007/fp6intro1.pdf
8. Nielsen: Hacking health: how consumers use smartphones and wearable tech to track their health. Nielsen (March 2015). www.nielsen.com/us/en/insights/news/2014/hacking-health-how-consumers-use-smartphones-and-wearable-tech-to-track-their-health.html
9. Terry, K.: Physicians warm to digital communications with patients (2014). www.medscape.com/viewarticle/826596
10. VICINITY Project, GA No.688467: Open virtual neighborhood network to connect IoT Infrastructures and smart objects. http://vicinity2020.eu/vicinity/
11. VICINITY Project: Pilea-Hortiatis (GR) eHealth & Assisted Living. http://vicinity2020.eu/vicinity/content/pilea-hortiatis-gr-%E2%80%93-ehealth-assisted-living
12. Walji, M., Sagaram, S., Sagaram, D., Meric-Bernstam, F., Johnson, C., Mirza N.Q., Bernstam, E.V.: Efficacy of quality criteria to identify potentially harmful information: a cross-sectional survey of complementary and alternative medicine web sites. J. Med. Internet Res. **6**(2:e21), 87–100 (2004)
13. Sagaram, S., Walji, M., Meric-Bernstam, F., Johnson, C., Bernstam, E.: Inter-observer agreement for quality measures applied to online health information. Stud. Health Technol. Inform. **107**(Pt.2), 1308–1312 (2004)

Are 5G Networks and the Neutral Host Model the Solution to the Shrinking Telecom Market

Ioannis Neokosmidis[1]([✉]), Theodoros Rokkas[1], Dimitris Xydias[1], Antonino Albanese[2], Muhammad Shuaib Siddiqui[3], Carlos Colman-Meixner[4], and Dimitra Simeonidou[4]

[1] inCITES Consulting SARL, Strassen, Luxembourg
i.neokosmidis@incites.eu
[2] ITALTEL, Castelletto, Milan, Italy
[3] Software Networks Area, Fundacio i2CAT, Barcelona, Spain
[4] High Performance Networks Group, University of Bristol, Bristol, UK

Abstract. 5G networks will offer advanced functionalities and features such as high throughput, low latency, security and reliability by leveraging technological advances like network virtualization, edge computing and network slicing. The latter will facilitate the entrance of new players in the value chain. Moreover, they will offer a means for network operators to change their business models in order to address revenue losses. The concept of a neutral host supported by the H2020 5GCity project seems to be a strong candidate for future business models helping network operators thrive in the new telecom era.

Keywords: 5G networks · Business model · Cloud computing · Neutral host NFV · SDN · Telecom market

1 Introduction

During the last decade, European telecom operators have been experiencing declines in their revenues, mainly because service prices stagnation, regulations, and an increasing demand of investments in their infrastructures. As a result, operators have been looking for innovative ways to turnaround this negative situation by considering the adoption of 5G networks given their technological, economical, and social values [1].

The 5G-PPP association has identified a series of specifications and KPIs [2] for 5G networks to be addressed by several ongoing initiatives and projects. The 5G networks KPIs are ultra-high data rates, low latency, reliability and, host neutrality. The last KPI will give a very important role to 5G technology in enabling new players from the vertical industries to enter the digital value chain, something that has not been done yet with the currently available technologies. This role will create significant social value through cutting-edge technological applications in various industries, such as medical care, transportation, and entertainment.

Hence, 5G networks are expected to offer new business opportunities and business models like neutral host to existing network operators. This can be attributed to the fact that 5G networks will make use of technological advances in network function

L. Iliadis et al. (Eds.): AIAI 2018, IFIP AICT 520, pp. 70–77, 2018.
https://doi.org/10.1007/978-3-319-92016-0_7

virtualization [3], software-defined networks (SDN) [4], edge computing, end-to-end network slicing and network analytics. Such innovative technologies will improve network performance and facilitate the development of sliceable applications and services.

This paper aims to investigate the neutral host business model, as proposed in the 5GCity project, along with the necessary changes that network operators need to make in their business models to thrive in the new digital era. The obtained results will be a valuable tool for decision makers, so to achieve the maximum exploitation of the technological advances of 5G and accelerate the return of network operators to revenue growth.

The objective of 5GCity [5], an innovation project financed within the 5G Public-Private Partnership (5GPPP) initiative by the European Commission (Horizon 2020 program), is the design, development, deployment and demonstration of a distributed cloud and radio platform for municipalities and infrastructure owners acting as 5G neutral hosts. The project's aim is to build and deploy a common, multi-tenant, open platform that extends the (centralized) cloud model to the extreme edge of the network, with demonstrations in three different cities (Barcelona, Bristol and Lucca). 5GCity will directly impact a large and varied range of actors: (i) telecom providers; (ii) municipalities; and (iii) several different vertical sectors utilizing the city infrastructure.

The rest of the paper is organized as follows: Sect. 2 presents the status of today's telecom market. Section 3 introduces the expected future of telecom networks along with the involved actors. Section 4 describes the required changes for network operators to increase their revenue. Section 5 introduces the role of a neutral host in a 5G Small Cell network. Finally, Sect. 6 concludes this work.

2   Status of Today's Telecom Market

The impact of the financial crisis of 2008 has different repercussions in EU based on each country's economic structure. As expected, southern European countries were strongly influenced by this crisis. While the growth of GDP in Greece remains negative, Italy and Spain have recovered the growth last year.

However, ICT networks provide the backbone for digital products and services that have the potential to support all aspects of our lives, and drive Europe's economic recovery [6]. Well-functioning markets deliver access to high-performance fixed and wireless broadband infrastructure, at affordable prices. Successive adaptations of the EU's telecoms rules combined with the application of EU competition rules, have been instrumental in ensuring that markets operate more competitively, bringing lower prices and better quality of service to consumers and businesses. Effective competition is a key driver for investment in telecoms networks.

Electronic communications sector represented 2,1% of EU's GDP in 2014, compared to 2,3% in 2013 and 2,7% in 2009. In 2014 the revenues of the electronic communications sector in the European Union were estimated at 300 billion euros while investment was about ~12% of the total turnover (Fig. 1).

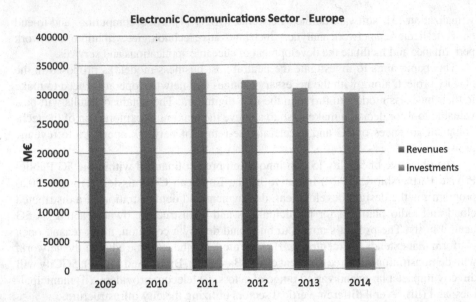

Fig. 1. Electronic communications sector revenues and investments (source: Digital Agenda Scoreboard)

According to inCITES Consulting connectivity database, Prognosis, both mobile and fixed service revenues were in decline in Western Europe for nearly a decade till 2016 (Fig. 2).

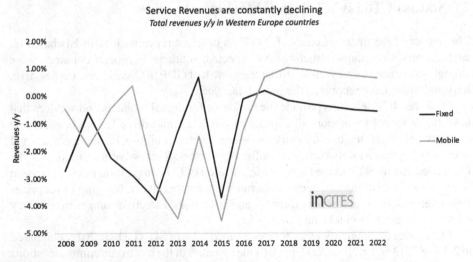

Fig. 2. Year-on-year service revenue trend for fixed and mobile markets in Western Europe (source: inCITES Consulting)

This can be attributed to the mobile termination rate cuts and other regulatory interventions (e.g. EU Zero Roaming) leading to ARPU squeeze as well as to the proliferation of bundles and decrease of voice traffic. Figure 3 illustrates the average revenue per user in the retail mobile market.

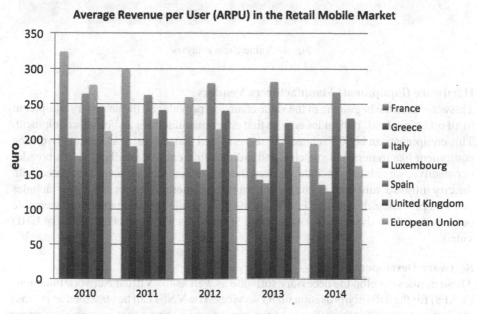

Fig. 3. Average revenue per user in the retail mobile market (source: Digital Agenda Scoreboard)

inCITES forecasts the service revenues to grow at a 0.8% CAGR in the mobile case and to drop at a −0.3% CAGR in the fixed case between 2017–22. It is evident that the forecasted increase in revenues is very small if one takes into account the ongoing growth in data traffic. According to Cisco Visual Networking Index (VNI), the global mobile data traffic grew an estimated 74% in 2015. Growth rates varied widely by region, with Central and Eastern Europe at 71% followed by Western Europe (52% in 2015). In 2015 mobile data traffic was 545.750 and 432.322 Terabytes per month in Central & Eastern Europe and Western Europe respectively (Statista).

3   The Future of Telecom Networks – Involved Actors

The value creation in the telecommunications market is no longer the case of a closed market limited to few players: new roles and relationships are evolved and become part of the new ecosystem. Each actor must understand its position to increase its value and maximize the potential revenues.

The following section describes the initial insights regarding the value chain analysis for future 5G networks. The involved actors and their relative position in the value chain is depicted in Fig. 4.

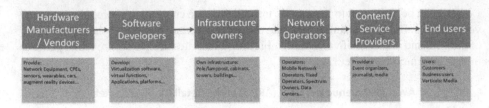

Fig. 4. Value chain analysis

Hardware (Equipment) Manufacturers/Vendors
This actor is on the beginning of the value chain and provides all the necessary equipment to all other involved. It includes entities that either manufactures and/or sells equipment. This equipment can be ICT related like servers, hard disk drives, RAM etc., networking equipment like routers and switches and radio equipment like small cells. In a broader perspective, we can also include vendors that manufacture equipment associated with the city infrastructure such as lampposts, cabinets, cameras, sensors etc. It also includes vendors providing devices for End Users such as mobile phones, tablets and wearable devices that allow the delivery of enhanced 5G services like augmented reality or UHD video.

Software Developers
These entities develop the necessary software as well as the Virtual Network Functions (VNFs) for the delivery/provision of 5G services. The VNFs can be classified as i) those that are necessary for the delivery of the service and ii) those that are complementary and are tailored to fulfil the requirements of users like the media vertical or immersive services. This type of actor also includes entities who develop applications, like for example video analytics or augmented reality software.

Infrastructure Owners
These entities own the necessary infrastructure that can be used for hosting the computing, storage and networking infrastructure. The available resources include space in street cabinets, lampposts or buildings along with power supply and connectivity facilities. These are necessary to power and interconnect the ICT equipment. Municipalities can be included in this category and are expected to play a significant role since they possess both facilities and ICT infrastructure. Municipalities will act as a Neutral Host providing wholesale access to interested parties (network operators). Thus, such entities will be of high importance since they enable network densification and keeping low costs.

Network Operators (ICT Infrastructure Providers)
This category includes all types of network operators like mobile and fixed, cloud providers, data centers that owns the physical resources of the network. It also includes entities that own spectrum licenses. This entity will receive wholesale access from Neutral Host in order to provide services to end-users.

Content/Service Providers

It includes entities that does not own network resources but use virtual resources to create and provide their own services. By taking advantage of the Neutral Host concept, service providers have a pool of different type of resources that can select and use to develop new and innovative services. The type of services they offer can be connectivity, Internet access, content distribution etc. They can develop their own content or come into agreement with other Content Providers or even End Users. They enter into Service Level Agreements with Network Operators to get access to the physical resources.

End Users

This term covers all short of users that range from simple users that seek only connectivity services to vertical industries that have more specific and tight requirements. They are the ultimate consumers of the services created in the telecommunication ecosystem. Furthermore, End Users can become content producers to Service Providers.

4 Mandatory Changes in Operators' Business Models

In this section, the necessary changes that will allow network operators to thrive in the new digital era are investigated and presented.

4.1 Network Operators to Exploit Their Strong Position as Network Owners

In the last years, network operators have seen OTTs and vendors gaining a big part of end-user relationships. Taking also into account that connectivity is no longer profitable, network operators arc seeking a role as intermediates between vendors and OTTs facilitating partnerships and adopting a wholesale and a "smart pipe" model towards success. In the so-called neutral host model, OTTs, virtual operators and third parties are leasing access from network operators in order to provide their services while vendors are attracted by operators' large scale. Moreover, manufacturers and vendors will be able to connect their devices in the new Internet of Things era. Network operators should resort to recent technologies such as network analytics, software defined networks and network virtualization to optimize network operation and improve its performance. By leveraging cloud computing, networks operators are aiming to a digital single market where they can provide their services remotely from any part of the value chain leading to significant savings due to economies of scale.

4.2 Networks Operators to Get Closer to Clients' Needs

Networks operators should leverage recent technological achievements in order to provide tailor-made personalized services to their customers. Networks operators are probably the only entity that is able to securely collect and analyze users' data. Using big data analytics, valuable knowledge can be extracted enabling them to adapt their products and investment plans in order to meet B2B and B2C requirements. Using advanced computing capabilities, networks operators can now adopt different (e.g. per usage) and/or hybrid pricing schemes and offer customer and price differentiation.

4.3 Required Investments

In order to stay on top of technological advances and achieve the aforementioned transformations, networks operators should also change their investment strategies. On the one hand, networks operators should definitely continue investing in infrastructure in order to expand their networks. Since this is a capital-intensive process, networks operators should resort to alternative funding schemes (e.g. network sharing and co-investments) and exploit governmental subsidies and PPPs. On the other hand, network investments should be accompanied by software-based investments which are essential for controlling and maintaining the network.

5   The Role of Neutral Host in 5G Networks – Potential Risks

In future 5G network deployments, Small Cells [7–9] are expected to play a significant role in reaching the KPIs as these are specified from 5G-PPP. However, Small Cells deployment usually requires locations with costly backhaul and power facilities, which might hinder the mass deployment of Small Cells. In addition, it should be highlighted that the deployment of "parallel" access networks will be prohibited especially in dense areas. Within future 5G infrastructures, network sharing should evolve beyond the traditional infrastructure sharing models used in previous generations, i.e. site, mast, RAN and core network sharing, towards cloudification, virtualization and holistic end-to-end network slicing.

Given this complex landscape, the business model of a neutral operator owning the infrastructure and providing wholesale access to mobile operators seems to be among the most promising ones. For example, a neutral host operator (i.e., the infrastructure owner) could deploy and manage Small Cells while leasing out slices of network capacity to the different 5G service providers on an equal basis to foster competition. However, the advantages of a neutral host operator model are accompanied by several risks related to the possibility of a monopolistic behavior. This contains the risk for abuse of dominant position. In such case, the neutral host operator may refuse to supply the necessary wholesale input, to proceed to excessive pricing as well as to demonstrate discrimination among operators/customers and/or set barriers to new entrants. In order to address these challenges, careful monitoring mechanisms are necessary. These will ensure the public/general interest as well as maximization of the social welfare. NRAs, NCAs, State Aid/PPP are authorities that can potentially undertake the monitoring processes with the first being the most appropriate due to its expertise on remedies such as price cap regulation, retail minus regulation, etc. that require cost accounting models and relative experience.

6 Conclusions

European telecom companies faced reductions in their revenue associated to variety of factors. 5G networks through a neutral host business model promises to revive opportunities for telecom operators to increase their revenue and new social and economic values for the society.

In this paper, we investigated the necessary changes that should be adopted by network operators to remain competitive by first reporting the status of the telecom market in decreasing revenues fashion. Then we describe the role of telecom networks and actors in the new digital. Followed by several guidelines that will be useful for network operators to adequate their business model by including the neutral host model supported by the H2020 5GCity project. Finally, we described the role of neutral host to address the deployment limitations of 5G networks along with their potential risks.

Acknowledgment. The research leading to these results has been supported by the EU funded H2020 5G-PPP project 5GCity (grant agreement No. 761508).

References

1. G. W. Report, "Identification and quantification of key socio-economic data for the Strategic Planning of 5G introduction in Europe," SMART 2014/0008 (2015)
2. https://5g-ppp.eu/kpis/
3. Mosharaf, N.M., Chowdhury, K., Boutaba, R.: A survey of network virtualization. Comput. Netw. **54**(5), 862–876 (2010)
4. Nunes, B.A.A., Mendonça, M., Ngyen, X.-N., Obraczka, K., Turletti, T.: A survey of software-defined networking: past, present, and future of programmable networks. IEEE Commun. Surv. Tutor. **16**(3), 1–18 (2014)
5. www.5gcity.eu
6. European Commission: Communication from the European Commission on "A Digital Single Market Strategy for Europe" [COM(2015) 192 final, 06.05.2015] (2015)
7. Small Cell Forum (SCF) Release 7.0: Document 055.07.01 – Small Cells and 5G Evolution: A Topic Brief. http://scf.io/en/documents/055__Small_cells_and_5G_evolution_a_topic_brief.php
8. Quek, T.Q.S., de la Roche, G., Güvenç, İ., Kountouris, M.: Small Cell Networks Deployment, PHY Techniques, and Resource Management. Cambridge University Press, Cambridge (2013)
9. Mahmoud, H.A., Guvenc, I.: A comparative study of different deployment modes for femtocell networks. In: Proceedings of IEEE Indoor Outdoor Femtocells (IOFC) Workshop (co-located with PIMRC 2009), Tokyo, Japan, pp. 1–5, September 2009

An Experimental Assessment of Channel Selection in Cognitive Radio Networks

Anna Umbert[1]([✉]), Oriol Sallent[1], Jordi Pérez-Romero[1], Juan Sánchez-González[1], Diarmuid Collins[2], and Maicon Kist[3]

[1] Universitat Politècnica de Catalunya (UPC), c/Jordi Girona, 1-3, 08034 Barcelona, Spain
annau@tsc.upc.edu

[2] CONNECT Centre for Future Networks, Trinity College Dublin (TCD), Dublin, Ireland
[3] Federal University of Rio Grande do Sul (UFRGS), Porto Alegre, Brazil

Abstract. The management of future networks is expected to fully exploit cognitive capabilities that embrace knowledge and intelligence, increasing the degree of automation, making the network more self-autonomous and enabling a personalized user experience. In this context, this paper presents the use of knowledge-based capabilities through a specific lab experiment focused on the Channel Selection functionality for Cognitive Radio Networks (CRN). The selection is based on a supervised classification that allows estimating the number of interfering sources existing in a given frequency channel. Four different classifiers are considered, namely decision tree, neural network, naive Bayes and Support Vector Machine (SVM). Additionally, a comparison against other channel selection strategies using Q-learning and game theory has also been performed. Results obtained in an illustrative and realistic test scenario have revealed that all the strategies allow identifying an optimum solution. However, the time to converge to this solution can be up to 27 times higher according to the algorithm selected.

Keywords: Channel selection · Classification · Cognitive Radio

1 Introduction

The increasing traffic demand will lead future wireless networks to face a severe shortage of spectrum, especially when considering the highly dense deployments of small cells envisaged for meeting the demands of future systems. Cognitive Radio Networks (CRN), based on the Cognitive Radio (CR) paradigm [1], will bring light to this problem. Briefly, CR observes the environment, analyzes these observations, makes decisions to intelligently configure certain radio parameters, and finally executes these decisions. Analysis and decision can be supported by means of learning mechanisms that exploit the knowledge obtained from the execution of prior decisions.

CRN concepts are also expected to play a relevant role in the context of future 5G (5th Generation) networks [2], which should include by design unprecedented network flexibility and highly efficient/adaptive network resource usage, including flexible

L. Iliadis et al. (Eds.): AIAI 2018, IFIP AICT 520, pp. 78–88, 2018.
https://doi.org/10.1007/978-3-319-92016-0_8

spectrum management. Thus, the introduction of intelligence in the network will be an important requirement. In this direction, the advent of big data analytics [3] will boost the extraction of the meaningful information from the available data, to support the use of cognitive capabilities both in the Radio Access Network (RAN) and in the Core Network.

Using knowledge-based procedures and Artificial Intelligence (AI) as key elements of cognition for supporting the optimization in future networks has been considered in the literature for the last several years. Specific algorithms for learning time domain traffic patterns and mobility patterns, respectively, have been proposed and analyzed [4, 5]. Similarly, in [6] a clustering strategy was proposed to identify the user's daily motifs and extract the personalised Quality of Service observed by a user when being connected to a real 3G/4G network. Nevertheless, the authors believe that one important reason for the (relatively) low penetration of AI concepts in this domain so far is due to the difficulty for the research community in general to test (and hopefully prove the validity of) potential solutions in realistic conditions. Clearly, AI-based knowledge discovery models (e.g. classification, prediction, clustering) can hardly be properly assessed in simulated environments, where many of the real-world effects are not retained. Instead, more solid results and conclusions can be derived from implementing such mechanisms in realistic conditions.

In this respect, WiSHFUL is a European project from the European Horizon 2020 Programme that focuses on speeding up the development and testing cycles of wireless solutions and, therefore, it offers a great opportunity to gain access to realistic data and measurements [7]. It defines software modules with unified interfaces that permit wireless developers to quickly implement and validate advanced wireless network solutions. The WiSHFUL project offers access to different advanced wireless testbeds, among them the IRIS testbed at Trinity College Dublin [8].

In this context, this paper describes a specific experiment using the IRIS testbed. The experiment focuses on the Channel Selection functionality for CRN, so that an access point decides the most appropriate channel to use within a band that is shared among multiple transmitters. This selection is based on a supervised classification that allows estimating the number of interfering sources existing in a given frequency channel. Specifically, four different classifiers have been implemented: decision tree, neural network, naive Bayes and Support Vector Machine (SVM). Additionally, a comparison against other channel selection strategies using Q-learning and game theory has also been performed. In this way, this experiment contributes to expand the capabilities of the existing WiSHFUL Intelligence framework [9] that offers an experimentation environment for early implementation and validation of end-to-end 5G solutions that improve resource utilization through advanced reconfigurability of radio and network settings.

The rest of the paper is organised as follows. Section 2 presents the IRIS testbed used for executing experiments. Section 3 discusses the considered approaches for channel selection. The experimental results obtained with these approaches are presented in Sect. 4, while Sect. 5 summarizes the main conclusions.

2   The IRIS Testbed

The IRIS testbed is the reconfigurable radio testbed at Trinity College Dublin [8]. It provides access to radio hardware that supports the experimental investigation of the interplay between radio capabilities and networks.

The testbed employs 18 ceiling or wall mounted Universal Software Radio Peripheral (USRP) N210s equipped with SBX daughterboard, reaching frequencies between 40 MHz and 4.4 GHz, and 4 other radio nodes not available within the WiSHFUL context, as underlying radio resources. All these elements are connected to a private computational cloud, allowing to deploy an array of computational environments. By default, each USRP device of the testbed is associated to a Virtual Machine (VM) that occupies 4 CPU cores and 4 GB of RAM from the computational cloud. Testbed access was supported by jFed Experimenter suite developed by the Fed4FIRE+ EU project.

For setting up and executing the experiments with the IRIS testbed, we modify the code and the configuration files in a remote local machine at Universitat Politècnica de Catalunya (UPC) premises, and then we upload the files to the testbed machines, we execute the test, and we download back the results files to our local machines. To perform these operations, a custom made code implemented with Python programming language that uses the WiSHFUL software framework and the Unified Programming Interface (UPI) functions and runs on the IRIS Testbed has been created.

Two different pieces of python code, namely the *wishful_controller* and the *agent*, have been used. The *wishful_controller* runs on a computer, whereas one *agent* runs on each radio node. The configuration of a radio node as a transmitter or receiver is made by the *wishful_controller* when the radio program is activated. The purpose of the *agent* is to connect to the *wishful_controller* and wait for instructions (passed through UPI calls). In turn, the *wishful_controller* executes the logic for controlling the experiment.

A deployment example of the experimentation framework is illustrated in Fig. 1. In this case, a scenario with three nodes acting as transmitters (AP1, AP2, and AP3) and three nodes acting as receivers (STA1, STA2 and STA3) is considered.

3   Experimenting Channel Selection Functionality Using the IRIS Testbed

The experiment considered here focuses on learning the interference characterisation and using the learnt information for supporting channel selection in CRN. Specifically, the approach consists in analyzing the environment where a given cell (or access point) is operating by performing both radio-frequency and performance measurements and, based on these measurements, to characterise the observed interference in terms of the number of interfering sources. To support this knowledge discovery, the capabilities of the IRIS testbed are extended through the inclusion of the RapidMiner tool [10]. It is a powerful all-in-one tool that features hundreds of pre-defined data preparation and machine learning algorithms to support data science projects.

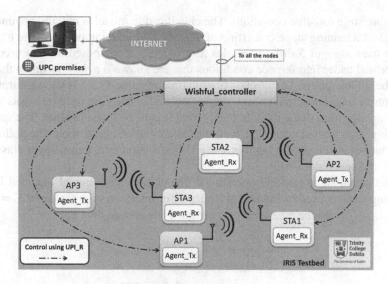

Fig. 1. Example of experimentation scenario

3.1 Learning Interference Characterisation

The example in Fig. 1 illustrates a scenario for learning interference characterization. Let us assume, as an example, that the receiver STA1 is connected to the transmitter AP1 operating at a given frequency. Simultaneously, the other transmitters (i.e. AP2 and AP3) may be operating in the same frequency, thus generating interference to STA1, or they may be operating in a different frequency, thus not generating interference. In this scenario, the objective of the considered experiment is to apply machine-learning based tools to smartly process the measurements performed by STA1 in order to characterize the existing interference. More specifically, it is proposed to use a supervised classification mechanism to estimate, based on the measurements of STA1, the number of interfering sources at a certain instant of time.

The classification is the process of finding a model or function that describes and distinguishes data classes or concepts. The obtained model (i.e. the classifier) is then used to determine the class to which an object belongs. The object is the entity to be classified and it is usually represented by a tuple that includes a set of attribute values (e.g. a tuple could be a set of measurements performed by a receiver and each of the measurements is an attribute). The classification process assumes that the possible classes are predefined in advance. Then, the classifier model is usually obtained from a supervised learning algorithm that analyses a set of training tuples associated with known classes.

Figure 2 illustrates the classification process. In general terms, the classifier takes as input a tuple of the form $X_t = \{x_{t,1}, x_{t,2}, ..., x_{t,M}\}$ with M different measurements performed by a receiver at time t. The objective of the classifier is to make an association between the input tuple X_t and the class $C(X_t)$ that specifies the number of interfering sources at time t. For that purpose the process involves the following steps:

1. Training stage (off-line operation): The classification model is initially obtained by means of a training stage consisting of a supervised learning process. The training stage uses as input S different tuples X_j $j = 1, ..., S$ composed of measurements performed under interference conditions that are known *a priori*, meaning that the number of interferers, i.e. the class of each training tuple $C(X_j)$, is known during the measurements. These tuples and their associated classes are used as inputs to the training algorithm that will build the internal structure of the classifier. The specific training algorithm depends on the considered classification tool. The following alternatives are considered in this study [12]: decision tree, naive Bayes classifier, SVM and neural network.

2. Classification stage (on-line operation): The classification model obtained in the training stage is used to estimate the number of interferers for any tuple $X_t = \{x_{t,1}, x_{t,2}, ..., x_{t,M}\}$ with the measurements obtained at a certain time t.

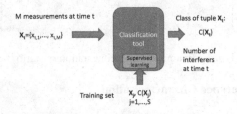

Fig. 2. Classification process

In the specific experiment on the IRIS testbed, we initially create tuples X_t with measurements of the throughput (*Th*) and Received Signal Strength Indicator (*RSSI*) at time t, i.e. $X_t = \{Th(t), RSSI(t)\}$ under different interference situations (with 0 interferers, 1 interferer and 2 interferers). During the training stage, each of these tuples and the number of interferers for each one are used to build a classification model. Then, during the classification stage, the model is used each time that the methodology needs to estimate the number of interferers for each new tuple of measurements.

3.2 Channel Selection

Channel selection (also denoted as carrier selection) is the mechanism used to decide the operating channel (i.e. center frequency and associated bandwidth) of a transmitter. A smart channel selection mechanism is relevant to facilitate the coexistence between multiple transmitters in wireless scenarios operating in unlicensed spectrum when there is little or no coordination between these transmitters. This could be the case of e.g. Wi-Fi networks or unlicensed LTE (LTE-U).

The design of a proper channel selection functionality can greatly improve the overall efficiency of a wireless system when using unlicensed spectrum, since it will impact on the overall interference experienced by the receivers and thus on the achieved throughput performance.

Under the above considerations, the purpose of the experiment considered here is to use the IRIS testbed to assess a channel selection algorithm (Algorithm 1) that exploits the extracted knowledge from the supervised classification process for characterizing the interference as explained in Sect. 3.1. For benchmarking purposes, a channel selection algorithm using Q-learning (Algorithm 2) and another one using game theory (Algorithm 3) have also been tested.

The general scenario assumes a total of T transmitters with their associated receivers and a total of K possible frequency channels. The considered channel selection algorithms are described in the following:

Algorithm 1: Supervised Classification-Based Channel Selection Algorithm

For the supervised classification-based channel selection algorithm for the i-th transmitter, $i = 1, ..., T$, it is assumed that the training stage explained in Sect. 3.1 has been executed previously to build the classifier. Then, each time step, the receiver measures the values of throughput and $RSSI$ for all the channels. Then, the classifier estimates the number of interferers in each of the channels. The estimated number of interferers is averaged considering a time window of N samples. The selected channel will be the one with minimum number of interferers. The process is subsequently repeated at the next time steps to consider possible changes in the environment (e.g. due to channel selections made by other transmitters) which could lead to new channel changes.

Algorithm 2: Q-Learning-Based Channel Selection Algorithm

Q-learning is a type of Reinforcement Learning (RL) technique [13] where learning is achieved through the interaction with the environment, so that the learner discovers which actions yield the most reward by trying them. In this way, each transmitter progressively learns and selects the channels that provide the best performance based on the previous experience. In the considered algorithm, described in detail in [14, 15], each transmitter i stores a value function $Q(i, k)$ that measures the expected reward (i.e. throughput) that can be achieved by using each channel k according to the past experience. Whenever a channel k has been used by the transmitter i, $Q(i, k)$ is updated following a single state Q-learning approach with null discount rate and learning rate α_L. Based on this, the channel selection decision-making follows the softmax policy with temperature τ.

Algorithm 3: Game Theory-Based Channel Selection Algorithm

In this algorithm, the channel selection problem is modelled as a game in which each transmitter/receiver pair is a player and the actions made by each player are the selected channels. Specifically, here we consider the Iterative Trial and Error Learning-Best Action (ITEL-BA) algorithm described in [16]. In ITEL-BA, each transmitter retains a benchmark action $a_{B,i}(t)$ (i.e. a benchmark channel to select) and the corresponding benchmark reward $r_{B,i}(t)$ as a reference to evolve the action selection strategy. The reward is measured as the obtained throughput averaged during a time window of N samples. At a certain time, a channel is chosen depending on the so-called mood of the player, which basically captures the degree of satisfaction of the player with the current benchmark action and benchmark reward. The mood $m_i(t)$ of player i at the beginning of time step t can be *content*, *discontent*, *hopeful* or *watchful*. The general idea is that a content player will be selecting the benchmark action most of the time, and will occasionally experiment with new actions according to a probability $\varepsilon << 1$ called exploration rate. Instead, a discontent player will try out new actions frequently, eventually becoming content. The *hopeful* and *watchful* moods correspond to transitional situations, triggered by changes in the behavior of other players (or in the environment), and they will facilitate updates in the values of the benchmark action and reward to cope with these changes. The reader is referred to [16] for a detailed specification of the ITEL-BA algorithm.

4   Results

The evaluation of the channel selection algorithms is performed using the set-up of the IRIS testbed illustrated in Fig. 1. It is considered that 3 nodes act as APs (AP1, AP2, AP3). Each APs has an associated receiver (STA1, STA2, STA3). There are 3 possible channels to select: Channel #1: 2890 MHz, Channel #2: 2900 MHz and Channel #3: 2910 MHz.

Initially, all the APs transmit on Channel #1. Subsequently, each AP can change channel being used according to the different channel selection algorithms explained in Sect. 3.2.

4.1   Algorithm 1: Supervised Classification-Based Channel Selection

Different executions are performed for each of the considered classifiers. The algorithm is tested with an averaging window of $N = 50$ samples. The results shown in Figs. 3, 4, 5 and 6 depict the channel number selected by each AP as a function of the number of channel selection decisions for the decision tree, naive Bayes, SVM and neural network classifiers, respectively. It is observed that, although all the APs start with the same Channel #1, in all the cases the APs are able to switch to a channel that is estimated by the classifier to be free of interferers. As a result, the system is able to find an optimum configuration in which each AP uses a different channel and correspondingly there is no interference. It is also worth observing that the naive Bayes and SVM classifiers are able to switch to a channel free of interferers very quickly, in just one channel selection decision. In the decision tree, naive Bayes and SVM classifiers, AP1 switches to Channel #3, AP2 switches to Channel #2 and AP3 remains in the same Channel #1. This solution is kept for the rest of the execution and no further changes are performed. In turn, focusing on the behavior of the decision tree classifier (see Fig. 3), it is observed that, due to the lower accuracy of this classifier, it requires a few more decisions to reach the optimum configuration in which each AP uses a different frequency. For example, it is observed that, at the beginning, AP3 makes a wrong decision by switching temporarily to Channel #3, which is being used by AP1, but then it moves to Channel #1. As for the neural network classifier, which also has lower accuracy, Fig. 6 reflects that, at the beginning, the APs quickly find a solution with different channels (i.e. AP1 using Channel #3, AP2 using Channel #2 and AP3 using Channel #1). However, after some time, AP2 makes a wrong decision and switches to the Channel #1 used by AP3. This situation is solved after 10 further decisions, when AP3 switches to Channel #2.

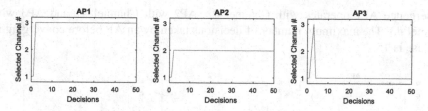

Fig. 3. Selected channel with Algorithm 1 and Decision Tree classifier for each AP

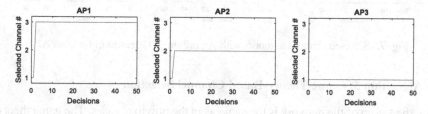

Fig. 4. Selected channel with Algorithm 1 and Naive Bayes classifier for each AP

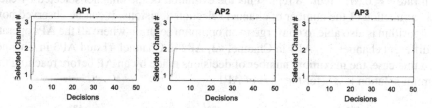

Fig. 5. Selected channel with Algorithm 1 and SVM classifier for each AP

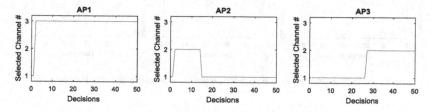

Fig. 6. Selected channel with Algorithm 1 and Neural Network classifier for each AP

4.2 Algorithm 2: Q-Learning-Based Channel Selection

The set-up for this execution is the same as for Algorithm 1, with all the three APs working initially in Channel #1. The Q-learning algorithm is configured with learning rate $\alpha_L = 0.1$, while the temperature parameter τ is initially 0.15 and is reduced in each decision following a logarithmic cooling approach as explained in [14]. Figure 7 depicts the evolution of the channels selected by each AP with the successive channel selection decisions. It is observed that after some fluctuations associated to the probabilistic behavior of the softmax decision-making criterion finally the experiment converges to a solution where each AP has selected a different channel. Specifically, after convergence AP1 operates with Channel #2, AP2 with Channel #1 and AP3 with Channel #3. The maximum number of decisions taken by an AP before converging in this case is 15.

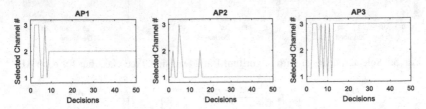

Fig. 7. Selected channel numbers with Algorithm 2 (Q-learning) for each AP

4.3   Algorithm 3: Game Theory-Based Channel Selection

Again, the set-up of the network is the same as in the previous cases. The game theory-based algorithm is configured with an averaging window of $N = 50$ samples and exploration rate $\varepsilon = 0.01$. Figure 8 represents the evolution of the channel selected by each AP as a function of the number of channel selection decisions. It can be observed how this algorithm is also able to converge to an optimum solution where all the APs operate in a different channel, i.e. AP1 in Channel #3, AP2 in Channel #1 and AP3 in Channel #2. In this case, the maximum number of decisions made by an AP before reaching the optimum solution is 27 (for the case of AP1).

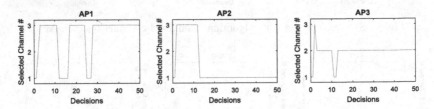

Fig. 8. Selected channel numbers with Algorithm 3 (game theory) for each AP

5   Conclusions

This paper has presented an experiment focusing on the channel selection functionality for Cognitive Radio Networks (CRN), so that an access point decides the most appropriate channel to use within a band that is shared among multiple transmitters. This selection has been based on a supervised classification that allows estimating the number of interfering sources existing in a given frequency channel. Specifically four different classifiers have been considered: decision tree, neural network, naive Bayes and Support Vector Machine (SVM). The channel selection algorithm exploits the estimation of the number of interferers to decide the most convenient channel to be used by a transmitter. Furthermore, a comparison against other Channel Selection strategies using Q-learning and game theory-based mechanisms has also been performed. Results in a scenario with

3 pairs of transmitter/receiver APs have revealed that all the considered algorithms for channel selection converge to an optimum solution where all the pairs operate in a different channel. Furthermore, it has been observed that the fastest convergence is achieved with the SVM and Naive Bayes classifiers, while the Game Theory and Q-learning based approaches exhibit slower convergence.

Acknowledgements. This work has been done using the IRIS testbed available through the WiSHFUL Platform. This work has been partly supported by the Spanish Research Council and FEDER funds under RAMSES and SONAR 5G grants (ref. TEC2013-41698-R and TEC2017-82651-R).

References

1. Mitola III, J.: Cognitive radio: an integrated agent architecture for software defined radio. Ph.D. dissertation, KTH Royal Institute of Technology (2000)
2. El Hattachi, R., Erfanian, J. (eds.): NGMN 5G White Paper. NGMN Alliance, February 2015. https://www.ngmn.org/fileadmin/ngmn/content/down-loads/Technical/2015/NGMN_5G_White_Paper_V1_0.pdf
3. Chih-Lin, I., Liu, Y., Han, S., Wang, S., Liu, G.: On big data analytics for greener and softer RAN. IEEE Access, August 2015. http://ieeexplore.ieee.org/document/7210136/
4. Pérez-Romero, J., Sánchez-González, J., Sallent, O., Agustí, R.: On learning and exploiting time domain traffic patterns in cellular radio access networks. Machine Learning and Data Mining in Pattern Recognition. LNCS (LNAI), vol. 9729, pp. 501–515. Springer, Cham (2016). https://doi.org/10.1007/978-3-319-41920-6_40
5. Sánchez-González, J., Pérez-Romero, J., Agustí, R., Sallent, O.: On learning mobility patterns in cellular networks. In: Iliadis, L., Maglogiannis, I. (eds.) AIAI 2016. IAICT, vol. 475, pp. 686–696. Springer, Cham (2016). https://doi.org/10.1007/978-3-319-44944-9_61
6. Sánchez-González, J., Sallent, O., Pérez-Romero, J., Agustí, R.: On extracting user-centric knowledge for personalised quality of service in 5G networks. In: IFIP/IEEE International Symposium on Integrated Network Management - 2nd International Workshop on Analytics for Network and Service Management, Lisbon, Portugal, May 2017
7. WiSHFUL. http://www.wishful-project.eu/
8. IRIS Testbed. https://iris-testbed.connectcentre.ie
9. D10.1 Design of software architecture for intelligent control and showcases. http://www.wishful-project.eu/sites/default/files/images/WiSHFUL_D10.1_Lead_iMinds_R_PU_2015-12-23_Final.pdf
10. RapidMiner. https://rapidminer.com/
11. Pérez-Romero, J., Sallent, O., Ferrús, R., Agustí, R.: Knowledge-based 5G radio access network planning and optimization. In: International Symposium on Wireless Communication Systems (ISWCS), Poznan, Poland, August 2016
12. Han, J., Kamber, M.: Data Mining Concepts and Techniques, 2nd edn. Elsevier, New York City (2006)
13. Sutton, R.S., Barto, A.G.: Reinforcement Learning: An Introduction. MIT Press, Cambridge (1998)
14. Sallent, O., Pérez-Romero, J., Ferrús, R., Agustí, R.: Learning-based coexistence for LTE operation in unlicensed bands. In: International Conference on Communications (Workshops), IEEE ICC 2015, 8–12 June 2015, London, United Kingdom. pp. 2307–2313 (2015)

15. Perez-Romero, J., Sallent, O., Ferrús, R., Agusti, R.: A robustness analysis of learning-based coexistence mechanisms for LTE-U operation in non-stationary conditions. In: 82nd Vehicular Technology Conference, IEEE VTC 2015-Fall, 6–9 September 2015, Boston, MA, pp. 1–5 (2015)
16. Pérez-Romero, J., Sallent, O., Ahmadi, H., Macaluso, I.: On modeling channel selection in LTE-U as a repeated game. In: Wireless Communications and Networking Conference, IEEE WCNC 2016, 3–6 April 2016, Doha, Qatar (2016)

Space/Time Traffic Fluctuations in a Cellular Network: Measurements' Analysis and Potential Applications

Juan Sánchez-González[✉], Oriol Sallent, and Jordi Pérez-Romero

Universitat Politècnica de Catalunya (UPC),
c/Jordi Girona, 1-3, 08034 Barcelona, Spain
juansanchez@tsc.upc.edu

Abstract. The characterization of the space/time traffic profiles in a cellular network can be of high interest for automating the operation of future networks, since the knowledge extracted from the traffic fluctuations in a cell and its neighbours can be effectively exploited by different optimisation functions. In this context, this paper takes as an input a set of real traffic measurements in a cellular network deployed in a large city and analyses, on a per cell basis, the traffic profile characteristics at different time scales (week, day, hour). Then, the analysis is extended to the space dimension by considering the traffic of one cell in relation to that of its neighbours. This allows identifying traffic complementarities between neighbour cells at different time scales that can be exploited by certain optimisation functions, as illustrated in the paper with specific examples.

Keywords: Space/time traffic analysis · Cellular networks · SON
Mobility Load Balancing · Coverage and capacity optimisation · Energy saving

1 Introduction

In the last years, cellular networks have witnessed an explosive increase in the traffic volume due to the massive penetration of new wireless devices (such as smartphones and tablets). It is envisaged that this trend will continue in the future with the emergence of new bandwidth-intensive applications such as high definition video, 3D, augmented reality/virtual reality, etc. and with the demand for wireless Machine-to-Machine communications. According to [1], the worldwide mobile devices are expected to consume more than 48.3 Exabytes per month by 2021, which represents a sevenfold increase between 2016 and 2021. To cope with these challenging requirements, research and standardization work is nowadays focused on the development of the 5th Generation (5G).

5G networks are expected to be characterized by unprecedented flexibility to support a wide range of requirements and network functionalities associated to different application scenarios, going beyond the provision of enhanced Mobile BroadBand (eMBB) services to incorporate services associated to other sectors such as automotive, utilities,

L. Iliadis et al. (Eds.): AIAI 2018, IFIP AICT 520, pp. 89–98, 2018.
https://doi.org/10.1007/978-3-319-92016-0_9

smart cities, etc. The resulting heterogeneity and the required flexibility will make the network planning and operation much more complex, thus claiming for an increase in the degree of automation of these processes.

Legacy systems such as 2G/3G/4G already started the path towards a higher degree of automation through the introduction of Self-Organizing Network (SON) functionalities [2]. However, nowadays, the volume and variety of measurement data that can be obtained from the mobile network is overwhelming. Due to the recent developments of big data technologies [3], it is envisioned that 5G SON will better exploit the huge amount of data available by a Mobile Network Operator (MNO) [4, 5]. The target is to efficiently handle this big amount of data and turn it into value by gaining insight and understanding data structures and relationships, extracting exploitable knowledge and deriving successful decision-making.

Obtaining knowledge of space/time traffic profiles can be of high interest for network optimisation since the analysis of traffic spatio/temporal fluctuations in a given cell and its neighbours can be effectively exploited by different decision making processes associated to the planning and operation of the network. In this direction, several works have proposed methodologies to analyse the base stations traffic to obtain knowledge of the network usage to be used for network optimization. As an example, [6] provides a geospatial and temporal characterization of application usage in a real 3G cellular data network. In particular, the paper studies where and when users are running the different services (e-mail, web-browsing, etc.) in order to improve the radio resource provision in the network. Similarly, [7] proposes a methodology to identify different types of cells (i.e. cells deployed in residential areas, commercial areas, etc.) by evaluating several features such as traffic fluctuation, user mobility, temporal pattern of traffic generation and user service preferences.

Some works, such as [8, 9], make use of real measurements to extract spatio-temporal traffic models that are used for traffic forecasting. The characterization and modelling of spatio-temporal fluctuations in the access network by analyzing real measurements in cellular networks has been addressed by [10–12]. In particular, according to [11], the spatial distribution of traffic can be assumed to be log-normal distributed around certain geographical areas with high traffic demands. However, the temporal evolution of traffic can be represented as the summation of different sinusoids with periods of 8, 12 and 24 h to capture the user social behavior, because mobile users tend to have repetitive behaviors in periods of one day, half a day and working hours. Some works make use of Artificial Intelligence mechanisms in order to extract knowledge of the time traffic evolution. As an example, [13] compares Support Vector Machine and K-means methodologies for the classification of cells with high load levels during all the day, cells with a peak load level in the morning and cells with a peak load level in the evening. Classification algorithms are used in [14] to identify cells with periods of low traffic level and cells with peaks of traffic and apply this knowledge in different management processes such as energy saving or spectrum planning. Similarly, [15] proposes an algorithm that exploits knowledge of spatio-temporal traffic fluctuations to save energy by switching off certain base stations without reducing the network capacity.

While the above papers have addressed different strategies to analyze the traffic in the different cells, none of the previous works have focused on the identification of spatio-temporal traffic complementarities among neighbor cells and how to exploit them for optimizing the operation of the network. In this context, this paper provides two main contributions. First, it presents a statistical analysis of a bunch of realistic traffic measurements obtained from hundreds of cells in a large city to evaluate at what extent fluctuations exist in real traffic when considering, on a per cell basis, the traffic profile characteristics at different time scales (week, day, hour). Second, the analysis is extended to incorporate the spatial dimension by illustrating, through several examples, some existing traffic complementarities between neighbour cells at different time scales. For each example, the paper discusses possible network reconfiguration actions that can make use of the identified complementarities.

The rest of the paper is organised as follows. Section 2 presents the statistical analysis of the real traffic measurements in the time domain, while Sect. 3 presents examples of traffic complementarities between cells and possible ways to exploit them for the optimisation of the radio resource usage. Finally, Sect. 4 summarizes the main conclusions.

2   Analysis of Traffic Measurements in Time

The available measurements have been obtained from 423 cells that belong to a real cellular network deployed in the city centre of one of the major cities in Spain. For each cell, the measurements have been recorded during one week in periods of 15 min. For the analysis of the time evolution of the cell traffic, different averaging periods (i.e. 2, 8 and 24 h) have been considered. Due to confidentiality reasons, the presented traffic load has been normalised. In any case, this normalisation does not affect the analysis of the results, since we are only interested in relative traffic variations between cells.

Considering the measurements of all the cells, Fig. 1 shows the 10th, 50th and 90th percentile of the normalised average daily traffic from Monday to Sunday (i.e. in the presented results, X^{th} percentile represents the average daily traffic that is not exceeded by X% of the cells). It is observed that, over 24 h period (i.e., on a per-day view) and over the whole scenario, traffic keeps at a rather constant level during weekdays and lowers during weekends. Nevertheless, the statistical analysis made at a shorter time scale provides further knowledge. As an example, Fig. 2 shows the 10th, 50th and 90th percentile of the

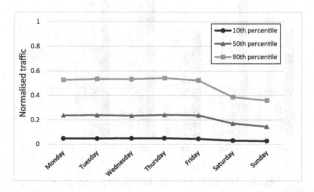

Fig. 1. 10th, 50th and 90th percentile of the average daily traffic.

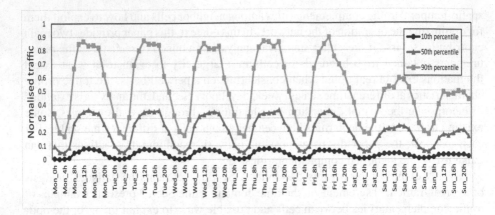

Fig. 2. 10th, 50th and 90th percentile of the average traffic over 2 h periods.

average traffic over 2 h periods and over the whole scenario from Monday to Sunday. This view allows observing intra-day traffic variations, exhibiting higher traffic levels during working hours (i.e., from 8AM to 6PM).

In order to assess at what extent the different cells exhibit different traffic behaviours, the average daily traffic per cell from Monday to Friday is analysed. For each day, each cell is classified as having low (L), medium (M) or high (H) traffic. Based on this, it is found that 84% of the cells are classified in the same category (L, M or H) every day from Monday to Friday. Therefore, the other 16% of the cells exhibit significant daily traffic variations during weekdays. Figure 3 depicts some examples of these cells. For example, Cell_264 has L traffic from Monday to Thursday and M traffic on Friday. In turn, Cell_93 has only H traffic on Thursday. In some cases, a reason to explain the traffic variation from one day to another can be found (e.g., Cell_93 is located in an area where there is a weekly street market on Thursday), while in other cases the source of the traffic fluctuation remains unclear.

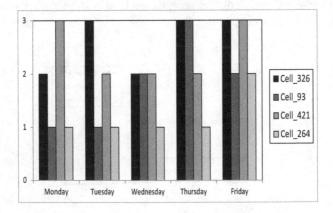

Fig. 3. Traffic level evolution during weekdays.

The average traffic over periods of 8 h (i.e. 0 h–8 h, 8 h–16 h and 16 h–24 h) has been also analysed from Monday to Friday. Again, for each period of 8 h, each cell is classified as having L, M or H traffic. Table 1 presents the percentage of cells classified in the same category every day from Monday to Friday and the percentage of cells classified differently in some days. It is observed that, at night, around 89% of the cells are classified equally (i.e. with L traffic) all days while more differences are observed in the evening.

Table 1. Percentage of cells classified under the same and under different categories in all the days from Monday to Friday.

Period	% of cells with the same traffic level (H, M or L) in all days	% of cells with different traffic levels in different days
Night (0 h–8 h)	89%	11%
Morning (8 h–16 h)	83%	17%
Evening (16 h–24 h)	74%	26%

Figure 4a and b show examples of cells with different classification on weekdays during the periods 8 h–16 h and 16 h–24 h, respectively. Note, for example, that Cell_264 has L traffic from Monday to Thursday while it has M traffic on Friday morning and H traffic on Friday evening. The reason of this behaviour is that Cell_264 is located in one of the most important entertainment and shopping areas of the city where the population density is higher especially on Friday evening. In turn, Cell_93 has a peak traffic on Thursday morning, while the traffic is M or L for the rest of the 8 h periods of the week. The H traffic on Thursday was already identified in Fig. 3. A closer look allowed identifying that the H traffic is mostly during the working hours, as the traffic increase is due to the presence of the weekly street market.

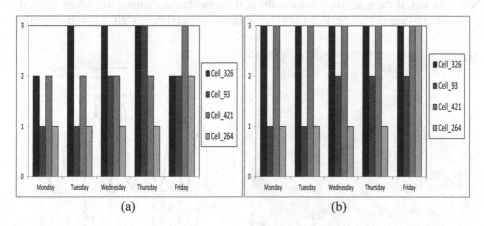

(a)   (b)

Fig. 4. Traffic level during weekdays: (a) in the period 8 h–16 h; (b) in the period 16 h–24 h

3   Analysis of Traffic Measurements in Time and Space

Obtaining knowledge of spatio-temporal traffic fluctuations and traffic complementarities between neighbour cells will clearly be very valuable for the optimisation of the radio resource usage in the different cells. Specifically, the identification of traffic complementarities can be helpful as an input for certain SON functions that automate the operation of the network (see e.g. [2, 16] for background reading about SON functions). In this respect, both self-optimization functions, which intend to tune certain network parameters according to specific performance targets, and self-planning functions, which intend to automate the decisions of deploying new nodes in the network, can benefit from the analysis of traffic in the different cells and the identification of traffic complementarities. Depending on the time scale of the discovered complementarities, different kind of actions over the network may be done.

In the following, some examples of traffic complementarities found in the analysed scenario are presented and possible network reconfiguration actions are discussed.

3.1   Case Study #1

Figure 5a presents a region with the geographical location of some cells of the network, while Fig. 5b shows the evolution of the daily and 2-h averaged traffic during the week in Cell_119 and Cell_1. It is observed that Cell_119 presents a high level of traffic during morning and evening and lower traffic values at night. In turn, Cell_1 is located in an area with lower population density and, consequently, it has lower traffic levels. If the traffic was analysed separately on a per-cell basis, the high traffic level experienced by Cell_119 would suggest a planning decision involving the deployment of a new cell in its proximity or an increase in the capacity of Cell_119, e.g. by deploying a new carrier. Nevertheless, if the analysis considers the complementarities among neighbour cells, it is possible to see in Fig. 5b, that the average traffic of neighbour Cell_1 is substantially

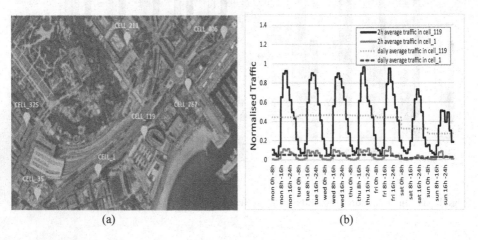

(a)   (b)

Fig. 5. (a) Considered scenario; (b) normalised daily and 2-h averaged traffic for Cell_1 and Cell_119.

lower than that of Cell_119 in all the considered time scales. As a result, the self-planning function can identify that no new cell is actually needed because the excess of traffic in Cell_119 can be absorbed by Cell_1. To achieve this, the network can rely on either the Coverage and Capacity Optimization (CCO) or the Mobility Load Balancing (MLB) self-optimization functions. Specifically, the CCO function can adjust the antenna tilts of the involved cells so that their coverage areas fit better their traffic demands. For example, the CCO function can decide an increase in the antenna tilt of Cell_119 and a reduction of the tilt of Cell_1. This would allow that more users in the area will tend to connect to Cell_1 and would reduce the overload situations of Cell_119. Alternatively, a similar effect can be obtained through the MLB function, which would adjust the cell reselection and handover thresholds to force that more users in the area connect through the less loaded Cell_1.

3.2   Case Study #2

Figure 6a presents the geographical location of several cells in an area in the city centre, while Fig. 6b shows the weekly and daily average traffic for Cell_202 and Cell_265. Although the weekly average traffic in both cells is very similar, the daily average traffic shows some complementarities between these two cells. As shown in Fig. 6b, Cell_265 has a relatively high load level on Friday and Saturday since this cell is located in an important shopping and entertainment street in the city, where people usually go shopping in the weekend. On the other hand, Cell_202 has higher traffic levels during the weekdays since it is located in a nearby business street, where people usually stay during working hours. Based on this, the system could rely on the CCO or MLB functions. For example, two different configurations could be considered for setting the antenna tilts and better adapt to the different traffic demands. On Friday and Saturday the selected configuration would consist in a higher tilt in Cell_265 and a lower one in Cell_202. This would allow shedding traffic from Cell_265 to Cell_202. For the rest of the days,

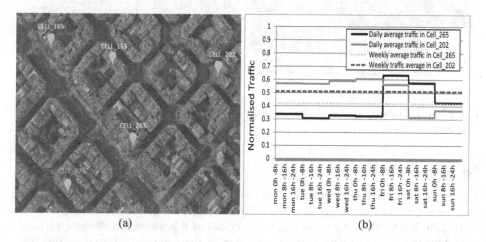

(a)   (b)

Fig. 6. (a) Considered scenario; (b) normalised weekly and daily averaged traffic for Cell_202 and Cell_265.

the configuration would consist in a lower tilt in Cell_265 and a higher one in Cell_202 in order to shed traffic from Cell_202 to Cell_265.

3.3 Case Study #3

Figure 7a shows the geographical locations of Cell_36 and Cell_49, while Fig. 7b presents the normalised daily and 8-h average traffic in both cells. Cell_36 is deployed in an entertainment area of the city with plenty of restaurants and shops, while Cell_49 provides coverage to some office buildings located in the harbour area. Although the daily average traffic from Monday to Thursday is very similar in Cell_36 and Cell_49, the traffic averaged over periods of 8 h reveals that there is a clear complementarity between the morning and evening traffic served by Cell_36 and Cell_49 in the weekdays. In particular, Cell_49 exhibits a substantially high traffic during mornings, while at the same time the traffic in Cell_36 is lower. The situation reverses during evenings and nights and during the weekend, when the traffic in Cell_36 is higher than that of Cell_49. The identification of this complementarity suggests that the high traffic situations in either one or the other cell could be solved by shifting traffic from the highly loaded cell to the less loaded one. Again, this can be achieved through the CCO/MLB functions, so that traffic would be shed from Cell_49 to Cell_36 in the morning while traffic would be shed from Cell_36 to Cell_49 in the evening and during the weekends.

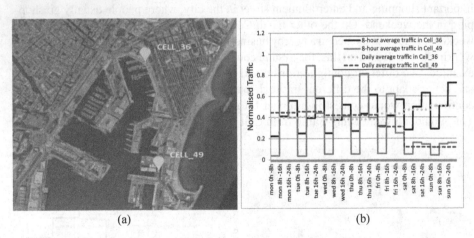

(a)   (b)

Fig. 7. (a) Considered scenario; (b) normalised daily and 8-h averaged traffic for Cell_36 and Cell_49.

3.4 Case Study #4

Figure 8a presents the geographical location of several cells in another area of the city center, while Fig. 8b presents the daily and 8-h average traffic in Cell_111 and Cell_286. It is worth noting that there are periods of 8-h where the average traffic is very low in Cell_111 (especially at night and in the weekend). Based on this, the energy saving self-optimization function can identify Cell_111 as a candidate cell to be switch off during these periods of time and serve this traffic from a neighbor cell (i.e. Cell_286 in this example).

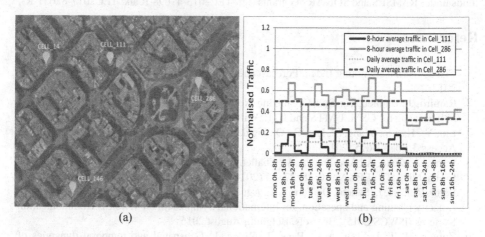

(a)   (b)

Fig. 8. (a) Considered scenario; (b) normalised daily and 8-h averaged traffic for Cell_111 and Cell_286.

4 Conclusions

This paper has presented a statistical analysis of spatio-temporal traffic fluctuations and complementarities among neighbour cells by processing real measurements obtained from hundreds of cells deployed in a large city. Besides well expected observations, such as that the average traffic per day keeps at a rather constant level during weekdays and that higher traffic levels are observed during working hours in case of shorter averaging periods (e.g. 2 h, 8 h), the measurements have revealed that around 16% of the studied cells present significant inter-day traffic variations during weekdays. In some cases, an explanation can be found (e.g. a street market that occurs on a specific day of the week in the area of the cell, thus causing a traffic increase on that day), while in other cases the explanation remains unknown.

The analysis has also jointly considered the traffic of a cell and its neighbours. This study has allowed the identification of some examples of areas exhibiting traffic complementarities among cells at different time scales. The detection of these complementarities can be valuable for supporting the operation of certain SON functions and optimizing the behaviour of the network. In particular, the presented examples illustrate situations in which the CCO/MLB functions can adjust the tilt or the handover and cell reselection thresholds to shift traffic from a highly loaded cell to a less loaded neighbour. The application of these actions avoids having to deploy a new cell to cope with the high load situations. Similarly, another example has illustrated the possibility of exploiting the traffic complementarities for energy saving purposes, identifying cells that can be switched-off during night periods.

Acknowledgements. This work has been supported by the EU funded H2020 5G-PPP project 5G ESSENCE under grant agreement 761592 and by the Spanish Research Council and FEDER funds under RAMSES and SONAR 5G grants (ref. TEC2013-41698-R and TEC2017-82651-R).

References

1. Cisco Visual Networking Index: Forecast and Methodology, 2016–2021, White Paper, June 2017
2. Ramiro, J., Hamied, K.: Self-Organizing Networks: Self-Planning, Self-Optimization and Self-Healing for GSM, UMTS and LTE. Wiley, Hoboken (2012)
3. Liu, Y., Han, S., Wang, S., Liu, G.: On big data analytics for greener and softer RAN. IEEE Access **3**, 3068–3075 (2015)
4. Imran, A., Zoha, A., Abu-Dayya, A.: Challenges in 5G: how to empower SON with big data for enabling 5G. IEEE Netw. **28**, 27–33 (2014)
5. Pérez-Romero, J., Sallent, O., Ferrús, R., Agustí, R.: Artificial intelligence-based 5G network capacity planning and operation. In: International Symposium on Wireless Communication Systems (ISWCS 2015), Brussels, Belgium, August 2015
6. Zubair, M., Ji, L., Liu, A.X., Pang, J., Wang, J.: Geospatial and temporal dynamics of application usage in cellular data networks. IEEE Trans. Mob. Comput. **14**(7), 1369–1381 (2015)
7. Ma, J., Ni, W., Yin, J., Lin, S., Cui, H., Liu, R.P., Fang, B.X.: Modelling social characteristics of mobile radio networks. In: International Conference on Communications (ICC 2015), London, United Kingdom, June 2015
8. Miao, D., Sun, W., Qin, X., Wang, W.: MSFS: multiple spatio-temporal scales traffic forecasting in mobile cellular network. In: 14th International Conference on Pervasive Intelligence and Computing, Auckland, New Zealand, August 2016
9. Xiu, F., Lin, Y., Huang, J., Wu, D., Shi, H., Song, J., Li, Y.: Big data drive mobile traffic understanding and forecasting: a time series approach. IEEE Trans. Serv. Comput. **9**(5), 796–805 (2016)
10. Lee, D., Zhou, S., Zhong, X., Niu, Z.: Spatial modeling of the traffic density in cellular networks. IEEE Wirel. Commun. **21**(1), 80–88 (2014)
11. Wang, S., Zhang, X., Zhang, J., Feng, J., Wang, W., Xin, K.: An approach for spatial-temporal traffic modeling in mobile cellular networks. In: International Teletraffic Congress (ITC), Ghent, Belgium, September 2015
12. Li, R., Zhao, Z., Zhou, X., Palicot, J., Zhang, H.: The prediction analysis of cellular radio access network traffic: from entropy theory to networking practice. IEEE Commun. Mag. **52**(6), 234–240 (2014)
13. Hammami, S.E., Afifi, H., Marot, M., Gauthier, V.: Network planning tool based on network classification and load prediction. In: IEEE Wireless Communications and Networking Conference (WCNC 2016), Doha, Qatar, April 2016
14. Pérez-Romero, J., Sánchez-González, J., Sallent, O., Agustí, R.: On learning and exploiting time domain traffic patterns in cellular radio access networks. Machine Learning and Data Mining in Pattern Recognition. LNCS (LNAI), vol. 9729, pp. 501–515. Springer, Cham (2016). https://doi.org/10.1007/978-3-319-41920-6_40
15. Kim, J., Lee, H.W., Chong, S.: Traffic-aware energy-saving base station sleeping and clustering in cooperative networks. IEEE Trans. Wirel. Commun. **17**(2), 1173–1186 (2017)
16. Aliu, O.G., Imran, A., Imran, M.A., Evans, B.: A survey of self organisation in future cellular networks. IEEE Commun. Surv. Tutor. **15**(1), 336–361 (2013)

MHDW

Detecting Question Intention Using a K-Nearest Neighbor Based Approach

Alaa Mohasseb[(✉)], Mohamed Bader-El-Den, and Mihaela Cocea

School of Computing, University of Portsmouth, Portsmouth, UK
{alaa.mohasseb,mohamed.bader,mihaela.cocea}@port.ac.uk

Abstract. The usage of question answering systems is increasing daily. People constantly use question answering systems in order to find the right answer for different kinds of information, but the abundance of available data has made the process of obtaining relevant information challenging in terms of processing and analyzing it. Many questions classification techniques have been proposed with the aim of helping in understanding the actual intent of the user's question. In this research, we have categorized different question types through introducing question type syntactical patterns for detecting question intention. In addition, a k-nearest neighbor based approach has been developed for question classification. Experiments show that our approach has a good level of accuracy in identifying different question types.

Keywords: Natural language processing · Question classification
Machine learning · Text mining · Information retrieval

1 Introduction

The usage of question answering systems is increasing daily, people make frequent use of question answering systems in order to find the right answer for different kinds of information. The goal of question classification process is to accurately assign labels to questions based on expected answer type.

Many questions classification techniques have been proposed with the aim of helping in understanding the actual intent of the user's question but the abundance of available data has made the process of obtaining relevant information challenging in terms of processing and analyzing it.

Recent studies classified different type of questions by using different machine learning algorithms such as Support Vector Machine (SVM) [3,6,8,17]. Other works like [9,19] used SVM in addition to other machine learning algorithms such as Naive Bayes, Nearest Neighbors and Decision Tree. Moreover, Neural Networks has been used as the machine learning algorithm in other works [15,16].

Furthermore, other methods such as features selection have been applied to obtain an accurate question classifier [6,7,9,18,19] used bag-of-words, Other works like [18] used semantic and syntactic features, Moreover, [6] used uni-gram and word shape feature.

© IFIP International Federation for Information Processing 2018
Published by Springer International Publishing AG 2018. All Rights Reserved
L. Iliadis et al. (Eds.): AIAI 2018, IFIP AICT 520, pp. 101–111, 2018.
https://doi.org/10.1007/978-3-319-92016-0_10

In this paper, we propose a method that automatically identifies and classifies users' questions intention using a k-nearest neighbor based approach based on the syntactical pattern of each type of question. In particular, we develop a framework which was adapted from [10,11] to test the performance of the proposed method. Experimental results show that our solution leads to accurate identification of different question types.

The rest of the paper is organized as follows: Sect. 2 outlines previous work on question classification. Section 3 provides a detailed description of the proposed question classification framework. Section 4 reports experimental results. Finally, Sect. 5 concludes the paper and outlines future work.

2   Related Work

In this section we outline previous work on questions classification methods and machine learning algorithms.

Recent studies classified different type of questions by using different machine learning algorithms. In [8] a statistical classifier has been proposed which is based on SVM and uses prior knowledge about correlations between question words and types in order to learn question word specific classifiers. They have stated that under such a statistical framework, any data set, question ontology, or set of features can be used.

Other works like [9,19] used SVM in addition to other machine learning algorithms. [9] proposed an approach for question classification through using machine learning. In this work three different classifiers were used, which are; Nearest Neighbors (NN), Nave Bayes (NB), and SVM using two kinds of features: bag-of-words and bag-of n grams. In order to train the learning algorithm, a set of lexical, syntactic, and semantic features were used, among which are the question headword and hypernym. Similarly, in [19] five machine learning algorithms were used, which are; NN, NB, Decision Tree (DT), Sparse Network of Winnows (SNoW), and SVM using two kinds of features: bag-of-words and bag-of-ngrams.

In addition, authors in [17] proposed a method of using a feature selection algorithm to determine appropriate features corresponding to different question types. Moreover, they design a new type of features, which is based on question patterns then applied a feature selection algorithm to determine the most appropriate feature set for each type of questions. The proposed approach was tested on the benchmark dataset TREC, using SVM for the classification algorithm.

SVM were also used in [3] for the classification of open-ended questions. They have stated that SVM could be trained to recognize the occurrence of certain keywords or phrases in a question class and then, based on the recurrence of these same keywords, be able to correctly identify a question as belonging to that class.

Another classification has been proposed in [4] using SVM. According to authors in this work enormous amount of time is required to create a rich collection of patterns and keywords for a good coverage of questions in an open-domain application, so they have used support vector machines for question classification. The goal is to replace the regular expression based classifier with a classifier that learns from a set of labeled questions and represented the questions as frequency weighted vectors of salient terms.

Moreover, works like [15,16] used Neural Networks as the machine learning algorithm. [15] proposed a neural network for question answering system, they have stated that the proposed network can process many complicated sentences and can be used as an associative memory and a question-answering system. In addition, the proposed network is composed of three layers and one network which are, Sentence Layer, Knowledge Layer, Deep Case Layer and Dictionary Network. The input sentences are divided into knowledge units and stored in the Knowledge Layer.

The proposed approach in [16] formulates the task as two machine learning problems which are, detecting the entities in the question, and classifying the question as one of the relation types in the knowledge base. Based on this assumption of the structure, this approach trains two recurrent neural networks and outperform state of the art by significant margins relative improvement.

Furthermore, other studies classified different type of question using different features selection like bag-of-words, semantic and syntactic features, and unigram and word shape feature.

Authors in [6] proposed head word feature which used two approaches to augment semantic features of such head words using WordNet. In addition, other standard features were augmented as well such as wh-word, unigram feature, and word shape feature.

In [18] a machine learning-based question-answering framework has been proposed, which integrates a question classifier with a simple document/passage retrievers, and proposed context-ranking models. This method provides flexible features to learners, such as word forms, syntactic features, and semantic word features. In addition, The proposed context-ranking model, which is based on the sequential labeling of tasks, this model combines rich features to predict whether the input passage is relevant to the question type.

Finally, works in [7] used machine learning approaches, namely, different classifiers and multiple classifier combination method by using composite statistic and rule classifiers, and by introducing dependency structure from Minipar and linguistic knowledge from Wordnet into question representation, in addition, features like the Dependency Structure, Wordnet Synsets, Bag-of-Word, and Bi-gram were used. Also a number of kernel functions were analysed and the influence of different ways of classifier combination, such as Voting, AdaBoost, ANN and TBL, on the precision of question classification.

3 Proposed Approach

In this section we introduce a K-nearest neighbor based approach using domain specific syntax information for question classification. The framework mainly relies on Question Type Syntactical Patterns. In the first part of this section question types that have been used are explained in detail; in the second section we introduce our syntactical patterns and in the third part we explain the structure of the proposed approach.

3.1 Question Types

Questions could be classified according to their intent into six categories; Factoid, Choice, Causal, Confirmation, Hypothetical and List; each of these types have their own structure and characteristics [12].

1. Factoid: this type begins with a question word such as *What, Where, Why, Who, Whose, When, Which,* as well as *How, how many, how often, how far, how much, how long, how old* and any kind of information is expected as an answer. For example *"what is a good blood pressure"*.
2. Choice: this type of question offers choices in the question. The question contains two (or more) presented options. These options are connected using the conjunction "OR". For example *"Which is better iphone or samsung? and why?"*.
3. Causal: starts with How or Why and requires explanation. For Example, *"why do earthquakes occur at destructive plate margins?"*.
4. Confirmation: this type of question begins with an auxiliary verb or linking verb for example *"is Frankfurt a city in Germany?"*, in addition, the question could start with negative auxiliary verb or linking verb. For example, *"wasn't Thomas Edison born in new jersey"*. The expected answer for this type of question is either Yes or No.
5. Hypothetical: hypothetical questions are asked to have a general idea of a certain situation. It is mainly "What would you do if/What would happen if" type of questions. For example *"what would you do if someone had a stroke?"*.
6. List: plural terms are a highly reliable indicator of this question, this type requires a list of entities or facts in answers. For example *"What countries are in Africa?"*.

3.2 Question Types Syntactical Patterns

The proposed framework mainly relies on the question types and the characteristics of each type discussed in Sect. 3.1. Using these characteristics we propose the formulation of syntactical patterns for each question; thus, these give us domain-specific information. Each syntactical pattern is composed of a sequence of term categories. These categories of terms are described below. For the purpose of constructing Question Type Syntactical Patterns, a random set of 3,000 questions has been selected from Yahoo Non-Factoid Question Dataset[1] and TREC 2007 Question Answering Data[2].

The categorization of terms in our solution is mainly based on the seven major word classes in English: Verb (V), Noun (N), Determiner (D), Adjective (Adj), Adverb (Adv), Preposition (P) and Conjunction (Conj). In addition to that, we added a category for question words that contains the six main question words (QW): how, who, when, where, what and which. Some word classes like

---

[1] https://ciir.cs.umass.edu/downloads/nfL6/.
[2] http://trec.nist.gov/data/qa/t2007_qadata.html.

Nouns consists of subclasses, such as Common Nouns (CN), Proper Nouns (PN), Pronouns (Pron) and Numeral Nouns (NN). Also, the Verb class has subclasses, such as Action Verbs (AV), linking Verbs (LV) and Auxiliary Verbs (AuxV).

Furthermore, the syntactical patterns of each question types have been identified by tagging each term in the question to one of the main word classes mentioned above, and then a further tagging is done to assign each term in the question to one of the domain specific term categories. For example, in the question *"who is Frida Kahlo"*, the terms will be tagged as follows: (a) *"who"* will be tagged to *"QW"*, (b) *"is"* is tagged to *"LV"* and (c) *"Frida Kahlo"* is tagged to *"PN"*.

Finally, after each term is tagged to one of the word classes, it will be tagged to the domain specific term category; the proposed categories are derived from the following topics;

1. *Health:* which includes specific terms related to health, medicine, beauty.
2. *Sports:* includes terms related to game and recreation, sports events, sports.
3. *Arts and entertainment:* consists of terms related to Entertainment, Celebrities Name, lyrics, Movies, Books, Authors.
4. *Food and drinks:* includes terms related to foods, drinks, recipe.
5. *Animals:* consists of terms related to Pets, wild animals.
6. *Science and math:* which includes specific terms related to Science, math.
7. *Technology and internet:* consists of terms related to Software and Applications, Site, Website, URL, Database and Servers.
8. *Society and culture:* includes terms related to Environment, Holidays, Months, history, political, Relationships, Family.
9. *News and events:* includes terms related to Newspapers, Magazines, Documents, events.
10. *Job, Education and Reference:* includes terms related to Careers, Institutions, Associations, Clubs, Parties, Foundations and Organizations.
11. *Business and Finance:* includes terms related to Money, company, products, Economy.
12. *Travel and places:* which includes specific terms related Geographical Areas, Transportation, Places and Buildings, Countries.

These categories help in the identification of the main topics that are found in most question answering systems. Terms categories have been created for the purpose of identifying the different type of questions. These terms have been constructed after the analysis of different datasets. For example, *"QW"* will be tagged to "Question Word Who" (QW_{Who}); *"LV"* will not be tagged to any further categories and *"PN"* will be tagged to "Proper Noun Celebrity" ($PN_{Celebrity}$). This step is executed by using a database that contains more than 10,000 terms [13].

3.3   Framework

To investigate the impact of using the domain specific syntax information on the classification performance, the following framework, shown in Fig. 1, has been developed. The proposed framework involves automatic identification and classification of user's questions using KNN approach which is based on the patterns described in the previous section. We illustrate the framework by using the following examples of question: *"is mercury a metal"* and *"what are the symptoms of diabetes"*.

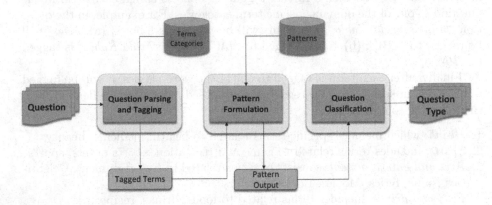

Fig. 1. Question classification framework

1. Question Parsing and Tagging:
   This step is mainly responsible for extracting users question terms. The system simply takes the question and parses to tag each term in the question to its terms' category.
   Question 1: is mercury a metal
   Terms extracted: is, mercury, a, metal

   Question 2: what are the symptoms of diabetes
   Terms extracted: what, are, the, symptoms, of, diabetes

   After parsing, each term in the question will be tagged to one of the terms category.
   The final tagging will be:

   Question 1 Terms Tagging:
   $is = LV$, $mercury = PN_{Science}$, $a = D$, $metal = CN_{Singular}$, where $PN_{Science}$ is Proper Noun Science and $CN_{Singular}$ is Common Noun Singular

   Question 2 Terms Tagging:
   $what = QW_{What}$, $are = LV$, $the = D$, $symptoms = CN_{Plural}$, $of = P$, $diabetes = CN_{Health}$, where CN_{Plural} is Common Noun Plural and CN_{Health} Common Noun Health.

2. Pattern Formulation

In this phase after tagging each term in the question, the pattern is formulated, as illustrated below for the two previously introduced questions.

Question 1 Pattern: $LV + PN_{Science} + D + CN_{Singular}$

Question 2 Pattern: $QW_{What} + LV + D + CN_{Plural} + P + CN_{Health}$

3. Question Classification

In this step the system first attempts to match the question with the most appropriate Question Type Pattern to determine the Question type. For the given examples.

Question 1 Type: Confirmation

Question 2 Type: List

Second, the system will match the question with the most appropriate Domain Category to determine the Question Domain Specific. This step is done by matching each words in the question with one of the Domain Specific Terms Categories Sect. 3.2 and the domain is selected based on the number of words related to a domain in each question. For the given examples.

Question 1 Domain Category: Science and math

Question 2 Domain Category: Health

This will result in the final classification of each question in which *Question 1* will be classified to $Confirmation\_Scienceandmath$ and *Question 2* will be classified to $List\_Health$

4 Experimental Evaluation

To test the accuracy of our proposed approach $1,160$ questions were randomly selected from Yahoo Non-Factoid Question and TREC 2007 Question Answering Data. Their distribution is given in Table 1.

K-Nearest Neighbor (KNN) was used as the machine learning algorithm for the automatic classification. The classification accuracy is obtained by using the implementation of the above algorithm from the Weka software [5]. The effectiveness of the classification was evaluated based on Precision, Recall and F-Measure, i.e. typical metrics for the evaluation of classifiers, using 10-fold cross-validation and value of $K = 1$. Furthermore, a comparison was done using different values of K to evaluated the classification accuracy when increasing the value of K from $K = 1$ to 10.

Table 2 presents the classification performance details (Precision, Recall and F-Measure) of the KNN classifier. Results show that KNN identified correctly (i.e. Recall) 82.8% of the questions when the value of $K = 1$.

Table 1. Data distribution

Question type	Total
Causal	31
Choice	12
Confirmation	321
Factoid	688
Hypothetical	7
List	101

KNN classified correctly 93.1% (Recall) of the confirmation questions and 92.2% of the factoid questions, on the other hand, classification accuracy (Recall) for causal, choice, hypothetical and list questions were lower. KNN could correctly classified 32.3% of the causal questions, 25% of the choice questions, 28.6% of the hypothetical questions and 12.9% of the list questions.

Table 2. KNN classifier performance with value of K = 1

Question types	Precision	Recall	F-measure
Causal	0.714	0.323	0.444
Choice	0.333	0.250	0.286
Confirmation	0.849	0.931	0.889
Factoid	0.853	0.922	0.886
Hypothetical	0.667	0.286	0.400
List	0.333	0.129	0.186
Overall	0.797	**0.828**	0.805

Figure 2 shows the impact of increasing the value of K, There is a marginal increase in the accuracy between k = 1, 2 and 3 in which K = 3 has the highest accuracy with 83.7% shown in Table 3, however, in terms of Recall for certain question categories such as causal, choice, hypothetical and list K = 1 performed better. In addition, when K = 4, 5 and 6 the accuracy slightly decreased while when the value of K = 6 and 7 the accuracy increased again but decreased with K = 9 and 10.

These results show that KNN deals well with confirmation and factoid questions. In addition, KNN could not distinguish between causal, choice, hypothetical and list type of questions and incorrectly classified most of them as confirmation and factoid questions. As shown in Table 1 the question dataset suffers from imbalance between the labels, as the number of the instances that belongs to one more classes is outnumbered by the instances that belong to other classes. This is know by the class imbalance problem and it normally hinders

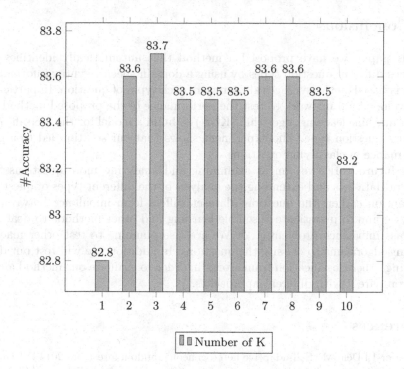

Fig. 2. Comparison of using different value of K

the classifiers ability in correctly predicting the instances that belongs to the minority class [14]. However, the proposed algorithms has been able to perform reasonably well over the minority classes as shown in Tables 2 and 3.

Overall, the results validate that questions Type Syntactical Patterns is an effective method for question classification as well as for the distinction between different question types.

Table 3. KNN classifier performance with value of K = 3

Question types	Precision	Recall	F-measure
Causal	0.714	0.161	0.263
Choice	1.000	0.083	0.154
Confirmation	0.870	0.938	0.903
Factoid	0.831	0.956	0.889
Hypothetical	1.000	0.143	0.250
List	0.385	0.050	0.088
Overall	0.802	**0.837**	0.795

5   Conclusions

In this paper, we have proposed a method that automatically identifies and classifies different question types by using a domain specific syntax information, which is based on the syntactical pattern of each types of question. In particular, we developed a framework to test the performance of the proposed method and used a machine learning algorithm (KNN) to build a model for the identification of user's question type. The experiment shows that our solution led to a good performance in classifying questions.

As future work, we aim at examining and analyzing more questions from different data-sets and extending the analysis of the different types of questions. As mention earlier, the questions dataset suffers form imbalance between the label, we aim to investigate ensemble learning and other methods to deal with the class imbalance problem [1,2]. We are also planning to test other machine learning algorithms to classify the questions. In addition, we will test our dataset using other classification frameworks in order to evaluate our method and be able compare it with different approaches.

References

1. Bader-El-Den, M.: Self-adaptive heterogeneous random forest. In: 2014 IEEE/ACS 11th International Conference on Computer Systems and Applications (AICCSA), pp. 640–646. IEEE (2014)
2. Bader-El-Den, M., Teitei, E., Adda, M.: Hierarchical classification for dealing with the class imbalance problem. In: 2016 International Joint Conference on Neural Networks (IJCNN), pp. 3584–3591. IEEE (2016)
3. Bullington, J., Endres, I., Rahman, M.: Open ended question classification using support vector machines. In: MAICS 2007 (2007)
4. Hacioglu, K., Ward, W.: Question classification with support vector machines and error correcting codes. In: Proceedings of the 2003 Conference of the North American Chapter of the Association for Computational Linguistics on Human Language Technology: companion volume of the Proceedings of HLT-NAACL 2003-short papers, vol. 2, pp. 28–30. Association for Computational Linguistics (2003)
5. Hall, M., Frank, E., Holmes, G., Pfahringer, B., Reutemann, P., Witten, I.H.: The weka data mining software: an update. ACM SIGKDD Explor. Newsl. 11(1), 10–18 (2009)
6. Huang, Z., Thint, M., Qin, Z.: Question classification using head words and their hypernyms. In: Proceedings of the Conference on Empirical Methods in Natural Language Processing, pp. 927–936. Association for Computational Linguistics (2008)
7. Li, X., Huang, X.J., WU, L.D.: Question classification using multiple classifiers. In: Proceedings of the 5th Workshop on Asian Language Resources and First Symposium on Asian Language Resources Network (2005)
8. Metzler, D., Croft, W.B.: Analysis of statistical question classification for fact-based questions. Inf. Retrieval 8(3), 481–504 (2005)
9. Mishra, M., Mishra, V.K., Sharma, H.: Question classification using semantic, syntactic and lexical features. Int. J. Web Seman. Technol. 4(3), 39 (2013)

10. Mohasseb, A., Bader-El-Den, M., Liu, H., Cocea, M.: Domain specific syntax based approach for text classification in machine learning context. In: 2017 International Conference on Machine Learning and Cybernetics (ICMLC), vol. 2, pp. 658–663. IEEE Systems, Man and Cybernetics (2017)
11. Mohasseb, A., Bader-El-Den, M., Kanavos, A., Cocea, M.: Web queries classification based on the syntactical patterns of search types. In: Karpov, A., Potapova, R., Mporas, I. (eds.) SPECOM 2017. LNCS (LNAI), vol. 10458, pp. 809–819. Springer, Cham (2017). https://doi.org/10.1007/978-3-319-66429-3_81
12. Mohasseb, A., Bader-El-Den, M., Cocea, M.: Question categorization and classification using grammar based approach. Inf. Process. Manag. (2018, under review)
13. Mohasseb, A., El-Sayed, M., Mahar, K.: Automated identification of web queries using search type patterns. In: WEBIST (2), pp. 295–304 (2014)
14. Perry, T., Bader-El-Den, M., Cooper, S.: Imbalanced classification using genetically optimized cost sensitive classifiers. In: 2015 IEEE Congress on Evolutionary Computation (CEC), pp. 680–687. IEEE (2015)
15. Sagara, T., Hagiwara, M.: Natural language neural network and its application to question-answering system. Neurocomputing **142**, 201–208 (2014)
16. Ture, F., Jojic, O.: Simple and effective question answering with recurrent neural networks. arXiv preprint arXiv:1606.05029 (2016)
17. Van-Tu, N., Anh-Cuong, L.: Improving question classification by feature extraction and selection. Indian J. Sci. Technol. **9**(17) (2016)
18. Yen, S.J., Wu, Y.C., Yang, J.C., Lee, Y.S., Lee, C.J., Liu, J.J.: A support vector machine-based context-ranking model for question answering. Inf. Sci. **224**, 77–87 (2013)
19. Zhang, D., Lee, W.S.: Question classification using support vector machines. In: Proceedings of the 26th Annual International ACM SIGIR Conference on Research and Development in Information Retrieval, pp. 26–32. ACM (2003)

Incremental Learning for Large Scale Classification Systems

Athanasios Alexopoulos[1], Andreas Kanavos[1,2]($\boxtimes$), Konstantinos Giotopoulos[2], Alaa Mohasseb[3], Mohamed Bader-El-Den[3], and Athanasios Tsakalidis[1]

[1] Computer Engineering and Informatics Department, University of Patras, Patras, Greece
{atalex,kanavos,tsak}@ceid.upatras.gr
[2] Technological Educational Institute of Western Greece, Patras, Greece
kgiotop@ceid.upatras.gr
[3] School of Computing, University of Portsmouth, Portsmouth, UK
{alaa.mohasseb,mohamed.bader}@port.ac.uk

Abstract. One of the main characteristics of our time is the growth of the data volumes. We collect data literally from everywhere; smart phones, smart devices, social media and the health care system, which defines a small portion of the sources of the big data. The big data growth poses two main difficulties, storing and processing them. For the former, there are certain new technologies that enable us to store large amounts of data in a fast and reliable way. For the latter, new application frameworks have been developed. In this paper, we perform classification analysis using Apache Spark in one real dataset. The classification algorithms that we have used are multiclass, and we are going to examine the effect of the dataset size and input features on the classification results.

Keywords: Apache Spark · Apache MLlib · Big data · Classification Computing performance · DataFrame · Spark SQL

1 Introduction

Nowadays, one of the most frequently used term is Big Data, which is utilized so as to define the increase of the data volumes, as modern datasets are ever expanding both in size and complexity. But with the rapid growth of the stored data, difficulties have appeared [11]. The first obvious problem deals with where to store these huge amounts of data, and then how to process them and retrieve the information they hide. Researchers soon found out that even storing data can easily outperform the capabilities of a single computer, no matter how sophisticated that could be. So they decided not to opt for the popular scale up solution but came up with the idea of scaling out. Instead of continuously updating a single computer, spreading the data or the computation to a cluster of computers interconnected via network, would prove handy.

© IFIP International Federation for Information Processing 2018
Published by Springer International Publishing AG 2018. All Rights Reserved
L. Iliadis et al. (Eds.): AIAI 2018, IFIP AICT 520, pp. 112–122, 2018.
https://doi.org/10.1007/978-3-319-92016-0_11

In order to solve the data storage problem, the idea of NoSQL, which stands for Not Only SQL, arose. Those database systems were originally supported and used by major Internet companies (Google, Amazon, Facebook), since they had difficulties in dealing with huge amounts of data with the conventional RDBMS solutions [12]. Somewhat similar, researchers cope the need of processing those data, with the use of cluster programming models[1]. In order to unify, and thus simplify, the mode to process big data, Apache Spark [19] project came up. This provides an efficient and scalable analysis of big data accordingly and can support a wide range of workloads as well.

Now that we have discussed how to store and process with big data, one query remains; what the origin of such data is. There is not a single answer to this question since we can collect data from everywhere and have ample forms. Ranging from a post or a tweet in social media, the graph that shows relations between persons who use the specific aspect of the media or share a trend, reviews of products, data collected from smart devices to even more sophisticated data like health records of patients.

In this paper we aim to perform classification analysis in a real dataset, using Apache Spark's MLlib, a machine learning library optimized for distributed systems. We investigate several classification models (Decision Trees, Random Forest, Logistic Regression) and the way they evolve along the size of the dataset.

The remainder of the paper is structured as follows: Sect. 2 presents the related work and cloud computing methodologies, while Sect. 3 presents the machine learning (e.g. classification) algorithms used in our proposed system. Section 4 presents the steps of training as well as the classification type, e.g. ternary. Moreover, Sect. 5 presents the evaluation experiments conducted and the results gathered. Ultimately, Sect. 6 presents conclusions and draws directions for future work.

2   Related Work

Data mining is an idea that came into existence during the 1990's and its main advantage is that it is suitable for discovering hidden patterns and other useful information from a known dataset. It provides the researcher with the tools to discover correlations that exist and where not obvious at first, and thus makes the task of Decision Making easier [6]. As Fayyad et al. stated [4], the knowledge discovery has a wide range of application areas, with marketing, finance (especially investment) and fraud detection defining a portion of them. The process of knowledge discovery is structured in several stages, the first of which is data selection. The preprocessing of data is bound to follow and the transformation of it into the appropriate format with the final stage of Data Mining, in which a suitable algorithm (or technique in general) is applied in order to extract the hidden information, in a form appropriate for future use [17].

There are several tools that encapsulate those principles, with Weka [5] being one of the most widely used and accepted in business and academia. Although

---

[1] https://en.wikipedia.org/wiki/NoSQL.

its popularity, it has the limitation of the capabilities of a single computer, in terms of memory and computational power. Using the notion of distributed computation, researchers came up with a distributed framework or Weka, the Distributed Weka Spark [9], which is implemented on top of Apache Spark.

In addition, frameworks like Hadoop, Apache Spark, Apache Storm as well as distributed data storages like HDFS and HBase are increasingly becoming popular, as they are engineered in a way that makes the process of very large amounts of data almost effortless. Such systems are gaining much attention and consecutively libraries (like Apache Spark's MLlib), which make the use of Machine Learning techniques possible in the cloud, are introduced.

One of the first widely used framework that supports data processing in a distributed manner across clusters of computers is Apache Hadoop [15], which makes use of the MapReduce paradigm. There were several efforts to use Hadoop for data mining problems, in [18] researchers implemented KD-tree algorithm on Hadoop, in [20] they developed a fast parallel k-means clustering algorithm based on MapReduce whereas in [8] the researchers developed Pegasus, a big graph mining tool built on MapReduce.

In social media analysis, a cloud-based architecture was proposed in [1] where authors aim at creating a sentiment analysis tool for Twitter data based on Apache Spark cloud framework. There, tweets are classified using supervised learning techniques and the classification algorithms are used for ternary classification. In addition, in [16], a survey of machine learning algorithms implemented on Apache Spark over DHT-structures (Distributed Hash Table) is presented; authors experimented across a POS dataset that had been stored in Cassandra with some of the most influential algorithms that have been widely used in the machine learning community. Finally, a novel distributed framework implemented in Hadoop as well as in Spark for exploiting the hashtags and emoticons inside a tweet is introduced in [7]. Moreover, Bloom filters are also utilized in order to increase the performance of the proposed algorithm.

2.1 Distributed Computing

In this section we will briefly discuss the tools we used to perform the analysis. As above mentioned, the classification analysis will be performed with the use of Apache Spark. For clarity reasons though, a brief mentioning of Spark's predecessor, Hadoop MapReduce, is vital and of essential importance.

2.2 MapReduce Model

MapReduce [3] is a programming technique used in distributed systems. Its main advantage being that it is easily scalable over a number of computing nodes. It consists of two main procedures, namely Map() and Reduce(), which is performed after the Map() job. A MapReduce program is executed in three stages the map, shuffle and reduce. In the map stage, the input data is split into a number of chunks and each chunk is sent to a mapper to execute the Map() algorithm. Its result is a set of $< key, value >$ pairs which, during the shuffle stage are grouped by the *key*, and each *key* is fed into the corresponding reducer in which they execute the Reduce() function.

2.2.1 Apache Spark

Apache Spark[2] [19] was founded in 2009 at the University of California, Berkley. Although it shares the same principles as Hadoop, its philosophy differs. It uses the abstraction of "Resilient Distributed Dataset" (RDD's), which represent a fault-tolerant correlation of elements, distributed across many compute nodes that can be manipulated in parallel. Using them, a wide range of tasks, including SQL, streaming, machine learning and graph processing, in a unified manner, can be captured. Its main advantage over MapReduce paradigm is that we don't have to flush the intermediate data to the disk, just to read them at the reduce stage, since it can perform iterative computations in memory, which can have a positive impact on the performance [14].

2.2.2 MLlib

Spark ships with MLlib[3], a distributed machine learning library [11]. It consists of implementations of common machine learning algorithms, that can be used with scalable environments, for several types of analysis including classification, regression, clustering and collaborative filtering. MLlib also includes Java, Scala and Python APIs.

3   Classification Models

In this section we will discuss the classification methods that we utilized. We examined multiclass classification, while the focus of the research concerned the way that the size of the dataset affected the computation time needed to perform each as well as the way the metrics evolved. As a quick reminder, classification is an instance of supervised learning, and its purpose is, based on previous knowledge (set of observations and the output class of each observation) to identify in which output class a new observation belongs.

3.1   Decision Trees

Decision Trees is a classification algorithm, which can be represented in a tree form [10]. The nodes of the tree represent the feature of the dataset, and depending on each feature's value we navigate through the tree structure until we reach a leaf, which represents the output classes. The root of the tree is the feature that best divides the training data, by minimizing a loss function. The procedure in following is recursively executed to each partition of the data to form the subtrees, until the training data is divided into subsets of the same class.

---

[2] http://spark.apache.org/.
[3] http://spark.apache.org/mllib/.

3.2   Random Forest

Random Forest is a generalization of a Decision Tree classifier [2]. It consists of a set of Decision Tree classifiers, so in order to classify for a new input we insert it in each tree of the forest, ending in the "vote" of an output class. The class that will receive the most votes, is the output class the Random Forest will return. To construct each tree, we sample with replacement a number of cases from the original data, equal to the number of trees our forest has, and then we use a subset of the features of that specific selection in order for the size level of tree to be increased.

3.3   Logistic Regression

Logistic Regression is a regression model that can be used when the dependent value (output class) is categorical. It uses a logistic function to express the relationship between the dependent value and the independent (features of each class). Apache Spark supports both binomial and multinomial logistic regression, in which case, assuming we have K output classes, one class is chosen as pivot, $K - 1$ models are created and the final result is the class with the largest probability among the $K - 1$ models.

3.4   One-Vs-Rest

The One-Vs-Rest (or One-Vs-All) classifier, uses a base classifier, that can efficiently perform binary classification and trains a single classifier per output class (considering the portion of the data that belong to that class as positive and the rest as negative). In order to determine the label of the output class, it uses the classifier with the highest confidence score.

3.5   Multilayer Perceptron

A Multilayer Perceptron is an artificial neuron network model used to map a set of input data (input classes) to a set of output classes. It consists of layers of nodes fully connected, with a certain weight, to the ones of the next level. Using back-propagation, a technique that changes the connection weights of each node to the ones of the next layer in order to minimize the output error, we can train the Multilayer Perceptron for a given dataset.

4   Implementation

Our approach follows the proposal of [4], as presented in Sect. 2. Firstly, we need to discuss the framework on which the computation took place.

The overall architecture of the proposed system is depicted in Fig. 1 taking into account the corresponding modules of our approach. Initially, a preprocessing step, as shown in the following subsection, is utilized and afterwards the classifiers for prediction scope are employed.

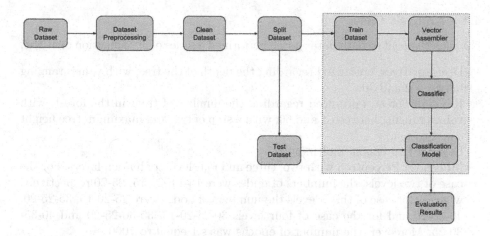

Fig. 1. Proposed System Architecture

The creators of Apache Spark have also founded Databricks that supplies researchers with a web based platform in which they can store and analyse their data with Spark. It offers researchers a mini cluster with 6 Gb of RAM for their analysis and also cloud storage. As programming language, Python (PySpark) was chosen.

The realistic dataset is the PAMAP dataset [13], also provided by UCL[4]. It contains 2.872.533 rows of data from 8 subjects and 12 different activities. The devices that were used to obtain those measurements were inertial measurement units in the ankle, chest and hand of the subject as well as a heart rate monitor. Since the dataset is realistic, some of the data were missing. There were two main reasons for that, data dropping due to using wireless sensors and problematic hardware setup. Also, there was another issue with the equipment used; the sampling frequency of the heart rate monitor was lower than the inertial measurement units. All those missing values were indicated as NaN.

Our first attempt to clean up the data was by withdrawing all the rows that contained at least one NaN value. As a result we had to withdraw 2.610.265 rows of data. To overcome this obstacle, we replaced all the intermediate NaN values of the heart rate monitor with the last known value. After that replacement, the dataset contained only 13.141 rows indicated as NaN, which we ignored in the final analysis.

In order to perform the analyses, we split the original data into segments of 5.000, 10.000, 25.000, 50.000, 75.000, 100.000, 200.000 rows. But, in order for the results to be comparable in each case, we had to keep the ratio of the number of instances that belong to a specific class to the total number of instances, stable. So, we calculated the fraction of each class in the original dataset, and at the examined cases we assured that each class had the same fraction of observations.

---

[4] http://archive.ics.uci.edu/ml/datasets/PAMAP2+Physical+Activity+Monitoring.

4.1 Analysis Cases

For each segment of both datasets we performed a series of classification analyses.

- Decision Trees, optimized regarding the depth of the tree, with values ranging between 2 and 30.
- Random Forest, optimized regarding the number of trees in the forest, with values ranging between 1 and 60, with a step of two and maximum tree height equal to ten.
- Logistic Regression, multinomial.
- Multilayer Perceptron with two, three and four levels of hidden layers. For the case of two levels, the numbers of nodes were 15-14, 20-15, 25-20 respectively, whereas for case of three levels the numbers of nodes were 25-20-15, 35-25-20, 40-30-20 and for the case of four levels 30-25-20-15, 35-30-25-20 and 40-35-30-25. Moreover, the number of epochs was set equal to 1000.

5 Evaluation

The results of our work are presented in the following Tables 1 to 5. Recall, Precision and F-Measure are used as the evaluation metrics of the different algorithms. Also, the time that was needed to train each classifier is presented, as well as information about the best settings.

In PAMAP Dataset, a series of classification analyses are conducted. In Table 1, the results of the Decision Tree classifier are presented. As the dataset increased in size, we kept getting higher scores, as expected. Worth noting is the fact that in this case, the height of the tree had the highest possible value in all cases, but its complexity increased since nodes kept increasing in number. Also, the computational time needed, as expected, kept rising with the size of the dataset, but not in a linear manner; when the size of the dataset increased by $40 times$ (from 5.000 rows to 200.000), the time needed nearly doubled.

Table 1. Decision Tree

Dataset size	Precision	Recall	F-Measure	Time	Depth	Number of nodes
5.000	0.862	0.859	0.860	0:15:25	17	731
10.000	0.923	0.923	0.923	0:17:21	16	1007
25.000	0.954	0.954	0.954	0:21:09	18	1625
50.000	0.966	0.966	0.966	0:24:44	25	2441
75.000	0.968	0.968	0.968	0:39:55	27	3363
100.000	0.981	0.981	0.981	0:41:43	27	3139
200.000	0.989	0.989	0.989	0:57:26	30	4083

Next, the Random Forest classifier (Table 2) is discussed. Again as the dataset size grew bigger, so did the metrics' scores. The only exception is the case of the 10.000 rows in which we had the best observed scores, but this might be caused by the split of the dataset. Overall, this classifier produced lower metrics compared with the Decision Tree classifier; the best F-Measure score is 76.7% while Decision Tree's was 90.0%. Furthermore, the training time of this classifier is overall higher than the Decision Tree one. When the size of the dataset increased 40 times, it needed 4 times more for the classifier to be trained.

Table 2. Random Forest

Dataset size	Precision	Recall	F-Measure	Time	Number of trees	Number of nodes
5.000	0.907	0.907	0.907	0:29:27	60	28908
10.000	0.927	0.925	0.926	0:36:01	50	28522
25.000	0.945	0.945	0.945	0:49:12	44	31618
50.000	0.953	0.953	0.953	1:04:11	42	35836
75.000	0.950	0.949	0.949	2:01:05	44	38600
100.000	0.958	0.958	0.958	2:28:11	48	45134
200.000	0.951	0.950	0.950	3:42:04	56	56274

The next classifier is the Multinomial Logistic Regression (Table 3), where there was no parameter optimization performed. With few exceptions, we can argue that as the dataset size increases, so do the metrics, although some fluctuation exists. The metrics' score is higher than the Random Forest classifier, but did not perform as well as Decision Trees. As for the scaling of time regarding the size of the dataset, for 20 times bigger dataset, from 10.000 to 200.000 rows, the classifier's training time increased by 7.5 times.

Table 3. Logistic regression

Dataset size	Precision	Recall	F-Measure	Time
5.000	0.858	0.861	0.860	0:00:26
10.000	0.861	0.862	0.861	0:00:26
25.000	0.814	0.818	0.816	0:00:32
50.000	0.803	0.807	0.804	0:00:42
75.000	0.802	0.806	0.803	0:01:00
100.000	0.825	0.828	0.826	0:01:14
200.000	0.800	0.804	0.802	0:01:56

The last classifier examined is One-Vs-All (Table 4). As the base classifier, we have chosen Logistic Regression. Its performance was rather poor, both in

Table 4. One-vs-All

Dataset size	Precision	Recall	F-Measure	Time
5.000	0.755	0.755	0.749	0:02:03
10.000	0.789	0.791	0.789	0:02:15
25.000	0.788	0.792	0.789	0:02:29
50.000	0.781	0.784	0.781	0:02:56
75.000	0.770	0.773	0.771	0:04:56
100.000	0.796	0.798	0.796	0:07:17
200.000	0.774	0.778	0.775	0:11:16

Table 5. Multilayer Perceptron

Dataset size	Precision	Recall	F-Measure	Time	Best layer
5.000	0.639	0.646	0.641	0:09:20	[31, 35, 25, 20, 12]
10.000	0.691	0.708	0.697	0:14:27	[31, 35, 25, 20, 12]
25.000	0.720	0.719	0.719	0:32:22	[31, 40, 30, 20, 12]
50.000	0.707	0.732	0.721	1:01:55	[31, 40, 30, 20, 12]
75.000	0.724	0.738	0.727	1:30:39	[31, 40, 30, 20, 12]
100.000	0.755	0.776	0.759	1:55:59	[31, 35, 25, 20, 12]
200.000	0.775	0.778	0.775	3:59:41	[31, 35, 25, 20, 12]

time needed to train and in the metrics' score. Examining again F-Measure, it achieved 79.5% while the Logistic Regression achieved 80.8%. Considering time scaling, with regards to the dataset size, for 20 times bigger dataset, the classifier's training time has been increased by 3.23 times, and in every case the training was 7 to 11 times higher.

Overall, it can be argued that the best choice in PAMAP dataset is the Decision Tree classifier, since it performed better in the metric scores from all other classifiers and its training time scaled well regarding the dataset size.

6 Conclusions and Future Work

In our work we delved into the performance of various classification algorithms in a distributed environment. Each classification method had strengths and limitations, depending on the dataset. The Decision Tree classifier outperformed all the other classification methods, which was a pleasant surprise.

As for future work, more datasets with the same classification methods to establish a better understanding, will be checked. Of course, the cluster on which we run the classification methods is another key aspect of the cloud computing in general, so checking the same or similar algorithms and dataset on different clusters may prove fundamental and reveal well-hidden secrets.

References

1. Baltas, A., Kanavos, A., Tsakalidis, A.K.: An apache spark implementation for sentiment analysis on twitter data. In: Sellis, T., Oikonomou, K. (eds.) ALGO-CLOUD 2016. LNCS, vol. 10230, pp. 15–25. Springer, Cham (2017). https://doi.org/10.1007/978-3-319-57045-7_2
2. Breiman, L.: Random forests. Mach. Learn. **45**(1), 5–32 (2001)
3. Dean, J., Ghemawat, S.: Mapreduce: simplified data processing on large clusters. Commun. ACM **51**(1), 107–113 (2008)
4. Fayyad, U.M., Piatetsky-Shapiro, G., Smyth, P.: From data mining to knowledge discovery in databases. AI Mag. **17**(3), 37–54 (1996)
5. Hall, M.A., Frank, E., Holmes, G., Pfahringer, B., Reutemann, P., Witten, I.H.: The WEKA data mining software: an update. SIGKDD Explor. **11**(1), 10–18 (2009)
6. Hand, D.J., Mannila, H., Smyth, P.: Principles of Data Mining. MIT Press, Cambridge (2001)
7. Kanavos, A., Nodarakis, N., Sioutas, S., Tsakalidis, A., Tsolis, D., Tzimas, G.: Large scale implementations for twitter sentiment classification. Algorithms **10**(1), 33 (2017)
8. Kang, U., Faloutsos, C.: Big graph mining: algorithms and discoveries. SIGKDD Explor. **14**(2), 29–36 (2012)
9. Koliopoulos, A., Yiapanis, P., Tekiner, F., Nenadic, G., Keane, J.A.: A parallel distributed WEKA framework for big data mining using spark. In: IEEE International Congress on Big Data, pp. 9–16 (2015)
10. Kotsiantis, S.B.: Supervised machine learning: a review of classification techniques. Informatica (Slovenia) **31**(3), 249–268 (2007)
11. Meng, X., Bradley, J.K., Yavuz, B., Sparks, E.R., Venkataraman, S., Liu, D., Freeman, J., Tsai, D.B., Amde, M., Owen, S., Xin, D., Xin, R., Franklin, M.J., Zadeh, R., Zaharia, M., Talwalkar, A.: Mllib: machine learning in apache spark. J. Mach. Learn. Res. **17**(1), 1235–1241 (2016)
12. Moniruzzaman, A.B.M., Hossain, S.A.: Nosql database: new era of databases for big data analytics - classification, characteristics and comparison. Int. J. Database Theor. Appl. **6**(4), 1–14 (2013)
13. Reiss, A., Stricker, D.: Introducing a new benchmarked dataset for activity monitoring. In: International Symposium on Wearable Computers (ISWC), pp. 108–109 (2012)
14. Shi, J., Qiu, Y., Minhas, U.F., Jiao, L., Wang, C., Reinwald, B., Özcan, F.: Clash of the titans: mapreduce vs. spark for large scale data analytics. PVLDB **8**(13), 2110–2121 (2015)
15. Shvachko, K., Kuang, H., Radia, S., Chansler, R.: The Hadoop distributed file system. In: IEEE 26th Symposium on Mass Storage Systems and Technologies (MSST), pp. 1–10 (2010)
16. Sioutas, S., Mylonas, P., Panaretos, A., Gerolymatos, P., Vogiatzis, D., Karavaras, E., Spitieris, T., Kanavos, A.: Survey of machine learning algorithms on spark over DHT-based structures. In: Sellis, T., Oikonomou, K. (eds.) ALGOCLOUD 2016. LNCS, vol. 10230, pp. 146–156. Springer, Cham (2017). https://doi.org/10.1007/978-3-319-57045-7_9
17. Witten, I.H., Eibe, F., Hall, M.A., Pal, C.J.: Data Mining: Practical Machine Learning Tools and Techniques. Morgan Kaufmann, Burlington (2016)

18. Yang, L., Shi, Z.: An efficient data mining framework on Hadoop using Java persistence API. In: 10th IEEE International Conference on Computer and Information Technology (CIT), pp. 203–209 (2010)
19. Zaharia, M., Xin, R.S., Wendell, P., Das, T., Armbrust, M., Dave, A., Meng, X., Rosen, J., Venkataraman, S., Franklin, M.J., Ghodsi, A., Gonzalez, J., Shenker, S., Stoica, I.: Apache spark: a unified engine for big data processing. Commun. ACM **59**(11), 56–65 (2016)
20. Zhao, W., Ma, H., He, Q.: Parallel K-means clustering based on mapreduce. In: Jaatun, M.G., Zhao, G., Rong, C. (eds.) CloudCom 2009. LNCS, vol. 5931, pp. 674–679. Springer, Heidelberg (2009). https://doi.org/10.1007/978-3-642-10665-1_71

Argumentative Discourse Concepts as Revealed by Traversing a Graph

Panagiotis Gourgaris[1], Andreas Kanavos[1,3(✉)], Nikos Karacapilidis[2],
and Vassilis Tampakas[3]

[1] Computer Engineering and Informatics Department, University of Patras,
Patras, Greece
{gourgaris,kanavos}@ceid.upatras.gr
[2] Department of Mechanical Engineering and Aeronautics, University of Patras,
Patras, Greece
karacap@upatras.gr
[3] Computer and Informatics Engineering Department,
Technological Educational Institute of Western Greece, Antirrion, Greece
vtampakas@teimes.gr

Abstract. Recent advances in computing and Internet technologies, together with the advent of the Web 2.0 era have resulted in the development of a plethora of online tools, such as forums and social networking applications, which offer people an unprecedented level of flexibility and convenience to participate in complex argumentative discourses of diverse interest. However, these tools do not enable an intelligent analysis of the related content. Aiming to address this issue, this paper presents preliminary work on the exploitation of Neo4j graph platform for managing well-established argumentation elements. The proposed high level and scalable approach facilitates the discovery of latent and arbitrarily long and complex argumentation in argument graphs, as well as its meaningful exploitation towards gaining insights.

Keywords: Argumentation · Collaborative Decision Making
Graph database · Knowledge graph · NoSQL

1 Introduction

Argumentation is ubiquitous in our everyday life. It might be argued, that every action can be modeled, up to an extent, as an argumentative discourse [13]. An array of examples of various importance and complexity can be pointed out: political and rhetoric argumentation, business negotiations, as well as questions such as "which movie shall we watch tonight", "which car should I buy", and so forth. All these are manifestations of an argumentation discourse.

This paper presents preliminary work on the exploitation of Neo4j for managing argumentation related data. Neo4j, a NoSQL graph database, stores data physically as a graph. Starting here from the notions portrayed in Dung's works

L. Iliadis et al. (Eds.): AIAI 2018, IFIP AICT 520, pp. 123–132, 2018.
https://doi.org/10.1007/978-3-319-92016-0_12

[1, 4–6], we try to map the various argumentation elements and their relations to a graph which is dynamically constructed during a discourse. Taking into account diverse argumentation concepts and approaches, our formalization elements are those described in the Hermes system [10]. Although here, instead of a tree, we loosen up the architecture and consider the whole issue formulation problem as a continuously expanding graph, following the generally accepted notions in argumentation. Given a knowledge graph formulated as an argumentation framework, we examine the possibility of a graph theoretic route that would yield some quantitative results.

Neo4j supports Cypher, a declarative, ASCII art, and pattern based query language for handling conceptual graphs. We try and relax the restrictions imposed by Dung's model for argument sets, in hope of finding a way to quantitatively assess the process of collaboratively formulating the understanding of an issue and reaching consensus. We aim to check whether the relaxed argumentation forms that we will use give a more probabilistic nature to argumentation acceptance and the assent of any issue considered. By including the human factor, our approach by design engulfs notions that we see in the value-based argumentation frameworks propositions and the labeling process for examining argument attacks.

1.1 Motivation and Contribution

Although the overall argumentation process does not necessarily consider large data sets, the rapid development of web technologies and social networks have resulted in the creation of a big volume of content. Opinions, emotions, ideas and thoughts can be extracted in order to explain, assist, and even predict human decision making. The Big data challenge lies in the efficient implementation of a framework for extracting large amount of data from the social media and adopt appropriate methodologies to process them. We can succeed in this by employing a Neo4j server and populating a graph database. The need for new database approaches, that goes beyond the relational one, was highlighted with the advent of Web 2.0, which is dominated by high volumes of unstructured or semi-structured and high order data. Those data can provide the knowledge on which computer formulated notions from argumentation theory like dialogues, value-based argumentation frameworks, argument schemes etc. can rely and give solutions.

The most commonly used tools for knowledge sharing cannot be considered deliberation tools. The problems they face are systemic, like signal-to-noise ratio, redundancy, repetition and balkanization. The main result is not having any debate and low quality of knowledge being spread, although one could contend that this was not their initial goal.

The remaining of this paper is organized as follows. Section 2 presents existing research and background topics on argumentation notions. Section 3 provides a description of Neo4j's basic elements. Section 4 discusses the proposed approach about how the knowledge graph should be created during the deliberation. Section 5 gives a road-map of challenges and comments on limitations of deliberation systems and Graph Databases. Finally, Sect. 6 provides concluding remarks and sketches our future work directions.

2 Argumentation Concepts

In this section we provide a description of some basic argumentation notions which sparked our study. Their direct relation with graph databases is what made us try and devise a deliberation schema based on a graph database back-end.

To start with, an *argumentation discourse* as a process towards reaching consent over a difference of opinions, has four *discussion stages* as portrayed in [7]:

1. **Confrontation Stage:** this is where doubt or the difference of opinions over a standpoint is brought forward.
2. **Opening Stage:** the departing point for the discussion. A common ground for a fruitful discussion must be reached and all parties, or protagonists, present their own assent towards a standpoint.
3. **Argumentation Stage:** the main discourse stage, where protagonists bring forth arguments to overcome any antagonists' doubts or critical reactions and antagonists are considering acceptance of the protagonists' argumentation.
4. **Concluding Stage:** at this stage, either a protagonist's standpoint is accepted by all parties, hence the antagonists' doubts are retracted, or a protagonist's standpoint is retracted. In any case, a conclusion must be reached and explicitly expressed.

Although these stages seem to have a logical ordering, a discourse need not pass through all of them -at least not explicitly- and not in this particular order. These stages could be easily matched with the diverse processes of deliberation systems; for example, threads in internet forums.

A finer structuring of the elements making up argumentation is enabled through Pollock's theory [14] for defeasible reasoning. Reasons - called arguments, by argumentation theorists - can be attacked by others, hence the use of the adjective defeasible. The main issue risen is when the argument is attacked. Or, in other words, in which way is it attacked? Pollock argues that two types of defeaters exist, namely *rebutting* and *undercutting*.

1. **Undercutting argument:** those attacking the connection of an argument and its conclusion. This is knowledge obtained that attacks the acceptance of the reason supporting a conclusion.
2. **Rebutted:** a reason supporting the opposite conclusion.

The work done by Dung [4] is where argumentation relates most with graph theory. Notions as *argumentation framework*, *conflict*, *relation* are explained in his paper. Specifically:

An *argumentation framework* is a pair

$$AF = \langle A, attacks \rangle$$

where A is a set of arguments and *attacks* is a binary relation defined on A. A framework can be represented as a directed graph $G = (V, E)$. A graph G consists of a set of vertices V and a set of edges E. Just like in an argumentation framework, the set of edges correspond to a set of pairs of vertices by means of a relation. Hence, for a set $A = \{a, b, c\}$, (a, b) denotes *a attacks b*.

As a starting point for a deliberation system in which a discourse can be unravelled, we use notions from Hermes [10]. Its framework is based on IBIS (Issue-Based Information System). The argument diagramming takes form through a framework consisting of *issues*, *alternatives*, *positions*, and *constraints*.

1. **Issues:** the problem to be solved.
2. **Alternatives:** the possible solutions to the problem.
3. **Positions:** the arguments as seen in Dung; they support or attack an alternative.
4. **Constraints:** a way to quantitatively weigh reasons; they have the form of a rule $(position_1, preference\_relation, position_2)$ with relations taking a value of *"more(less) important than"* or *"equally important"*.

3   Neo4j Graph Database

Our work aims to build innovative tools that give an overall view of data-intensive and cognitively-complex discourses, while also efficiently handle the diversity of requirements concerning their analysis and meaningful interpretation. By having such a roadmap, one can assess all dialectical rules and constructs. Fallacies and impediments which contradict the whole process can be more evident; and in the end, reaching a solution regarding the issues at hand [17], hopefully could become a lot easier. By using a graph database, one can store relationships between data. This unique characteristic makes them ideal for our purposes.

To our knowledge, Neo4j has not been used for such an endeavor. Examples of use cases include real-time recommendation systems, social network analysis, network and IT operations. It provides production grade front- or back-end social graph storage. Moreover, it offers graph analytics similar to link prediction, shortest paths, clustering coefficient, and minimum spanning trees, bolstering the potential of graph tools including NetworkX, machine learning frameworks like Graphlab, and distributed processing systems such as Spark [12,16]. In a context where (i) data are highly connected amongst them, (ii) relationships are often created, erased and updated, and (iii) relationships are the elements that actually trigger insights, graph databases are the solution to handling the big data as well as the real-time aspect of today's deliberation systems.

The fundamental units that form a graph are *nodes* and *relationships*. In Neo4j, both can have properties. Entities of a domain are represented by nodes, albeit relationships can be used too, depending on the formulation and domain of the problem. In addition, multiple *labels* can be attached to nodes. The nature of the questions we want to answer, based on our data, will define the various structures of our graph.

Neo4j's data model is similar to the entity relationship diagram. Concretely, *nodes* can be considered as the entities in the graph. So, for example in the statement *"Panos and Andreas are friends and Panos owns a Brand1 car with plate number AF-101 and Andreas owns a Brand2 car with plate number BD-101"*, Panos, Andreas and the cars are all distinct entities, hence will be distinct nodes in our graph.

Labels state the role of a node making them essentially the entity type identifiers. As an excellent paradigm for the statement above, we can locate two labels for nodes, *person* and *car*.

Relationships are any interactions between nodes, usually identified as verbs. They are considered to be directed and have a start node and an end node. In our example statement, those would be *friend of* and *owns*.

Properties are attributes of nodes and relationships. They are *key-value* pairs attached to them, helping us to quantitatively answer questions regarding our database. In these settings, the "Panos" node which is labeled as a *person*, can have a set of properties like *name : Panos, age* : 35. Also the relationship *friend of* can have a pair of *since:MM/DD/YYYY* as its property.

Again, we can easily see that depending on the problem (or domain), the same statement might yield a different data model. For example, although in our previous analysis the plate numbers could simply be a property of nodes labeled as *car*, in another approach specific license plates could be nodes themselves.

The way we put all this to use is through the Cypher language, which was built grounded on the simple SQL clauses and has lots of graph domain additional ones. A simple occurrence for our little dataset above could be:

```
match (p:Person)-[:FRIEND]->(f:Person)
where p.name='Panos'
return f.name
```

which would return all names of nodes that the Panos node has a relationship of $FRIEND$. The basic idea is that initially one forms a math statement which will return a subgraph and then applies an action on it. Another example is:

```
match ()-[:FRIEND]->()<-[:FRIEND]-(f)
return f.name
```

which would return the names of all nodes that have a relationship of type $FRIEND$ with some common node. Considering this from an argumentative perspective, these could be two arguments *a, c* attacking the same argument *b*, which could constitute an "accrual of reasons".

4   Proposed Schema

In this section, we present our approach for a schema that could work as a knowledge graph for a Collaborative Decision Making system. We will be using argumentation elements based on those of Hermes [10], in following put them in a Neo4j's context, and finally try to address the problem formulation task. We will be presenting the elements and notions using graph lingo.

Our scheme has three types of nodes and four types of relationships. All relationships (edges) in Neo4j are directed. Incidentally, if a node u points to a node v, then u is a child of v and v is a parent of u.

4.1   Nodes

The types of nodes used in the present schema are *issues*, *alternatives* and *arguments*.

Issues, here noted as S_j, are equivalent to *standpoints* (the problem being debated). In Hermes [10], they refer to decisions to be made; in this paper, we prefer keeping a more argumentative perspective for notations, as this mental disposition helps with the rest of our descriptions. Issues can also be parents for other issues.

Alternatives, here noted as C_i, are children nodes of *issues*. An *alternative* is a proposition, considered to be a potential solution to the parent issue.

Arguments can be children of both *alternatives* and *issues*. Depending on the relationship between two arguments, a new issue can be automatically raised.

4.2   Relationships

We have four types of relationships depending on their start and end node.
Relationship H between an alternative C_i and an issue S_j:

$$C_i \; H \; S_j, \; with \; H \; \epsilon \; \{ALTERNATIVE\_TO\}$$

Relationship Ω between an argument a or an issue S_k and an issue S_j:

$$\{a, S_i\} \; \Omega S_j, \; with \; \Omega \; \epsilon \; \{RAISES\}$$

Relationship Υ between an argument a and another one b:

$$a \; Y \; b, \; with \; \Upsilon \; \epsilon \; \{REBUTS, UNDERCUTS\}$$

Relationship X between an argument a and an alternative C_i:

$$a \; X \; C_j, \; with \; X \; \epsilon \; \{ATTACK, SUPPORT\}$$

Some characteristics of the above relationships are:

1. All relationships are non symmetric.

2. A *rebuttal* automatically raises a new issue. We consider it to be a new issue and view it as a new dispute that needs to be resolved through negotiations.
3. Also, when an argument a rebuts another b, then the two must have opposing relationships with their common alternative parent. So:

$$if(a, ATTACK, Ci) and (a, REBUTS, b), then we must have (b, SUPPORT, Ci).$$

4. Upon the creation of a rebutting relationship, a new issue S_j concerning it as well as the relationship $(a, RAISES, S_j)$ is created.

4.3   Example

Figure 1 illustrates the main Neo4j web interface. The graph depicted in Fig. 1 is more clearly shown in following Fig. 2. There, a draft example of a simple argumentation over the question *"Should I buy car Model1 of Brand1?"* is considered.

In addition, two alternatives are presented, namely *"Yes"* and *"No"*. These two alternatives often correspond to two different opinions. Another user supports *"Yes"* with an argument *"Low price compared to others"*. After that, an argument rebutting it (*"Very expensive for what is provides"*) is expressed and a new issue with the title *"Price comparison"* is created. Likewise, we see that the argument *"Engines of Model1 from Brand1 burn oil"* supports *"No"*, while another, arguing *"Engines of Model1 since 2008 are fixed"*, undercuts it.

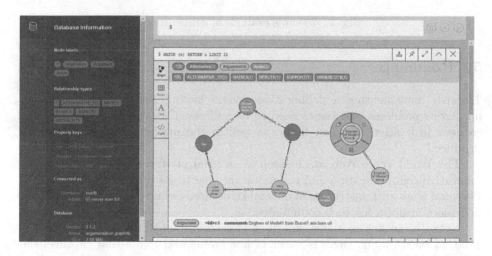

Fig. 1. The web interface of Neo4j administrator panel.

While not fully visible in this simple example, we will be forming our argumentation map with the dialectic systems in mind. Although the time aspect of time-centric systems might be considered by others to generate non-structured data, it is the authors' opinions that it could be an asset, adding to the knowledge that can be obtained from the graph.

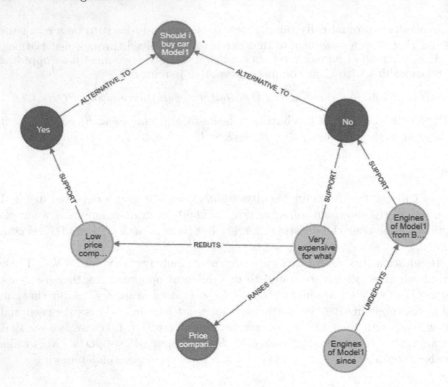

Fig. 2. A simple example of deliberation.

5 Roadmap

Towards implementing a deliberation system having Neo4j as its backbone, numerous problems and issues need to be addressed. In such systems, one has to bear in mind the human factor as well as the mechanics of how data are produced.

The World Wide Web can be seen as an ideal platform for enhancing argumentative communication and collaboration, due to its ubiquity and openness. Personal blogs and unstructured or semi-structured online discussion forums can provide a medium for such communication.

Notwithstanding opinions and discussions may be identified by their topics, time, or participants, there is a lack of fine-grained structure that captures the way that different facts, opinions, and arguments relate to one another and, as such, contribute to the overall picture. An example is considered in [3], where Deme is specifically designed for supporting democratic, small to medium-sized group deliberation.

By far, the most used systems are those that formulate the deliberation process via sharing content also known as time-centric systems, e.g. wikis, blogs, forums and emails. Data is most commonly in the form of free text and the way people create content does not give a structured result. The size and creation processes of data are the main reasons of problems such as duplication, balkanization as well as the very low signal-to-noise ratio. Also, the only two valid ways of handling the plethora of data and any redundancy as a result, is to either impose restrictions prior to making any post publicly available -perhaps if designated members moderate discussions, or to manually assess all data after the knowledge database is created; in either way, the amount of human labor can become enormous.

A number of highly-structured argument-based deliberation support systems (ADSS) have been already proposed. These suffer from two key limitations: first, they usually support a small number of participants; in addition, most of them target specific domains, such as education, or academic research. Moreover, highly-structured ADSSs based on client-server architectures, are usually designed for small to medium-sized groups and are therefore not easily scalable [8].

Another limitation of existing structured ADSSs is that they subscribe to specific theories of argumentation and decision-making. While the majority of these systems may be suitable for specific domains, an outstandingly truly global-scale argumentation infrastructure must allow for a variety of reasoning patterns to spark interaction. Such reasoning patterns are known in argumentation theory as argumentation schemes [18]. By incorporating such methodologies, the non-collaborativeness problem with large scale tools [11] can be efficiently addressed.

Authors in [15] present theoretical and software foundations for a World Wide Argument Web (WWAW). Concretely, WWAW can be considered as a large-scale Web of inter-connected arguments posted by individuals to express their opinions in a rather structured manner. ArgDF, a pilot Semantic Web-based system is presented, through which users can create arguments using different argumentation schemes and can query arguments using a Semantic Web query language.

6 Conclusions and Future Work

We have presented preliminary work on the exploitation of Neo4j for managing argumentation related data. As future work, we intend to enhance the framework in order to perform meaningful numeric evaluations. More specifically, we will examine whether all types of nodes can have such capabilities. Furthermore, we will try to address several issues that deliberation systems face; heavy dependency on manual moderating work -either during or after the system launch - has to be thoroughly tackled. A very good example regarding this issue is the user incentives of Stack Overflow[1]. In addition to reputation votes, there are about 90 badges a user wins for completing milestones.

Another addition to our framework concerns the argumentation structures [2]. This could help arguments being posted in order to be regarded more as evidence rather than as simple bias, thus adding to the overall credibility of the

---

[1] https://stackoverflow.com/.

system. The ultimate goal after dealing with these issues would be the development of an online argumentation platform for generic, large-scale deliberating purposes [9].

References

1. Bondarenko, A., Dung, P.M., Kowalski, R.A., Toni, F.: An abstract, argumentation-theoretic approach to default reasoning. Artif. Intell. **93**, 63–101 (1997)
2. Craven, R., Toni, F.: Argument graphs and assumption-based argumentation. Artif. Intell. **233**, 1–59 (2016)
3. Davies, T., O'Connor, B., Cochran, A., Effrat, J.J., Parker, A., Newman, B., Tam, A.: An online environment for democratic deliberation: motivations, principles, and design. CoRR abs/1302.3912 (2013)
4. Dung, P.M.: On the acceptability of arguments and its fundamental role in non-monotonic reasoning, logic programming and n-person games. Artif. Intell. **77**(2), 321–357 (1995)
5. Dung, P.M., Kowalski, R.A., Toni, F.: Dialectic proof procedures for assumption-based, admissible argumentation. Artif. Intell. **170**(2), 114–159 (2006)
6. Dung, P.M., Mancarella, P., Toni, F.: Computing ideal sceptical argumentation. Artif. Intell. **171**(10–15), 642–674 (2007)
7. van Eemeren, F.H., Grootendorst, R.: A Systematic Theory of Argumentation: The Pragma-Dialectical Approach. Cambridge University Press, Cambridge (2004)
8. Gordon, T.F.: An open, scalable and distributed platform for public discourse. In: Informatik, pp. 232–234 (2003)
9. Gürkan, A., Iandoli, L., Klein, M., Zollo, G.: Mediating debate through on-line large-scale argumentation: evidence from the field. Inf. Sci. **180**, 3686–3702 (2010)
10. Karacapilidis, N.I., Papadias, D.: Computer supported argumentation and collaborative decision making: the HERMES system. Inf. Syst. **26**(4), 259–277 (2001)
11. Klein, M.: Enabling large-scale deliberation using attention-mediation metrics. Comput. Support. Coop. Work (CSCW) **21**(4–5), 449–473 (2012)
12. Panzarino, O.: Learning Cypher. PACKT Publishing, Birmingham (2014)
13. Perelman, c: The new rhetoric. In: Bar-Hillel, y (ed.) Pragmatics of Natural Languages. SYLI, vol. 41, pp. 145–149. Springer, Dordrecht (1971). https://doi.org/10.1007/978-94-010-1713-8_8
14. Pollock, J.L.: Defeasible reasoning. Cogn. Sci. **11**(4), 481–518 (1987)
15. Rahwan, I., Zablith, F., Reed, C.: Laying the foundations for a world wide argument web. Artif. Intell. **171**(10–15), 897–921 (2007)
16. Robinson, I., Webber, J., Eifrem, E.: Graph Databases. O'Reilly, Sebastopol (2013)
17. Toulmin, S.E.: The Uses of Argument. Cambridge University Press, Cambridge (2003)
18. Walton, D., Reed, C., Macagno, F.: Argumentation Schemes. Cambridge University Press, Cambridge (2008)

Query Disambiguation Based on Clustering Techniques

Panagiota Kotoula and Christos Makris[✉]

Department of Computer Engineering and Informatics, University of Patras,
Rio, 26500 Patras, Greece
{kotoula,makri}@ceid.upatras.gr

Abstract. In this paper, we describe a novel framework for improving information retrieval results. At first, relevant documents are organized in clusters utilizing the containment metric along with language modeling tools. Then the final ranked list (ascending/descending order) of the documents that will be returned to the user for the specific query, is produced. To achieve that, firstly we extract the scores between the clusters and the query representations and then we combine the internal rankings of the documents inside the clusters using these scores as weighting factor. The method employed is based in the exploitation of the inter-documents similarities (lexical and/or semantics) after a sophisticated preprocessing. The experimental evaluation demonstrates that the proposed algorithm has the potential to improve the quality of the retrieved results.

Keywords: Query disambiguation · Information retrieval
Query reformulation · Clustering · Containment · Semantics

1 Introduction

One of the most popular research issues has always been the subject of improving the quality of ranking in Information Retrieval results. To this extent, information need is expressed through the form of queries submitted against a search engine or platform with the purpose of receiving any available information related to the query (Baeza-Yates and Ribeiro-Neto 2011; Manning et al. 2008). The problem or the challenge in this process is the search machine's potential and capability to respond and deliver the fittest set of information for the specific query, if this information actually exists.

On the other hand, users that post their queries are not specialists but instead plain, every day users that are not usually aware of the best format to provide their input query either because they do not leverage the full potential of the search platform or because they cannot express their intention clearly. The search engine's greatest challenge is then, to understand this user's intention through this given input, the query, that is to disambiguate the terms that synthesize the query and attempt to satisfy the query request.

The disambiguation process in information retrieval concerns both the way the query is approached as well as the way that the retrieved documents are processed.

L. Iliadis et al. (Eds.): AIAI 2018, IFIP AICT 520, pp. 133–145, 2018.
https://doi.org/10.1007/978-3-319-92016-0_13

Effective retrieval functions and techniques have been mostly derived from the class of probabilistic models and several approaches have been successfully implemented towards this direction (Baeza-Yates and Ribeiro-Neto 2011; Croft et al. 2009).

Recently, the aforementioned models have been combined with the cluster-based retrieval approach. Clustering depends on the relationship between document and query processing. If documents' processing depends on the query, then clustering can be seen as gathering all documents related to this query under the same cluster. Otherwise, documents can be clustered according to the relation between their content information based on lexical or semantic similarities and independent to the query. The level of similarity decided will provide the different number of clusters for a given corpus and will utilize the overlapping and redundant information present in the documents. This kind of retrieval is based on the hypothesis that similar documents can satisfy the same query or queries (Jardine and van Rijsbergen 1971; van Rijsbergen 1979). Moving in this line of thought recently researches have depicted that if good clusters can be designed then the retrieval performance will be improved (Raiber and Kurland 2014).

In this paper we propose a framework in order to improve query search results by leveraging specific types on information representation along with selecting the proper clustering algorithm to organize the documents. Our approach examines query-independent document processing and representation resulting to a lexical based inter-document similarity in order to form the clusters. The key of improvement in our results is the use of a generalized structural unit, namely *gloss*, derived from WordNet's thesaurus hierarchy (Fellbaum 1998; Princeton WordNet Gloss Corpus 2008) instead of words, namely *senses*. Usual problems like frequent irrelevant terms are faced effectively since the generalized approach we design elevates the terms that have the most similar sense(s) between each other throughout the document and when gathered they actually represent its content due to their semantics. Our final result is the list of documents returned for the query as an improved ranking.

The paper is organized as follows: in Sect. 2 we present a brief survey on similar techniques, while in Sect. 3 we describe an outline of our approach. In Sect. 4 we describe the lexical and semantics processing of the documents and in Sect. 5 we conclude the document processing presenting the clustering along with the techniques for evaluating internal scores of the contained documents. In Sect. 6 we process the query and explain the reformulation. Finally, in Sect. 7 we describe our ranking technique along with comparing our result with other techniques and platforms in Sect. 8 and conclude our research in Sect. 9.

2 Related Work

Many researches have been developed regarding document and query processing in terms of query disambiguation techniques. Most of them use additional databases that extend the analysis from the standard search engines. These databases are known as thesaurus or ontologies and are basically lexical databases (mainly for the English language) providing extra information and tools for analyzing content and query processing like sets of synonyms, antonyms, definitions and other data, all derived from a hierarchical structure.

In these researches the various processing rules and techniques are applied mostly in conjunction with the WordNet (Princeton University) (Fellbaum 1998; Princeton WordNet Gloss Corpus 2008) ontology, along with probability distribution models to smooth and arrange the results. Most of our techniques were inspired or derived from the work of (Giakoumi et al. 2015) that raise the question of whether the texts and the query should be approached with dependency between each other or not. In any case, texts are being scored in respect to one global lexicon and clusters are being formed through KL-Divergence (Kullback and Leibler 1951). Throughout the process, TF-IDF and SMLE (Smoothed Maximum Likelihood Estimate) models provide the necessary smoothing of the contained information.

In other articles like (Makris et al. 2014; Plegas and Stamou 2012; Agrawal et al. 2009; Angel and Koudas 2011) processing focuses around information redundancy. These techniques leverage greedy algorithms like MAXI-MAXU (Maximum k-Intersection, Maximum k-Union), to allocate the maximum intersection of similar information between pairs of documents. Upon locating the same context, a new document is being created that contains this context once along with any new information contained in the texts that participated in the intersection process over the specified threshold. The newly created content is being checked with the coherence metric that concludes whether the derived text is logical and valid.

In a series of additional papers, (Kanavos et al. 2013; Makris et al. 2013; Makris and Plegas 2013; Raviv et al. 2016), a recent and interesting approach is being explored to provide further information in text and terms annotation. The process of Wikification leverages the structure of Wikipedia pages in order to assign additional weights in the scores assigned to terms through WordNet's disambiguation process. Further clustering of the texts is being performed in these papers too, using n-tuples. Finally, using the TAGME (Ferragina and Scaiella 2010) technique in conjunction with WordNet results, the final score is assigned to the texts before being returned for a specific query.

Moreover (Levi et al. 2016; Raviv et al. 2016) explored language models, clustering and Wikification techniques in order to improve the retrieval performance. Our work can be considered to act complementarily to these attempts since it explores the use of WordNet and its glosses as an extra refined mechanism.

3   Outline of the Approach

The disambiguation process in information retrieval concerns both the way the query is approached as well as the way that the retrieved documents/ pages are handled from the (any) search engine. In order to decide how this process can be better applied, in terms of a source corpus or a web search in respect to a specific query, we define the way to modify and represent these documents appropriately while reformulating the query at the same time.

At first, we process the documents and we consider this step as completely independent from the query. The reason for this decision is an intuitive thought which dictates that *given a specific query, the chances to find an answer for it and this answer to be ideal are very low*; on the other hand, given a document we can extract one or more queries that can find their ideal answer(s) inside the document they represent.

For text processing we use the *WordNet 2.1* ontology by choosing to extract the *glosses* from the hierarchy. The *glosses* are sentences that describe the various *senses* also included in this model. That way we insert the idea of generality in our technique; in other words we define a new generalized structural unit to represent our texts. We examine and evaluate the use of *glosses* due to their structural position inside the *WordNet* model. As such instead of limited and isolated *senses*, we elevate the use of *glosses* with the purpose of adding or **discovering** additional (important per case) information for the terms that are contained in the text.

A significant step in our approach is *document clustering* based on the *containment* metric. Through *clustering* we target to achieve the maximum possible concentration of the same or similar content of all documents under the same interface (representation). This interface/ representation is the lexicon of the *cluster,* based on the documents it contains. This lexicon is being forwarded later in the process in order to be compared with the various representations of the query. At the same time, the documents inside these clusters also receive a score independently of the query.

The query is being processed in a similar way – like the documents – through *WordNet 2.1* ontology information extraction. It is then reformulated and through the *glosses*, extracted from its terms, various representations are being produced (all possible combinations between *glosses* of each term).

In the final stage of our processing, we produce the final ranked list (ascending/ descending order) applied on the documents that will be returned to the user for the specific query. To achieve that, firstly we extract the scores between the clusters and the query representations and then we combine them through the *Borda Count* Method (Kozorovitzky, and Kurland 2011) providing the final ranking order of the documents to return.

For the implementation of this research's algorithm we created and used tools in *JAVA* and *Python* in an end-to-end application so that the largest part of the process to be automated and user's interference to be minimum.

4   Language Model Processing of Documents

4.1   Document Representation

We begin our document representation technique using natural language processing based on NLTK tools (Bird et al. 2016) and OpenNLP (OpenNLP 2016) trained models to extract the terms from the documents and lemmatize them. The output of these steps are being forwarded to WordNet 2.1 interface, where for each document, the contained words one by one are set as input in the thesaurus.

To select the appropriate sense or senses from the WordNet schema we utilize the Wu & Palmer similarity measure (Wu and Palmer 1994) which is depicted below:

$$similarity(c_i, c_j) = \frac{2depth(LCA(c_i, c_j))}{depth(c_i) + depth(c_j)},$$

where we define *depth* () as the depth of the node inside the ontology and as *LCA* () the lowest common ancestor of the two senses c_i, c_j in the hierarchy, for the terms t_i, t_j. We use the above algorithm because we do not know a priori the fittest sense for each incoming term and Wu & Palmer provide us the ones for which the similarity is maximized. The similarity is calculated over the senses but the algorithm moves one step further and retrieves from the WordNet ontology the respective gloss that the sense belongs to.

To this point, we have extracted all the necessary information from the WordNet schema and assigned these sets of glosses (sentences) to each one of the retrieved documents. Each document is now being represented by a set of glosses retrieved for its terms instead of the more common methods that stop to the retrieval of senses only. The main advantage of our approach is that there is no need to perform extensive smoothing techniques like TF-IDF. That is because by extracting a more generalized description for each term, the words inside the document that concern the actual concept will finally be expressed by more similar or the same glosses and as such collect the majority of the content. Instead, words that do not contribute to the overall conceptual representation will eventually be limited to minimum frequency in the following steps.

4.2   Language Model for Internal Scoring of Documents in a Cluster

In the next step, we represent the information contained inside the documents with a language modelling approach that aims to conclude scores for each document given a larger set of glosses contained in a fixed vocabulary V.

Given a constructed fixed vocabulary V, the idea is to calculate a probability measure over strings that belong to it (Manning et al. 2008). In this work, we construct these vocabularies V containing a fixed set of sentences and calculate the probability of those sentences to exist inside the document. Since our unit for representation is no longer one word but instead a set of words, we apply the same rules for calculating the probability metric over sentences (sets of strings).

For each document and for each contained sentence we calculate these probabilities using the SMLE model (Smoothed Maximum Likelihood Estimate). SMLE model adjusts the representation of the document in respect to the frequency of its contained sentences, in other words based on the number of occurrences of each sentence s in the fixed vocabulary V:

$$M_d^{SMLE}(s) = \begin{cases} \frac{f_{s,d}}{l_d} - c, & \text{if } s \in d \\ eps, & \text{if } s \ni d \end{cases}, \quad \forall s \in V,$$

where $f_{s,d}$ is the number of occurrences of sentence s in document d and l_d is the number of terms contained in both d and V; also, *eps* is a very small quantity of the order of 10^{-10} and c is estimated as:

$$c = eps * \frac{|V| - n_d}{|V|},$$

where $|V|$ is the number of sentences in vocabulary V and n_d the number of sentences both in the vocabulary V and the document d.

The Smoothed version of MLE containing quantities *eps* and c is performed in order to avoid the zero probability problem of MLE, that is:

$$M_d^{MLE}(s) = 0, \forall s \in V \ \& \ \forall s \ni d$$

Using the SMLEs produced we can then calculate the document's score against the fixed vocabulary V by adding these sub-SMLEs for all contained sentences inside the document representation.

5 Clustering

5.1 Containment

Documents are now represented by probability distributions and we can focus on how to leverage the similar ones in order to proceed with further clustering them. For this step we chose to use a simple but efficient metric known as *Containment* (Broder et al. 1997) accompanied with the K. To examine whether a document d_1 is contained inside another document d_2 we use the following formula:

$$Containment(d_1, d_2) = \frac{|S(d_1) \cap S(d_2)|}{|S(d_1)|},$$

where $S(d_i)$ is the set of glosses that the document d_i contains. Containment is being calculated from both directions and we keep the one that produces the higher score. The maximum value for the containment is 1.0 which means that document d_1 is fully contained inside document d_2. The result in each comparison is rounded up to one decimal and the measure is calculated for all possible pairs of documents – removing from the final set those with containment equal to zero 0.0.

5.2 Containment Based Clustering

Having extracted the containment scores between all pairs of documents and keeping only the directions that produce the largest scores we now proceed to the clusters. Specifically, each cluster will be formed by those documents that the containment score between them belongs to a specific pre-defined set of values. One document may be present in more than one clusters.

For the final clustering of documents we have three tools: the content (containment), the value of the SMLE and the mapping between senses and glosses. We choose to use the simplest approach, namely the containment, to divide the texts into clusters. Specifically, having each time one hundred documents for processing we can put clusters of ten/fifteen documents setting containments limits in the range intervals of 0.1 units to meet separately all possible spaces between 0.1 and 0.9. The number of fifteen documents per cluster emerged after experiments. As for the other two metrics, the SMLE will be used for the internal ranking of documents within the cluster so that to get the final ranking of the representations of the query, in the last step of our processing. Finally, the mapping between concepts and glosses on the subject, can be used for further analysis but we stop at this point because we aim to end use only glosses. Nevertheless, one can combine senses and glosses and produce information more well defined to the nature of documents. Such information can produce more glosses for the representation of documents, to combine concepts from each other so that the glosses to be more targeted. We leave this as a matter of future research.

Returning to the clustering we develop the algorithm to extract clusters according to the analysis we did earlier. First, we define the first cluster with documents having containments between the 0.8 and 0.9 interval. Then we repeat this step every 0.1 units: 0.6–0.7, 0.4–0.5, 0.2–0.3 and 0.1.

In particular we run the list of document pairs and using their containment metric we pick up initially all pairs of values in the content space 0.8–0.9. Then we collect all the documents whose containment has values between 0.6–0.7. There is always the case of a document from the previous calculated interval, to appear and we permit this as case, considering that this raises the chances of finding more similarity between query and representation of a cluster because of the extra vocabulary the document adds to that cluster. We repeat the same procedure for the remaining intervals. When we completed the separation in the first cluster, we can reduce even more the documents per cluster and display different documents for the same intervals.

The distribution of the documents inside the clusters resembles a normal one; clusters produced for scores between 0.3 and 0.7 contain larger numbers of documents than clusters near the edge with scores 0.2 to 0.1 or 0.8 to 1.0 as shown in Fig. 1:

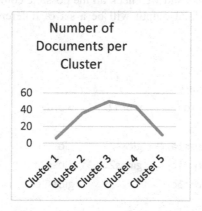

Fig. 1. Normal distribution of contained documents

Finally, based on the SMLE language model d, the score for each document inside the cluster is being produced. The fixed vocabulary V for each cluster which is used for this score is derived from the separate vocabularies of all documents contained in this cluster. The glosses occur one time at most since the global cluster vocabulary must not contain redundant information. The score for each document varies per cluster it belongs to.

It is important to mention two key characteristics for the above process:

1. The score for each document is produced based on the fixed vocabulary of each cluster it belongs to as such one document may have more than one scores based on the clusters it belongs to.
2. The option to create sub clusters is also utilized in our approach and the technique aims to create a more uniform representation inside the clusters in respect to the number of contained documents. It proves that the aforementioned technique performs worse than the normal distribution.

6 Query Processing

To process the query we follow the same lexical and language model probability approaches, where we tokenize the input, lemmatize the separate terms and provide them as input to WordNet 2.1 in order to retrieve the respective glosses. In the document processing we chose to keep those glosses, whose senses produced the highest scores for the terms. For the query we choose to keep all glosses produced by the WordNet 2.1 schema. Our intuition behind this decision is that the user who posed the query might have had in mind any specific intention out of various possible ones; so, if a query can mean a lot of different things we have to keep all those meanings instead of just some.

In the final step of this process we reformulate the query by producing all possible glosses for each of its terms and we check all the possible combinations between them as shown if Fig. 2. The final output will be a set of different query representations containing glosses.

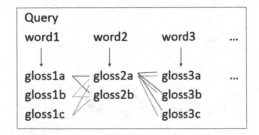

Fig. 2. Normal distribution of contained documents

7 Ranking

To produce the final list of documents that will be returned to the user, our algorithm calculates a similarity score between the global fixed vocabulary V of each cluster and each of the query representations. We annotate the query representations as: $q_i, 1 < q < Q$, where Q is the total number of query representations. Each cluster's vocabulary is annotated as: $c_i, 1 < i < C$, where C is the total number of clusters. At the first step we produce the similarity measurement score between the two quantities for each query representation and each cluster's vocabulary.

A lot of techniques have been developed for lexical similarities over the years basically for application over characters between words. In our framework we adjusted a few of them to be performed over sentences – words instead of characters and sentences instead of words. We concluded in the use of two methods: *Positional N-Grams* similarity and *Levenshtein Distance*. The *N-Gram* similarity was used with position $n = 4$. The advantage of the use of the aforementioned similarity techniques is that they offer the possibility of two sentences to be partially similar and not totally the same. Between the two techniques, N-Gram executes in lesser time than *Levenshtein Distance* and produces better similarity scores. Based on comparing every representation q_i with every cluster C_j, there will be produced *Similarities*: S_{ij}:

Query representation	Cluster	Similarity between query and cluster
q_1	Cluster C_1	S_{11}
	Cluster C_2	S_{12}
	...	......
q_2	Cluster C_1	S_{21}
	Cluster C_2	S_{22}
	...	......

Then we adjust the ranking based on the documents of every cluster. As we already described the internal ranking of documents in each cluster employs SMLE and the containment metric.

Ranking in each cluster	Query + Cluster: S_{ij} combination
doc_1	S_{12}
doc_2	
doc_3	
doc_7	S_{31}
doc_8	
doc_9	
doc_1	
doc_2	S_{13}
...	...

The final score of each document is produced through Borda Count that combines the similarity between clusters and query representations with the internal document score as produced in each cluster. In particular the combined lists correspond to every distinct combination of cluster and query representation, the lists are ranked according to the internal scores of the document in each cluster and during the combination we use as extra weight the similarity between the query and the clusters.

8   Experimental Evaluation

To perform our evaluation we explored 20 web queries from TREC 2012 WebTracks. We selected queries with the best characteristics against WordNet 2.1 and in respect to the quality of their corpus, in order to perform the experiments. All tracks use the 1 billion page ClueWeb09 (http://lemurproject.org/clueweb09/) dataset and contain a diversity task that contains a ranked list of documents that covers the query topic avoiding information redundancy. TREC assessors have assigned appropriate relevance judgement scores for the documents related to each of the queries. For our results we have employed Google and AOL search engines and for each we have retained the top 100 pages returned. Common identifier of the quality of the results (both for our algorithm as well as for the Google and AOL engines results) is the N-DCG metric (Baeza Yates and Ribeiro-Neto 2011; Manning et al. 2008).

Each query is being examined against WordNet and confirmed that all of its terms extract the necessary information – otherwise the query is dismissed. We retrieved up to 200 documents from the ClueWeb09 corpus related to each query. For the clustering of the documents we used the containment metric and created the clusters based on the following sets of values: 0.8–1.0, 0.6–0.7, 0.4–0.5, 0.2–0.3 and 0–0.1. To measure the efficiency of our method we used (a) the relevance judgement scores from TREC 2012 specialists and (b) the N-DGC, Normalized Discounted Cumulative Gain metric.

When comparing our algorithm with the ideal list of documents returned for each query we have a success of 75% in a very well controlled environment where: (i) the stop words list is extended to contain additional words based on the previous results, (ii) clustering is preserved in the values presented above, (iii) queries selected have documents with strict normal distribution of scores, (iv) we keep all glosses for the query terms and (v) we change the threshold in our ranking techniques per case. The following Fig. 3 represents the most representative samples of our results with scores [0, 4]. In the vertical axis 0 indicates no relativity at all between the document and the query and 4 is the highest relativity between them. In the horizontal axis, reside the documents evaluated for the query.

Finally, our algorithm was assessed against Google and AOL results for the same queries. The vertical axis in the following Fig. 4, shows the N-DCG metric and the horizontal contains the 20 queries. From the results, our algorithm performs much better than Google (69%) and better than AOL (71%).

Google decides the returned list through Page Rank and focuses on user "clicks" as well as the incoming and outgoing links between pages. As such pages with lesser interactions between each other are hardly going to be presented in the list. On the other hand, the close values between our algorithm (75%) and AOL – which are both higher than Google's - could be explained through the use of a common technique between the two approaches which is the clustering of the pages before they are returned for a specific query. Finally, we perform a soft comparison of our algorithm with the techniques and approaches presented in the related researches (Giakoumi et al. 2015; Plegas and Stamou 2012) to further evaluate our algorithm. Our test range was much more limited than the ones used in the aforementioned paper as such the results are inconclusive. Specifically, our algorithm seems to perform 5%–10% better but the

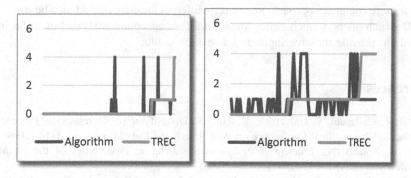

Fig. 3. Algorithm evaluation against TREC assessment.

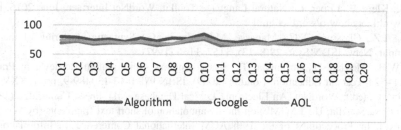

Fig. 4. Algorithm evaluation against Google and AOL.

queries used are not the same nor in the same extensive number. At the same time, the range of the corpus used in our experiments is significantly smaller mainly due to the limited capacity and related resources used for our research as such further experiments are necessary to conclude.

9   Conclusions

In this paper we presented a framework in an attempt to improve the quality in the retrieval performance of search engines. The novel approach of our research is the use of a more generalized structure unit, namely gloss, in order to represent our texts throughout language and probabilistic models in conjunction with a lately very effective technique – clustering. Our main goal in this approach is to introduce a more generalized way of modeling the input in a conceptual way in order to enforce the inclusion of independent modules, re-usable and easily attached to different methods and techniques. This way a model can be flexible enough to be attached in a variety of approaches. At the same time, our algorithm needs further improvement. In our approach the most significant one concerns the use of WordNet where the interface for the input has limited options; a different lemmatizer of stemmer could be developed to provide the words to WordNet in a better comprehensive and pos-tagged way without losing information. To this extend someone can further enhance the scores by applying the Wikification techniques in the final document ranking.

In a more complex approach, an entirely different thesaurus could also be used, like YAGO which offers a much better framework for conceptual analysis but so far lacks the tools to provide massive input and assess its results.

References

Agrawal, R., Collapudi, S., Halverson, A., Ieong S.: Diversifying search results. In: Proceedings of the 2nd International Conference on Web Search and Data Mining, pp. 5–14 (2009)

Angel, A., Koudas, N.: Efficient diversity-aware search. In: Proceedings of the SIGMOD Conference, pp. 781–792 (2011)

Baeza-Yates, R.A., Ribeiro-Neto, B.A.: Modern Information Retrieval - The Concepts and Technology Behind Search, 2nd edn. Pearson Education Ltd., Harlow (2011). ISBN 978-0-321-41691-9

Bird, S., Klein, E., Loper, E.: Natural Language Toolkit, WordNet Interface, June 2016. http://www.nltk.org/howto/wordnet.html

Broder, A.Z., Glassman, S.C., Manasse, M.S., Zweig, G.: Syntactic clustering of the web. Comput. Netw. ISDN Syst. **29**(8–13), 1157–1166 (1997)

Croft, W.B., Metzler, D., Strohman, T.: Search Engines - Information Retrieval in Practice, pp. 1–524. Pearson Education, London (2009). ISBN 978-0-13-136489-9, pp. I–XXV

Fellbaum, C. (ed.): WordNet, An Electronic Lexical Database. MIT Press, Cambridge (1998)

Ferragina, P., Scaiella, U.: TAGME: on-the-fly annotation of short text fragments (by Wikipedia entities). In: Proceedings of the 19th ACM International Conference on Information and Knowledge Management (CIKM 2010), pp. 1625–1628. ACM, New York (2010)

Giakoumi, I., Makris, C., Plegas, P.: Language Model and Clustering based Information Retrieval. In: Proceedings of the 11th International Conference on Web Information Systems and Technologies, WEBIST 2015 pp. 479–486 (2015)

Jardine, N., van Rijsbergen, C.J.: The use of hierarchical clustering in information retrieval. Inf. Storage Retr. **7**, 217–240 (1971)

Kanavos, A., Makris, C., Plegas, Y., Theodoridis, E.: Extracting knowledge from web search engine using wikipedia. In: Iliadis, L., Papadopoulos, H., Jayne, C. (eds.) EANN 2013. CCIS, vol. 384, pp. 100–109. Springer, Heidelberg (2013). https://doi.org/10.1007/978-3-642-41016-1_11

Kozorovitzky, A.K., Kurland, O.: Cluster-based fusion of retrieved lists. In: SIGIR 2011, pp. 893–902 (2011)

Kullback, S., Leibler, R.A.: On information and sufficiency. Ann. Math. Stat. **22**(1), 79–86 (1951)

Levi, O., Raiber, F., Kurland, O., Guy, I.: Selective cluster-based document retrieval. In: CIKM 2016, pp. 1473–148 (2016)

Makris, C., Plegas, Y., Stamatiou, Y.C., Stavropoulos, E.C., Tsakalidis, A.K.: Reducing redundant information in search results employing approximation algorithms. In: Decker, H., Lhotská, L., Link, S., Spies, M., Wagner, R.R. (eds.) DEXA 2014. LNCS, vol. 8645, pp. 240–247. Springer, Cham (2014). https://doi.org/10.1007/978-3-319-10085-2_22

Makris, C., Plegas Y., Theodoridis, E.: Improved Text Annotation with Wikipedia Entities. In: SAC 2013 Proceedings of the 28th Annual ACM Symposium on Applied Computing, pp. 288–295 (2013)

Makris, C., Plegas, Y.: Algorithms and Techniques of Personalized Search in Internet Environments Using Underlying Semantics. University of Patras, Department of Computer Engineering and Informatics, July 2013

Manning, C.D., Raghavan, P., Schütze, H.: Introduction to Information Retrieval, pp. 1–482. Cambridge University Press, Cambridge (2008). pp. I-XXI

OpenNLP 1.5: Pre-Trained Models for 1.5 Series, June 2016. http://opennlp.sourceforge.net/models-1.5/

Plegas, Y., Stamou, S.: Reducing Information Redundancy in Search Results. J. Am. Soc. Inform. Sci. Technol. **63**(8), 1581–1592 (2012). https://doi.org/10.1002/asi

Princeton WordNet Gloss Corpus (January 2008): WordNet Gloss Disambiguation Project, Sponsored by ARDA/DTO, SRI's AQUAINT Project. http://wordnet.princeton.edu/glosstag.shtml Accessed July 2016

Raiber, F., Kurland, O.: The correlation between cluster hypothesis tests and the effectiveness of cluster-based retrieval. In: SIGIR. ACM, pp. 1155–1158 (2014)

Raviv, H., Kurland, O., Carmel, D.: Document retrieval using entity-based language models. In: SIGIR 2016, pp. 65–74 (2016)

Rebele, T., Suchanek, F., Hoffart, J., Biega, J., Kuzey, E., Weikum, G.: YAGO: a multilingual knowledge base from wikipedia, wordnet, and geonames. In: Groth, P., Simperl, E., Gray, A., Sabou, M., Krötzsch, M., Lecue, F., Flöck, F., Gil, Y. (eds.) ISWC 2016. LNCS, vol. 9982, pp. 177–185. Springer, Cham (2016). https://doi.org/10.1007/978-3-319-46547-0_19

van Rijsbergen, C.J.: Information Retrieval, 2nd edn. Butterworths, London (1979)

Wu, Z., Palmer, M.: Verbs semantics and lexical selection. In: Proceedings of the 32nd Meeting of Association of Computational Linguistics, pp. 133–138 (1994)

Automatic Selection of Parallel Data
for Machine Translation

Despoina Mouratidis$^{(\boxtimes)}$ ⓘ and Katia Lida Kermanidis ⓘ

Department of Informatics, Ionian University,
7 Pl. Tsirigoti, 49100 Corfu, Greece
{cl2mour, kerman}@ionio.gr

Abstract. Nowadays machine translation is widely used, but the required data for training, tuning and testing a machine translation engine is often not sufficient or not useful. The automatic selection of data that are qualitatively appropriate for building translation models can help improve translation accuracy. In this paper, we used a large parallel corpus of educational video lecture subtitles as well as text posted by students and lecturers on the course fora. The text is quite challenging to translate due to the scientific domains involved and its informal genre. We applied a random forest classification schema on the output of three machine translation models (one based on statistical machine translation and two on neural machine translation) in order to automatically identify the best output. The unorthodox language phenomena observed as well as the rich-in-terminology scientific domains addressed in the educational video lectures, the language-independent nature of the approach, and the tackled three-class classification problem constitute innovative challenges of the work described herein.

Keywords: Machine learning · Educational data · Data selection
Machine translation · Random forests

1 Introduction

In recent years, many people, companies and organizations make use of machine translation (MT) solutions. MT software has been improving, and researchers are trying to generate the best translation of a source text. The use of MT is said to have become an indispensable tool, not only for scientific purposes, but also for the general public. Moreover, automatic translation contributes decisively to the learning process, since it can extend the learning target group by breaking the language barrier and enhancing access to the educational material. To this end, the European project TraMOOC (Translation for Massive Open Online Courses) [10] aims at improving the translation process, and overcoming the language barriers in online educational content.

After almost half a century that statistical approach prevailed in MT [9], a new method, the neural – based approach, appeared. This, in contrast to statistical machine translation (SMT) implemented by using parallel text corpora to calculate probabilities, generates much more accurate translations. More specifically, neural machine translation (NMT) implements deep learning techniques to teach text translations by taking on existing statistical models as a basis. Also, NMT is able to use algorithms to train itself with linguistic rules [3].

Certainly, many challenges occur in the translation process. Additionally, it should be noted that there is difficulty in translation out of domain data. Therefore, there is a large amount of data to be translated. For large sentences, an extension of the classical neural encoder-decoder can be used, taking into account only the words which have information relevant to the target word and not the whole sentence [1]. Post-editing and data selection are two ways to reduce the data (i.e. choosing only quality parallel segments) without hurting translation quality. Many online MT platforms now prompt users to improve the proposed translation themselves [12]. This may be a solution to improve translation models, but it also creates a multitude of data that needs to be evaluated regarding usability. On the other hand, data selection methods can be used to recognize the useful and non-useful features in parallel segments. Research has shown that when models are trained with less, but more accurate, data, their performance improves [17].

In this paper, we consider data selection as a classification problem and we explore the idea of using three translation prototypes for our experiments, one based on SMT and the other two based on NMT. The contribution of this paper is multi-fold:

- the educational content domain comprises scientific fields that involve a high degree of terminology and unknown words. This phenomenon requires a set of robust learning features to represent the parallel text segments.
- the informal genre (spontaneous speech transcriptions and forum text) presents linguistic phenomena that are unorthodox and ungrammatical, like repetitions, interjections, fillers, truncated utterances etc., posing a challenge to the automatic identification of grammatical utterances.
- the proposed approach is language independent. All linguistic features are based on string similarity and no morphosyntactic information is incorporated in any form.
- a metalearner (Random Forest) is employed for data classification, for the first time for the task at hand to the authors' knowledge, in order to tackle the aforementioned challenges.

2 Experimental Setup

This section describes the corpora, tools and the classification process used.

2.1 Corpus

The parallel corpus we worked on was provided from the TraMOOC project. As already mentioned, the corpus includes lecture speech transcriptions and text posted by class participants on course fora. The source corpus consists of 2,687 segments (sentences) in English (Src). For each of these segments, three translation outputs into Greek are available, generated by three prototypes (Trans1, Trans2, Trans3), whereas one reference translation (Ref) from a professional translator is also provided. Translation model 1 (Trans1) used the open-source phrase-based SMT toolkit Moses [8], the translation models 2 (Trans2) and 3 (Trans3) used the NMT Nematus toolkit [15]. Trans1 is a statistical based prototype trained on both in- and out-of-domain data. Trans2 is trained on the same data as Trans1 and uses labels to identify and remember the domain, while Trans3 is the result of training with more in-domain data providing via crowdsourcing, weight tying, layer normalization, and improved domain adaptation. Out of domain data included widely known corpora e.g. Europal, JRC-Acquis, OPUS, WMT News corpora etc. In domain data included TED, QED corpus, Coursera etc. [11].

Data pre-processing included the removal of symbols (for example #, $), and some alignment corrections, so that each segment is mapped to its Src, Ref, Trans1, Trans2 and Trans3 variations.

A challenge was the translation of entities like URLs, mathematical expressions and rare words. The first two entity types were copied to the translation output by some prototypes (Trans2 & Trans3, and Trans3 respectively), while the third type is tackled by the third prototype by word division in order to improve MT output [16].

2.2 Annotation

Two Greek linguists have annotated each segment with A, B or C depending on whether Trans1, 2 or 3 is more similar to Ref respectively. We observe low annotation percentage for class A (17%) compared with class B (37%) and C (46%). This confirms the superiority of the NMT vs. SMT models. At this point, it's important to notice that the two annotators gave different answers in 82 of the 2,687 segment cases. For the different answers, the annotators had a discussion and finally agreed on one common label.

We present five segments and their Trans1-2-3 and Ref translations (Table 1), the sixth segment is an example of disagreement of two linguistics.

Table 1. Segment examples from source, Trans1, Trans2, Trans3 and Ref.

ID	Source	Trans1	Trans2	Trans3	Ref
1	The archplot refers to the classical design of a story and has been called by many names.	Η archplot αναφέρεται στην κλασική σχεδιασμό μιας ιστορίας και έχει κληθεί με πολλά ονόματα.	Το αρχαϊκό σχέδιο αναφέρεται στον κλασικό σχεδιασμό μιας ιστορίας και έχει κληθεί από πολλά ονόματα.	Η αρχική πλοκή αναφέρεται στον κλασικό σχεδιασμό μιας ιστορίας και έχει ονομαστεί από πολλά ονόματα.	Η κύρια πλοκή αναφέρεται στην τυπική διαμόρφωση μιας ιστορίας και έχει πάρει πολλά ονόματα.
2	A bit of gaming history: Which now famous video game character made his/her first appearance in the 1981 "Donkey Kong" arcade game?	Ένα κομμάτι της ιστορίας παιχνιδιών: Η οποία τώρα διάσημο βιντεοπαιχνίδι χαρακτήρας έκανε την πρώτη της εμφάνιση στο 1981 "DonkeyKong" βιντεοπαιχνίδι;	Ένα κομμάτι της ιστορίας του παιχνιδιού: Που τώρα ο διάσημος video-παιχνίδι χαρακτήρας έκανε την πρώτη του εμφάνιση το 1981 στο βιντεοπαιχνίδι του DoneyKong;	Ένα κομμάτι ιστορίας παιχνιδιών: Το οποίο τώρα ο διάσημος χαρακτήρας του βιντεοπαιχνιδιού έκανε την πρώτη του εμφάνιση στο παιχνίδι "DonkeyKong" παιχνίδι;	Λίγη ιστορία παιχνιδιών: Ποιος/α σημερινός γνωστός χαρακτήρας βιντεοπαιχνιδιού εμφανίστηκε για πρώτη φορά το 1981 στο «Donkey Kong»;
3	This is where studying critical thinking can help.	Εδώ είναι που σπουδάζουν σειρά μαθημάτων Κριτική Σκέψη μπορεί να βοηθήσει.	Εδώ είναι που η μελέτη της κρίσιμης σκέψης μπορεί να βοηθήσει.	Εδώ είναι που η μελέτη της Κριτικής Σκέψης μπορεί να βοηθήσει.	Σε αυτό το σημείο οι σπουδές στην Κριτική Σκέψη μπορούν να βοηθήσουν.

(continued)

Table 1. (*continued*)

ID	Source	Trans1	Trans2	Trans3	Ref
4	Upload the essay as a zip file including the Statement of Authorship.	Ανέβασε το δοκίμιο ως ταχυδρομικό φάκελο, συμπεριλαμβανομένης της δήλωσης Niemann.	Ανέβαζε την εργασία ως φερμουάρ, συμπεριλαμβανομένης της δήλωσης του αρχαίου πλοίου.	Ανεβάστε την έκθεση ως ένα αρχείο zip συμπεριλαμβανομένου της δήλωσης του διατάκτη.	Ανεβάστε την έκθεση ως συμπιεσμένο αρχείο συμπεριλαμβανομένης της Δήλωση Συγγραφικής Πατρότητας.
5	You need to get the audience to want to "lean into the screen".	Θα πρέπει να πάρετε το κοινό να θέλουν να "λιτή στην οθόνη".	Πρέπει να κάνεις το κοινό να θέλει να "λυγίσει στην οθόνη".	Πρέπει να κάνεις το κοινό να θέλει να "γείρει στην οθόνη".	Θα πρέπει να κάνετε το κοινό να θέλει να « μπει στην οθόνη» .
6	For anybody interested in deeper exploration of the origins of storytelling please check-out Professor Hobohm's full lecture on the topic that we added below.	Για όποιον ενδιαφέρεται για βαθύτερη εξερεύνηση του προέλευση της αφήγησης παρακαλώ ελέγξτε-out o καθηγητής Hobohm είναι γεμάτο διάλεξη για το θέμα που προσθέσαμε παρακάτω.	Για οποιονδήποτε ενδιαφέρεται για βαθύτερη έρευνα για την προέλευση της αφήγησης, παρακαλώ εξετάστε την πλήρη διάλεξη του καθηγητή Hobohm για το θέμα που προσθέσαμε από κάτω.	Για οποιονδήποτε ενδιαφέρεται για βαθύτερη εξερεύνηση της καταγωγής της αφήγησης, παρακαλώ ελέγξτε την πλήρη διάλεξη του καθηγητή Χόμπομ για το θέμα που προσθέσαμε παρακάτω.	Όποιος ενδιαφέρεται για πιο διεξοδική έρευνα σχετικά με την προέλευση της αφήγησης παρακαλώ ρίξτε μια ματιά σε όλη τη διάλεξη του καθηγητή Hobohm πάνω στο θέμα που προσθέσαμε από κάτω.

ID 1: (i) *archplot*: No translation by Trans1 (not found). Trans2 and Trans3 correctly separate the two synthetics. Trans2 translates the first synthetic as a main word (αρχαϊκό = *archaic*), common in historical contexts, but not correct in this segment. Trans3 finds the meaning of the prefix: arch- (archi › αρχή, αρχική).

(ii) *has been called*: the three trans didn't change the passive into the active form. Trans1 and 2 gave the most common meaning (κληθεί). Nevertheless, the more successful translation of Trans3 (ονομαστεί) makes a pleonasm with the object (ονόματα), Ref's choice being the correct (πάρει).

ID 2: (i) *which*: None of the three Trans translated correctly this question word, not being the first word of the segment.

(ii) Trans1 incorrectly connected *which* to history giving the same grammatical gender (ιστορία...η οποία). Trans2 chose the sometimes confusing, but very common, που (not the question word πού). Trans3 incorrectly connected *which* to *a bit* giving the same grammatical gender (κομμάτι...το οποίο).

(iii) *now*: None of the three Trans translated it as an adjective.

(iv) Trans1 and Trans2 didn't connect the word *game* to *character* as a genitive case (παιχνίδι...χαρακτήρας), as was done correctly by Trans3 (χαρακτήρας βιντεοπαιχνιδιού).

ID 3: (i) *This is where*: no metaphorical sense by the three Trans.

(ii) *studying*: the same translation by Trans2 and Trans3 (μελέτη), but not expressing the action, the process, as a verb would have done. Trans1 uses a verb (σπουδάζουν) and the sense of "process" is given also by adding an object but the syntax generates a pleonasm (σπουδάζουν σειρά μαθημάτων) and the syntax of the segment is incorrect.

ID 4: (i) *Authorship*: Trans1 translated this word by the word *Niemann* that is non-existing in the source segment. It's important to note that we find the *Niemann Statement* in Harvard and other contexts and this is relevant with essays and authors. Very interesting, (but the result is completely false) is also the Trans2 translation process: from the basic meanings of the whole word (*authorship* =origin, source)

Trans2 uses a synonym: αρχαίου (ancient), but at the same time it separately translates the second synthetic of the word (-ship) to give the common phrase: αρχαίου πλοίου.

(ii) *essay*: Trans1 gives the main meaning of the word (δοκίμιο), but the Trans2 and Trans3 choices are also correct (εργασία, έκθεση), Trans3 choice being Ref's choice.

(iii) *zip file*: Trans1 translates *zip* by the common adjective of *file*, but here it is irrelevant: ταχυδρομικό. The Trans2 translation (φερμουάρ) is completely irrelevant here, but very common in other contexts. Trans3 correctly doesn't translate *zip* in this context.

ID 5: (i) *get*: Trans1 gives the most common translation (πάρετε), but it is not correct here. Trans2 and Trans3 correctly translate this multi-sense word.

(ii) *You*: Only Trans1 correctly translates *You* as a plural pronoun.

(iii) *lean*: None of the three Trans is correct *(λιτή, λυγίσει, γείρει)* compared to Ref's correct choice (μπει). The word here has a very special metaphorical meaning: "to enter". The sense of "motion" of the preposition *into*, in the Source text, is partly conveyed in Trans3 (γείρει).

ID 6: Annotator 1 labeled Trans2 as the better translation for the following reasons: (1) έρευνα is a better translation for *exploration* in this segment, as the main meaning of the word (εξερεύνηση) here is not precise, (2) προέλευση for the word *origins* is the best translation in this segment and is the same as the Ref tranlation, (3) εξετάστε is not the best translation for *check-out* in this segment but is better than ελέγξτε, because its meaning is not the primary one (i.e. check) but closer to other secondary meanings of *check*, like "note" or "hold". By *check-out*, in combination with the word *whole*, the writer here means: "read" or better "study and keep in mind", but it can't be translated so, as it is far from the meaning of *check*, (4) Trans2 kept the proper noun *Hobohm* in Latin letters, like Ref, and as it is considered to be good practice for dealing with proper nouns from one language to another.

Annotator 2 labeled Trans3, as the better translation for the following reasons: (1) εξερεύνηση is the exact meaning of "exploration", in combination with its prepositional phrase *of the origins*, implying "deeper research" (εξερεύνηση being more exploratory than a simple research (έρευνα)), (2) της καταγωγής is the primary and most common meaning for *of the origins*, as it refers to "the first appearance", to "the creation" of the subjective genitive: *storytelling*, (3) Trans3 changed the Latin into Greek letters for the proper noun: Χόμπομ, as the target language is Greek, and it is common practice to do so.

2.3 Features

We considered the task at hand as a classification problem with three output (class) values, so we represented each segment as a tuple (Src, Trans1-2-3, Ref). Each tuple was modeled as a feature-value vector, while the features are based on string similarity, they contain no form of morhosyntactic information, and are therefore language independent. The feature set was based on the work by Barrón-Cedeño et al. [2] and Pighin et al. [13]. Feature values were calculated using MATLAB.

Basic-Simple Features

These are simple string similarity features. Levenshtein distance is a string similarity metric, which calculates the minimum number of single-character changes required to change one word into the other. Also, another string similarity metric was used to determine if Trans 1-2-3 is contained in Ref (Containment c) [5].

- Length (in number of words) of Src-Trans1-Trans2-Trans3-Ref.
- Length in words of Trans1, Trans2, Trans3, Ref divided by Src, also for Trans1, Trans2, Trans3 divided by Ref.
- Length in characters divided by length in words for Src, Trans1, Trans2, Trans3 and Ref.
- Levenshtein distance of Trans1, Trans2, Trans3 divided by Length of words and characters of Trans1, Trans2, Trans3.
- Number of words that exist in Trans and do not exist in the Ref divided by the number of words in Trans (and vice versa).
- Containment c of Trans1-Ref, Trasn2-Ref, Trans3-Ref [5].
- Ratio of (third bullet)'s resulting features between (Trans1-Trans2-Trans3, Src), (Ref, Src), and (Trans1-Trans2-Trans3, Ref).
- Longest word for Src, Trans1, Trans2, Trans3 and Ref.
- Longest word in Trans1, Trans2, Trans3 divided by Src and Ref and longest word in Ref divided by longest word in Src.
- If Ref = Trans1 or Trans2 or Trans3, then True, otherwise False, if Src = Trans1 or Trans2 or Trans3, then True, otherwise False.

Noise-Based Features

- If Src is a one word string then True, otherwise False.
- If Src is a string of more than five words then True, otherwise False.
- If Src is a string with length six to ten words then True, otherwise False.
- If Src is a string with length up to eleven words then True, otherwise False.
- If Src, Trans1, Trans2, Trans3, Ref has a word with length 10 to 14 characters then True otherwise False. We did the same with word length 15 to infinity.
- If Src or Trans1 or Trans2 or Trans3 has a word of three repeated characters then True, otherwise False.

Similarity-Based Features

- The length factors (LF-defined in [14]), LF(Ref, Trans1), LF(Ref, Trans2) and LF (Ref, Trans3) are calculated.
- Using the LF (described above), if LF(Ref, Trans1) > LF(Ref, Tans2) then True, otherwise False. The same comparison is performed on LF(Ref, Trans2) and LF (Ref, Trans3), as well as on LF(Ref, Trans1) and LF(Ref, Trans3) (and vice versa).

2.4   Results

We have nominal and numeric features. We normalized the numeric features so that their values range between 0 and 1, by using the Feature scaling method. We decided to use the Weka machine learning workbench [18] for training and testing our dataset. We used evaluation measures that are common in classification, and adopted from Information Retrieval. The first measure is Precision, that is True Positive / (True Positive + False Positive). The second measure is Sensitivity - (Recall), that is True Positive / (True Positive + False Negative).

Given the challenges governing the genre and the domain of the data, we decided to apply a meta-learner for increased robustness. We chose the Random Forest classifier, due to their using the Law of Large Numbers and the ability to avoid overfitting [4], and achieving high generalization accuracy. Random Forests implement an ensemble learning schema that generates multiple decision trees during training, and constructs a combination of the classification outputs of each tree model for prediction. We set the number of iterations (number of trees to be constructed) to 65. Each tree was constructed while considering 20 random features. We employed 10 fold cross validation as testing mode. The minority class (A) causes problems in the classification process: the classification algorithms give low accuracy as they tend to classify the new unseen segments in the majority class [7]. In order to improve the accuracy of the classifier for the minority class (precision 49%, recall 22%), we used the Smote filter [6], which is an over-sampling approach for creating new synthetic training data. Smote combines the feature values of minority class examples with the feature values of their nearest neighbor examples ($n = 5$) in order to produce new examples of the minority class. The Smote process is applied only on the training data. Using Smote, the segments of class A doubled in number, and the total number of segments reached 3150. We observed that we had better results when we used RandomForest_Smote including all the features as seen in Table 2.

Table 2. Precision and recall of our experiments.

Classifier : RandomForest				
Class	Precision	Recall	Number of features	Number of instances
A	49%	22%	82	2687
B	46%	36%	82	2687
C	50%	70%	82	2687
Classifier : RandomForest_Smote				
A	77%	63%	82	3150
B	44%	32%	82	3150
C	50%	68%	82	3150

It is noted that the results obtained are satisfactory, given that in our experiment we had three classification values, in contrast to related research that targeted a binary class output [2]. Moreover, the features we used are simple string comparison features, and they are language independent, including no morphosyntactic information in any form.

It is noted that the results obtained are satisfactory, given that in our experiment we had three classification values, in contrast to the [2] research. In addition, the features we used are simple string comparison features, and they are language independent.

We observed in the table that when we applied RandomForest before the Smote filtering, the classifier correctly classified 22% of A segments for Class A (Trans1), 36% of B segments for Class B (Trans2) and 70% of C segments for Class C (Trans3). After the Smote process, a major change is observed in Class A, where the percentage increased to 64%. For classes B and C we did not notice any particular changes. What is remarkable is that when the classifier does not sort correctly, it usually classifies the segments from one neural model to another (60% B -> C and 25% C -> B), and a much smaller percentage to the statistical model (7% C -> A and 8% B -> A) as well. In total, we can see in the figure below (Fig. 1) the percentages of incorrectly classified instances.

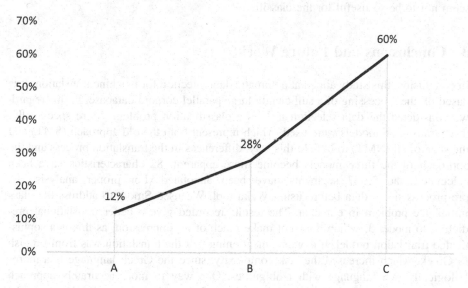

Fig. 1. Total percentages for incorrectly classified instances.

The majority of incorrectly classified instances from classes A and B, were classified by Random Forest in class C (60%). For classes A and C 28% were misclassified into B. We observe a low percentage, only 12%, of misclassifications from classes B and C to class A.

We note that Trans1 does not apply the basic syntactic rules, i.e. the subject-verb agreement, the subject-predicate agreement, as well as the modifiers agreements (attributive adjectives, predicate adjectives). Non-agreement is also observed in genitive constructions (possessive case, subjective and objective genitives), when of course there is not *of* (genitive case) or *by*. However, it has been found that Trans1 has, in many cases, a richer vocabulary than Trans2 and Trans3. In addition, Trans1 retains the main names, as Trans2 also does, in the Latin script, as it is considered right, and does the same in words not existing in its vocabulary, avoiding false and unrelated translations, as in Trans2 and Trans3 sometimes occurs. Trans2 applies the above agreements, but not always successfully. Trans2 disposes quite satisfactory vocabulary, but not always about words that having more than two basic meanings. However, as it has been said, Trans2 translates all the common words, even those that do not exist in its vocabulary, breaking up compound words into their components and translating them, but, in some cases, this translation is wrong. Trans3 applies the above agreements more successfully than Trans2, it translates more successfully the components of compound words, but, as it has been said, Trans3 lags somewhat to the vocabulary richness.

It is important to know which features are more important to the classifier, so we tried the attribute evaluator technique (in Weka). Ratio of length in words and ratio of length in characters seem to be functional, as well as the Length Factor (LF), as we have described in Sect. 2.3. On the other hand, comparisons, like if Ref = Trans1-2-3, seem not to be so useful for the classifier.

3   Conclusions and Future Work

In conclusion, this study aimed at automatic data selection for machine translation. It is based on the processing of a sufficiently large parallel corpora database. In this regard, we considered the data selection task as a classification problem. More specifically, three translation models were used, which represent both the old approach (SMT) and the state of art (NMT) to MT. In this way, differences in the translation process and the approach of the three models become more apparent. 82 characteristics have been calculated and 2,687 segments have been annotated. For proper analysis, we pre-processed our data before using Weka tool. We used Smote to address the class imbalance problem in our data. The results recorded give a better translational prediction to model 3, which does not make much of an impression, as this is a sophisticated translation model. It is worth mentioning that the translation was from English to Greek, which increased the task complexity, since the Greek language is a morohologically rich language with ambiguities. One way to more accurately approach ambiguities in the future might be the use of data categorization. For example, grammatical categorization may prove far superior to the lexical features employed herein, an approach that has already been considered for the Greek language [19]. Furthermore, it could be studied whether the use of in-depth features influences the translation process, such as etymology, that is believed to be of great help for the Greek language.

It is worth asking ourselves whether we can find similar results amongst other language pairs, and this may be a new field for study.

References

1. Bahdanau, D., Cho, K., Bengio, Y.: Neural machine translation by jointly learning to align and translate. In: Proceedings of 3th International Conference on Learning Representations, pp. 1–15. ICLR, San Diego (2015)

2. Barrón-Cedeño, A., Màrquez Villodre, L., Henríquez Quintana, C.A., Formiga Fanals, L., Romero Merino, E., May, J.: Identifying useful human correction feedback from an on-line machine translation service. In: Proceedings of 23rd International Joint Conference on Artificial Intelligence, pp. 2057–2063. AAAI Press, Beijing (2013)
3. Bentivogli, L., Bisazza, A., Cettolo, M., Federico, M.: Neural versus phrase-based machine translation quality: a case study. In: Proceedings of the 2016 Conference on Empirical Methods in Natural Language Processing, pp. 257–267. ACL, Austin (2016)
4. Breiman, L.: Random forests. Mach. Learn. 45(1), 5–32 (2001)
5. Broder, A.Z.: On the resemblance and containment of documents. In: Proceedings of the Compression and Complexity of Sequences, pp. 21–29. IEEE Computer Society Washington, Washington (1997)
6. Chawla, N.V., Bowyer, K.W., Hall, L.O., Kegelmeyer, W.P.: SMOTE: synthetic minority over-sampling technique. J. Artif. Intell. Res. 16, 321–357 (2002)
7. Daskalaki, S., Kopanas, I., Avouris, N.: Evaluation of classifiers for an uneven class distribution problem. Appl. Artif. Intell. 20(5), 381–417 (2006)
8. Koehn, P., Hoang, H., Birch, A., Callison-Burch, C., Federico, M., Bertoldi, N., Dyer, C.: Moses: open source toolkit for statistical machine translation. In: Proceedings of the 45th Annual Meeting of the ACL on Interactive Poster and Demonstration Sessions, pp. 177–180. ACL, Prague (2007)
9. Koehn, P., Och, F.J., Marcu, D.: Statistical phrase-based translation. In: Proceedings of the 2003 Conference of the North American Chapter of the Association for Computational Linguistics on Human Language Technology, pp. 48–54. ACL, Edmonton (2003)
10. Kordoni, V., Birch, L., Buliga, I., Cholakov, K., Egg, M., Gaspari, F., Georgakopoulou, Y., Gialama, M., Hendrickx, I.H.E., Jermol, M., Kermanidis, K., Moorkens, J., Orlic, D., Papadopoulos, M., Popovic, M., Sennrich, R., Sosoni, V., Tsoumakos, D., Van den Bosch, A., van Zaanen, M.; Way, A.: TraMOOC (Translation for Massive Open Online Courses): providing reliable MT for MOOCs. In: Proceedings of the 19th Annual Conference of the European Association for Machine Translation (EAMT), pp. 376–400. European Association for Machine Translation (EAMT), Riga, (2016)
11. Miceli Barone, A.V., Haddow, B., Germann, U., Sennrich, R.: Regularization techniques for fine-tuning in neural machine translation. In: Proceedings of the 2017 Conference on Empirical Methods in Natural Language Processing, pp. 1489–1494. ACL, Copenhagen (2017)
12. Peris, Á., Cebrián, L., Casacuberta, F.: Online Learning for Neural Machine Translation Post-editing. Cornell University Library arXiv preprint 1, pp. 1–12 (2017). arXiv:1706.03196
13. Pighin, D., Màrquez, L., May, J.: An analysis (and an annotated corpus) of user responses to machine translation output. In: Proceedings of the 8th International Conference on Language Resources and Evaluation, pp. 1131–1136. European Language Resources Association (ELRA), Istanbul (2012)
14. Pouliquen, B., Steinberger, R., Ignat, C.: Automatic identification of document translations in large multilingual document collections. In: Proceedings of the International Conference Recent Advances in Natural Language Processing (RANLP), pp. 401–408. Recent Advances in Natural Language Processing (RANLP), Borovets (2003)
15. Sennrich, R., Firat, O., Cho, K., Birch-Mayne, A., Haddow, B., Hitschler, J., Junczys-Dowmunt, M., Läubli, S., Miceli Barone, A., Mokry, J., Nădejde, M.: Nematus: a toolkit for neural machine translation. In: Proceedings of the EACL 2017 Software Demonstrations, pp. 65–68. ACL, Valencia (2017)
16. Sennrich, R., Haddow, B., Birch, A.: Neural machine translation of rare words with subword units. In: Proceedings of the 54th Annual Meeting of the Association for Computational Linguistics, pp. 1715–1725. ACL, Berlin (2016)

17. Sharaf, A., Feng, S., Nguyen, K., Brantley, K., Daumé III, H.: The UMD neural machine translation systems at WMT 2017 bandit learning task. In: Proceedings of the Conference on Machine Translation (WMT), pp. 667–673. ACL, Copenhagen (2017)
18. Singhal, S., Jena, M.: A study on WEKA tool for data preprocessing, classification and clustering. Int. J Innovative Technol. Explor. Eng. (IJITEE) 2(6), 250–253 (2013)
19. Stamatatos, E., Fakotakis, N., Kokkinakis, G.: Automatic text categorization in terms of genre and author. Comput. Linguist. 26(4), 6–15 (2000)

The Biomolecular Computation Paradigm: A Survey in Massive Biological Computation

Georgios Drakopoulos[1]([✉]), Dimitrios Tsolis[2], Antonia Stefani[3]([✉]),
and Phivos Mylonas[1]([✉])

[1] Department of Informatics, Ionian University,
Plateia Tsirigoti 7, Kerkyra 49100, Hellas
{c16drak,fmylonas}@ionio.gr
[2] Department of Cultural Heritage Management and New Technologies,
University of Patras, G. Seferi 2, Agrinio 30100, Hellas
dtsolis@upatras.gr
[3] Hellenic Open University, Tsamadou 13-15, Achaia 26222, Hellas
stefani@eap.gr

Abstract. Biomolecular computation is the scientific field focusing on the theory and practice of encoding combinatorial problems in ordinary DNA strands and applying standard biology lab operations such as cleansing and complementary sequence generation to them in order to compute an exact solution. The primary advantage offered by this computational paradigm is massive parallelism as the solution space is simultaneously searched. On the other hand, factors that need to addressed under this model are the DNA volume growth and computational errors attributed to inexact DNA matching. Biomolecular computation additionally paves the way for two- and three-dimensional self assemblying biological tiles which are closely linked at a theoretical level to a Turing machine, establishing thus its computational power. Applications include medium sized instances of TSP and the evaluation of the output of bounded fan-out Boolean circuits.

Keywords: Biomolecular computation · DNA computation
Computing paradigm · Computational media · Parallel computing
CREW PRAM · TSP · Boolean circuits
Nondeterministic Turing machine

1 Introduction

The seminal paper [19] is widely known for essentially establishing the field of quantum computing. However, a lesser known offshoot is *biomolecular computing*, alternatively known as *DNA computing*. The founding notions of this computational paradigm were presented in [2], where it was proposed that regular DNA strands can represent combinatorial inputs instead of the functions of

Published by Springer International Publishing AG 2018. All Rights Reserved
L. Iliadis et al. (Eds.): AIAI 2018, IFIP AICT 520, pp. 157–167, 2018.
https://doi.org/10.1007/978-3-319-92016-0_15

a living organism. Then standard lab operations can be applied to these strands in order to extract strands containing a solution. As a concrete application, the TSP was solved exactly through a brute force methodology in a medium sized graph $G = (V, E)$ in $O(|V| + |E|)$ elementary operations and $O(\log |V|)$ DNA strands, indicating the potential of massive parallelism. This was repeated in [32] with a different algorithmic approach though in the sequence of lab operations, establishing the fact that novel and efficient algorithms are also necessary in this computational paradigm.

The primary objective of this survey is to concisely summarize the principles and notions of the paradigm of biomolecular computing with an emphasis on the potential for massively parallel computations. The latter may well serve in the dawn of the big data and 5 V era as an unconventional inspiration for the designers of parallel algorithms or distributed systems.

The remaining of this survery is structured as follows. Section 2 summarizes the principal concepts of biomolecular computing, the connections to known computational models, and describes computational applications not examined elsewhere in this survey. The elementary operations, advantages, and disadvantages of the biomolecular paradigm are explained in Sect. 3. The most important application, namely TSP, is described in Sect. 4. The parallelism potential is explored in Sect. 5, while factors working against the computation scale up are investigated in Sects. 6 and 7. The main points are summarized in Sect. 8 and certain conclusions are drawn. Finally, Table 1 summarizes the survey notation.

Table 1. Survey notation.

Symbol	Meaning
$\triangleq$	Definition or equality by definition
$\lceil s \rceil, \lfloor s \rfloor$	DNA strand s in 5-3 and 3-5 direction respectively
$\bar{s}$	Complementary DNA strand of s in 5-3 direction
$|s|$	Length (number of bases) of DNA strand s
$s_1 \parallel s_2$	Strands s_1 and s_2 match completely
$s_1 \sqsupset s_2$	Strand s_2 matches to the right side of s_1
$s_1 \sqsubset s_2$	Strand s_2 matches to the left side of s_1
$s_1 \sqcup s_2$	Strand s_2 matches to a middle segment of s_1
$s_1 \nparallel s_2$	Strands s_1 and s_2 do not match
$s_1 \cap s_2 = k$	Strands s_1 and s_2 overlap in k bases
$|S|$	Cardinality of set S
$\mathrm{E}[X]$	Mean value of random variable X
$\mathrm{Var}[X]$	Variance of random variable X

2   Previous Work

As stated earlier, the groundwork for the paradigm of biomolecular computing was laid in [2] followed by [32]. Soon, notions and applications emerged as noted in the early surveys [40,45,47]. The computational power of the paradigm is explored in [6,9] and its limits in [18]. The enormous potential for parallelism is highlighted in [21–24,43]. The notion of self assembly was applied to this paradigm in [1,31,48]. According to this principle, which is reminiscent of non-supervised learning, DNA tiles in a test tube given proper mobility conditions and time can attach themselves to tiles or strands containing fully or partial complementary sequences without human intervention in two [50,51] or three dimensions [28]. Issues pertaining to complexity of the biomolecular paradigm are examined from various viewpoints in [4,29,46].

Another way to examine the potential and the complexity of biomolecular computation is through the simulation of the operation of sequential, bounded fan-in Boolean circuits with DNA strands as first shown in [3,36] and described in detail in the follow up work [39]. Questions regarding the complexity of constructing and evaluating the output of such circuits are addressed in [34,35,37], whereas self assembling circuits are investigated in [38].

Among the algorithmic applications of biomolecular computation are the brute force parallel solution of k-SAT in [13] and in [5], dynamic programming on the Cell Matrix architecture [49], and splicing systems [11]. Shortest path algorithms implemented in biomolecular elementary operations are presented in [33] and in [42]. Length bounded computing with DNA strands and its connections to space complexity are explored in [20]. An evolutionary algorithm also expressed these operations is described in [12].

Finally, steps regarding the implementation of a DNA computer are given in [25,26,41,44], although these proposals vary. DNA operations can be also simulated over Neo4j with properties in edges corresponding to physical or chemical DNA properties in an approach similar to the one presented in [30] for implementing persistent data structures. Concerning software, a fully functional graphical computing environment for biomolecular computation is described in [10]. It also includes DNA C, a C variant which is a combination of the C constructs pertaining to integers with an extension implementing the fundamental operations of biomolecular computing. The exclusion of floating point arithmetic should not come as a surprise, since biomolecular computation is discrete in nature and has been so far applied only in combinatorial problems. Nonetheless, should the need arise, floating point numbers can be approximated fairly well by rationals or by continued fractions. For instance, the golden ratio φ is represented by the infinite fraction[1]

$$\varphi = 1 + \cfrac{1}{1 + \cfrac{1}{1 + \cfrac{1}{1 + \dots}}} \tag{1}$$

---

[1] OEIS sequence A000012.

3 Paradigm Notions

3.1 Definition

Knowledge transfer and inspiration between computer science and biology has been fruitful. This relationship has already resulted in bioinformatics, connectomics, and computational biology. One of them, with direct reference to the everyday laboratory handling of DNA strands, is the paradigm of biomolecular computation which can be formally defined as

Definition 1. *Biomolecular computing is the art and science of using DNA strands as computational medium to appropriately encode candidate solutions to (possibly intractable for a Turing machine) combinatorial problems and using standard biological laboratory techniques in order to select an exact solution.*

From Definition 1 follows that any DNA encoding corresponds strictly to candidate solutions of a combinatorial problem and not to the design and functions of a living being. Also, the difference from the fields of bioinformatics and computational biology should be clear. Although the inspiration, terminology, and implementation are biological, the paradigm is definitiely computational as the objective is to codify and efficiently solve instances of intractable, at least under the conventional Turing machine model, combinatorial problems.

3.2 Abstract DNA Operations

Under the biomolecular computation paradigm the elementary operations applied to the DNA strands in the test tube are the following.

- **Initialize** (T_0): Crate a test tube T_0 containing each admissible candidate solution for a combinatorial problem according to a probability distribution, usually the uniform one.
- **Copy**(T_0, T_1): Copy the contents of T_0 to the tube of T_1.
- **Merge**(T_0, T_1): Mix the contents of T_0 and T_1 to T_0.
- **Detect**(T_0): Examine whether T_0 is empty.
- **Select**(T_0, s_0): Extract s_0, if present, from T_0.
- **Extract**(ℓ): Extract strands of length ℓ.
- **Cleavage**(s_0, σ_0): Slice s_0 according to the shorter template strand σ_0.
- **Anneal**(s_0): Create double DNRA strands from a single one.
- **Denature**(s_0): Create single DNA strands from a double one.
- **Ligate**(T_0): Create bonds between double strands inside tube T_0.

The basic storage unit in this paradigm is the test tube which may contain a fixed volume of DNA strands. The latter are not necessarily of the same type. In fact, the opposite is quite common as the tube contains the results of a sequence of lab operations applied to a set of candidate solutions. It is only after the end of these operations where the solution, if any, to the instance at hand is extracted and cultivated that a test tube may contain only copies of a single strand.

4 TSP

Perhaps the most well known biomolecular algorithm is the one shown in algorithm 1 for solving TSP for a graph $G = (V, E)$. Notice this is a brute force method which can be used among others to discover community structure in graphs as in [15,27]. However, this approach could not be a basis for heuristic techniques such as those in [16,17]. The primary characteristic of algorithm 1 is that all paths of length j are created in j steps. Assume that each vertex is encoded with b_v and each edge with b_e bases. Each vertex v_k has a unique coding s_k in DNA bases, while the edge (v_i, v_j) is encoded as the concatenation of $\bar{s}_i$ and $\bar{s}_j$.

Algorithm 1. TSP expressed in biomolecular operations

Require: tubes T_0, T_v with encoded vertices; tube T_e with encoded edges
Ensure: a Hamilton circle is found
1: **initialize**(T_0)
2: **for** $j \leftarrow 1$ **to** $|V|$ **do**
3:     **merge**(T_0, T_e)
4:     **merge**(T_0, T_v)
5:     **ligate**(T_0)
6: **end for**
7: **extract**($|V| (b_v + b_e)$)
8: **denature**(T_0)
9: **return detect**(T_0)

---

5 Parallelism

Theoretically, the biomolecular computation paradigm can be reduced to simulating a CREW PRAM, a version of RAM with $P > 1$ processors and M memory locations where multiple processors can read the same memory address but only one can write any given time at a given memory address. The CREW PRAM operation set LOAD, READ, WRITE as well as the memory configuration of this machine can be simulated by a sequence of biomolecular operations as shown in [46] through a sequence of successive configurations of length $O(\log(PM))$ each. Starting from a random configuration, mixing a sequence of admissible configurations, at the expense of a multiplicatively growing volume, finally yields one superconfiguration of concatenated configurations representing a desired sequence of computation, assuming that one can be found. By repeatedly applying cleavage operations, the individual configurations are extracted.

Another way to quantify the actual parallelism offered by the biomolecular paradigm is to use Amdahl's law as a benchmark

$$\Gamma \triangleq \frac{1}{(1 - \gamma_0) + \dfrac{\gamma_0}{s}}, \qquad 0 \leq \gamma_0 < 1 \tag{2}$$

where Γ is the actual speedup, γ_0 is the parallelizable part of the task, and s is the speedup of that part. Thus, the size of the parallelizable part plays a crucial role and essentially defines how much can be actually sped up as for infinite s

$$\Gamma \to \frac{1}{1 - \gamma_0} \tag{3}$$

6   Error Free Computations

6.1   Overview

Errors in the biomolecular computation can be classified into two broad categories. The first source of errors lies in the encoding of candidate solutions as there can be partial DNA matches which may eventually create false final solutions, in other words creating false positives. Moreover, the elementary operations described above may not be executed with absolute sucess due to a number of factors. This might create depending on the nature of the operations involved either false positives or false negatives.

6.2   Encoding

Concerning the solution encoding, an obvious approach might be to choose an encoding with controllable redundancy β_0. Namely, each bit of information is expressed with $\alpha_0 = 1 + \beta_0$ bits in total and on average. Thus, the ratio ρ_0 of original to redundant information is

$$\rho_0 \triangleq \frac{1}{\beta_0} = \frac{1}{\alpha_0 - 1} < 1 \tag{4}$$

For instance, in a graph problem with $|V|$ if each vertex normally requires $\lceil \log|V| \rceil$ bits to encode, then it would require α_0 times as much.

Regarding the number of false negatives or false positives, it can be argued that it is proportional to the partial matches of DNA strings. While there is a case where an intended match of two DNA strands s_1 and s_2 fails, strand mismatches denoted by $s_1 \nparallel s_2$ can be considered accurate for the most part. On the contrary, partial matches either from left or from right are with high probability indicators of failed operations, especially if the two strands overlap in only a few bases. For a single biomolecular step in the same test tube T_0, let

$$
\begin{aligned}
u &= |s_1 \parallel s_2| \\
u_r(k) &= |s_1 \sqsupset s_2, s_1 \cap s_2 = k| \\
u_l(k) &= |s_1 \sqsubset s_2, s_1 \cap s_2 = k| \\
u_m &= |s_1 \sqcup s_2| \\
u_o &= |s_1 \nparallel s_2|
\end{aligned}
\tag{5}
$$

denote respectively the number of DNA perfect matches, right and left matches in k bases, middle matches and no matches. Thus, in a single biomolecular step the ratios of true matches Q^+ and true mismatches Q^- are

$$Q^+ \triangleq \frac{u + u_m}{u + u_m + \sum_{k=1}^{|s_2|} u_r(k) + \sum_{k=1}^{|s_2|} u_l(k)}$$

$$Q^- \triangleq \frac{u_o}{u_o + \sum_{k=1}^{|s_2|} u_r(k) + \sum_{k=1}^{|s_2|} u_l(k)} \qquad (6)$$

Another way to assess the reliability of a sequence of n_0 biomolecular operations is the following. Let π_k be the success probability of each operation. The success probability π^+ by the product rule, assuming operation independence, is

$$\pi^+ \triangleq \prod_{k=1}^{n_0} \pi_k = \pi_1 \dots \pi_{n_0} \qquad (7)$$

Thus, if $\mu_1 \leq \pi_k \leq \mu_2$, then the following bounds can be derived

$$e^{-n_0 \mu_2} \leq \pi^+ \leq e^{-n_0 \mu_1} \qquad (8)$$

Perhaps a more accurate way to assess the average value of π^+ is to consider the geometric mean of the sequence

$$\bar{\pi} \triangleq \left(\prod_{k=1}^{n_0} \pi_k \right)^{\frac{1}{n_0}} = \mu_1 \left(\prod_{k=1}^{n_0} \left(1 + \frac{\eta_k}{\mu_1} \right) \right)^{\frac{1}{n_0}}, \quad \pi_k = \mu_1 + \eta_k \qquad (9)$$

6.3   Trials

Due to the nature of the actual biological operations, they are not always executed with absolute correctness. This can be attributed to a number of reasons including the age, technology, and condition of lab equipment, the chemistry and quantity of DNA strands themselves, the nature of bonds between strands, and lab conditions such as radiation and electomagnetic pulses of various frequences. As a result, a strand encoding an invalid solution can emerge from the test tubes or a strand containing the solution can be missed in them [7,8].

The geometric distribution models sequences of test outcomes where the probability of success is p_0. Its probability mass function is defined as

$$\text{prob}\{X = k\} \triangleq p_0(1 - p_0)^k, \quad k \in \mathbb{Z}^+ \qquad (10)$$

The interpretation of X is that it models the number of failed attempts of an experiment before the single successful outcome of that experiment. The mean value of this distribution is readily calculated in equation (11).

$$\text{E}[X] \triangleq \sum_{k=0}^{+\infty} k \, \text{prob}\{X = k\} = \frac{1 - p_0}{p_0} = e^{\text{logit}(1-p_0)} \qquad (11)$$

The logit $(\cdot)$ function is the inverse of the sigmoid function extensively used to train deep recurrent and tensor stack networks [14] expresses the logarithm of the odds of a single Bernoulli trial. Also is a special case of a link function to the generalized linear model and leads to the logistic regression, commonly found in deep learning applications.

The variance of X is its mean value scaled by the success probabilty p_0. This is coherent with intuition, since the larger p_0, the fewer attempts are required to achieve success and the number of failed attempts will be close to zero.

$$\mathrm{Var}\,[X] \triangleq \sum_{k=0}^{+\infty} (k - \mathrm{E}\,[X])^2 \,\mathrm{prob}\,\{X = k\} = \frac{1 - p_0}{p_0^2} = \frac{\mathrm{E}\,[X]}{p_0} \qquad (12)$$

7   Volume Considerations

The major practical limitation of biomolecular computation is the volume neces-sary to represent each candidate solution. This is limited not only by the volume of the test tube, but also by the encoding which, in turn, implies a redundancy rate to ensure higher operation success probabilites. If V_0 is the hard limit for the test tube volume, α_0 the encoding redundancy factor, n is the number of candidate solutions, and ℓ_0 the solution length, then

$$V_0 \geq (a_0 n \ell_0)^{1+\epsilon} \Leftrightarrow n \leq \frac{1}{a_0 \ell_0} V_0^{\frac{1}{1+\epsilon_0}} \qquad (13)$$

where ϵ_0 is a constant which depends on a number of diverse factors such as lab temperature and tube technology. If a biomolecular computation requires J_0 steps to complete, then the required volume grows exponentially. Then, the above limit should be modified as

$$n \leq \frac{1}{a_0 \ell_0} V_0^{\frac{1}{J_0(1+\epsilon_0)}} \qquad (14)$$

8   Conclusions

This survey explores the foundations, applications, and limits of biomolecular computation which represents an alternative computational paradigm. The lat-ter is based on the handling of potentially very long strands of ordinary DNA using standard biology lab operations such as annealing, generating a comple-mentary strand, selecting a strand, or concatenating two strands. These strands do not codify the inner workings of any living organism. Instead, they contain a suitably selected representation of a computational problem. By selecting an appropriate representation of an input instance, a plethora of various output instances are created by a series of biological operations. Although a fraction of the abovementioned output instances may contain incomplete operations and must be removed by cleansing operations, their majority will contain with high probability a solution.

Acknowledgments. The financial support by the European Union and Greece (Partnership Agreement for the Development Framework 2014–2020) under the Regional Operational Programme Ionian Islands 2014–2020 for the project "Smart vine variety selection and management using ICT - EYOINOS" is gratefully acknowledged.

References

1. Adleman, L., Cheng, Q., Goel, A., Huang, M.D., Kempe, D., De Espanes, P.M., Rothemund, P.W.K.: Combinatorial optimization problems in self-assembly. In: STOC, pp. 23–32 (2002)
2. Adleman, L.M.: Molecular computation of solutions to combinatorial problems. Nature **369** (1994)
3. Amos, M., Dunne, P.E.: DNA simulation of Boolean circuits. In: Proceedings of 3rd Annual Genetic Programming Conference, pp. 679–683 (1997)
4. Amos, M., Gibbons, A., Dunne, P.E.: The complexity and viability of DNA. In: Biocomputing and emergent computation: Proceedings of BCEC97 (1997)
5. Baum, E.B., Boneh, D.: Running dynamic programming algorithms on a DNA computer. DNA Based Comput. **II**(44), 77–80 (1999)
6. Beigel, R., Fu, B.: Solving intractable problems with DNA computing. In: IEEE Conference on Computational Complexity, p. 154 (1998)
7. Bijlani, R., Cheng, Y., Pearce, D.A., Brooks, A.I., Ogihara, M.: Prediction of biologically significant components from microarray data: independently consistent expression discriminator (ICED). Bioinformatics **19**(1), 62–70 (2003)
8. Boneh, D., Dunworth, C., Lipton, R.J., Sgall, J.: Making DNA computers error resistant. DNA Based Comput. **II**(44), 163–170 (1996)
9. Boneh, D., Dunworth, C., Lipton, R.J., Sgall, J.: On the computational power of DNA. Discrete Appl. Math. **71**(1–3), 79–94 (1996)
10. Carroll, S.: A complete programming environment for DNA computation. In: Workshop Non-Silicon Comp. NSC-1, pp. 46–53 (2002)
11. Dassen, J.: Molecular computation and splicing systems. Master's thesis, Leiden University (1996)
12. Deaton, R., Murphy, R.C., Rose, J.A., Garzon, M., Franceschetti, D.R., Stevens, S.: A DNA based implementation of an evolutionary search for good encodings for DNA computation. In: International Conference on Evolutionary Computation, pp. 267–271. IEEE (1997)
13. Díaz, S., Esteban, J.L., Ogihara, M.: A DNA-based random walk method for solving k-SAT. In: Condon, A., Rozenberg, G. (eds.) DNA 2000. LNCS, vol. 2054, pp. 209–220. Springer, Heidelberg (2001). https://doi.org/10.1007/3-540-44992-2_14
14. Drakopoulos, G.: Knowledge mining with tensor algebra. Tech. rep., Ionian University October 2017. https://doi.org/10.13140/RG.2.2.25548.92803
15. Drakopoulos, G., Kanavos, A., Karydis, I., Sioutas, S., Vrahatis, A.G.: Tensor-based semantically-aware topic clustering of biomedical documents. Computation **5**(3), 34 (2017)
16. Drakopoulos, G., Kanavos, A., Tsakalidis, A.: A Neo4j implementation of fuzzy random walkers. In: SETN May 2016
17. Drakopoulos, G., Kanavos, A., Tsakalidis, K.: Fuzzy random walkers with second order bounds: an asymmetric analysis. Algorithms **10**(2), 40 (2017)
18. Dunne, P.E., Amos, M., Gibbons, A.: Boolean transitive closure in DNA (1998)
19. Feynman, R.P.: There is plenty of room at the bottom. Eng. Sci. **23**(5), 22–36 (1960)

20. Fu, B., Beigel, R.: Length bounded molecular computing. BioSyst. **52**(1), 155–163 (1999)
21. Gehani, A., Reif, J.: Micro flow bio-molecular computation. Biosyst. **52**(1), 197–216 (1999)
22. Gorban, A.N., Gorbunova, K.O., Wunsch, D.C.: Liquid brain: the proof of algorithmic universality of quasichemical model of fine-grained parallelism. Neural Netw. World **11**(4), 391–412 (2001)
23. Gusfield, D.: Algorithms on Strings, Trees and Sequences: Computer Science and Computational Biology. Cambridge University Press, Cambridge (1997)
24. Henaut, A., Contamine, D.: Computation with DNA. Tech. rep., Rapport de recherche - Institut national de recherche en informatique et en automatique (1996)
25. Hinze, T., Sturm, M.: Towards an in-vitro implementation of a universal distributed splicing model for DNA computation. In: Proceedings of Theorietag pp. 185–189 (2000)
26. Hoheisel, J.D., Vingron, M.: DNA chip technology. Biospektrum **4**, 17–20 (1998)
27. Kanavos, A., Drakopoulos, G., Tsakalidis, A.: Graph community discovery algorithms in Neo4j with a regularization-based evaluation metric. In: WEBIST, April 2017
28. Ming-Yang, K., Ramachandran, V.: DNA self-assembly for constructing 3D boxes. In: Eades, P., Takaoka, T. (eds.) ISAAC 2001. LNCS, vol. 2223, pp. 429–441. Springer, Heidelberg (2001). https://doi.org/10.1007/3-540-45678-3_37
29. Karp, R.M., Kenyon, C., Waarts, O.: Error resilient DNA computation. In: SODA, pp. 458–467 (1996)
30. Kontopoulos, S., Drakopoulos, G.: A space efficient scheme for graph representation. In: ICTAI. IEEE, November 2014
31. LaBean, T.H., Yan, H., Kopatsch, J., Liu, F., Winfree, E., Reif, J.H., Seeman, N.C.: Construction, analysis, ligation, and self-assembly of DNA triple crossover complexes. J. Am. Chem. Soc. **122**(9), 1848–1860 (2000)
32. Lipton, R.J.: Speeding up computations via molecular biology. DNA Based Comput. **27**, 67–74 (1995)
33. Narayanan, A., Zorbalas, S.: DNA algorithms for computing shortest paths. In: Proceedings of Genetic Programming, vol. 718, p. 723 (1998)
34. Ogihara, M.: Relating the minimum model for DNA computation and Boolean circuits. In: Proceedings of the 1st Annual Conference on Genetic and Evolutionary Computation, vol. 2, pp. 1817–1821. Morgan-Kaufmann Publishers Inc. (1999)
35. Ogihara, M., Ray, A.: Circuit evaluation: Thoughts on a killer application in DNA computing. Comput. Bio-Molecules. Theor. Exp. 111–126 (1998)
36. Ogihara, M., Ray, A.: DNA-based self-propagating algorithm for solving bounded-fan-in Boolean circuits. Genet. Program. **98**, 725–730 (1998)
37. Ogihara, M., Ray, A.: The minimum DNA computation model and its computational power. In: Unconventional Models of Computation, pp. 309–322 (1998)
38. Ogihara, M., Ray, A.: Executing parallel logical operations with DNA. In: Proceedings of the 1999 Congress on Evolutionary Computation, vol. 2, pp. 972–979. IEEE (1999)
39. Ogihara, M., Ray, A.: Simulating Boolean circuits on a DNA computer. Algorithmica **25**(2–3), 239–250 (1999)
40. Pisanti, N.: DNA computing: a survey. Bull. EATCS **64**, 188–216 (1998)
41. Qiu, Z.F., Lu, M.: Take advantage of the computing power of DNA computers. In: Rolim, J. (ed.) IPDPS 2000. LNCS, vol. 1800, pp. 570–577. Springer, Heidelberg (2000). https://doi.org/10.1007/3-540-45591-4_78

42. Reif, J.H.: Paradigms for biomolecular computation. In: First International Conference on Unconventional Models of Computation, pp. 72–93 (1998)
43. Reif, J.H.: Parallel biomolecular computation: models and simulations. Algorithmica **25**(2), 142–175 (1999)
44. Reif, J.H.: Successes and failures. Science **296**, 478–479 (2002)
45. Reif, J.H.: The emergence of the discipline of biomolecular computation in the US (2002). http://citeseer.nj.nec.com/reif02emergence.html
46. Reif, J.H.: The design of autonomous DNA nanomechanical devices: walking and rolling DNA. In: Hagiya, M., Ohuchi, A. (eds.) DNA 2002. LNCS, vol. 2568, pp. 22–37. Springer, Heidelberg (2003). https://doi.org/10.1007/3-540-36440-4_3
47. Rooß, D.: Recent developments in DNA computing. In: Proceedings of the 27th International Symposium on Multiple Valued Logic, pp. 3–9 (1997)
48. Rothemund, P.W., Winfree, E.: The program-size complexity of self-assembled squares. In: STOC, pp. 459–468. ACM (2000)
49. Wang, B.: Implementation of a dynamic programming algorithm for DNA Sequence alignment on the Cell Matrix architecture. Master's thesis, Utah State University, Department of Computer Science (2002)
50. Wąsiewicz, P., Borsuk, P., Mulawka, J.J., Węgleński, P.: Implementation of data flow logical operations via self-assembly of DNA. In: Rolim, J., et al. (eds.) IPPS 1999. LNCS, vol. 1586, pp. 174–182. Springer, Heidelberg (1999). https://doi.org/10.1007/BFb0097898
51. Yan, H., LaBean, T.H., Feng, L., Reif, J.H.: Directed nucleation assembly of DNA tile complexes for barcode-patterned lattices. Proc. Natl. Acad. Sci. **100**(14), 8103–8108 (2003)

How Much Different Are Two Words with Different Shortest Periods

Mai Alzamel[1], Maxime Crochemore[1,2], Costas S. Iliopoulos[1],
Tomasz Kociumaka[3], Ritu Kundu[1], Jakub Radoszewski[1,3(✉)],
Wojciech Rytter[3], and Tomasz Waleń[3]

[1] Department of Informatics, King's College London, London, UK
{mai.alzamel,maxime.crochemore,costas.iliopoulos,ritu.kundu}@kcl.ac.uk
[2] Université Paris-Est, Marne-la-Vallée, France
[3] Faculty of Mathematics, Informatics and Mechanics, University of Warsaw,
Warsaw, Poland
{kociumaka,jrad,rytter,walen}@mimuw.edu.pl

Abstract. Sometimes the difference between two distinct words of the same length cannot be smaller than a certain minimal amount. In particular if two distinct words of the same length are both periodic or quasiperiodic, then their Hamming distance is at least 2. We study here how the minimum Hamming distance $dist(x, y)$ between two words x, y of the same length n depends on their periods. Similar problems were considered in [1] in the context of quasiperiodicities. We say that a period p of a word x is *primitive* if x does not have any smaller period p' which divides p. For integers p, n ($p \leq n$) we define $\mathcal{P}_p(n)$ as the set of words of length n with primitive period p. We show several results related to the following functions introduced in this paper for $p \neq q$ and $n \geq \max(p, q)$.

$$\mathcal{D}_{p,q}(n) = \min \{ dist(x, y) \ : \ x \in \mathcal{P}_p(n), \ y \in \mathcal{P}_q(n) \},$$
$$N_{p,q}(h) = \max \{ n \ : \ \mathcal{D}_{p,q}(n) \leq h \}.$$

1 Introduction

Consider a word x of length $|x| = n$, with its positions numbered 0 through $n - 1$. We say that x has a period p if $x_i = x_{i+p}$ for all $0 \leq i < n - p$. Our work can be seen as a quest to extend Fine and Wilf's Periodicity Lemma [14], which is a ubiquitous tool of combinatorics on words.

Lemma 1 (Periodicity Lemma [14]). *If a word x has periods p and q and $|x| \geq p + q - \mathrm{GCD}(p, q)$, then x also has a period $\mathrm{GCD}(p, q)$.*

Other known extensions of this lemma include a variant with three [10] and an arbitrary number of specified periods [11,16,17,23], the so-called new periodicity

---

W. Rytter—Supported by the Polish National Science Center, grant no 2014/13/B/ST6/00770.

L. Iliadis et al. (Eds.): AIAI 2018, IFIP AICT 520, pp. 168–178, 2018.
https://doi.org/10.1007/978-3-319-92016-0_16

lemma [3,13], a periodicity lemma for repetitions that involve morphisms [19], and extensions into periodicity of partial words [4–9,22], into abelian [12] and k-abelian [18] periodicity, into bidimensional words [20], and other variations [15,21].

We say that a word x of length n is *periodic* if it has a period p such that $2p \leq n$. For two words x and y of length n, by $dist(x,y)$ we denote their Hamming distance being the number of positions $i = 0,\ldots,n-1$ such that $x_i \neq y_i$. The following folklore fact gives a lower bound on how different are two distinct periodic words. Its proof can be found in [1].

Fact 2. *If x and y are distinct periodic words of the same length, then $dist(x,y) \neq 1$.*

We present several generalizations of this fact.

Results similar to Fact 2 were presented recently in the context of quasiperiodicity [1]. We say that a word x has a *cover* u if each position in x is located inside an occurrence of u in x. The word x is called *quasiperiodic* if it has a cover u other than x. In [1] the following generalization of Fact fct:folklore was shown: $dist(x,y) > 1$ for any two distinct quasiperiodic words x, y of the same length. This type of fact has potential applications; see [2].

There is a quantitative difference between periods and covers. For example, there are words x and y of length 1024 with shortest covers of length 4 and 5, respectively, and $dist(x,y) = 2$:

$$x = (abaa)^{256} \quad \text{and} \quad y = aaba(abaa)^{255}$$

with covers $abaa$ and $aabaa$. However, if x and y are words of length 1024 with shortest periods 4 and 5, respectively, then we must have $dist(x,y) \geq 357$.

We say that a period p of a word x is *primitive* if no proper divisor of p is a period of x, i.e., if $p' \mid p$ and p' is a period of x, then $p' = p$. We define

$$\mathcal{P}_p(n) = \{\, |x| = n,\ p \text{ is a primitive period of } x \,\}.$$

The ultimate goal of this work is a characterization of the function $\mathcal{D}_{p,q}$ defined for $p \neq q$ and $n \geq \max(p,q)$ as:

$$\mathcal{D}_{p,q}(n) = \min\{\, dist(x,y) \ : \ x \in \mathcal{P}_p(n), y \in \mathcal{P}_q(n) \,\}.$$

As $\mathcal{D}_{p,q}$ is non-decreasing for given p,q, it can be described by the following auxiliary function:

$$N_{p,q}(h) = \max\{\, n \ : \ \mathcal{D}_{p,q}(n) \leq h \,\}.$$

One can note that Lemma 1 can be equivalently formulated as $N_{p,q}(0) < p+q-\mathrm{GCD}(p,q)$ (Fig. 1). Similarly, an equivalent formulation of Fact 2 is $N_{p,q}(1) < 2q$.

Fine and Wilf [14] also proved that the bound $p+q-\mathrm{GCD}(p,q)$ of Lemma 1 cannot be improved. Consequently, $N_{p,q}(0) = p + q - \mathrm{GCD}(p,q) - 1$. On the other hand, we show that $N_{p,q}(1) = 2q - 1$ only for $p \mid q$. Hence, the bound $N_{p,q}(1) < 2q$ of Fact 2 is not tight in general.

Our Results. In Sect. 2 we consider the case that $p \mid q$. In the remaining sections, we only consider the case of $p < q$ and $p \nmid q$. In Sect. 3 we show exact values of the function $\mathcal{D}_{p,q}$ for $p + q - \mathrm{GCD}(p,q) \leq n \leq 2q$. In Sect. 4, we show the following bounds valid for abitrary $n \geq q$:

$$\left\lfloor \frac{n-q}{p} \right\rfloor \leq \mathcal{D}_{p,q}(n) \leq 2 \left\lceil \frac{n-q}{p} \right\rceil .$$

We also prove an alternative bound $\mathcal{D}_{p,q}(n) \geq \left\lfloor \frac{2n}{p+q} \right\rfloor$ valid for $n \geq p + q$.

h	$N_{3,4}(h)$	example
1	6	$a\,a\,b\,a\,a\,b$ $a\,a\,b\,a\,a\,a$
2	8	$a\,a\,b\,a\,a\,b\,a\,a$ $a\,a\,b\,a\,a\,a\,b\,a$
3	10	$a\,a\,b\,a\,a\,b\,a\,a\,b\,a$ $a\,a\,b\,a\,a\,a\,b\,a\,a\,a$
4	11	$a\,a\,b\,a\,a\,b\,a\,a\,b\,a\,a$ $a\,a\,b\,a\,a\,a\,b\,a\,a\,a\,b$
5	17	$a\,a\,b\,a\,a\,b\,a\,a\,b\,a\,a\,b\,a\,a\,b\,a\,a$ $a\,a\,b\,a\,a\,a\,b\,a\,a\,a\,b\,a\,a\,a\,b\,a\,a$

h	$N_{2,3}(h)$	example
0	3	$a\,b\,a$ $a\,b\,a$
1	4	$a\,b\,a\,b$ $a\,b\,a\,a$
2	5	$a\,b\,a\,b\,a$ $a\,b\,a\,a\,b$
3	9	$a\,b\,a\,b\,a\,b\,a\,b\,a$ $a\,b\,a\,a\,b\,a\,a\,b\,a$
4	10	$a\,b\,a\,b\,a\,b\,a\,b\,a\,b$ $a\,b\,a\,a\,b\,a\,a\,b\,a\,a$
5	11	$a\,b\,a\,b\,a\,b\,a\,b\,a\,b\,a$ $a\,b\,a\,a\,b\,a\,a\,b\,a\,a\,b$
6	15	$a\,b\,a\,b\,a\,b\,a\,b\,a\,b\,a\,b\,a\,b\,a$ $a\,b\,a\,a\,b\,a\,a\,b\,a\,a\,b\,a\,a\,b\,a$
7	16	$a\,b\,a\,b\,a\,b\,a\,b\,a\,b\,a\,b\,a\,b\,a\,b$ $a\,b\,a\,a\,b\,a\,a\,b\,a\,a\,b\,a\,a\,b\,a\,a$

Fig. 1. Upper table: values of $N_{3,4}(h)$ for $h = 1, \ldots, 5$ together with pairs of words of length $N_{3,4}(h)$ that have the Hamming distance h. Lower table: values of $N_{2,3}(h)$ for $h = 0, \ldots, 7$.

2 Preliminaries

Let us consider a finite alphabet Σ. If x is a word of length $|x| = n$, then by $x_i \in \Sigma$ for $i = 0, \ldots, n - 1$ we denote its ith letter. We say that a word v is a factor of a word x if there exist words u and w such that $x = uvw$. A factor v is called a prefix of x if u is an empty word in some such decomposition and a suffix if w is an empty word in some such decomposition. By $x[i..j]$ we denote the factor $x_i \ldots x_j$.

If $x_i = x_{i+p}$ for all $0 \le i < n - p$ for some integer p, then p is called *a period* of x and the prefix of x of length p is called *a string period* of x. If x has period p, then y is called a *periodic extension of x with period p* if y also has period p and has x as a prefix.

We say that a period p is *primitive* if no proper divisor of p is a period of x. Note that the shortest period (denoted $p = \mathbf{per}(x)$) is always primitive.

We say that a word x is *primitive* if there exists no other word u and integer $k > 1$ such that $x = u^k$. Note that p is a primitive period of x if and only if the corresponding string period is a primitive word. Two words x and y are each other's cyclic rotations if there exist words u and v such that $x = uv$ and $y = vu$. In this case we also say that $|u|$ is the shift between x and y.

For a sequence of positive integers $(a_1, \ldots, a_m)$, we define a $(a_1, \ldots, a_m)$-*decomposition* of a word x as a sequence of consecutive factors of x of lengths $a_1, \ldots, a_m, a_1, \ldots, a_m, \ldots$ The sequence ends at the last *complete* factor that can be cut out of x; see Fig. 2 for an example.

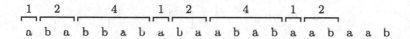

Fig. 2. The $(1, 2, 4)$-decomposition of *ababbabababaabababaabaab* is *a ba bbab a ba abab a aab*.

If $p \mid q$, we can give a simple complete characterization of functions $N_{p,q}$ and $\mathcal{D}_{p,q}$.

Fact 3. *If $p \mid q$ and $p < q$, then $\mathcal{D}_{p,q}(n) = \left\lfloor \frac{n}{q} \right\rfloor$ and $N_{p,q}(h) = q \cdot (h + 1) - 1$.*

Proof. We first show that $\mathcal{D}_{p,q}(n) \ge \left\lfloor \frac{n}{q} \right\rfloor$. Consider a positive integer n, words $x \in \mathcal{P}_p(n)$, $y \in \mathcal{P}_q(n)$, and the (q)-decompositions of x and y: $\alpha_1, \ldots, \alpha_k$ and $\beta_1, \ldots, \beta_k$. Observe that $\alpha_1 = \ldots = \alpha_k$ and $\beta_1 = \ldots = \beta_k$ because q is a period of both x and y, but $\alpha_1 \ne \beta_1$ because q is a primitive period of y, but not a primitive period of x. Hence, $dist(x, y) \ge k$.

As for the other inequality on $\mathcal{D}_{p,q}(n)$, let us take $x = (a^{p-1}b)^{\lfloor n/p \rfloor} a^{n \bmod p}$ and let y be the word that is obtained from x by changing the letters at positions $i \equiv q - 1 \pmod{q}$ from b to c. Then $dist(x, y) = \left\lfloor \frac{n}{q} \right\rfloor$.

Finally, the formula for $N_{p,q}(h)$ follows directly from the other one. □

Henceforth, we will always assume that $p \nmid q$ and $q \nmid p$.

3   Exact Values for Small n

Let us start with the following useful lemma.

Lemma 4. *Let x be a word of length n and let y by its cyclic rotation by s characters. If $x \neq y$, then $dist(x, y) \geq 2$. Moreover, there are two mismatches between x and y located at least $GCD(n, s)$ positions apart.*

Proof. Note that $y_i = x_{(i+s) \bmod n}$ for $0 \leq i < n$. Since $x \neq y$, we have $x_a \neq y_a = x_{(a+s) \bmod n}$ for some position a. Let k be the smallest positive integer such that $x_a = x_{(a+ks) \bmod n}$. Due to $x_{(a+s) \bmod n} \neq x_a$ and $x_{(a+ns) \bmod n} = x_a$, we have $1 < k \leq n$. Let $b = (a + (k-1)s) \bmod n$. Note that $x_b \neq x_a = x_{(b+s) \bmod n} = y_b$. Hence, a and b are positions of two distinct mismatches between x and y. Moreover, $b \equiv (a + (k-1)s) \bmod n \equiv a \pmod{GCD(n, s)}$. Consequently, these two mismatches are indeed located at least $GCD(n, s)$ positions apart. □

For an illustration of the following Lemma 5, see Fig. 3.

Lemma 5. *Consider positive integers p, q satisfying $p < q$ and $p \nmid q$. Let x and y be words of length n such that $p + q - GCD(p, q) \leq n \leq q + p\lceil \frac{q}{p} \rceil - 1$, p is a period of x, and q is a period of y but not a period of x. Then*

$$dist(x, y) \geq \left\lfloor \frac{n-q}{p} \right\rfloor + \left\lfloor \frac{n-q+GCD(p,q)}{p} \right\rfloor .$$

Proof. Let $u = x[0..p-1]$ and let v be the cyclic rotation of u by q characters. Note that u is a string period of x, so $u \neq v$; otherwise, q would be a period of x. Consequently, Lemma 4 provides two distinct indices a, b such that $u_a \neq v_a$, $u_b \neq v_b$, and $a \leq b - GCD(p, q) < p - GCD(p, q)$. Let us define

$$A = \left\{ kp + a : 0 \leq k < \left\lfloor \frac{n-q+GCD(p,q)}{p} \right\rfloor \right\},$$

$$B = \left\{ kp + b : 0 \leq k < \left\lfloor \frac{n-q}{p} \right\rfloor \right\}.$$

Observe that

$$\max A = \left\lfloor \frac{n-q+GCD(p,q)}{p} \right\rfloor p - p + a \leq n - q + GCD(p,q) - p + a < n - q$$

and

$$\max B = \left\lfloor \frac{n-q}{p} \right\rfloor p - p + b \leq n - q - p + b < n - q.$$

Moreover,

$$\max A \leq \left\lfloor \frac{p\lceil q/p \rceil - 1 + GCD(p,q)}{p} \right\rfloor p - p + a = \left\lceil \frac{q}{p} \right\rceil p - p + a < q + a \leq q + \min(A \cup B),$$

and

$$\max B \leq \left\lfloor \frac{p\lceil q/p \rceil - 1}{p} \right\rfloor p - p + b = \left\lceil \frac{q}{p} \right\rceil p - p < q \leq q + \min(A \cup B).$$

Consequently, for each $i \in A \cup B$, there are positions x_i and x_{i+q}, and all these $2(|A| + |B|)$ positions are distinct. Moreover, observe that for $i \in A$, we have $x_i = u_a \neq v_a = x_{i+q}$, while for $i \in B$, $x_i = u_b \neq v_b = x_{i+q}$. Thus, for $i \in A \cup B$, we have $x_i \neq x_{i+q}$, but $y_i = y_{i+q}$; hence $x_i \neq y_i$ or $x_{i+q} \neq y_{i+q}$. The positions we consider are distinct, so $dist(x,y) \geq |A \cup B| = |A| + |B| = \left\lfloor \frac{n-q}{p} \right\rfloor + \left\lfloor \frac{n-q+\mathrm{GCD}(p,q)}{p} \right\rfloor$, as claimed.   □

For an illustration of the following Lemma 6, see Figs. 4 and 5.

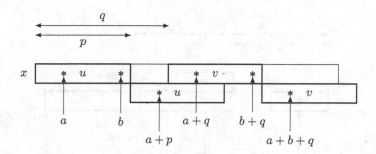

Fig. 3. Illustration of the equalities in the bound in Lemma 5 for $\lceil \frac{q}{p} \rceil = 1$.

Lemma 6. *Consider coprime integers p, q satisfying $1 < p < q$. Let w be a word of length $p + q - 2$ with periods p and q, but without period 1. Moreover, let n be an integer such that $p + q - 1 \leq n \leq q + \lceil \frac{q}{p} \rceil p - 1$, and let x and y be periodic extensions of w of length n preserving periods p and q, respectively. Then $\mathbf{per}(x) = p$, $\mathbf{per}(y) = q$, and*

$$dist(x,y) \leq \left\lfloor \frac{n-q}{p} \right\rfloor + \left\lfloor \frac{n-q+1}{p} \right\rfloor,$$

Proof. Claim. If a position i satisfies $i < q$ or $(i-q) \bmod p < p-2$, then $x_i = y_i$.

Proof. The claim is clear for $i < q+p-2$ since due to the common prefix of x and y. Thus, we consider a position $i = q+kp+r$ with $1 \leq k < \lceil \frac{q}{p} \rceil$ and $0 \leq r < p-2$. We have $x_{q+kp+r} = x_{q+r} = y_{q+r} = y_r = x_r = x_{kp+r} = y_{kp+r} = y_{q+kp+r}$. This is because positions $r < kp+r < q+r$ are within the common prefix of x and y.   □

Consequently,

$$dist(x,y) \leq \{i : q \leq i < n \wedge (i-q) \bmod p \geq p-2\} =$$
$$\{j : 0 \leq j < n-q \wedge j \bmod p = p-1\} + \{j : 0 \leq j < n-q \wedge j \bmod p = p-2\} =$$
$$\left\lfloor \frac{n-q}{p} \right\rfloor + \left\lfloor \frac{n-q+1}{p} \right\rfloor,$$

as claimed. Next, we prove that $p' := \mathbf{per}(x)$ is equal to p. Note that $p' \leq p$ by definition of x. For a proof by contradiction, suppose that $p' < p$. Note that w has periods p' and q. Moreover, $|w| = p + q - 2 \geq p' + q - 1$, so $\mathrm{GCD}(p', q)$ is a period of w. Moreover, $n \geq p+q-1 \geq p+\mathrm{GCD}(p',q)-1$, so $\mathrm{GCD}(\mathrm{GCD}(p',q),p)$

is a period of x. However, $\text{GCD}(\text{GCD}(p',q),p) = \text{GCD}(p',\text{GCD}(q,p)) = 1$ is not a period of w, which is a prefix of x.

Similarly, suppose that $q' := \mathbf{per}(y) < q$. We observe that $|w| = p+q-2 \geq p+q'-1$, so $\text{GCD}(p,q')$ is a period of w. Moreover, $n \geq p+q-1 \geq \text{GCD}(p,q')+q-1$, so $\text{GCD}(\text{GCD}(p,q'),q)$ is a period of y. However, $\text{GCD}(\text{GCD}(p,q'),q) = \text{GCD}(q',\text{GCD}(p,q)) = 1$ is not a period of w, which is a prefix of y.   □

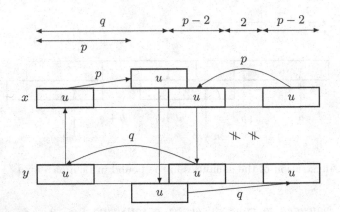

Fig. 4. Illustration of the equalities in the lower bound in Lemma 6 for $n = q + 2p - 2$.

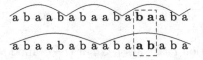

Fig. 5. A periodic prefix of a Fibonacci word and a power of a Fibonacci word that differ only at two positions.

Theorem 7. *If $p < q$, $p \nmid q$, and $p+q-\text{GCD}(p,q) \leq n \leq q + \lceil \frac{q}{p} \rceil p - 1$, then*

$$\mathcal{D}_{p,q}(n) = \left\lfloor \frac{n-q}{p} \right\rfloor + \left\lfloor \frac{n+\text{GCD}(p,q)-q}{p} \right\rfloor. \tag{1}$$

Proof. Lemma 5 gives a lower bound of $\mathcal{D}_{p,q}(n)$. Our upper bound is based on Lemma 6. Let $d = \text{GCD}(p,q)$, $p' = \frac{p}{d}$, $q' = \frac{q}{d}$, and $n' = \lfloor \frac{n}{d} \rfloor$. Observe that $1 < p' < q'$ and $p' + q' - 1 \leq n' \leq q' + \lceil \frac{q'}{p'} \rceil p' - 1$. Hence, Lemma 6 results in strings x', y' with of length n' with shortest periods p' and q' respectively, and with $dist(x',y') \leq \left\lfloor \frac{n'-q'}{p'} \right\rfloor + \left\lfloor \frac{n'-q'+1}{p'} \right\rfloor = \left\lfloor \frac{n-q}{p} \right\rfloor + \left\lfloor \frac{n-q+\text{GCD}(p,q)}{p} \right\rfloor$.

Let c be a character occurring neither in x' nor in y'. Let us define x and y so that $x_{id+d-1} = x'_i$ and $y =_{id+d-1} = y'_i$, and $x_j = y_j = c$ if $j \bmod d \neq d-1$. Note that $dist(x, y) = dist(x', y')$ and $|x| = |y| = n$. Also, observe that due to the choice of the character c, all periods of x and y are larger than dn' or multiples of d. Consequently, $\mathbf{per}(x) = d\mathbf{per}(x') = dp' = p$ and $\mathbf{per}(y) = d\mathbf{per}(y') = dq' = q$. This completes the construction.   □

Corollary 8. *The formula (1) of Theorem 7 applies for $p + q - \mathrm{GCD}(p, q) \leq n \leq 2q$.*

Fact 9. *The function $\mathcal{D}_{p,q}(n)$ is non-decreasing for $n \geq p + q - \mathrm{GCD}(p, q)$. Moreover:*

$$\mathcal{D}_{p,q}(n) = h \iff N_{p,q}(h-1) < n \leq N_{p,q}(h)$$
$$N_{p,q}(h) = n \iff \mathcal{D}_{p,q}(n) = h < \mathcal{D}_{p,q}(n+1)$$

4 Bounds for $\mathcal{D}_{p,q}(n)$ for Arbitrary n

Lemma 10. *Let p, q be integers such that $p < q$ and $p \nmid q$. Moreover, let x and y be words of length $n \geq q$ such that p is a period of x, and q is a period of y but not of x. Then $dist(x, y) \geq \left\lfloor \frac{n-q}{p} \right\rfloor$.*

Proof. Since q is not a period of x, we have $x_i \neq x_{i+q}$ for some position i, $0 \leq i < n - q$. Consider a set $J = \{j : 0 \leq j < n - q \wedge j \equiv i \pmod{p}\}$. Since p is a period of x, we have $x_j \neq x_{j+q}$ for each $j \in J$; on the other hand, $y_j = y_{j+q}$, so $x_j \neq y_j$ or $x_{j+q} \neq y_{j+q}$. Moreover, $p \nmid q$ implies that the positions $j, j + q$ across $j \in J$ are pairwise distinct. Consequently, $dist(x, y) \geq |J| \geq \left\lfloor \frac{n-q}{p} \right\rfloor$.   □

Theorem 11. *If $p < q$, $p \nmid q$, and $n \geq p + q$, then $\left\lfloor \frac{n-q}{p} \right\rfloor \leq \mathcal{D}_{p,q}(n) \leq 2\left\lceil \frac{n-q}{p} \right\rceil$.*

Proof. The lower bound follows directly from Lemma 10. The upper bound is obtained using words $(x, y) \in \mathcal{S}_{p,q,n}$ with string periods $a^{p-1}b$ and $(a^{p-1}b)^k a^r$ where $q = kp + r$. Indeed, x and y agree on the first q positions. After that, inside each pair of corresponding fragments of length at most p they have at most 2 mismatches.   □

Remark 12. In general, it is not true that $\mathcal{D}_{p,q}(n) \geq \lceil \frac{n-q}{p} \rceil$. For example, words $x = cacbcacbcacbcacbcac$ and $y = cacbcacacbcacacbcac$ of length 19, with shortest periods $p = 4$ and $q = 6$, respectively, satisfy $dist(x, y) = 3 < \lceil \frac{19-6}{4} \rceil$.

Theorem 13. *If $p < q$ and $p \nmid q$ and $n \geq p + q$, then $\mathcal{D}_{p,q}(n) \geq \left\lfloor \frac{2n}{p+q} \right\rfloor$.*

Proof. We use the following claim:

Claim. If $p < q$ and $p \nmid q$, then

(a) $N_{p,q}(1) = q + p - 1$,
(b) $N_{p,q}(2) = q + 2p - \text{GCD}(p, q) - 1$.

Proof. Observe that $q + p \leq q + 2p - \text{GCD}(p, q) \leq q + \lceil \frac{q}{p} \rceil p - 1$, so the values below are within the scope of Theorem 7. We have:

$$\mathcal{D}_{p,q}(q + p - 1) = \left\lfloor \frac{p-1}{p} \right\rfloor + \left\lfloor \frac{p + \text{GCD}(p,q) - 1}{p} \right\rfloor = 0 + 1 = 1$$

$$\mathcal{D}_{p,q}(q + p) = \left\lfloor \frac{p}{p} \right\rfloor + \left\lfloor \frac{p + \text{GCD}(p,q)}{p} \right\rfloor = 1 + 1 = 2.$$

This concludes the proof of part (a).

$$\mathcal{D}_{p,q}(q + 2p - \text{GCD}(p, q) - 1) = \left\lfloor \frac{2p - \text{GCD}(p,q) - 1}{p} \right\rfloor + \left\lfloor \frac{2p-1}{p} \right\rfloor = 1 + 1 = 2$$

$$\mathcal{D}_{p,q}(q + 2p - \text{GCD}(p, q)) = \left\lfloor \frac{2p - \text{GCD}(p,q)}{p} \right\rfloor + \left\lfloor \frac{2p}{p} \right\rfloor = 1 + 2 = 3.$$

This concludes the proof of part (b).   □

Consider words $x \in \mathcal{P}_p(n)$, $y \in \mathcal{P}_q(n)$ and their $(p + q)$-decompositions: $\alpha_1, \ldots, \alpha_k$ and $\beta_0, \ldots, \beta_{k-1}$. If $\alpha_i = \beta_i$ for some $1 \leq i \leq k$, then, by the Periodicity Lemma, both α_i, β_i have period $\text{GCD}(p, q)$; consequently, both x and y have period $\text{GCD}(p, q)$, a contradiction. Hence, part (a) of the claim implies $dist(\alpha_i, \beta_i) \geq 2$ for each $i = 1, \ldots, k$.

Let α_{k+1} and β_{k+1} be the suffixes of x and y starting immediately after the last factors of the corresponding decompositions. If $|\alpha_{k+1}| < \frac{p+q}{2}$, then we already have that

$$dist(x, y) \geq 2 \left\lfloor \frac{n}{p+q} \right\rfloor = \left\lfloor \frac{2n}{p+q} \right\rfloor.$$

Otherwise, by part (b) of the claim applied for the words $\alpha_k \alpha_{k+1}$ and $\beta_k \beta_{k+1}$, we have

$$dist(x, y) \geq 2 \left(\left\lfloor \frac{n}{p+q} \right\rfloor - 1 \right) + 3 = 2 \left\lfloor \frac{n}{p+q} \right\rfloor + 1 = \left\lfloor \frac{2n}{p+q} \right\rfloor.$$

In both cases we obtain the desired inequality.   □

5   Conclusions

The paper studies the following general type of question:

> How much dissimilar in a whole should be two objects which are different in some specific aspect?

The answer to this type of question heavily depends on the studied type of the objects. Thus sometimes the answer is completely trivial; for example, two different strings of the same length may differ at only a single position. In this work we show that if we consider different strings of the same length that are additionally periodic, then the implied number of positions where the two strings must differ can be large. The exact number depends on the length of the strings and on their periods.

References

1. Amir, A., Iliopoulos, C.S., Radoszewski, J.: Two strings at Hamming distance 1 cannot be both quasiperiodic. Inf. Process. Lett. **128**, 54–57 (2017)
2. Amir, A., Levy, A., Lubin, R., Porat, E.: Approximate cover of strings. In: Kärkkäinen, J., Radoszewski, J., Rytter, W. (eds.) 28th Annual Symposium on Combinatorial Pattern Matching, CPM 2017, 4–6 July 2017, Warsaw, Poland, vol. 78 of LIPIcs, pp. 26:1–26:14. Schloss Dagstuhl - Leibniz-Zentrum fuer Informatik (2017)
3. Bai, H., Franek, F., Smyth, W.F.: The new periodicity lemma revisited. Discrete Appl. Math. **212**, 30–36 (2016)
4. Berstel, J., Boasson, L.: Partial words and a theorem of Fine and Wilf. Theor. Comput. Sci. **218**(1), 135–141 (1999)
5. Blanchet-Sadri, F., Bal, D., Sisodia, G.: Graph connectivity, partial words, and a theorem of Fine and Wilf. Inf. Comput. **206**(5), 676–693 (2008)
6. Blanchet-Sadri, F., Corcoran, K., Nyberg, J.: Fine and Wilf's periodicity result on partial words and consequences. In: Loos, R., Fazekas, S.Z., Martín-Vide, C., (eds.) Proceedings of the 1st International Conference on Language and Automata Theory and Applications, LATA 2007, Report 35/07, pp. 115–126. Research Group on Mathematical Linguistics, Universitat Rovira i Virgili, Tarragona (2007)
7. Blanchet-Sadri, F., Hegstrom, R.A.: Partial words and a theorem of Fine and Wilf revisited. Theor. Comput. Sci. **270**(1–2), 401–419 (2002)
8. Blanchet-Sadri, F., Oey, T., Rankin, T.D.: Fine and Wilf's theorem for partial words with arbitrarily many weak periods. Int. J. Found. Comput. Sci. **21**(5), 705–722 (2010)
9. Blanchet-Sadri, F., Simmons, S., Tebbe, A., Veprauskas, A.: Abelian periods, partial words, and an extension of a theorem of Fine and Wilf. RAIRO - Theor. Inf. Appl. **47**(3), 215–234 (2013)
10. Castelli, M.G., Mignosi, F., Restivo, A.: Fine and Wilf's theorem for three periods and a generalization of Sturmian words. Theor. Comput. Sci. **218**(1), 83–94 (1999)
11. Constantinescu, S., Ilie, L.: Generalised Fine and Wilf's theorem for arbitrary number of periods. Theor. Comput. Sci. **339**(1), 49–60 (2005)
12. Constantinescu, S., Ilie, L.: Fine and Wilf's theorem for Abelian periods. Bull. EATCS **89**, 167–170 (2006)
13. Fan, K., Puglisi, S.J., Smyth, W.F., Turpin, A.: A new periodicity lemma. SIAM J. Discrete Math. **20**(3), 656–668 (2006)
14. Fine, N.J., Wilf, H.S.: Uniqueness theorems for periodic functions. Proc. Am. Math. Soc. **16**(1), 109–114 (1965)
15. Giancarlo, R., Mignosi, F.: Generalizations of the periodicity theorem of Fine and Wilf. In: Tison, S. (ed.) CAAP 1994. LNCS, vol. 787, pp. 130–141. Springer, Heidelberg (1994). https://doi.org/10.1007/BFb0017478
16. Holub, S.: On multiperiodic words. ITA **40**(4), 583–591 (2006)
17. Justin, J.: On a paper by Castelli, Mignosi, Restivo. ITA **34**(5), 373–377 (2000)
18. Karhumäki, J., Puzynina, S., Saarela, A.: Fine and Wilf's theorem for k-Abelian periods. Int. J. Found. Comput. Sci. **24**(7), 1135–1152 (2013)
19. Manea, F., Mercaş, R., Nowotka, D.: Fine and Wilf's theorem and pseudo-repetitions. In: Rovan, B., Sassone, V., Widmayer, P. (eds.) MFCS 2012. LNCS, vol. 7464, pp. 668–680. Springer, Heidelberg (2012). https://doi.org/10.1007/978-3-642-32589-2_58

20. Mignosi, F., Restivo, A., Silva, P.V.: On Fine and Wilf's theorem for bidimensional words. Theor. Comput. Sci. **292**(1), 245–262 (2003)
21. Mignosi, F., Shallit, J., Wang, M.: Variations on a theorem of Fine & Wilf. In: Sgall, J., Pultr, A., Kolman, P. (eds.) MFCS 2001. LNCS, vol. 2136, pp. 512–523. Springer, Heidelberg (2001). https://doi.org/10.1007/3-540-44683-4_45
22. Smyth, W.F., Wang, S.: A new approach to the periodicity lemma on strings with holes. Theor. Comput. Sci. **410**(43), 4295–4302 (2009)
23. Tijdeman, R., Zamboni, L.Q.: Fine and Wilf words for any periods II. Theor. Comput. Sci. **410**(30–32), 3027–3034 (2009)

Non-coding RNA Sequences Identification and Classification Using a Multi-class and Multi-label Ensemble Technique

Michalis Stavridis[1], Aigli Korfiati[1,2], Georgios Sakellaropoulos[1], Seferina Mavroudi[2,3], and Konstantinos Theofilatos[2(✉)]

[1] School of Medicine, University of Patras, Patras, Greece
`michailstavridis@yahoo.com, gsak@med.upatras.gr`
[2] InSyBio Ltd., Winchester, UK
`{a.korfiati,s.mavroudi,k.theofilatos}@insybio.com`
[3] Department of Social Work, School of Sciences of Health and Care, Technological Educational Institute of Western Greece, Patras, Greece

Abstract. High throughput sequencing RNA-sequencing technologies and modern in silico techniques have expanded our knowledge on short non-coding RNAs. These sequences were initially split into various categories based on their cellular functionality and their sequential, thermodynamic and structural properties believing that their sequence can be used as an identifier to distinguish them. However, recent evidence has indicated that the same sequences can act and function as more than one type of non-coding RNAs with a striking example of mature microRNA sequences which can also be transfer RNA fragments. Most of the existing computational methods for the prediction of non-coding RNA sequences have emphasized on the prediction of only one type of noncoding RNAs and even the ones designed for multiclassification do not support multiple labeling and are thus not able to assign a sequence to more than one non-coding RNA type. In the present paper, we introduce a new multilabel- multiclass method based on the combination of multiobjective evolutionary algorithms and multilabel implementations of Random Forests to optimize the feature selection process and assign short RNA sequences to one or more non-coding RNA types. The overall methodology clearly outperformed other machine learning techniques which were used for the same purpose and it is applicable to data coming from RNA-sequencing experiments.

Keywords: Multi-label classification · Non-coding RNAs
Multi-objective optimization · Random forests · Dimensionality reduction

1 Introduction

Non-coding RNAs (ncRNAs) are RNA fragments that are not translated to proteins [1]. Small ncRNAs typical size is of 18–35 nucleotides (nt) and long-non-coding RNAs (lncRNAs) can be more than 200 nt (e.g., enhancer RNA – eRNA) [2]. The transfer

L. Iliadis et al. (Eds.): AIAI 2018, IFIP AICT 520, pp. 179–188, 2018.
https://doi.org/10.1007/978-3-319-92016-0_17

RNA (tRNA) or the ribosomal RNA (rRNA) have been the subject of several studies and this has established their well-accepted functional roles in cells. However, over the past few years, advances on sequencing biotechnologies and other improvements on experimental protocols led to the elucidation of more ncRNA categories, the most prominent being: microRNAs (miRNAs), small nuclear RNAs (snRNAs), small nucleolar RNAs (snoRNAs), small inferring RNAs (siRNAs), piwi-interacting RNAs (piRNAs), ti-RNAs, spli-RNA, tRNA fragments (tRfs) and others to be identified [3].

Recently, transcriptomics analysis using RNA-seq data has also become the state-of-the-art procedure for identifying and annotating functionally ncRNA molecules. However, since ncRNA transcripts are drastically different from mRNAs, the majority of 'general-purpose' bioinformatics programs face limitations and are not well suited for discovering effectively ncRNAs from RNA-seq [4]. To mitigate this problem, several computational methods have been tailored to the needs of ncRNA data analysis.

NcRNAs were initially split into various categories based on their cellular functionality and their sequential, thermodynamic and structural properties believing that their sequence can be used as an identifier to distinguish them. However, recent evidence has indicated that the same sequences can act and function as more than one type of ncRNAs with a striking example of mature microRNA sequences which can also be transfer RNA fragments. Most of the existing computational methods for the prediction of non-coding RNA sequences have emphasized on the prediction of only one type of ncRNAs [5] and even the ones designed for multiclassification, do not support multiple labeling and are thus not able to assign a sequence to more than one non-coding RNA types.

For each one of the aforementioned short non-coding RNA types, a variety of computational methods exists for their prediction [6]. These are split into the computational methods which are designed to be specific to one type of short ncRNAs and the ones which can predict more than one type of short ncRNAs [7]. The first category of methods presents increased classification performances but their applicability is limited as they cannot be used to analyze on a single run a large transcriptomic dataset and to predict different types of short ncRNAs. Moreover, most of the methods belonging to the second category exclude from their analysis significant types of short ncRNAs, while others are based on data mining in existing repositories and thus they cannot extend the current knowledge on short ncRNAs. Finally, most of these methods use the same features for all the different types of short ncRNAs. Another important drawback of existing methodologies is that they consider the different types of non-coding RNAs as separate forcing every RNA sequence to be classified in only one type of non-coding RNAs. However, as already mentioned, recent evidence has proven that this does not hold since tRNA fragments can have the same sequence as miRNAs [8]. If we add this fact to the previously known one that several types of non-coding RNAs are generated from pruning other types of non-coding RNAs, as in the case of pre-miRNAs and mature miRNAs, then a need for a multilabel computational method is raised to treat these data effectively.

In the present paper, we introduce a new multilabel, multiclass method called Multi-label GARF, which combines multi-objective evolutionary algorithms with multi-label Random Forest implementations. In particular, it uses a Pareto-based multi-objective optimization to select the optimal subset of features to be used as inputs, to select the most suitable implementation of Random Forests for every dataset and to optimize its parameters. This optimization process is being guided by 7 fitness functions which are evaluating the solutions based on the classification performance of the Random Forest models extracted from them, and based on their simplicity in terms of the number of selected inputs and their number of random trees. The multi-objective optimization framework, by design avoids local optimal solutions promoting the optimal exploration of the search space.

For the problem of classifying the RNA sequences to non-coding RNA types, for the purposes of the present manuscript, a new dataset was constructed with pre-miRNAs, mature miRNAs, snoRNAs, tRNAs, tRFs, rRNAs, pseudo hairpins and random RNA sequences. All these sequences were pairwise compared to locate similar sequences and for some of them multiple labels were assigned by this process. For all the sequences of the dataset, 58 sequential, thermodynamical and structural features were calculated including most significant features from existing non-coding RNA classification methods. The proposed solution was applied on this dataset and its performance was compared with existing state-of-the-art multi-label methods. Multi-label GARF significantly outperformed other methods in terms of classification performance on the testing dataset. Its performance surpassed 60% of the very strict multi-label accuracy metric which considers a sample to be classified correctly only if all its labels have been predicted correctly. It is noteworthy than none of the random RNA sequences were assigned to any of the non-coding RNA types and this makes the final predictive models suitable for screening RNA-seq reads for non-coding RNA sequences.

2 Materials and Methods

RFAM database [9] was used to download mature miRNA (1865), pre-miRNA (2547), tRNA (12522), rRNA (25723) and snoRNA (12522) sequences. Moreover, tRNA fragments (tRFs) were downloaded from MINTbase [10] and tRFdb [11]. In order to train and test effectively the machine learning classifiers, the random undersampling method was applied randomly selecting only 1865 sequences of each category to be included in the final dataset since this is the plurality of the minority class. The produced dataset was extended with 1865 pseudo hairpin sequences constructed following the method described in [12] and 1865 random RNA-sequences of lengths from 20 to 200.

These sequences were pairwise compared to identify equal or similar sequences allowing total 2 mismatches belonging to more than one categories or sequences which can be found within other sequences. This analysis was conducted to assign multiple labels to these types of sequences.

As a next step for all of these sequences 58 structural, sequential and thermodynamic features were calculated using InSyBio ncRNAseq tool [13]. The final dataset was split in training and testing set with 2/3 of its sequences being assigned to the training set and the remaining 1/3 to the test set. This split was conducted randomly but reassuring that 1:1 proportion is maintained for every class in the dataset.

The proposed designed and implemented method is a hybrid method which solves on parallel the problems of dimensionality reduction and multiple labels classification.

In specific the proposed method, Multi-Label GARF, is an ensemble dimensionality reduction technique which utilizes a multiobjective evolutionary algorithm [14] for the identification of the optimal feature subset to be used as input to the classifiers as well as for the selection of the most suitable type of Random Forests classifier [15] to be used and its optimal parameters.

The multi-objective evolutionary framework used for this implementation was based on the multi-objective evolutionary algorithm initially applied in [16] for the optimiza-tion of the preprocessing pipeline for the analysis of Mass Spectrometry data. This is based on a Pareto-optimization technique to allow fast convergence to good exploration properties and effective handling of the contradictory goals of minimizing the number of used features, maximizing the accuracy of the classifiers and minimizing the complexity of the classifier to achieve better generalization properties.

The algorithm starts by randomly initializing a first population of solutions which are represented as float vectors. These vectors consist of (i) float variables for the parameter number of random trees to be used and the minimum number of samples assigned per leaf to control the splitting process on Random Forests, (ii) a float variable to choose between the two alternative multi-label Random Forest algorithms (a value greater than 0.5 indicates the selection of method 2 and a value less than 0.5 indicates the selection of method 1) and 58 float variables for deciding if a feature will be selected as input or not (values greater than 0.5 forces a feature to be used as input). The float vectors of the population are initialized randomly with values from the normal distri-bution with mean equal to $min\_value + (max\_value - min\_value)/2$ and variance $(max\_value - min\_value)/2$, where max_value is the maximum allowed value of an optimization variable and min_value is its minimum allowed value.

For the variation of the population of solutions in order to create new solutions, crossover and mutation operators are sequentially applied. Regarding the crossover operators, two crossover methods are used with probabilities which are also provided by the user (45% probability for two-point crossover operator, 45% probability for arith-metic crossover and 10% for not applying crossover operator were used for this imple-mentation). For the mutation, the Gaussian mutation operator is applied since it is the most suitable operator for the float representation scheme which is adopted in the proposed algorithm with mutation probability 1%.

To better handle the multiple objectives of the current problem, the selection process was based on a multi-objective optimization method. The first step is to calculate the number of Pareto frontiers (sets of solutions where no solution is better than other solu-tions in the same set to all optimization goals). To calculate the Pareto frontiers, the efficient and fast solution described in [17] was used. An initial fitness value is then assigned to every solution equal to the reverse order of the parent front to which it has been assigned by the previous step. Next, the method calculates solution niches by grouping together solutions according to their similarity. The fitness values of every solution in a given niche are divided by the variable m (average similarity of every solution) which is calculated by performing pairwise comparisons of all solutions of the niche calculating their geometrical distances and calculating the mean pairwise distance of them. These fitness values are then tuned according to the number of solutions belonging to each niche. Roulette Wheel Selection is then used to select the population of the next generation. The best solution passes as it is to the next generation.

The total fitness value is calculated with the weighted sum of the optimization goals with the weights pre-defined by the user. The specific fitness functions (FF) which were used for multi-label GARF algorithm were the following:

$$FF1 = \frac{1}{1 + \text{Number of selected features}}$$

$$FF2 = \text{Classification Accuracy}$$

$$FF3 = \text{Hamming Loss Classification Metric}$$

$$FF4 = \frac{1}{1 + \text{Number of trees used by Random Forests}}$$

$$FF5 = \frac{\text{Average number of samples per node Split in Random Trees}}{\text{Total Number of samples}}$$

$$FF6 = \text{Recall Classification Metric}$$

$$FF7 = \text{Precision Classification Metric}$$

Fitness function 1 aims at the minimization of the selected features in order to increase the interpretability of the classifier. Fitness functions 4 and 5 were used to promote solutions which lead to simpler models to present better generalization properties. The rest of the fitness functions are employed to increase the algorithm's classification performance.

The algorithm was terminated when the population of solutions is deemed as converged (the similarity among the solutions surpasses a predefined threshold) or when the maximum number of generations is reached.

The multi label Random Forest classifiers implementation was based on sklearn python library [18] using two different approaches regarding the function used to measure the quality of a split in the process of generating the trees of random forests. The first method is called Gini and uses the Gini impurity function [19] and the second method uses the information gain function [20].

The overall pipeline of the multi-label GARF is depicted in Fig. 1.

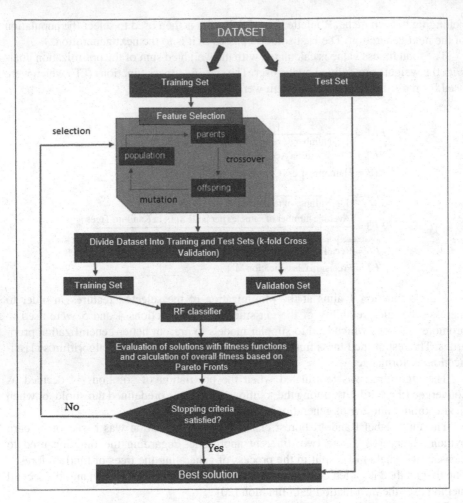

Fig. 1. Flowchart of proposed method: multi-label GARF

3   Experimental Results

All features of the dataset were arithmetically normalized to the interval [−1, 1] and missing values were imputed using KNN-Impute method [21]. Then the Multi-label GARF and other multi-label methods were used to train multi-label classification models using the training dataset. The trained classification models were applied on the testing dataset and Table 1 presents the Accuracy and Hamming-Loss metric for every model.

The state of the art multi-label models which were used for comparison reasons were the Random Forest implementation of sklearn library, the extra trees algorithm [22], the multi-label KNN [23], a Decision Tree algorithm [24] and the Binary Relevance algorithm [25]. For all these algorithms, all features were used as inputs and they were tested using their default parameters.

Table 1. Comparative results on the classification of non-coding RNA sequences using the proposed technique and other existing machine learning techniques compatible with multi-label datasets.

Method	Accuracy (mean − SD)	Hamming-Loss Metric (mean − SD)
Multi-label GARF	**61% − 0.3461**	**0.051 − 0.002529**
Random forest	28% − 0.0002	0.010 − 0.000061
Extra trees	12% − 0.0002	0.009 − 0.000062
Multi label KNN	1% − 0.0008	0.010 − 0.000006
Decision tree	29% − 0.0004	0.010 − 0.000007
Binary relevance	22% − 0.0005	0.012 − 0.000005

Regarding the Multi-label GARF algorithm, after extensive testing in the training set, a population of 50 individuals was used and a maximum number of 200 generations was set for the termination criterion. Further increase in the number of generations did not improve the results. Mutation Probability was set to 1%. Moreover, during its training phase internal 5-fold cross validation was applied using the training dataset. In order to take into account, the stochastic nature of this method we run the experiments 25 times and the results of Table 1 are the mean values together with their standard deviation (SD). The goal significances for the fitness functions 2, 3, 6, 7 were set to 1.5 and for the other goals to 1. By this way we are setting for the final ordering of the solutions, classification performance to be twice as significant as the goals of minimizing the classification model's complexity.

The best solution uncovered by Multi-label GARF method among all runs used the Gini metric for splitting criterion on the random tree nodes, 8637 number of random trees, 3 as minimum number of samples assigned per leaf and 27 features were selected. Moreover, a closest examination on the results indicated that none of the random RNA sequences was assigned to any of the non-coding RNA types by the multi-label GARF method.

Multi-label GARF significantly outperformed the other examined methods in terms of classification performance on the testing dataset. Its performance was over 60% of the very strict multi-label accuracy metric which considers a sample to be classified correctly only if all its labels have been predicted correctly. None of the other examined methods presented accuracy more than 30%.

Finally, it is noteworthy than none of the random RNA sequences were assigned to any of the non-coding RNA types and this makes the final predictive models suitable for screening RNA-seq reads for non-coding RNA sequences.

4   Discussion

Predicting and classifying short ncRNAs is of crucial importance for systems biology and translational medicine to: (i) allow the prediction of new ncRNA molecules for human or other not well studied organisms (including the human microbiome), (ii) ease the analysis of high throughput sequencing experiments by allowing for the efficient identification and quantification of non-coding RNAs without the need of analyzing them separately by modifying samples with specialized libraries and (iii) enable the understanding of ncRNAs functionality. To the best of our knowledge, most existing methods are offering prediction of very limited number of non-coding RNA categories with most of them emphasizing on miRNAs. Moreover, all existing methods do not take into account the fact that some sequences may be assigned to more than one ncRNA categories while some ncRNA sequences are being generated from pruning other ncRNAs.

In the present work, we have attempted to overcome these difficulties by proposing a unified multi-label multi-classification algorithmic framework which combines multi-label Random Forests with a multi-objective optimization algorithm to find the optimal classification model with the minimum number of inputs. To test the proposed solution, we generated the first multi-label dataset for non-coding RNAs mining information from several databases and compared the proposed solution with other state-of-the-art multi-label classification models. The multi-label GARF clearly outperformed all other methods in both classification metrics used. Moreover, on this specific dataset none random RNA sequence was assigned to any type of non-coding RNAs. Furthermore, the additional labels which are assigned by it in some of the sequences which maintained the strict metric of multi-label accuracy in approximately 60% should be further explored in the future as meaningful information could reside on them about other functionalities that could be performed by the same sequences or parts of them.

The fact that the proposed technique was able to train models that can predict non-coding RNAs within longer RNA sequences makes it appropriate for being applied directly on the reads extracted from deep RNA-sequencing experimental techniques. As an example, in the case of identifying miRNAs from RNA-sequencing, a common problem is whether to search for pre-miRNAs or for mature miRNAs since both types of RNA sequences can be detected in a biosample. The extracted predictive models from the present paper can solve efficiently this problem as well as the problem that non-coding RNAs are most of the time only a subset of a read being generated by sequencing technologies. Thus, an interesting future direction includes testing and validating the performance of the proposed method directly on sequences exported from RNA-sequencing experiments. Moreover, despite the promising results of the proposed model, its performance can be further improved by including even more features as potential inputs (e.g. existence of clover structure). Finally, the current implementation can be expanded to allow for the prediction of other types of non-coding RNAs such as scRNAs and diRNAs.

References

1. Costa, V., Angelini, C., De Feis, I., Ciccodicola, A.: Uncovering the complexity of transcriptomes with RNA-Seq. J. Biomed. Biotechnol. **10**, 19 p. (2010). Article ID 853916, https://doi.org/10.1155/2010/853916
2. Kang, W., Friedländer, M.R.: Computational pre-diction of miRNA genes from small RNA sequencing data. Front. Bioeng. Biotechnol. **3**, 7 (2015)

3. Veneziano, D., Di Bella, S., Nigita, G., Laganà, A., Ferro, A., Croce, C.M.: Noncoding RNA: current deep sequencing data analysis approaches and challenges. Human Mutat. **37**(12), 1283–1298 (2016)
4. Conesa, A., Madrigal, P., Tarazona, S., Gomez-Cabrero, D., Cervera, A., McPherson, A., Szcześniak, M.W., Gaffney, D.J., Elo, L.L., Zhang, X., Mortazavi, A.: A survey of best practices for RNA-seq data analysis. Genome Biol. **17**(1), 13 (2016)
5. Li, Y., Zhang, Z., Liu, F., Vongsangnak, W., Jing, Q., Shen, B.: Performance comparison and evaluation of software tools for microRNA deep-sequencing data analysis. Nucleic Acids Res. **40**(10), 4298–4305 (2012)
6. Aghaee-Bakhtiari, S.H., Arefian, E., Lau, P.: miRandb: a resource of online services for miRNA research. Brief. Bioinform. bbw109 (2017). https://doi.org/10.1093/bib/bbw109
7. Washietl, S., Will, S., Hendrix, D.A., Goff, L.A., Rinn, J.L., Berger, B., Kellis, M.: Computational analysis of noncoding RNAs. Wiley Interdiscip. Rev.: RNA **3**(6), 759–778 (2012)
8. Venkatesh, T., Suresh, P.S., Tsutsumi, R.: tRFs: miRNAs in disguise. Gene **579**(2), 133–138 (2016)
9. Griffiths-Jones, S., Moxon, S., Marshall, M., Khanna, A., Eddy, S.R., Bateman, A.: Rfam: annotating non-coding RNAs in complete genomes. Nucleic Acids Res. **33**(suppl_1), D121–D124 (2005)
10. Pliatsika, V., Loher, P., Magee, R., Telonis, A.G., Londin, E., Shigematsu, M., Kirino, Y., Rigoutsos, I.: MINTbase v2.0: a comprehensive database for tRNA-derived fragments that includes nuclear and mitochondrial fragments from all The Cancer Genome Atlas projects Nucleic Acids Res. PubMed, PMID:29186503 (2017)
11. Kumar, P., Mudunuri, S., Anaya, J., Dutta, A.: tRFdb: a database for transfer RNA fragments. Nucleic Acids Research (Database Issue) (2014). https://doi.org/10.1093/nar/gku1138
12. Kleftogiannis, D., Theofilatos, K., Likothanassis, S., Mavroudi, S.: YamiPred: a novel evolutionary method for predicting pre-miRNAs and selecting relevant features. IEEE/ACM Trans. Comput. Biol. Bioinform. (TCBB) **12**(5), 1183–1192 (2015)
13. Korfiati, A., Theofilatos, K., Alexakos, C., Mavroudi, S.: InSyBio ncRNASeq: a web tool for analyzing non-coding RNAs. EMBnet. J. **23**, e882 (2017)
14. Abraham, A., Jain, L.: Evolutionary multiobjective optimization. In: Abraham, A., Jain, L., Goldberg, R. (eds.) Evolutionary Multiobjective Optimization: Theoretical Advances and Applications, pp. 1–6. Springer, London (2005). https://doi.org/10.1007/1-84628-137-7_1
15. Breiman, L.: Random forests. Mach. Learn. **45**(1), 5–32 (2001)
16. Corthesy, J., Theofilatos, K., Mavroudi, S., et al.: An adaptive pipeline to maximize isobaric tagging data in large-scale MS-based proteomics. J. Proteome Res. (2017). Under Second Review at February 2018
17. Mishra, K.K., Harit, S.: A fast algorithm for finding the non dominated set in multiobjective optimization. Int. J. Comput. Appl. **1**, 35–39 (2010)
18. http://scikit-learn.org/stable/modules/generated/sklearn.ensemble.RandomForestClassifier.html. Accessed on December 2017
19. Modarres, R., Gastwirth, J.: A cautionary note on estimating the standard error of the gini index of inequality. Oxford Bull. Econ. Stat. **68**(3), 385–390 (2006). https://doi.org/10.1111/j.1468-0084.2006.00167
20. Liu, F., Zhang, X., Ye, Y., Zhao, Y., Li, Y.: MLRF: multi-label classification through random forest with label-set partition. In: Huang, D.-S., Han, K. (eds.) ICIC 2015. LNCS (LNAI), vol. 9227, pp. 407–418. Springer, Cham (2015). https://doi.org/10.1007/978-3-319-22053-6_44
21. Zhang, S.: Nearest neighbor selection for iteratively kNN imputation. J. Syst. Softw. **85**(11), 2541–2552 (2012)

22. Geurts, P., Ernst, D., Wehenkel, L.: Extremely randomized trees. Mach. Learn. **63**(1), 3–42 (2006)
23. Zhang, M.L., Zhou, Z.H.: ML-KNN: a lazy learning approach to multi-label learning. Pattern Recognit. **40**(7), 2038–2048 (2007)
24. Vens, C., Struyf, J., Schietgat, L., Džeroski, S., Blockeel, H.: Decision trees for hierarchical multi-label classification. Mach. Learn. **73**(2), 185 (2008)
25. Luaces, O., Díez, J., Barranquero, J., del Coz, J.J., Bahamonde, A.: Binary relevance efficacy for multilabel classification. Prog. Artif. Intell. **1**(4), 303–313 (2012)

A Multi-metric Algorithm for Hierarchical Clustering of Same-Length Protein Sequences

Sotirios–Filippos Tsarouchis[1], Maria Th. Kotouza[1(✉)] (iD),
Fotis E. Psomopoulos[1,2] (iD), and Pericles A. Mitkas[1]

[1] Electrical and Computer Engineering, Aristotle University of Thessaloniki,
54124 Thessaloniki, Greece
sotitsar@ece.auth.gr, {maria.kotouza,
fpsom}@issel.ee.auth.gr, mitkas@auth.gr
[2] Institute of Applied Biosciences, Centre for Research and Technology Hellas,
57001 Thessaloniki, Greece

Abstract. The identification of meaningful groups of proteins has always been a major area of interest for structural and functional genomics. Successful protein clustering can lead to significant insight, assisting in both tracing the evolutionary history of the respective molecules as well as in identifying potential functions and interactions of novel sequences. Here we propose a clustering algorithm for same-length sequences, which allows the construction of subset hierarchy and facilitates the identification of the underlying patterns for any given subset. The proposed method utilizes the metrics of sequence identity and amino-acid similarity simultaneously as direct measures. The algorithm was applied on a real-world dataset consisting of clonotypic immunoglobulin (IG) sequences from Chronic lymphocytic leukemia (CLL) patients, showing promising results.

Keywords: Hierarchical clustering · Amino acid sequences
Sequence similarity · Sequence identity

1 Introduction

One of the main challenges in computational biology concerns the extraction of useful information from biological data. This requires the development of tools and methods that are capable of uncovering trends, identifying patterns, forming models, and obtaining predictions of the system [1]. The majority of such tools and methods exist within the field of data mining. Clustering [2] is a data mining task that divides data into several groups using similarity measures, such that the objects within a cluster are highly similar to each other and dissimilar to the objects belonging to other clusters based on that metric. From a machine learning perspective, the search for meaningful clusters is defined as unsupervised learning due to the lack of prior knowledge on the number of clusters and their labels. However, clustering is a widely used exploratory tool for analyzing large datasets and has been applied extensively in numerous biological, genomics, proteomics, and various other omics methodologies [3]. Genomics is one of the most important domains in bioinformatics, whereas the number of sequences available is increasing exponentially [1]. Often the first step in sequence analysis, clustering can help organize sequences into

L. Iliadis et al. (Eds.): AIAI 2018, IFIP AICT 520, pp. 189–199, 2018.
https://doi.org/10.1007/978-3-319-92016-0_18

homologous and functionally similar groups, can improve the speed of data processing and analysis, and can assist the prediction process.

There have been several approaches in the past, attempting to address the issue of identifying meaningful groupings of sequences of identical lengths. While sequence clustering has a long history in the field of bioinformatics ([4, 5]), there are few attempts in literature that can be successfully applied to sequences of the same length. One of the most notable approaches is the Teiresias algorithm [6, 7], that discovers rigid patterns (motifs) in biological sequences based on the observation that if a pattern spans many positions and appears exactly k times in the input, then all fragments (sub patterns) of the pattern have to appear at least k times in the input. The main drawback of this algorithm is that pairwise comparisons are employed between all the sequences of the dataset, leading to an exponential increase in execution time and memory requirements for large-scale datasets.

In this paper, we introduce a method for clustering amino acid sequences of identical length, using an approach that does not demand pairwise comparisons between the sequences, but it is instead based on the usage of a matrix that contains the amino acid frequencies for each position of the target sequences.

2   Methodology

The proposed clustering method uses both sequence identity and amino-acid similarity as similarity measures to form the clusters (both concepts are further defined below). Ultimately, a binary top-down tree is constructed by consecutively dividing the frequency amino acid matrix of a given cluster into two sub-matrices, until only two sequences remain at each cluster at the leaf-level.

2.1   Binary Tree Construction

The first phase consists of a top down hierarchical clustering method. Hierarchical clustering is one of the most commonly used approaches for sequence clustering [8]. At the beginning of the process, it is assumed that all N sequences belong to a single cluster, which is consequently split recursively while moving along the different levels of the tree. Ultimately, the constructed output of the clustering process is presented as a binary tree. The right side of the tree is expected to be much longer than the left side due to the constraints posed by the split process; the sequences with the highest similarity percentage at a specific sequence position are assigned to the right side, whereas the remaining sequences are assigned to the left. The process of this phase (Algorithm 1, Fig. 2) can be formally described in the following steps and further detailed below:

1. Create frequency and frequency-similarity based matrix (*FM*, *FSM*)
2. Compute average identity of the matrices ($\overline{id}$, $\overline{idS}$)
3. Split each frequency matrix into two sub matrices
4. Update the Level matrix and the Identity matrices (*Y*, *I*, *IS*)
5. Check for branch break.

'Volume' classes		'Hydropathy' classes					
	in Å³	Hydrophobic		Neutral		Hydrophilic	
Very large	189-228	F	W	Y			
Large	162-174	I L	M			K R	
Medium	138-154	V			H	E	Q
Small	108-117		C P	T		D	N
Very small	60-90	A	G	S			
		Aliphatic	Sulfur	Hydroxyl	Basic	Acidic	Amide
				Uncharged	Charged		Uncharged
		Nonpolar			Polar		

Fig. 1. The 11 IMGT Physicochemical classes for the 20 amino acids [9]. (Color figure online)

Step 1: Frequency amino acid and frequency-similarity based amino acid matrix.
The first aims to construct a frequency amino acid matrix. This is defined as a 2-dimensional matrix, with number of rows equal to the number of the different amino acids (i.e. 20 rows) and number of columns equal to the length (L) of the sequences provided as input. Each element (i,j) of the matrix corresponds to the number of times amino acid i is present in position j for all sequences. The count matrix (CM) contains the absolute values, whereas the frequency matrix (FM) contains the corresponding frequencies (Eq. 1). In addition to CM, a second frequency matrix is constructed using the same approach, but instead of the 20 amino acids, groups of similar amino acids are used under given schemes. As a use case in this paper, the 11 IMGT physicochemical classes are taken into consideration, as shown in Fig. 1, and an 11 x L frequency matrix is constructed.

$$FM = CM/N \tag{1}$$

Step 2: Compute Identity. The identity is a similarity metric that is computed for each cluster based on the corresponding amino-acid frequency matrix. This metric, calculated as a percentage, indicates how compact the cluster is. Its maximum value (100%) corresponds to the case when the number of unique sequences that belong to a cluster is equal to one. The overall identity is equal to the average identity of each position in the given sequence (Eq. 2), and it is produced based on the $CThr$ matrix, that contains only the elements of the amino acid matrix (CM) that correspond to amino acids that appear more than once in the corresponding column (Eq. 3).

$$\overline{id} = \left(\sum_{j=1}^{L} max(CThr[,j])/N\right)/L \tag{2}$$

$$CThr[i,j] = \begin{cases} CM[i,j], & if\ CM[i,j] > 1 \\ 0, & if\ CM[i,j] \le 1 \end{cases},\ i = 1,..,20,\ j = 1,..,L \tag{3}$$

Steps 3–4: Split of Frequency Matrices. Each cluster is divided into two distinct subsets according to the following criteria and in the order that they are listed:

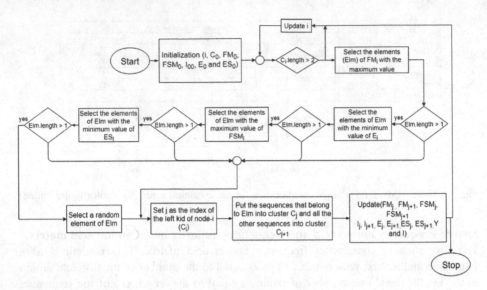

Fig. 2. Block diagram of the tree construction.

1. Select the element of the frequency amino acid matrix with the highest percentage. An example of the division of *cluster0* using this criterion is shown in Fig. 3.
2. If there exist more than one columns of the frequency amino acid matrix that contain the same highest percentage value, the selection is applied using the entropy criterion, defined below.
3. In the case where more than one columns exhibit the exact same entropy value, criterion 1 is applied to the frequency similarity amino acid matrix.
4. In the case of non-unique columns, criterion 2 is applied to the frequency similarity amino acid matrix.
5. If the number of columns is still more than one, one column from the above sub group of columns is randomly selected.

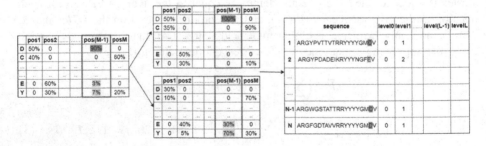

Fig. 3. The division of Cluster 0 using the first criterion.

Entropy criterion. The entropy is computed for each column of the frequency matrix and represents the diversity of the column. A lower entropy value indicates a more homogeneous column, therefore the column with the lowest entropy value is selected during the splitting process.

$$E[j] = \sum_{i=1}^{20} k, \; j = 1, \ldots, L, \text{ where } k = \begin{cases} 0, \text{ if } FM[i,j] = 0 \\ 1, \text{ if } FM[i,j] \neq 0 \end{cases} \tag{4}$$

Step 5: Branch Breaking. Acluster is no further divided into subsets when the number of sequences that belong to the cluster is less than 3.

2.2   Software Implementation

The algorithm outlined in the paper is implemented in R, a programming language that is widely used for statistical computing, graphics and data analytics. In order to produce an interactive and user-friendly tool, thus making it easier for users to interact with the data, the analysis, and the visualization of the results, an R Shiny application was built using the shiny package. In practical terms, a Shiny App is a web page/ UI connected to a computer running a live R session (Server). The users can select personalized parameters via the UI. These parameters are passed on to the Server, where the actual calculations are performed and the UI's display is updated according to the produced results.

R Shiny applications consist of at least two R scripts; the first one implements the User Interface (ui.R) by controlling the layout of the page using html commands and other nested R functions, and handles the input parameters provided by the users. The second script implements the Server (server.R) and contains essential commands and instructions on how to build the application and process the data. Except from those two essential scripts, a helper script is defined (helpers.R), which includes all the functions needed for further processing of the data and achieving the desirable plot formats.

Apart from the shiny package, several other packages have been utilized in order to add further functionality to the application and visualize the produced results. Indicatively, the DiagrammeR, data.tree and collapsibleTree libraries were very useful towards the visualization of the constructed tree. The latter is more interactive and gives the user the opportunity of collapsing branches and focusing on the branch or level of interest. Another special graph of our application is the logo graph, which contains the common letters of a specific cluster or level and can be produced through the use of the ggseqlogo library. Finally, our R Shiny Application is publicly available from the following URL:

https://github.com/mariakotouza/H-CDR3-Clustering.

Algorithm 1: Binary Tree Construction

N: Number of sequences
TL: Number of tree levels
Y: The Level matrix
I: The Identity matrix of FM
IS: The Identity matrix of FSM
Input: (X: Vector Nx1)
Output: (Y: Table NxTL, I, IS: Table NxTL)
1. **Initialization:**
1.1   Put all sequences into cluster C_0
1.2   Compute the frequency amino acid matrix FM_0
1.3   Compute the frequency similarity based amino acid matrix FSM_0
1.4   Compute Initial Identity id_{00}, idS_{00}
1.5   Compute Initial Entropy E_0 and ES_0
2. **Iteration:**
        Repeat for every new cluster-i
*.1   Compute the level that C_i belongs to
        Criteria for Division
*.2   Select $cell_i$ of FM_i or FSM_i according to the following criteria:
*.2.1   Elm ← the elements of FM_i with the maximum value
*.2.2   **if** Elm.length < 2 **then**
*.2.3 $cell_i$ ← Elm
*.2.4   Go to step *.3
        end if
*.2.5   Elm ← the elements of Elm with the minimum value of E_i
*.2.6   **if** Elm.length < 2 **then**
*.2.7 $cell_i$ ← Elm
*.2.8   Go to step *.3
        end if
*.2.9   Elm ← the elements of Elm with the maximum value of FSM_i
*.2.10 **if** Elm.length < 2 **then**
*.2.11 $cell_i$ ← Elm
*.2.12   Go to step *.3
        end if
*.2.13 Elm ← the elements of Elm with the minimum value of ES_i
*.2.14 **if** Elm.length < 2 **then**
*.2.15 $cell_i$ <- random element of Elm
        end if
        Division
*.3   j ← index of the left child of node-i (C_i)
*.4   Put the sequences that belong to $cell_i$ into cluster C_j
*.5   Put all the other sequences into cluster C_{j+1}
*.6   Compute the frequency amino acid matrixes FM_j and FM_{j+1}
*.7   Compute the frequency-similarity based amino acid matrixes FSM_j and FSM_{j+1}
*.8   Compute Identity id_j, id_{j+1}, idS_j and idS_{j+1}
*.9   Compute Entropy E_j and E_{j+1}
*.10   Fill in column Y[,level] with C_j or C_{j+1}
*.11   Fill in column I[,level] with id_j or id_{j+1} and column IS[,level] with idS_j or idS_{j+1}
*.12   Check if we have reached leaf
        End
3.   return Y, I

3 Results

Our method was applied on a real-world dataset comprising 123 clonotypic immunoglobulin (IG) amino acid sequences (deduced from the corresponding IG gene rearrangement sequences) from patients with chronic lymphocytic leukemia (CLL). All sequences utilized the IGHV4-34 gene with 111 (90.2%) being assigned to 6 distinct biologically relevant groups (subsets), and had an identical length of 20 amino acids. These subsets are characterized by the presence of common amino acid sequence patterns within the VH CDR3 of the clonotypic IG. Subset #4 is a major subset and patients belonging to this subset display an indolent clinical course, while the other subsets are minor. In detail, 101 sequences were assigned to subset #4, 2 to subset #207, 2 to subset #4-34/20-1, 4 to subset #4-34-16, 2 to subset #4-34-18 whereas 12 sequences carried heterogeneous receptors and, thus, were not assigned to any subset.

Through the application of our tool, a binary tree with 19 levels was constructed (Fig. 5). The average value and the standard deviation of each level's identity using the 20 amino-acid and the 11 IMGT Physicochemical classes are summarized in Table 1. The table shows that the identity value increased towards the leaves of the tree. Notably, when the 11 classes were used instead of the individual amino-acids, the total identity value was a little higher as expected.

Table 1. Average and standard deviation identity and similarity value of the clusters of the 19 tree levels.

	Identity Mean Value	Identity Standard Deviation	Similarity Mean Value	Similarity Standard Deviation
Level.0	0.000	NA	0.000	NA
Level.1	5.000	0.000	7.500	3.535
Level.2	38.750	41.708	41.250	39.660
Level.3	34.166	33.078	37.500	31.741
Level.4	37.500	25.083	41.500	25.500
Level.5	55.500	31.837	61.000	28.848
Level.6	71.875	29.753	79.375	23.969
Level.7	65.833	31.211	71.666	26.204
Level.8	66.666	26.394	72.500	22.079
Level.9	68.125	23.594	78.125	19.628
Level.10	70.833	24.579	77.500	18.907
Level.11	73.750	20.310	80.000	16.903
Level.12	75.000	15.811	80.500	14.615
Level.13	79.583	15.877	84.166	13.953
Level.14	80.416	13.221	83.333	12.851
Level.15	85.000	12.792	86.250	13.164
Level.16	86.250	111.505	87.083	11.957
Level.17	87.500	9.414	88.750	8.822
Level.18	93.750	7.723	94.166	7.334
Level.19	98.000	4.216	98.000	4.216

In more detail, both Average Identity and Average Similarity values are equal to zero at the root of the tree and they almost consistently increase at each level, reaching the value of 98 percent on level 19. At any given point, the Average Similarity value is equal or greater than the Average Identity value, which is reasonable assuming that every similarity group contains one or more individual letters. Regarding the Identity Standard Deviation and Similarity Standard Deviation, it can be observed that both have an initial value of NA at the root, they are slightly increased for levels 1 and 2 and then their values decrease for every level until reaching the leaves. This is an expected outcome of the process, since the standard deviation is a measure of how spread out numbers are. Finally, the Identity Standard Deviation is equal to or greater than Similarity Standard Deviation, because the number of individual letters is greater than the number of similarity groups and therefore the amount of spread is higher.

Figure 4 shows the logos of four clusters from four different levels of the tree. The size of each amino-acid indicates the percentage of its occurrence at the specific position of the CDR3 sequence, whereas the color of the amino-acid represents the IMGT Physicochemical class it belongs to. The color code used for the logo figures is consistent with the color scheme shown in Fig. 1.

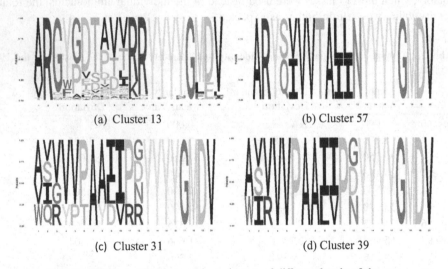

(a) Cluster 13   (b) Cluster 57

(c) Cluster 31   (d) Cluster 39

Fig. 4. CDR3 region logos of four clusters of different levels of the tree.

Subset #4 is the largest subset in the present data series comprising 101 clonotypic IG sequences. Most of them (93/101, 92%) formed cluster 13, at level 4 of the clustering process, with level 0 being the root of the tree. Cluster 13 also included 3 non-subset IG sequences. The identity and similarity rates of this cluster were 20% and 30%, respectively. The CDR3 of cluster 13 is 20 amino acids long and consisted of 4 conserved positions and 16 positions that are characterized by variability. Subset #4-34/20-1 consisted of 2 clonotypic IG sequences. These sequences were grouped together at level 9 (cluster 57) with high identity and similarity rates (80% and 95%, respectively). Only 4 positions of the CDR3 were encoded by different amino acids: A

R Y _ _ V V T A _ _ N Y Y Y Y G M D V. More uniform groups and less variability at a position level is noticed at higher levels of clustering. Consequently, identity and similarity rates increase from one level to another. Subset #4-34-16 consisted of 4 clonotypic IG sequences. Three out of 4 IG sequences (75%) were grouped together at level 5 forming cluster 31 with 45% identity and 50% similarity. Cluster 31 also included a non-subset IG sequence. At the next level of clustering (level 6) the sequences assigned to subset #4-34-16 (3/4, 75%) formed cluster 39 with higher identity and similarity rates (70%|80%). Six positions were characterized by variability.

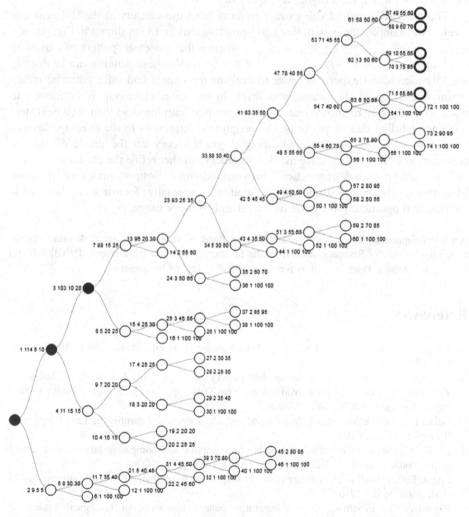

Fig. 5. The binary tree with 12 levels and values for each cluster with the format [cluster id, number of cluster sequences, identity, similarity]

4 Discussion

In this study, we applied a new clustering technique to 123 immunoglobulin (IG) sequences of the CDR3 region from patients with chronic lymphocytic leukemia (CLL), all of which express the IGHV4-34 gene. This is a hierarchical method that constructs a top-down binary tree by iteratively breaking the amino-acid frequency matrix into two sub-matrices and using identity and amino-acid similarity as measures for the clustering. The results of this analysis showed that the identity value increases as one transitions from the root towards the leaves of the tree. In the case when the 11 IMGT Physicochemical classes were used instead of the 20 individual amino-acids, the identity value was a little higher as expected.

The proposed method can extract patterns from the clusters at the different tree levels. For example, the pattern that corresponds to cluster 13 (as shown in Fig. 4a) is _ R _ _ _ _ _ _ _ _ _ _ _ Y _ Y _ G _ _ _ _, whereas the consensus pattern of cluster 39 (Fig. 4d) is _ _ _ V V P A A _ _ P _ Y Y Y Y G M D V. These patterns can be directly used by biomedical experts in order to evaluate the cluster and infer potential meaningful interaction at the amino acid level. In our case, clustering is performed to discover previously unknown patterns (unsupervised learning) and then, as a next step, sequence labeling can be performed to assign new sequences to the existing classes.

Future steps involve the application of graph theory on the produced tree, in conjunction with string distance metrics, in order to further refine the clustering process and uncover potential connections between different clusters/ nodes of the tree. Moreover, additional testing will be required, especially focusing on large-scale datasets and optimizing the code for speed and memory usage.

Acknowledgments. The authors would like to thank Katerina Gemenetzi, Andreas Agathangelidis and Kostas Stamatopoulos from the Institute of Applied Biosciences (INAB|CERTH) for providing the dataset as well as for their critical review of the paper.

References

1. Pedro Larranaga, R.S., Robles, V.: Machine learning in bioinformatics. Brief. Bioinform. **7**, 86–112 (2006)
2. Berkhin, P.: A survey of clustering data mining techniques. In: Kogan, J., Nicholas, C., Teboulle, M. (eds.) Grouping Multidimensional Data, pp. 25–71. Springer, Berlin (2006). https://doi.org/10.1007/3-540-28349-8_2
3. Belacel, N., Cuperlovic-Culf, M.: Clustering: Unsupervised Learning In Large Screening Biological Data (2010)
4. Li, W., Godzik, A.: Cd-hit: a fast program for clustering and comparing large sets of protein or nucleotide sequences. Bioinformatics **22**(13), 1658–1659 (2006)
5. Edgar, R.C.: Search and clustering orders of magnitude faster than BLAST. Bioinformatics **26** (19), 2460–2461 (2010)
6. Rigoutsos, I., Floartos, A.: Combinatorial pattern discovery in biological sequences: The TEIRESIAS algorithm. Bioinformatics (Oxford, England), **14**, 55–67 (1998)

7. Darzentas, N., Hadzidimitriou, A., Murray, F., Hatzi, K., Josefsson, P., Laoutaris, N., Moreno, C., Anagnostopoulos, A., Jurlander, J., Tsaftaris, A., Chiorazzi, N., Belessi, C., Ghia, P., Rosenquist, R., Davi, F., Stamatopoulos, K.: A different ontogenesis for chronic lymphocytic leukemia cases carrying stereotyped antigen receptors: molecular and computational evidence. Leukemia **24**, 125–132 (2010)
8. Cai, Y., Zheng, W., Yao, J., Yang, Y., Mai, V., Mao, Q., Sun, Y.: ESPRIT-forest: parallel clustering of massive amplicon sequence data in subquadratic time. PLoS Comput. Biol. **13**, e1005518 (2017)
9. IMGT, The International ImMunoGeneTics Information System. (http://www.imgt.org)

Towards String Sanitization

Oluwole Ajala[✉], Hayam Alamro, Costas Iliopoulos, and Grigorios Loukides

Department of Informatics, King's College London, London, UK
{oluwole.ajala,hayam.alamro,costas.iliopoulos,
grigorios.loukides}@kcl.ac.uk

Abstract. An increasing number of applications, in domains ranging from bio-medicine to business and to pervasive computing, feature data represented as a long sequence of symbols (string). Sharing these data, however, may lead to the disclosure of sensitive patterns which are represented as substrings and model confidential information. Such patterns may model, for example, confidential medical knowledge, business secrets, or signatures of activity patterns that may risk the privacy of smart-phone users. In this paper, we study the novel problem of concealing a given set of sensitive patterns from a string. Our approach is based on injecting a minimal level of uncertainty to the string, by replacing selected symbols in the string with a symbol "∗" that is interpreted as any symbol from the set of possible symbols that may appear in the string. To realize our approach, we propose an algorithm that efficiently detects occurrences of the sensitive patterns in the string and then sanitizes these sensitive patterns. We also present a preliminary set of experiments to demonstrate the effectiveness and efficiency of our algorithm.

Keywords: String · Sanitization · Data privacy

1 Introduction

Data that are used in a number of applications such as mining and web analysis often come in the form a long sequence of events. In many of these applications, such as biomedical informatics, network analysis, and marketing, the patterns of interest in analysis come in the form of consecutive symbols, i.e., substrings of the long sequence (string). At the same time, the data also contains patterns (substrings) that represent confidential information that must be protected before the data are published (released) for analysis. Examples of such information are medical knowledge (diagnosis and medications) and business secrets.

In this work, we study the general problem of sanitizing a string. The problem deviates from existing works, which focus on the sanitization of event sequences, or relational tables (i.e., collections of records). We formalize the problem of protecting a string by *sanitizing* (i.e., concealing) a given set of sensitive patterns that represent confidential information. To achieve this, we replace selected

ⓒ IFIP International Federation for Information Processing 2018
Published by Springer International Publishing AG 2018. All Rights Reserved
L. Iliadis et al. (Eds.): AIAI 2018, IFIP AICT 520, pp. 200–210, 2018.
https://doi.org/10.1007/978-3-319-92016-0_19

symbols in all occurrences of the sensitive patterns in the string with a symbol "*". That is, we inject uncertainty in the string. This clearly reduces the usefulness of the protected string in applications. Thus, in our problem, we aim to conceal the sensitive patterns while preserving the utility of the string as much as possible. As we show, the problem is NP-hard. To address the problem, we propose an algorithm, called *SSA* (String Sanitization Algorithm) that first efficiently detects occurrences of the sensitive patterns in the string and then sanitizes these sensitive patterns. The detection of the sensitive patterns is performed by the Aho-Corasick algorithm [3], which takes linear time in the length of the string. The sanitization of the sensitive patterns is performed by a greedy algorithm that is inspired by the well-known greedy algorithm for the Set Cover (*SC*) problem [5]. This algorithm is called SanitizeClusters, and it works by iteratively replacing the symbol that is contained in the largest number of currently unprotected sensitive patterns with the special symbol "*".

We also present a preliminary set of experiments to demonstrate the effectiveness and efficiency of our algorithm. In our experiments, we apply the algorithm to a commonly used sequential dataset and study empirically its effectiveness in terms of preserving data utility, as well as its efficiency. Our results show that the algorithm can sanitize the dataset in less than 10 ms and produce a sanitized dataset with a small number of occurrences of the symbol "*".

The organization of the rest of the paper is as follows. Section 2 summarizes the related work and state of art of this current research. In Sect. 3, we present our preliminaries containing formal definitions and an overview of the problem statement. We highlight our approach in Sect. 4, where we present our algorithms, their implementation and examples. We present a preliminary experimental evaluation of our approach in Sect. 5. Finally, we conclude and discuss future work in Sect. 6.

2   Related Work

Data sanitization is an important methodology to protect data, by means of concealing confidential knowledge in the form of user-specified patterns. Most existing sanitization approaches are applied to a collection (multi-set) of transactions [15,19,20], sequences [2,8,11], or trajectories [2] and prevent the mining of frequent sensitive patterns [2,8,19] or association rules [15,20], by applying deletion. To preserve utility, these approaches attempt to minimize the total number of deleted items (events) [8] and/or changes in the frequency of non-sensitive patterns [2], as well as in the output of frequent pattern [8,11,19] or association rule [15,20] mining. We share the utility goal of [8], but contrary to all these approaches, we consider a long string of events.

This is somewhat similar to the work of [13], which considered a sequence of events that are associated with time points. However, our work differs from that of [13] along two important dimensions. The first dimension is related to the type of data considered. Specificailly, we consider a string (sequence of symbols), whereas the work of [13] considers a sequence of multisets of symbols, where each multiset is associated with a time point. The second dimension is related to the problem considered. Specifically, the problem we aim to solve requires concealing sensitive strings (i.e., sequences of consecutive symbols that can potentially contain gaps), while minimizing the total number of deleted events. On the ontrary, the problem of [13] requires concealing single events (symbols), while preserving the distribution of event in the entire sequence. Also, we consider a sensitive string concealed when it does not appear in the entire string (i.e., has frequency zero), whereas the work of [13] considers a sensitive event concealed when its frequency in the event sequence is below a given threshold in any prefix of the sequence. The two problems also belong to different complexity classes; our problem is strongly NP-hard, as we show, and thus cannot be solved optimally in polynomial time, whereas the problem in [13] is weakly NP-hard and thus admits a pseudopolynomial time optimal algorithm.

Anonymization is a different methodology to protect data, whose goal is not to conceal given sensitive patterns but to preserve the privacy of individuals, whose information is contained in the data, by preventing inferences of the identity and/or sensitive information of these individuals. Most anonymization approaches are applicable to a collection of transactions [4,9], trajectories [1,16], or sequences (with [18] or without [14] time points), each of which is associated with a different individual. Another category of approaches anonymizes an individual's time-series [17] or event sequence [10], using differential privacy [7]. Anonymization approaches guard against the disclosure of an individual's identity [1,14] and/or sensitive information [1,4,10,17,18]. However, they cannot be applied to our problem, because their privacy models do not conceal the sensitive patterns in a long string, which we require to preserve privacy. Suppressing sensitive patterns from an infinite event sequence has been studied in [12,21]. These works aim to achieve privacy by minimizing the number of occurrences of sensitive patterns, while preserving the occurrences of certain nonsensitive patterns that are specified by data owners. Both types of patterns are sets of events. Thus, these works are not applicable to our problem, because they consider different type of data and have different utility goals.

3   Background and Problem Definition

3.1   Background

We begin with basic definitions and notation from [6]. Let $x = x[0]x[1]\ldots x[n-1]$ be a *string* of length $|x| = n$ over a finite ordered alphabet. We consider the case of strings over an *integer alphabet*: each letter is replaced by its lexicographical rank in such a way that the resulting string consists of integers in the range $\{1,\ldots,n\}$. For two positions i and j on x, we denote by $x[i\ldots j] = x[i]\ldots x[j]$ the *factor* (sometimes called *substring*) of x that starts at position i and ends at position j (it is of length 0 if $j < i$), and by ε the *empty string* of length 0. We recall that a *prefix* of x is a factor that starts at position 0 ($x[0\ldots j]$) and a *suffix* of x is a factor that ends at position $n-1$ ($x[i\ldots n-1]$). A prefix (resp. suffix) is said to be *proper* if it is any prefix (resp. suffix) of the string other than the string itself. For example, any of the strings in {a,ac, acc, accg} (respectively, {ccgt, cgt, gt, t}) is a proper prefix (respectively, suffix) of the string *accgt*.

We denote with S a string that we aim to protect and with $\mathcal{S}$ the set of symbols contained in S. To protect the string S, we conceal a set of substrings, $SP = \{sp_1, \ldots, sp_n\}$, of S. We refer to the substrings of SP as sensitive patterns, and we denote the set of symbols $\cup_{i \in [1,n]} sp_i$ with $\mathcal{SP}$. To conceal a sensitive pattern sp_i, we replace at least one symbol in it with a symbol $* \neq \varepsilon$. This process constructs a *sanitized* sensitive pattern sp_i' corresponding to sp_i. If sp_i occurs multiple times in the string S, we replace each occurrence of sp_i with sp_i'. Doing this for every sensitive pattern in SP constructs a *sanitized* string S' corresponding to S. Clearly, we cannot be certain about the symbols that were replaced by the symbol "$*$" in the sanitized string S'. This helps preserving privacy, because a recipient of S' interprets "$*$" as any symbol of $\mathcal{S}$ (assuming that $\mathcal{S}$ is public knowledge and contains more than one symbol).

3.2 Problem Definition

In this section, we formally define the probem we study and show that it is NP-hard.

Problem 1 (Optimal String Sanitization (OSS)). Given a string S and a set of sensitive patterns $SP = \{sp_1, \ldots, sp_n\}$, construct a *sanitized* string S' from S, such that: (I) S' contains no $sp_i \in SP$, $i \in [1, n]$, as a substring, (II) S' contains each sanitized pattern, sp_i', $i \in [1, n]$, that is constructed from sp_i by replacing at least one symbol in sp_i with the symbol $*$, as a substring, and (III) the number of occurrences (multiplicity) of the symbol $*$ in S' is minimum.

Theorem 1. *The OSS problem is NP-hard.*

Proof. The proof is by reducing the NP-hard Set Cover (SC) problem to OSS. The SC problem is defined as follows. Given a universe of elements $U = \{u_1, \ldots, u_n\}$ and a collection $L = \{L_1, \ldots, L_m\}$ such that each $L_j \in L$ is a subset of U, find a subcollection $L' \subseteq L$, such that: (I) L' covers all elements of U (i.e., $\cup_{L_j \in L'} L_j = U$), and (II) the number of subsets in L' is minimum.

We map a given instance $\mathcal{I}_{SC}$ of SC to an instance $\mathcal{I}_{OSS}$ of the OSS problem, in polynomial time, as follows:

I Each element $u_i \in U$ is mapped to a sensitive pattern $sp_i \in SP$, so that covering the element u_i corresponds to constructing a santized pattern sp_i' from sp_i.

II Each subset $L_j = \{u_1, \ldots, u_r\} \in L$ is mapped to a set $SP_j = \{sp_1, \ldots, sp_r\}$ $\subseteq SP$ of sensitive patterns which have a common symbol $s_j \in \mathcal{S}$, so that selecting L_j corresponds to constructing a set of sanitized patterns $\{sp_1', \ldots, sp_r'\}$ by replacing the common symbol s_j of the patterns in SP_j with the symbol $*$.

In the following, we prove the correspondence between a solution L' to the given instance $\mathcal{I}_{SC}$ of SC and a solution S' to the instance $\mathcal{I}_{OSS}$.

We first prove that, if L' is a solution to $\mathcal{I}_{SC}$, then S' is a solution to $\mathcal{I}_{OSS}$. Since $\cup_{L_j \in L'} = U = \{u_1, \ldots, u_n\}$, a sanitized sensitive pattern sp'_i is constructed for each sensitive pattern sp_i in SP. Thus, S' contains no sensitive pattern in SP as a substring, and it contains each sanitized sensitive pattern sp'_i that corresponds to a sensitive pattern sp_i, $i \in [1, n]$, as a substring. Since the number of subsets in L' is minimum and each $L_j \in L'$ leads to the replacement of the common symbol s_j of the patterns in SP_j with $*$, the sensitive patterns in SP are sanitized with the minimum number of occurrences of the symbol $*$. Furthermore, all occurrences of a sensitive pattern sp_i must be replaced with its corresponding sensitive pattern sp'_i. Thus, the number of occurrences of the symbol $*$ contained in the sanitized string S' is minimum, and S' is a solution to $\mathcal{I}_{OSS}$.

We now prove that, if S' is a solution to $\mathcal{I}_{OSS}$, then L' is a solution to $\mathcal{I}_{SC}$. Since S' is a solution to $\mathcal{I}_{OSS}$, each sensitive pattern in SP is sanitized, which implies that L' covers all elements of U. In addition, the number of occurrences of the symbol $*$ in S' is minimum. This implies that the sensitive patterns in SP are sanitized with the minimum number of occurrences of the symbol $*$ and hence the number of selected subsets in L' is minimum. Thus, L' is a solution to $\mathcal{I}_{SC}$.   □

4   String Sanitization Algorithm

This section discusses the String Sanitization Algorithm (SSA), which aims to solve the OSS problem. The algorithm is based on: (i) the *Aho-Corasick* string matching algorithm whose objective is to efficiently detect the occurrences of all sensitive patterns in the string, (ii) the SetIntersection algorithm whose objective is to organize sensitive patterns into clusters based on the symbols they share, and (iii) the SanitizeClusters algorithm whose objective is to perform the sanitization of the sensitive patterns in each cluster by replacing selected symbols in the patterns by the symbol "$*$".

4.1   Aho-Corasick Algorithm

The Aho-Corasick algorithm [3] is a well-known, efficient algorithm for detecting all occurrences of a finite set of patterns $P = \{p_1, \ldots, p_k\}$ in a given text T. Both patterns and T are strings. The algorithm constructs a finite state machine (FSM) automaton for the set of patterns P, which is used to perform pattern matching on the text T (i.e., find the symbol of T at which each occurrence of each pattern in P occurs in T). The benefit of the Aho-Corasick algorithm is that it works in linear time (when the string is independent of the number of patterns, as in our case). Specifically, the worst-case time complexity of the algorithm is $O(|T| + \sum_{i \in [1,k]} |p_i| + \mathcal{M}_{P,T})$, where $|T|$ denotes the length of T, $\sum_{i \in [1,k]} |p_i|$ denotes the the total length of the patterns in P, and $\mathcal{M}_{P,T}$ denotes the number of occurrences of patterns in P in the text T. This is typically much faster than the naive solution of detecting the occurrences of each pattern in P independently, which takes $O(\sum_{i \in [1,k]} |p_i| \cdot |T|)$ time.

In this work, we use the Aho-Corasick algorithm to detect all occurrences of sensitive patterns $\{sp_1, \ldots, sp_n\}$ in the string S, which is needed to before sanitizing the sensitive patterns (i.e., replacing at least one symbol in each sensitive pattern with $*$, in all occurrences of the sensitive pattern in the string). Thus, the worst-case time complexity of the Aho-Corasick algorithm in our case is $O(|S| + \sum_{i \in [1,m]} |sp_i| + \mathcal{M}_{SP,S})$, where $|s|$ is the length of the string S, $\sum_{i \in [1,m]} |sp_i|$ is the total length of the sensitive patterns in SP, and $\mathcal{M}_{SP,S}$ is the number of occurrenses of sensitive patterns in SP in S. Since the sensitive patterns have generally a small number of occurrences (since they model confidential knowledge), the Aho-Corasick algorithm is a good choice for detecting the occurrences of sensitive patterns in the OSS problem.

4.2   SetsIntersection Algorithm

After applying the *Aho-Corasick* algorithm to the string S, all occurrences of each sensitive pattern $sp_i \in SP$ are contained in $Occ(SP)$. We denote the j-th occurrence of sensitive pattern sp_i in the string S with $Occ(sp_i, j)$. If the sensitive pattern sp_i is a substring $sp_i[l \ldots l']$ of S, we denote its occurrence with the positions l and l'. Given $Occ(SP)$ and SP, the SetsIntersection algorithm begins by creating an empty two-dimensional array A. Then, it fills A by iterating over each sensitive pattern sp_i and creating a cluster C that contains sp_i together with all other sensitive patterns that share a position with sp_i. The set of sensitive patterns in C is added into the first element of A. The second element of A contains either the first position of each occurrence of a sensitive pattern, if the cluster contains only one sensitive pattern (i.e., no other sensitive pattern shares symbols with the sensitive pattern in the cluster), or the common positions of all occurrences of the sensitive patterns in C otherwise. After considering all sensitive patterns, the algorithm returns the array A.

4.3   SanitizeClusters Algorithm

This algorithm gets as input the array A created by the SetsIntersection algorithm, together with the string S. First, it initializes the sanitized string S' with the original string S. Then, in the for loop, it iteratives over each cluster (set of sensitive patterns contained in the first element of each record in the array A), and it sanitizes the sensitive patterns in the cluster. The sanitization of the sensitive patterns in the cluster (see do while loop) is performed until every sensitive pattern in the cluster has at least one symbol replaced by $*$. To sanitize the sensitive patterns in the cluster, the algorithm finds the most frequent position p corresponding to the sensitive patterns in the cluster and replaces the position with $*$ in S'. If there are more than one most frequent positions, the algorithm selects the last position, for efficiency. After all clusters are sanitized, the algorithm returns the sanitized string S'.

Algorithm 1. SetsIntersection

1: **Input:** sensitive patterns SP, $Occ(SP)$ containing all occurrences of each sensitive pattern in the string S.
2: **Output:** 2D array A. The i-th record of A contains two elements: the first is the cluster i (set of sensitive patterns), and the second is the positions of S that these sensitive patterns share.
3: Create empty 2D array A
4: **for each** sensitive pattern $sp_i \in SP$
5:    create new cluster C_j that contains sp_i
6:    Add into C_j all sensitive patterns that share a position with sp_i
7:    $A[j][0] \leftarrow C_j$
8:    **if** C_j contains one sensitive pattern **then**
9:        $A[j][1] \leftarrow$ first position of each occurrence of the sensitive pattern
10:   **else**
11:       $A[j][1] \leftarrow$ all common positions of each occurrence of the sensitive patterns in C_j and the first position of each occurrence of a sensitive pattern in C_j
12:   **end if**
13: **return** A

Algorithm 2. SanitizeClusters

1: **Input:** Array A created by Algorithm 1, string S
2: **Output:** Sanitized string S'
3: $S' \leftarrow S$
4: **for each** cluster C contained in the first column of A
5:    **do**
6:        $p \leftarrow$ most frequent position in C (break ties with last most frequent position)
7:        Replace p with $*$ in S'
8:    **while** a sensitive pattern in C does not have at least one symbol replaced with $*$ in S'
9: **return** S'

4.4 SSA Algorithm

We are now ready to present the SSA algorithm. The algorithm gets as input the string S and the set of specified sensitive patterns SP, and it begins by calling the Aho-Corasick algorithm, to obtain a set of positions $Occ(SP)$, for each sensitive pattern in SP. Then, SSA calls the SetsIntersection algorithm using $Occ(SP)$ and SP, to create the array A that organizes the sensitive patterns into clusters that are associated with their corresponding positions. Next, the array A together with the string S is given as input to the SanitizeClusters algorithm, which produces the sanitized string S'. Last, the SSA algorithm returns S'.

Algorithm 3. *SSA* (String Sanitization Algorithm)

1: **Input:** String S, set of sensitive patterns SP
2: **Output:** Sanitized string S'
3: $Occ(SP) \leftarrow$ Aho-Corasick(S, SP)
4: $A \leftarrow$ SetsIntersection($SP, Occ(SP)$)
5: $S' \leftarrow$ SanitizeClusters(A, S)
6: **return** S'

4.5 Example of Applying *SSA*

Suppose we have the string $S = \{aatccagcaactagaattgcaagcctcaaaact\}$, and the set of sensitive patterns $SP = \{sp_1, \ldots, sp_5\} = \{ag, caa, aac, aact, aag\}$, as shown in Fig. 1.

Fig. 1. Occurrences of sensitive patterns $sp_1, \ldots, sp_5$ in the string S.

The *SSA* algorithm will first execute the *Aho-Corasick algorithm* to obtain $Occ(SP)$, as shown in Fig. 2. After that, the SetsIntersection will be executed to create clusters of sensitive patterns and find the common positions of all occurrences of the sensitive patterns in each cluster (i.e., positions in S that are shared by all patterns in the cluster), if the cluster contains more than one sensitive patterns, or the first position of all occurrences of the sensitive pattern,

Occurences	start position	end position
$Occ(sp_1, 1)$	5	6
$Occ(sp_2, 1)$	7	9
$Occ(sp_3, 1)$	8	10
$Occ(sp_4, 1)$	8	11
$Occ(sp_1, 2)$	12	13
$Occ(sp_2, 2)$	19	21
$Occ(sp_5, 1)$	20	22
$Occ(sp_2, 3)$	26	28
$Occ(sp_3, 2)$	29	31
$Occ(sp_4, 2)$	29	32

Fig. 2. $Occ(SP)$ constructed by output of the Aho-Corasick algorithm. $Occ(sp_i, j)$ refers to the j-th occurrence of the sensitive pattern sp_i in the string S and corresponds to a a pair of positions denoting the positions at which the occurrence of sp_i starts and ends in S.

cluster	positions
$\{sp_1\}$	**5, 12**
$\{sp_2, sp_3, sp_4\}$	**8, 9**
$\{sp_2, sp_5, sp_1\}$	20, **21**
sp_2	**26**
sp_3, sp_4	29, 30, **31**

Fig. 3. Array A constructed by the SetIntersection algorithm. The position deleted by the SanitizeClusters appears in bold.

otherwise. The 5 clusters, together with their corresponding positions in the string S are returned as an array A, as illustrated in Fig. 3.

After that, the SanitizeClusters algorithm will consider each cluster and replace the most frequency of its corresponding positions in the string S with *, until all occurrences of all sensitive patterns in the cluster are sanitized (i.e., they have at least one of their positions replaced with *). The positionts that will be replaced with * are shown in bold in Fig. 3. Then, the SanitizeClusters algorithm will return the sanitized string S', which is produced by replacing the selected positions with *. The sanitized string S' is shown in Fig. 4. Last, S' is output by the SSA algorithm.

```
0 1 2 3 4 5 6 7 8 9 10 11 12 13 14 15 16 17 18 19 20 21 22 23 24 25 26 27 28 29 30 31 32
a a t c c * g c a * c t * g a a t t g c a * g c c t * a a a a * t
```

Fig. 4. Sanitizing sensitive patterns in a given text string after applying SSA

5   Experimental Evaluation

In this section, we evaluate SSA in terms of efficiency (running time) and utility (total number of deleted symbols). We did not compare against existing sanitization methods, as they cannot address the OSS problem. The dataset used was the Activities of Daily Living (ADL) dataset. This dataset is available from the UCI repository (https://archive.ics.uci.edu/ml/), and it has been used in prior works on data sanitization [13]. Based on this dataset, the following results were obtained:

Num. of sens. patterns	Total length of sens. patterns	Num. of *s	Time (in ms)
5	9	694	5.25
10	17	694	5.75
15	33	447	5.87

Fig. 5. Results for dataset for activity brushing of teeth.

Num. of sens. patterns	Total length of sens. patterns	Num. of *s	Time (in ms)
5	11	134	5.60
10	17	219	5.75
15	33	220	5.82

Fig. 6. Results for dataset for activity drinking glass.

Num. of sens. patterns	Total length of sens. patterns	Num. of *s	Time (in ms)
5	9	607	5.5
10	17	682	5.77
15	33	895	5.82

Fig. 7. Results for dataset for activity climbing stairs.

As can be seen from Figs. 5, 6, and 7, the algorithm is reasonably efficient, requiring no more than 10 ms to sanitize the set of sensitive patterns, which contains no more than 15 patterns. Furthermore, as expected, the runtime generally increases with the number of sensitive patterns, because, the more sensitive patterns we have, the larger their sum of lengths are (shown as total length of sensitive patterns in the tables).

In addition, the algorithm does not replace a large number of symbols with *. Specifically, the number of symbols that were replaced was no more than 895. As expected, the number of symbols that were replaced generally increases with the number of specified sensitive patterns. For example, it increases from 607 to 895 in Fig. 7. However, this was not true in Fig. 5, because in this experiment the sensitive patterns that were added as the number of sensitive patterns increased from 5 to 15 did not have many of their symbols selected for replacement by the algorithm.

6   Conclusion and Future Work

String sanitization is a necessary task in applications that feature sequences containing confidential information. This paper studied the problem of how to efficiently sanitize a string by replacing a small number of selected symbols contained in sensitive patterns with a special character "*". To deal with the problem, we proposed an algorithm SSA that fuses two sub-algorithms, one for detecting occurrences of sensitive patterns in the string, and another for sanitizing the sensitive patterns. The proposed algorithm was implemented and evaluated using the ADL dataset. Our results demonstrate the efficiency and effectiveness of our approach. Being the first work on addressing the problem of sanitizing a string, this work opens up a number of interesting avenues for future investigation. These include: (i) examining how to preserve the utility of the sanitized string in analytics or mining applications, (ii) developing algorithms for sanitizing strings that do not fit into the main memory, and (iii) performing

210   O. Ajala et al.

an evaluation of the algorithm using sensitive patterns that are specified by experts and model their privacy requirements (e.g., as in [9,16]).

References

1. Abul, O., Bonchi, F., Nanni, M.: Never walk alone: uncertainty for anonymity in moving objects databases. In: ICDE, pp. 376–385 (2008)
2. Abul, O., Bonchi, F., Giannotti, F.: Hiding sequential and spatiotemporal patterns. TKDE **22**(12), 1709–1723 (2010)
3. Aho, A., Corasick, M.J.: Efficient string matching: an aid to bibliographic search. Commun. ACM **18**(6), 333–340 (1975)
4. Chen, R., Mohammed, N., Fung, B.C.M., Desai, B.C., Xiong, L.: Publishing set-valued data via differential privacy. PVLDB **4**(11), 1087–1098 (2011)
5. Cormode, G., Karloff, H., Wirth, A.: Set cover algorithms for very large datasets. In: CIKM, pp. 479–488 (2010)
6. Crochemore, M., Hancart, C., Lecroc, T.: Algorithm on Strings. Cambridge University Press, Cambridge (2007)
7. Dwork, C.: Differential Privacy. In: Bugliesi, M., Preneel, B., Sassone, V., Wegener, I. (eds.) ICALP 2006. LNCS, vol. 4052, pp. 1–12. Springer, Heidelberg (2006). https://doi.org/10.1007/11787006_1
8. Gkoulalas-Divanis, A., Loukides, G.: Revisiting sequential pattern hiding to enhance utility. In: KDD, pp. 1316–1324 (2011)
9. Gkoulalas-Divanis, A., Loukides, G.: Utility-guided clustering-based transaction data anonymization. Trans. Data Priv. **5**(1), 223–251 (2012)
10. Götz, M., Nath, S., Gehrke, J.: MaskIt: privately releasing user context streams for personalized mobile applications. In: SIGMOD, pp. 289–300 (2012)
11. Gwadera, R., Gkoulalas-Divanis, A., Loukides, G.: Permutation-based sequential pattern hiding. In: ICDM, pp. 241–250 (2013)
12. He, Y., Barman, S., Wang, D., Naughton, J.F.: On the complexity of privacy-preserving complex event processing. In: PODS, pp. 165–174 (2011)
13. Loukides, G., Gwadera, R.: Optimal event sequence sanitization. In: Proceedings of the 2015 SIAM International Conference on Data Mining, pp. 775–783 (2015)
14. Monreale, A., Pedreschi, D., Pensa, R.G., Pinelli, F.: Anonymity preserving sequential pattern mining. Artif. Intell. Law **22**(2), 141–173 (2014)
15. Oliveira, S.R.M., Zaïane, O.R.: Protecting sensitive knowledge by data sanitization. In: ICDM, pp. 211–218 (2003)
16. Poulis, G., Skiadopoulos, S., Loukides, G., Gkoulalas-Divanis, A.: Apriori-based algorithms for km-anonymizing trajectory data. Trans. Data Priv. **7**(2), 165–194 (2014)
17. Rastogi, V., Nath, S.: Differentially private aggregation of distributed time-series with transformation and encryption. In: SIGMOD, pp. 735–746 (2010)
18. Sherkat, R., Li, J., Mamoulis, N.: Efficient time-stamped event sequence anonymization. ACM Trans. Web **8**(1), 4:1–4:53 (2013)
19. Sun, X., Yu, P.: A border-based approach for hiding sensitive frequent itemsets. In: ICDM, pp. 426–433 (2005)
20. Verykios, V.S., Emagarmid, A.K., Bertino, E., Saygin, Y., Dasseni, E.: Association rule hiding. TKDE **16**(4), 434–447 (2004)
21. Wang, D., He, Y., Rundensteiner, E., Naughton, J.F.: Utility-maximizing event stream suppression. In: SIGMOD, pp. 589–600 (2013)

Efficient Recognition of Abelian Palindromic Factors and Associated Results

Costas S. Iliopoulos and Steven Watts[✉]

Department of Informatics, King's College London, London, UK
{costas.iliopoulos,steven.watts}@kcl.ac.uk

Abstract. A string is called a *palindrome* if it reads the same from left to right. In this paper we define the new concept of an *abelian palindrome* which satisfies the property of being abelian equivalent to some palindrome of the same length. The identification of abelian palindromes presents a novel combinatorial problem, with potential applications in filtering strings for palindromic factors. We present an algorithm to efficiently identify abelian palindromes, and additionally generate an *abelian palindromic array*, indicating the longest abelian palindrome at each location. Specifically, for an alphabet of size $|\Sigma| \leq \log_2(n)$ and after $\mathcal{O}(n)$ time preprocessing using $\mathcal{O}(n + |\Sigma|)$ space, we may determine if any factor is abelian palindromic in $\mathcal{O}(1)$ time. Additionally, we may determine the abelian palindromic array in $\mathcal{O}(|\Sigma|n)$ time. We further specify the algorithmic complexity when this condition on alphabet size $|\Sigma|$ is relaxed.

1 Introduction

The identification of palindromic factors in strings, has been a much studied area of stringology, due to the interesting combinatorial aspects and the strong ties with genetic analysis, where palindromes often correspond to significant structures in DNA [3].

Variations of the palindrome identification problem have been frequently introduced, for example Karhumäki and Puzynina presented results on k-abelian palindromes on rich and poor words [2]. Holub and Saari considered the problem as applied to binary words, investigating the properties of palindromic factors of binary strings [4].

We introduce our own simple modification to the problem, yet to be explored, namely abelian palindromes. Though an interesting combinatorial problem in it itself, an efficient method of detecting abelian palindromes can potentially provide a filter by which ordinary palindromic factors may be deduced. This follows from the fact that an ordinary palindrome must necessarily also be an abelian palindrome, and therefore the search space may be reduced if non abelian palindromes can be efficiently dismissed.

© IFIP International Federation for Information Processing 2018
Published by Springer International Publishing AG 2018. All Rights Reserved
L. Iliadis et al. (Eds.): AIAI 2018, IFIP AICT 520, pp. 211–223, 2018.
https://doi.org/10.1007/978-3-319-92016-0_20

Likewise, the abelian palindromic array may potentially be used to assist in the calculation of the ordinary palindromic array, for the purpose of performing a greedy factorisation of a string into ordinary palindromes. This follows from the fact that the abelian palindromic array provides an upper bound for the equivalent value in the ordinary palindromic array.

The rest of this paper is organised as follows. In Sect. 2, we present basic definitions and notation on strings as well as definitions and results on abelian palindromes. Section 3 presents various data structures and algorithmic tools used in our final algorithms. In Sect. 4, a detailed implementation of our algorithms are presented, the first being identification of abelian palindromes, the second being the generation of the abelian palindromic array. Our concluding remarks are noted in Sect. 5. Additionally, the pseudocode of our implementation may be found in Sect. 6.

2   Preliminaries

2.1   Basic Terminology

We begin with basic definitions and notation from [1]. Let $x = x[0]x[1]\ldots x[n-1]$ be a *string* of length $|x| = n$ over a finite ordered alphabet. We consider the case of strings over an *integer alphabet* Σ: each character may be replaced by its lexicographical rank in such a way that the resulting string consists of integers in the range $\{0,\ldots,n-1\}$. We use $\text{ORD}(x[i])$ to refer to the lexicographical rank of the character $x[i]$. We use $\Sigma[i]$ to refer to the ith character of Σ, i.e. $\Sigma[\text{ORD}(x[i])] = x[i]$. For example, for the alphabet $\Sigma = \{\text{a},\text{c},\text{g},\text{t}\}$ we have $\text{ORD}(\text{g}) = 2$ and $\Sigma[2] = \text{g}$.

For two positions i and j on x, we denote by $x[i\mathinner{..}j] = x[i]\ldots x[j]$ the *factor* (sometimes called *substring*) of x that starts at position i and ends at position j (it is of length 0 if $j < i$), and by ε the *empty string* of length 0. We recall that a *prefix* of x is a factor that starts at position 0 ($x[0\mathinner{..}j]$) and a *suffix* of x is a factor that ends at position $n-1$ ($x[i\mathinner{..}n-1]$).

Let y be a string of length m with $0 < m \le n$. We say that there exists an *occurrence* of y in x, or, more simply, that y *occurs in* x, when y is a factor of x. Every occurrence of y can be characterised by a starting position in x. Thus we say that y occurs at the *starting position* i in x when $y = x[i\mathinner{..}i+m-1]$.

We denote the *reverse* string of x by x^R as the string obtained when reading x from right to left, i.e. $x^R = x[n-1]x[n-2]\ldots x[1]x[0]$. We say a string x is a *palindrome* when $x = x^R$.

We make use of the bit-wise *exclusive or* (XOR) operation between two binary strings x and y of the same length $|x| = |y|$, denoted $x \oplus y$. This adheres to the standard definition of XOR on two binary strings, i.e. $z[i] = (x[i] + y[i]) \pmod 2$ where $z = x \oplus y$. We may similarly apply the XOR operation to integers, $x, y \in \mathbb{Z}$ by converting x and y to their respective binary equivalents, performing the XOR operation, and converting the binary result into an integer. For example, given $x = 5, y = 11$ we have $x \oplus y = 5 \oplus 11 = 0101 \oplus 1011 = 1110 = 14$.

2.2 Abelian Palindromes

The concept of abelian strings relates to the idea of disregarding the order of appearance of characters in a string, and concerning ourselves only with the number of occurrences of each character within the string. With this in mind, we wish to define the concept of an *abelian palindrome*. To facilitate this, we must first recall the definition of a *Parikh Vector*.

Definition 1. *The Parikh vector $\mathcal{P}(T)$ of a string T over the alphabet Σ, is a vector of size $|\Sigma|$ which enumerates the number of occurrences of each character of the alphabet in T. If the character $c \in \Sigma$ has ordinality $i = \text{ORD}(c)$ in the lexicographical ordering of the alphabet Σ, then $\mathcal{P}(T)[i]$ stores the number of occurrences of c in T.*

We say that two strings T_1 and T_2 are abelian equivalent *denoted $T_1 \approx_p T_2$ if and only if they have the same Parikh vector, i.e. are permutations of each other.*

For example, the string $T_1 = $ accgta has the Parikh vector $\mathcal{P}(T_1) = (2, 2, 1, 1)$. The string $T_2 = $ gactcac has the same Parikh vector and thus $T_1 \approx_p T_2$. We may now define the concept of an abelian palindrome.

Definition 2. *A string T is an* abelian palindrome *if and only if there exists some palindrome P such that $P \approx_p T$.*

Note that in general, a string T will more easily satisfy the abelian palindromic property over the palindromic property. This comes as a direct result of Lemma 1, which follows clearly from Definition 2.

Lemma 1.

$$T \text{ palindromic} \implies T \text{ abelian palindromic} \qquad (1)$$
$$T \text{ not abelian palindromic} \implies T \text{ not palindromic} \qquad (2)$$

Proof. Assume T is palindromic, choose $P = T$. Therefore we have $P = T \approx_p T$. Thus T is abelian palindromic and Statement 1 is proven. Statement 2 follows as the contrapositive of Statement 1. $\qquad \square$

3   Tools

3.1   Initial Observations

We wish to efficiently identify abelian palindromic factors within a string. To enable this, we define some further concepts and auxiliary data structures.

From Definition 2, it is clear that whether a string T is an abelian palindrome is dependant on the values in its Parikh vector $\mathcal{P}(T)$, specifically the number of values that are odd or even. We use $|\mathcal{P}(T)|$ to refer to the total number of values in $\mathcal{P}(T)$, and further use $|(\mathcal{P}(T))|_{\text{odd}}$ and $|(\mathcal{P}(T))|_{\text{even}}$ to refer to the number of odd and even values in $\mathcal{P}(T)$ respectively. This notation allows us to succinctly describe the defining quality of an abelian palindrome in Lemma 2.

Lemma 2. T *abelian palindromic* $\Longleftrightarrow 0 \le |(\mathcal{P}(T))|_{odd} \le 1$.

Proof. We refer to the length of T as n. We call $T_l = T[0 \mathinner{\ldotp\ldotp} \lfloor \frac{n-1}{2} - 1 \rfloor]$ the *left half* of T and $T_r = T[\lceil \frac{n-1}{2} + 1 \rceil \mathinner{\ldotp\ldotp} n-1]$ the *right half* of T. Note that if n is even, $T = T_l\,T_r$. If n is odd, $T = T_l\,c\,T_r$ where $c = T[\frac{n-1}{2}]$. For an ordinary palindrome P, it is clear that if a character s occurs m times in P_l it must correspondingly occur m times in P_r, to preserve the palindromic property of P.

We first show that if T is an abelian palindrome, the number of odd values in the Parikh vector $|(\mathcal{P}(T))|_{odd}$ can not exceed 1 by contradiction. Let us assume that $|(\mathcal{P}(T))|_{odd} > 1$. In this case, we have at least 2 different characters $s_1, s_2 \in \Sigma$ with an odd number of occurrences in T. For any permutation of the characters in T, at least one of these two characters must have all its occurrences contained entirely within T_l and T_r, and we call this character s. The character s therefore occurs $2m$ times in T where m is the number of occurrences of s in T_l. Therefore s has an even number of occurrences, which leads us to a contradiction. Therefore we conclude that $0 \le |(\mathcal{P}(T))|_{odd} \le 1$.

We now show that we can always form a palindrome from a permutation of T when $0 \le |(\mathcal{P}(T))|_{odd} \le 1$. In the notation below we use P_l^R to represent the reversal of P_l.

Let us assume $|(\mathcal{P}(T))|_{odd} = 0$. In this case, $\mathcal{P}(T)$ contains only even values. We distribute the characters evenly to form an even length palindrome P such that $P \approx_p T$ as follows (with braces under characters indicating the number of repetitions of that character):

$$P_l = \underbrace{\Sigma[0]}_{\frac{1}{2}\mathcal{P}(T)[0]} \quad \underbrace{\Sigma[1]}_{\frac{1}{2}\mathcal{P}(T)[1]} \quad \cdots \quad \underbrace{\Sigma[|\Sigma|-1]}_{\frac{1}{2}\mathcal{P}(T)[|\Sigma|-1]}$$

$$P = P_l\,P_l^R$$

Now let us assume $|(\mathcal{P}(T))|_{odd} = 1$. In this case, $\mathcal{P}(T)$ contains a single odd entry corresponding to some character $c = \Sigma[i]$. We distribute the characters evenly, placing the character c at the centre, to form an odd length palindrome P such that $P \approx_p T$ as follows:

$$P_l = \underbrace{\Sigma[0]}_{\frac{1}{2}\mathcal{P}(T)[0]} \quad \cdots \quad \underbrace{\Sigma[i-1]}_{\frac{1}{2}\mathcal{P}(T)[i-1]} \quad \underbrace{\Sigma[i+1]}_{\frac{1}{2}\mathcal{P}(T)[i+1]} \quad \cdots \quad \underbrace{\Sigma[|\Sigma|-1]}_{\frac{1}{2}\mathcal{P}(T)[|\Sigma|-1]} \quad \underbrace{\Sigma[i]}_{\frac{1}{2}(\mathcal{P}(T)[i]-1)}$$

$$P = P_l\,\Sigma[i]\,P_l^R$$

Thus we have shown that $0 \le |(\mathcal{P}(T))|_{odd} \le 1$ is both a necessary and sufficient condition for T to be an abelian palindrome. Therefore Lemma 2 follows. $\qquad\square$

3.2   Prefix Parity Integer Array

We aim to describe a new data structure that will prove useful in recognising palindromic factors, beginning with some new definitions.

Lemma 2 provides us with a useful criterion by which we can seek longest abelian palindromes. We first provide some additional definitions which will prove useful.

Definition 3. *A prefix Parikh vector* $\mathcal{P}_i(T)$ *of a string* T *is the Parikh vector of the ith prefix of* T:

$$\mathcal{P}_i(T) = \mathcal{P}(T[0..i]) \; for \; 0 \leq i \leq n-1$$

Definition 4. *A parity vector* $\mathbb{P}(T)$ *of a string* T *over the alphabet* Σ *is a bit vector of length* Σ *which indicates the parity (even or odd) of the number of occurrences of each character of* Σ *in* T *(0 indicates **even**, 1 indicates **odd**):*

$$\mathbb{P}(T)[i] = \mathcal{P}(T)[i] \quad (\bmod \; 2)$$

Definition 5. *A prefix parity vector* $\mathbb{P}_i(T)$ *of a string* T *is the parity vector of the ith prefix of* T:

$$\mathbb{P}_i(T) = \mathbb{P}(T[0..i]) \; for \; 0 \leq i \leq n-1$$

Definition 6. *A parity integer* $\hat{\mathbb{P}}(T)$ *of a string* T *over the alphabet* Σ *is a decimal integer representing the value of the parity vector* $\mathbb{P}(T)$ *when interpreted as a binary number, with the order of magnitude of each bit determined by the lexicographical order of the alphabet* Σ:

$$\hat{\mathbb{P}}(T) = \sum_{i=0}^{|\Sigma|-1} 2^i \times \mathbb{P}(T)[i]$$

Definition 7. *A prefix parity integer* $\hat{\mathbb{P}}_i(T)$ *of a string* T *is the parity integer of the ith prefix of* T:

$$\hat{\mathbb{P}}_i(T) = \hat{\mathbb{P}}(T[0..i]) \; for \; 0 \leq i \leq n-1$$

Definition 8. *The prefix parity integer array* $\hat{\mathbb{P}}_A(T)$ *of a string* T *of length* n *is an integer array of length* n, *which contains the value of* $\hat{\mathbb{P}}_i(T)$ *at each position* i:

$$\hat{\mathbb{P}}_A(T)[i] = \hat{\mathbb{P}}_i(T)$$

The prefix parity integer array $\hat{\mathbb{P}}_A(T)$ (example: see bottom of Fig. 1) is the key to identifying longest abelian palindromes in a string T. To observe this, we note that the Parikh vector of a factor of T can be determined by evaluating the difference between the two prefix Parikh vectors at the start and end indexes of the factor. The parity vector and parity integer of a factor can also be determined in a similar way, by employing the bit-wise exclusive or (XOR) operation. We summarise these observations in Lemma 3.

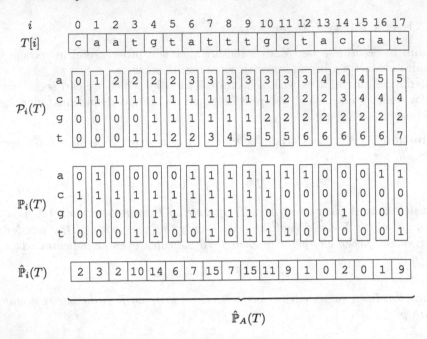

Fig. 1. Example of prefix Parikh vectors, prefix parity vectors and prefix parity integers.

Lemma 3. *Given a string T:*

$$\mathcal{P}(T[i..j]) = \mathcal{P}_j(T) - \mathcal{P}_{i-1}(T) \tag{1}$$

$$\mathbb{P}(T[i..j]) = \mathbb{P}_j(T) \oplus \mathbb{P}_{i-1}(T) \tag{2}$$

$$\hat{\mathbb{P}}(T[i..j]) = \hat{\mathbb{P}}_j(T) \oplus \hat{\mathbb{P}}_{i-1}(T) \tag{3}$$

Proof. Given a factor $F = T[i..j]$ we have $T[0..j] = T[0..i-1]\,F$. Therefore it follows that $\mathcal{P}(T[0..j]) = \mathcal{P}(T[0..i-1]) + \mathcal{P}(F) \implies \mathcal{P}(F) = \mathcal{P}(T[0..j]) - \mathcal{P}(T[0..i-1])$. Thus Statement 1 is proven.

Statement 2 follows from Statement 1 by observing that the truth table for the XOR operator is analogous to the parity table for the subtraction operator (when we interpret 0 as even, 1 as odd):

$-$	even	odd		$\oplus$	0	1
even	even	odd		0	0	1
odd	odd	even		1	1	0

Note that subtraction (mod 2) and XOR are both commutative operations, and therefore the order of operations is unimportant for both tables.

Statement 3 is simply an alternative formulation of Statement 2 in the form of parity integers instead of parity vectors. □

Given $\hat{\mathbb{P}}_A(T)$, it now becomes simple to verify whether a factor $T[i \,..\, j]$ is an abelian palindrome, i.e. $0 \leq |\mathcal{P}(T[i \,..\, j])|_{\text{odd}} \leq 1$.

Lemma 4. *Given a text T over the alphabet Σ, the following holds:*

$$T[i \,..\, j] \text{ abelian palindromic} \iff \hat{\mathbb{P}}_j(T) \oplus \hat{\mathbb{P}}_{i-1}(T) \in \{0\} \cup \{2^0, 2^1, \ldots, 2^{|\Sigma|-1}\}$$

Proof. The lemma follows from the application of previously defined lemmas. We use brackets under runs of characters to indicate the length of that run of characters:

$T[i \,..\, j]$ is abelian palindromic

$$\underset{\text{Lem. 2}}{\iff} 0 \leq |\mathcal{P}(T[i \,..\, j])|_{\text{odd}} \leq 1$$

$$\iff |\mathcal{P}(T[i \,..\, j])|_{\text{odd}} = 0 \ \vee \ |\mathcal{P}(T[i \,..\, j])|_{\text{odd}} = 1$$

$$\underset{\text{Def. 4}}{\iff} \mathbb{P}(T[i \,..\, j]) = \underbrace{0 \ldots 0}_{|\Sigma|} \ \vee \ \mathbb{P}(T) \in \{\underbrace{0 \ldots 0}_{|\Sigma|-1}1, \underbrace{0 \ldots 0}_{|\Sigma|-2}10, \ldots, 1\underbrace{0 \ldots 0}_{|\Sigma|-1}\}$$

$$\underset{\text{Def. 6}}{\iff} \mathbb{P}(T[i \,..\, j]) = 0 \ \vee \ \hat{\mathbb{P}}(T) \in \{2^0, 2^1, 2^2, \ldots, 2^{|\Sigma|-1}\}$$

$$\underset{\text{Lem. 3}}{\iff} \hat{\mathbb{P}}_j(T) \oplus \hat{\mathbb{P}}_{i-1}(T) \in \{0\} \cup \{2^0, 2^1, \ldots, 2^{|\Sigma|-1}\}$$

□

Lemma 4 immediately leads us to Lemma 5, which allows us to identify the longest factor of a string T starting at i which is abelian palindromic.

Lemma 5. *Given a text T over the alphabet Σ, the longest abelian palindromic factor of T occurring at position i is $T[i \,..\, j]$ where j satisfies the following:*

$$j = \max\{j' : \hat{\mathbb{P}}_{j'}(T) \in M(T, i)\}$$

$$M(T, i) = \{\hat{\mathbb{P}}_{i-1}(T) \oplus k : k \in \{0\} \cup \{2^0, 2^1, \ldots, 2^{|\Sigma|-1}\}\}$$

For a given string T and position i, we call $M(T, i)$ the match set.

Proof. For a fixed i, the longest $T[i \,..\, j]$ which is abelian palindromic is found by determining the largest j, such that i and j satisfy the condition in Lemma 4. We may derive the match set $M(T, i)$ from this condition by employing the fact that XOR is commutative:

$$\hat{\mathbb{P}}_{j'}(T) \oplus \hat{\mathbb{P}}_{i-1}(T) \in \{0\} \cup \{2^0, 2^1, \dots, 2^{|\Sigma|-1}\}$$

$$\Longleftrightarrow \exists k \in \{0\} \cup \{2^0, 2^1, \dots, 2^{|\Sigma|-1}\} \text{ such that } \hat{\mathbb{P}}_{j'}(T) \oplus \hat{\mathbb{P}}_{i-1}(T) = k$$

$$\Longleftrightarrow \exists k \in \{0\} \cup \{2^0, 2^1, \dots, 2^{|\Sigma|-1}\} \text{ such that } \hat{\mathbb{P}}_{j'}(T) = \hat{\mathbb{P}}_{i-1}(T) \oplus k$$

$$\Longleftrightarrow \mathbb{P}_{j'}(T) \in \{\hat{\mathbb{P}}_{i-1}(T) \oplus k : k \in \{0\} \cup \{2^0, 2^1, \dots, 2^{|\Sigma|-1}\}\} = M(T, i)$$

Thus for a given i, the largest j' satisfying the above condition gives us the j corresponding to the largest abelian palindromic factor $T[i \mathinner{..} j]$. $\qquad\square$

3.3   Rightmost Array

We describe a simple data structure that will prove useful for identifying longest abelian palindromes (Fig. 2).

Definition 9. *The* rightmost array $\mathcal{R}(A)$ *of an integer array A of length n over the alphabet $\{0, \dots, n-1\}$ stores at position i the index of the rightmost occurrence of the integer i in A. If there is no occurrence of i in A then $A[i] = -1$. Formally stated:*

$$\mathcal{R}(A)[i] = k \quad \Longleftrightarrow \quad A[k] = i \wedge A[k'] \neq i \ \forall k' > k$$

$$\mathcal{R}(A)[i] = -1 \Longleftrightarrow A[k] \neq i \ \forall k$$

i	0	1	2	3	4	5	6	7	8	9	10	11	12	13	14	15	16	17
$A[i]$	2	3	2	10	14	6	7	15	7	15	11	9	1	0	2	0	1	9
$\mathcal{R}(A)[i]$	15	16	14	1	-1	-1	5	8	-1	17	3	10	-1	-1	4	9	-1	-1

Fig. 2. Example of rightmost array.

4   Algorithms

4.1   Abelian Palindromic Factor Recognition

ABELIAN PALINDROMIC FACTOR RECOGNITION
Input: A string T of length n.
Output: A function $\mathrm{F} : \{0 \mathinner{..} n-1\} \times \{0 \mathinner{..} n-1\} \to \{\texttt{true}, \texttt{false}\}$ where $F(i, j)$ returns $\texttt{true}$ if $T[i \mathinner{..} j]$ is abelian palindromic and $\texttt{false}$ if $T[i \mathinner{..} j]$ is not abelian palindromic, in $\mathcal{O}(1)$ time.

Our algorithm to generate a function recognising abelian palindromic factors, relies on the construction of the prefix parity integer array $\hat{\mathbb{P}}_A(T)$. As shown in Lemma 4, we are able to determine if $T[i..j]$ is abelian palindromic by evaluating the truthfulness of the expression $\hat{\mathbb{P}}_j(T) \oplus \hat{\mathbb{P}}_{i-1}(T) \in \{0\} \cup \{2^0, 2^1, \ldots, 2^{|\Sigma|-1}\}$.

Given $\hat{\mathbb{P}}_A(T)$, this expression may be evaluated in $\mathcal{O}(1)$ time for a given i and j. This follows from the fact that XOR is a constant time operation. Additionally, we may check if an integer is a power of 2 in constant time by employing the (mod 2) operation.

It is important to note, that these operations are constant time under the assumption that their arguments do not exceed the maximum word size w of the computer implementation used. If we assume that the alphabet size is bounded by the logarithm of n, then this assumption holds, i.e. $|\Sigma| \leq \log_2(n)$. Alternatively, the limitation on $|\Sigma|$ need not depend on n, and may instead be expressed in terms of the word size w of a machine. If the word size is w, we may assume these operations are constant for an alphabet size $|\Sigma| \leq w$. For a larger $|\Sigma|$, the expression in Lemma 4 may be evaluated in $\mathcal{O}(\frac{|\Sigma|}{w})$ time.

We now consider the construction of $\hat{\mathbb{P}}_A(T)$. It is possible to construct the array directly while maintaining a single instance of $\hat{\mathbb{P}}_i(T)$, by Lemma 6.

Lemma 6.

$$\hat{\mathbb{P}}_A(T)[0] \quad = 2^{\mathrm{ORD}(T[0])}$$
$$\hat{\mathbb{P}}_A(T)[i] \quad = \hat{\mathbb{P}}_A(T)[i-1] + (2\,\mathbb{P}_i(T)[\mathrm{ORD}(T[i])] - 1) \times 2^{\mathrm{ORD}(T[i])} \quad 0 < i \leq n-1$$

Proof. The case for $\hat{\mathbb{P}}_A(T)[0]$ is trivially true. We note that $\hat{\mathbb{P}}_A(T)[i] = \hat{\mathbb{P}}_i(T)$ is an integer representation of $\mathbb{P}_i(T)$ interpreted as a binary string. $\mathbb{P}_i(T)$ and $\mathbb{P}_{i-1}(T)$ differ by a single bit flip, corresponding to the character encountered at $T[i]$. Therefore by Definitions 6 and 7, $\hat{\mathbb{P}}_i(T)$ and $\hat{\mathbb{P}}_{i-1}(T)$ will accordingly differ by a single power of 2, specifically $2^{\mathrm{ORD}(T[i])}$.

Whether $2^{\mathrm{ORD}(T[i])}$ should be added or subtracted is dependant on the current parity of the character $T[i]$. This is determined by $\mathbb{P}_i(T)[\mathrm{ORD}(T[i])]$, with 1 corresponding to addition $(+1)$ and 0 corresponding to subtraction (-1).

Thus the mapping $2b - 1$ where $b \in \{0, 1\}$ is the most recently flipped bit $b = \mathbb{P}_i(T)[\mathrm{ORD}(T[i])]$, indicates the appropriate addition $(+1)$ or subtraction (-1). $\qquad\square$

With this iterative equation for $\hat{\mathbb{P}}_A(T)$, we now have all the tools necessary to efficiently determine abelian palindromic factors and solve the problem as stated. We formalise the result in Theorem 1.

Theorem 1. *Given a string T of length n over the alphabet Σ, after $\mathcal{O}(n)$ time preprocessing and $\mathcal{O}(n + |\Sigma|)$ space, we may perform queries to determine if $T[i..j]$ is abelian palindromic in $\mathcal{O}(1)$ time when $|\Sigma| \leq \log_2(n)$.*

Additionally with no constraint on the size of Σ, with $\mathcal{O}(\frac{|\Sigma|}{w}n)$ time preprocessing we may perform such queries in $\mathcal{O}(\frac{|\Sigma|}{w})$ time, where w is the computer word size.

Proof. By using Lemma 6 we may iteratively construct $\hat{\mathbb{P}}_A(T)[i]$ from $\hat{\mathbb{P}}_A(T)[i-1]$ in $\mathcal{O}(1)$ time at each step, while maintaining the Σ-sized data structure $\mathbb{P}_i(T)$, resulting in a total time complexity $\mathcal{O}(n)$ and space complexity $\mathcal{O}(n + |\Sigma|)$ to construct $\hat{\mathbb{P}}_A(T)$.

By evaluating the expression on $\hat{\mathbb{P}}_A(T)$ in Lemma 4, we may then determine if $T[i..j]$ is abelian palindromic. Evaluating this expression may be performed in $\mathcal{O}(1)$ time when the number of bits required to store $\hat{\mathbb{P}}_i(T)$ is no larger than a single computer word w, i.e. when $|\Sigma| \leq \log_2(n) \leq w$. In general, $\hat{\mathbb{P}}_i(T)$ may be stored in $|\Sigma|$ bits, requiring $\lceil \frac{|\Sigma|}{w} \rceil$ words to store, and thus a multiplying factor of $\mathcal{O}(\frac{|\Sigma|}{w})$ time is required for all operations involving $\hat{\mathbb{P}}_i(T)$, both when constructing $\hat{\mathbb{P}}_A(T)$ and when evaluating the expression in Lemma 4, corresponding to a single query.   □

4.2   Abelian Palindromic Array Algorithm

ABELIAN PALINDROMIC ARRAY
Input: A string T of length n.
Output: An array P of size n such that $A[i]$ stores the length of the longest abelian factor of T occurring at position i, i.e. as a prefix of $T[i..n-1]$.

Our algorithm to generate the abelian palindromic array makes use of Theorem 1 and the rightmost array described in Definition 9. We also make use of Lemma 7.

Lemma 7. *The abelian palindromic array P of a string T satisfies:*

$$P[i] = \max\{\mathcal{R}(j) : j \in M(T, \hat{\mathbb{P}}_A(T)[i])\}$$

Where M is the match set as described in Lemma 5.

Proof. Lemma 5 indicates that the longest abelian palindromic factor occurring at i is $T[i..j]$ where j is the index of the rightmost prefix parity integer with a value contained in the match set $M(T, i)$.

By Definition 9, this rightmost j can be found by taking the largest value obtained when querying the rightmost array with every member of the match set.   □

Theorem 2. *Given a string T of length n over the alphabet Σ, we may determine the abelian palindromic array of T in $\mathcal{O}(|\Sigma|n)$ time and $\mathcal{O}(n + |\Sigma|)$ space, when $|\Sigma| \leq \log_2(n)$.*

Proof. Via the proof in Theorem 1 we are able to calculate the prefix parity integer array $\hat{\mathbb{P}}_A(T)$ in $\mathcal{O}(n)$ time and with $\mathcal{O}(n + |\Sigma|)$ space.

Since $|\Sigma| \leq \log_2(n)$, we know all values of $\mathcal{R}(A)[i] \in \{-1, 0, \ldots, n-1\}$. Therefore the rightmost array $\mathcal{R}(\hat{\mathbb{P}}_A(T))$ may be calculated in $\mathcal{O}(n)$ time, by parsing $\hat{\mathbb{P}}_A(T)$ from right to left and storing any new values encountered. Full details are available in the pseudocode in Sect. 6.

We now apply Lemma 7, which enables us to determine the longest abelian palindromic factor occurring at i by performing $|\Sigma|$ constant time queries. Thus a total of $\mathcal{O}(|\Sigma|n)$ constant time queries are required, and the total time complexity to generate the abelian palindromic array is $\mathcal{O}(|\Sigma|n)$.   □

5   Conclusion

We have presented two algorithms, the first for recognising whether or not a factor is abelian palindromic, and the second for generating an array which provides the length of the longest abelian palindromic factor at each position in a string.

The proposed algorithms are both dependant on a new data structure called the prefix parity integer array, requiring $\mathcal{O}(n)$ time to compute for a string with an alphabet size $|\Sigma| \leq \log_2(n)$. Additional complexity is required to determine the longest abelian palindromic factor for each position, namely $\mathcal{O}(|\Sigma|n)$ time.

The main improvement in this work, would be to remove the need for the current requirement that $|\Sigma| \leq \log_2(n)$, in order to obtain our current best complexity time. This appears to be a reasonable goal.

6   Pseudocode

Algorithm. Abelian Palindromes

```
1: function GETPREFIXPARITYINTEGERARRAY(T, Σ)
2:     n = |T|
3:     σ = |Σ|
4:     A = integer array of length n filled with 0          ▷ stores final result
5:     B = integer array of length σ filled with 0          ▷ stores powers of 2
6:     B[0] = 1
7:
8:     for i = 1 to σ − 1 do
9:         B[i] = 2 × B[i − 1]
10:    end for
11:
12:    ℙ = boolean array of length σ filled with 0
13:    prev = 0
14:
15:    for i = 0 to n − 1 do
16:        if ℙ[ORD(T[i])] == 1 then          ▷ ORD is the 0-indexed lexicographical order
17:            A[i] = prev − B[ORD(T[i])]
18:        else
19:            A[i] = prev + B[ORD(T[i])]
20:        end if
21:
22:        ℙ[ORD(T[i])] = not ℙ[ORD(T[i])]          ▷ not 1 = 0, not 0 = 1
23:        prev = A[i]
24:    end for
25:
26:    return A
27: end function
```

Algorithm. Abelian Palindromes

```
1: function GETRIGHTMOSTARRAY(A)
2:     n = |A|
3:     R = integer array of length n filled with -1          ▷ stores final result
4:
5:     for i = n − 1 to 0 do          ▷ parses A from right to left
6:         if R[A[i]] == −1 then
7:             R[A[i]] = i
8:         end if
9:     end for
10:
11:    return R
12: end function
```

Algorithm. Abelian Palindromes

```
 1: function GETMATCHSET(x, n)
 2:     M = integer array of length n + 1 filled with 0          ▷ stores final result
 3:
 4:     for i = 0 to n − 1 do
 5:         M[i] = x ⊕ 2^i                                        ▷ XOR operation
 6:     end for
 7:
 8:     M[n] = x
 9:
10:     return M
11: end function
```

Algorithm. Abelian Palindromes

```
 1: function GETABELIANPALINDROMICARRAY(T, Σ)
 2:     n = |T|
 3:     σ = |Σ|
 4:     A = GETPREFIXPARITYINTEGERARRAY(T, Σ)
 5:     R = GETRIGHTMOSTARRAY(A)
 6:     P = integer array of length n filled with 0              ▷ stores final result
 7:
 8:     for i = 0 to n − 1 do
 9:         M = GETMATCHSET(A[i − 1], σ)                          ▷ A[−1] defined as 0
10:
11:         rightmostMatch = −1
12:
13:         for each match in M do
14:             if R[match] > rightmostMatch then
15:                 rightmostMatch = R[match]
16:             end if
17:         end for
18:
19:         if rightmostMatch > i − 1 then
20:             P[i] = rightmostMatch − i + 1
21:         else
22:             P[i] = 0
23:         end if
24:     end for
25:
26:     return P
27: end function
```

References

1. Crochemore, M., Hancart, C., Lecroq, T.: Algorithms on Strings. Cambridge University Press, Cambridge (2007)
2. Karhumäki, J., Puzynina, S.: On k-abelian palindromic rich and poor words. In: Shur, A.M., Volkov, M.V. (eds.) DLT 2014. LNCS, vol. 8633, pp. 191–202. Springer, Cham (2014). https://doi.org/10.1007/978-3-319-09698-8_17
3. Subramanian, S., Chaparala, S., Avali, V., Ganapathiraju, M.K.: A pilot study on the prevalence of DNA palindromes in breast cancer genomes. BMC Med. Genomics 9(3), 73 (2016)
4. Holub, Š., Saari, K.: On highly palindromic words. Discrete Appl. Math. 157(5), 953–959 (2009)

HEALTHIOT

Recommender Systems for IoT Enabled m-Health Applications

Seda Polat Erdeniz[1](✉), Ilias Maglogiannis[2](✉), Andreas Menychtas[3],
Alexander Felfernig[1], and Thi Ngoc Trang Tran[1]

[1] Graz University of Technology, 8010 Graz, Austria
{spolater,alexander.felfernig,ttrang}@ist.tugraz.at
[2] Department of Digital Systems, University of Piraeus, 18532 Piraeus, Greece
imaglo@unipi.gr
[3] Bioassist, 11524 Athens, Greece
amenychtas@bioassist.gr
http://ist.tugraz.at, http://cbml.ds.unipi.gr, http://bioassist.gr

Abstract. *Recommender systems* can help to more easily identify relevant artifacts for users and thus improve user experiences. Currently recommender systems are widely and effectively used in the e-commerce domain (online music services, online bookstores, etc.). On the other hand, due to the rapidly increasing benefits of the emerging topic *Internet of Things (IoT)*, recommender systems have been also integrated to such systems. IoT systems provide essential benefits for human health condition monitoring. In our paper, we propose new recommender systems approaches in IoT enabled mobile health (m-health) applications and show how these can be applied for specific use cases. In this context, we analyze the advantages of proposed recommendation systems in *IoT enabled m-health applications*.

1 Introduction

Empowering and motivating people is a major challenge. This becomes especially crucial when it comes to the health and the physical condition of an individual [23]. It is a well-known fact that the average human lifetime is increasing. Living longer implies the risk of age related health problems that reduce significantly the quality of life. Therefore, many people need to improve and maintain their independence, functional capacity, health status as well as their physical, cognitive, mental and social wellbeing. Modern mobile and sensor technologies enable the recording of all kinds of data related to a person's daily lifestyle, such as exercises, steps taken, body weight, food consumption, blood pressure, cigarettes smoked, etc. This type of self-data tracking is often referred as the *Quantified-Self* concept [23].

Recent works have shown that tracking measurements such as step counts, spent calories and body weight are very effective to make the user conscious of its importance and it may lead to lifestyle changes by motivating a person

L. Iliadis et al. (Eds.): AIAI 2018, IFIP AICT 520, pp. 227–237, 2018.
https://doi.org/10.1007/978-3-319-92016-0_21

to engage in physical exercise [15]. Additionally, by tracking measurements over time, he/she gets insights regarding his/her progress and he/she is able to experience the direct relation between his efforts and the actual outcome. For instance, going for jogging twice a week leads to a decrease of body fat percentage [19].

As an emerging topic, the Internet of Things (IoT) [2,10,18] represents a networked infrastructure of connected different types of devices. In this context, a huge amount of services and applications is created which makes the identification of the relevant ones a challenging task. Several IoT solutions have been proposed to implement the concept of *Quantified-Self* and related challenges in the areas of health care and assisted living [14,17,26]. AGILE[1] is an EU-funded project aiming to build a modular hardware and software gateway for IoT with support for protocol interoperability, device and data management, IoT applications execution, and external Cloud communication. The main concept behind AGILE is to enable users to easily build IoT applications and control connected devices through a modular IoT gateway and a set of full stack (OS, runtime and applications) IoT software components. One of five pilot projects of AGILE is *Quantified-Self* which is an IoT enabled m-health (mobile health) system based on the AGILE gateway environment.

In the AGILE project, we have developed new *recommendation approaches* especially useful in IoT scenarios [7,8,24]. *Recommender systems* [11] suggest items (alternatives, solutions) which are potential interest for a user. Examples of related questions are: *which book should be purchased?, which test method should be applied?, which method calls are useful in a certain development context?* or *which applications are of potential interest for the current user?* A recommender system can be defined as *any system that guides a user to interesting or useful objects for the user in a large space of possible options or that produces such objects as output* [6].

In this paper, we propose new recommendation approaches in the IoT enabled m-health domain based on our example domain *Quantified-Self*. In *Quantified-Self*, we collect patients data using variety of IoT technologies. Based on the measured patients information, our proposed recommender provides life quality increasing solutions both to patients and physicians.

The remainder of this paper is organized as follows. First of all, we give an overview of the state of the art in recommendation technologies in IoT enabled m-health (Sect. 2). In Sect. 3, we introduce the example application *Quantified-Self*, thereafter we explain our proposed recommendation approaches for each use case based on the sample dataset from *Quantified-Self* (Sect. 4). Finally, in Sect. 5 we conclude our work with a discussion of issues for future work.

2   Related Work

IoT-based applications enable a deeper understanding for recommender systems which can primarily be explained by the availability of heterogeneous

---

[1] AGILE (An Adaptive & Modular Gateway for the IoT) is an EU-funded H2020 project 2016–2018 – see http://agile-iot.eu/.

information sources [1,9,29]. Thanks to this ongoing IoT revolution, huge amounts of data are being collected in clinical databases representing patients' health states. Sensor-based Internet-enabled devices equipped with radio frequency identification (RFID) [25] tags and other communication enablers [3] are opening up exciting new ways of innovative recommendation applications in the health domain. Hence, required digital information is already available for patient-oriented decision making. This means, when this data can be used by recommendation algorithms, very important results can be obtained [3].

In [28], authors propose to centralize personal health records (PHR) using a system which allows access for the owner as well as for authorized health professionals. In this system, recommender systems may support patients with additional laymen-friendly information helping to better comprehend their health status as represented by their record.

PHR management systems may fail to satisfy the individual medical information needs of their users. Personalized recommendations could solve this problem. In [27], a ranking procedure based on a health graph is proposed which enables a match between entries of a PHR management system and health information artifacts. This way, the user of such a system can obtain individualized health information he might be interested in.

Researchers have indicated that integrated medical information systems are becoming an essential part of modern healthcare systems. Such systems have evolved to an integrated enterprise-wide system. In particular, such systems are considered as a type of enterprise information system or enterprise resource planning (ERP) [13] system addressing healthcare industry sector needs. As part of efforts, nursing care plan recommender systems can provide clinical decision support, nursing education, clinical quality control, and serve as a complement to existing practice guidelines [5]. The authors of [5] exploit correlations among nursing diagnoses, outcomes and interventions to create a recommender system for constructing nursing care plans.

In [21], a health recommendation system architecture is proposed using rough sets, survival analysis approaches and rule-based expert systems to recommend clinical examinations for patients or physicians from patients' self reported data. Such data can be treated as condition attributes, while *survival time* from a follow-up study can be treated as the target function.

Authors of [4] propose the application of IoT for personalized healthcare in smart homes. An IoT architecture is presented which enables such healthcare services. Continuous monitoring of physical parameters and processing of the medical data form the basis of smarter, connected and personalized healthcare. The core functionalities of the IoT architecture are exposed using Restful web services.

In this paper, we apply recommendation techniques which are also applied in these related works. The added value in our work is especially the differentiation in recommended items indeed. We propose two new recommenders for our IoT project which recommends new apps, healthcare devices, and physical activity plans for patients.

3   Example Domain: Quantified-Self

Quantified-Self is used as an example domain to explain our proposed recommendation approaches throughout this paper. The realization of *Quantified-Self* concept requires the integration of several m-health and IoT elements (see Fig. 1), where proposed applications are orchestrated around the AGILE Gateway [16]. The gateway connects to the home network and through the gateway's management user interface, the owner has access to all provided features, such as reporting and visualization tools, can manage (store/view/edit) their data and define an access policy to share data with their social network contacts. Wearable activity trackers and medical sensors automatically communicate with the gateway whenever within range, and upload the most recent data. Integration with cloud platforms allows data synchronization between the gateway and the owner's online profile, which enables the user to access their data through a web application. In addition, health and activity data can be downloaded to the gateway from the owner's personal accounts on relevant platforms.

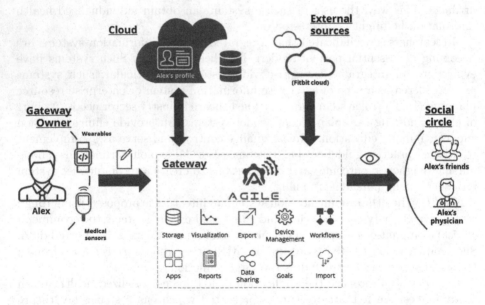

Fig. 1. Software architecture of *Quantified-Self* on the basis of the AGILE gateway.

As illustrated in Fig. 1, each user of the *Quantified-Self* application is provided with a set of activity tracking devices and biosignals sensors (such as oximeters[2], blood pressure monitors[3] or glucometers[4]), to monitor their daily

---

[2]   https://en.wikipedia.org/wiki/Pulse_oximetry.
[3]   http://bestreviews.com/best-blood-pressure-monitors.
[4]   https://en.wikipedia.org/wiki/Glucose_meter.

physical activity and physical condition. All activity data and biosignal measurements are stored locally, on the user's gateway. Users are able to visualize and manage their data, create reports and export the data from the gateway or even import past data from other cloud services they might have used before, such as Fitbit[5], GoogleFit[6], etc. In parallel, motion and lifestyle data can be processed and analyzed on the gateway, so as personalized recommendations are sent to the user's smart phone in order to encourage them to reach their physical activity goals. Moreover, users are able to share their activity data and achievements with certain people/users from their social circle, including relatives, friends and most importantly their physicians.

The *Quantified-Self* concept is targeting data acquisition on aspects of a person's daily life in terms of inputs (e.g. food consumed, quality of surrounding air), states (e.g. mood, arousal, blood oxygen levels), and performance (mental and physical activities) through a modern, health centric, social and mobile enabled, communication platform that resides in the gateway (in terms of collecting and visualizing data). The application is developed using the AGILE environment and software stack, and uses the communication modules of the gateway to collect data from self-tracking devices of users: wristbands or smart watches, weighting scales, oximeters, blood pressure monitors, etc. In addition, the cloud integration modules are exploited for periodically importing activity data and biosignals from other providers and applications through their public APIs.

Since the implementation of the aforementioned application is ongoing and the number of users who are currently using it is limited, an extended dataset from an established m-health solution [17,20] has been used as the knowledge base for our recommender. The main dataset consists of the "biosignal" measurements of patients and elders, which are acquired directly from the biosignal sensors that users are equipped with. Both in the present *Quantified-Self* solution and the application which provided the knowledge base, sensors that are used support wireless communication, and particularly Bluetooth, for simplified integration of the sensors, and for seamless, real-time synchronization of measurement data. The sensors currently supported are the following: *activity trackers, pulse oximeters, blood pressure monitors, weighing scales, spirometers, glucometers, and thermometers.* These sensors measure the following biosignal types: *step count, heart rate (bpm), oxygen saturation (%), blood pressure (mmHg), FEV1 (L), peak flow (L/min), blood glucose levels (mg/dL), and body temperature (Celsius/Fahrenheit).* It should be noted though that the modular design that has been followed, enables the potential integration of additional devices in the same application, which may require different operational workflows and communication patterns.

The biosignals' dataset includes approximately half million records of the aforementioned biosignals from one hundred users in a time frame of three years. Besides the biosignal data, the knowledge base includes information for users'

---

[5] https://www.fitbit.com/at/home.
[6] https://www.google.com/fit/.

demographics (gender, age, location), as well as their personal health record (lab results, medication and allergies). In order to ensure the smooth communication between the different components of the system, and for the smooth data integration with external systems well established data models have been used. Therefore in the proposed approach, all components and workflows which require data exchange and/or storage follow the *Fast Healthcare Interoperability Resources Specification (FHIR)*[7].

4 Recommendation Systems in Quantified-Self

We explain our proposed recommendation approaches for *IoT enabled m-health applications* based on the given example domain *Quantified-Self*. The increasing trend of using *Quantified-Self* solutions is also helpful for this improvement. The utilization of recommendation technologies is essential for improving the health conditions of individuals. The users of *IoT enabled m-health applications* can get recommendations for new activity plans, IoT enabled m-health devices, applications, healthy nutritions. All these recommendations help the users to enhance their life style and reach their target health conditions easier than before. These recommendations indeed play an important role like a *personal trainer* or *personal coach*.

4.1 Use Case - 1: *Virtual Coach*

In order to motivate subscribers/users for sportive activities, *Quantified-Self - Virtual Coach* collects demographic information (age, location, physical condition, medical history, chronic diseases, etc.) of each user. It stores user profiles on its online server and a recommender engine calculates the similarities between users based on their demographic data. Using the similar users' information, a new activity plan (how often, what to measure, which activities) or a new IoT device (a wristband, step counter watch, etc.) can be recommended to users.

In this case, a recommender engine uses *Collaborative Filtering* as the recommendation technology to find similarities between users. *Quantified-Self - Virtual Coach* recommends new activities or new devices to users based on these similarities. *Collaborative Filtering* [12] is based on the idea of promotion, where the opinion of similar users are considered. These users are also denoted as the *nearest neighbors* which means these are the users who have similar preferences compared to the current user. The first step of a collaborative filtering recommender is to identify the *k-nearest neighbors*[8] and to guess the preferences of the current user using the purchased items by nearest neighbors.

There are several similarity metrics in the context of collaborative filtering scenarios for determining nearest neighbors [11]. For the purposes of our example, we use a simplified formula that supports the identification of *k-nearest neighbors*[9] (see Formula 1).

---

[7] https://www.hl7.org/fhir/.
[8] k represents the number of users with similar profile or purchased items compared to the current user.
[9] For simplicity we assume $k = 1$.

Table 1. Profiles of users are stored in the online server of the recommender engine in anonymous mode (without their names, addresses, etc.).

Profiles of users							
	Demographics				Devices		
Profile	Age	Gender	Location	Chronic diseases	Oximeter	Wristband	BPM device
user-1	Young	Male	Urban	Asthma	✓	✓	-
user-2	Middle	Female	Suburban	Diabetics	-	-	✓
user-3	Elder	Male	Suburban	Diabetics	-	✓	-
Active user	Young	Female	Urban	Asthma	-	✓	-

$$similarity(user_a, user_b) = \frac{1}{1 + \Sigma^n_{property=1} |eval(user_a) - eval(user_b)|} \quad (1)$$

When Formula 1 is applied to the example of Table 1, *property* becomes *demographics* and *devices* of users. Thus, for the seven properties (age, gender, location, chronic diseases, oximeter, wristband, BPM (hearth beats per minute) device) of each user, the calculation result of *eval(user_a) - eval(user_b)* for the ith property is 0 if their values are same, otherwise it is 1. For instance, for the first property *age*, the calculation result of *eval(user_1) - eval(user_2)* is 1, because age of *user_1* is *young* whereas age of *user_2* is *middle*. Since they do not have the same values, their difference is 1. For another instance, for the sixth property *wristband*, the calculation result of *eval(user_1) - eval(user_2)* is 1, because the usage of oximeter of *user_1* is ✓ whereas for *user_3* it is ✓. Since they have the same values, when *property* = 5, the result of *eval(user_1) - eval(user_3)* is 0. In Table 1, user-1 (the *nearest neighbor*) has demographics which are similar to those of the current user. Consequently, a collaborative recommender proposes devices to the current user which have been investigated by the nearest neighbor (e.g., an *oximeter* device is recommended to the current user).

4.2 Use Case - 2: *Virtual Nurse*

Quantified-Self - Virtual Nurse motivates different types of chronic patients (i.e diabetes, asthma, cancer, cardiovascular) to reach their goals on the basis of a recommended plan. It collects the measured data of patients and checks their health conditional targets. If the measured values are very far from their expected (target) values, then some specific recommendations can be placed for those patients. The recommendations should be personalized and related to the base line of each user's data, which will be permanently updated.

The patient medical data includes the personalized models that shows the behavioral responses of the patients versus the coach interventions to discover best-practices and measure adherence. The recommender could act as a decision support system that gathers information from the patient, finds an activity plan that matches with the available objectives and offers a personalized list. A physician might intervene (semi-supervised recommendation) to select the collected information that are more related with the wellbeing of the patient.

In this case, the recommender engine uses *Content-based Filtering* as the recommendation technology to find a related plan based on the user data. *Quantified-Self - Virtual Nurse* recommends new activity plans to users based on their actual and expected measurements. *Content-based Filtering* [22] is based on the assumption of monotonic personal interests. For example, users interested in the topic *sports devices* are generally not changing their interests so often but keep their interests in the same topic. The basic approach of content-based filtering is to compare the content of already used items with new items that can potentially be recommended to the user.

Table 2. Actual and expected (targets) measurements of patient-1. The targets of the available activity plans are also represented. Arrows denote increase($\uparrow$)/decrease($\downarrow$)/stay($\longleftrightarrow$) targets of a plan. For instance, plan-2 is targeting to decrease the blood pressure and weight. Therefore, plan-2 includes activities which can decrease these two parameters.

Medical data of a patient and possible activity plans			
	Systolic blood pressure (mm Hg)	Heart-rate (bpm)	Weight (kg)
Targets of plan-1	$\downarrow$	$\downarrow$	$\downarrow$
Targets of plan-2	$\downarrow$	$\longleftrightarrow$	$\downarrow$
Targets of plan-3	$\longleftrightarrow$	$\downarrow$	$\longleftrightarrow$
Targets of plan-4	$\longleftrightarrow$	$\longleftrightarrow$	$\uparrow$
Targets of patient-1	120.00 ($\downarrow$)	70.00 ($\downarrow$)	80.00 ($\downarrow$)
Actuals of patient-1	142.00	91.00	108.00

A simplified example of a related recommendation approach is given in Table 2. When applying a content-based filtering based approach, recommended items (plans) are determined on the basis of the similarity of the patient's targets and available plans. Similar to collaborative filtering, there are different types of similarity metrics [11]. For the purposes of our examples, we introduce a simplified formula that supports the identification of, for example, relevant plans for the patient-1 (see Formula 2).

$$similarity(patient, plan) = \frac{\#(targets(patient) \cap targets(plan))}{\#(targets(patient) \cup targets(plan))} \quad (2)$$

Formula 2 determines the similarity on the basis of the targets of plans and targets of *patient-1*. For instance, the similarity between *patient-1* and *plan-3* is calculated as 0.33 where $\#(targets(patient) \cap targets(plan)) = 1$ since there is only 1 same target (target for hearth-rate) and $\#(targets(patient) \cup targets(plan)) = 3$ where the number of targets for both is three (systolic blood pressure, hearth-rate, and weight). In our example of Table 2, *plan-1* has the highest similarity with the targets of *patient-1*, therefore *plan-1* is recommended to *patient-1*.

5 Conclusions and Future Work

The utilization of recommender systems is considered essential for improving the health conditions of individuals. In this paper, We proposed two new recommenders for our IoT project which recommends new apps, healthcare devices, and physical activity plans for patients. We analyzed the applicabilities and the advantages of recommendation technologies in *IoT enabled m-health applications* by showing examples on the pilot application (*Quantified-Self*) of our project (*AGILE*). We have proposed two recommendation use cases *Virtual Coach* and *Virtual Nurse* which help users/patients to improve their health conditions. This improvement is provided by correct device or sportive activity recommendations for users by *Virtual Coach*, and correct activity plan recommendation for patients by *Virtual Nurse*. As future work, we will implement mentioned recommender engines for *Quantified-Self* system and analyze the results in the bases of changes in the health data of users. Besides, we plan to detect anomalies in *Quantified-Self* activity plans and send additional recommendations to users/physicians.

References

1. Amato, F., Mazzeo, A., Moscato, V., Picariello, A.: A recommendation system for browsing of multimedia collections in the Internet of Things. In: Bessis, N., Xhafa, F., Varvarigou, D., Hill, R., Li, M. (eds.) Internet of Things and Inter-Cooperative Computational Technologies for Collective Intelligence, Studies in Computational Intelligence, vol. 460. Springer, Heidelberg (2013). https://doi.org/10.1007/978-3-642-34952-2_16
2. Atzori, L., Iera, A., Morabito, G.: The Internet of Things: a survey. Comput. Netw. **54**, 2787–2805 (2010)
3. Chen, H., Chiang, R.H., Storey, V.C.: Business intelligence and analytics: from big data to big impact. MIS Q. **36**(4), 1165–1188 (2012)
4. Datta, S.K., Bonnet, C., Gyrard, A., Da Costa, R.P.F., Boudaoud, K.: Applying Internet of Things for personalized healthcare in smart homes. In: 2015 24th Wireless and Optical Communication Conference (WOCC), pp. 164–169. IEEE (2015)
5. Duan, L., Street, W.N., Xu, E.: Healthcare information systems: data mining methods in the creation of a clinical recommender system. Enterp. Inf. Syst. **5**(2), 169–181 (2011)
6. Felfernig, A., Burke, R.: Constraint-based recommender systems: technologies and research issues. In: ACM International Conference on Electronic Commerce (ICEC 2008), pp. 17–26, Innsbruck, Austria (2008)
7. Felfernig, A., Erdeniz, S.P., Azzoni, P., Jeran, M., Akcay, A., Doukas, C.: Towards configuration technologies for IoT gateways. In: 18th International Configuration Workshop, p. 73 (2016)
8. Felfernig, A., Erdeniz, S.P., Jeran, M., Akcay, A., Azzoni, P., Maiero, M., Doukas, C.: Recommendation technologies for IoT edge devices. Procedia Comput. Sci. **110**, 504–509 (2017)

9. Frey, R., Xu, R., Ilic, A.: A novel recommender system in IoT. In: 5th International Conference on the Internet of Things (IoT 2015), pp. 1–2, Seoul, South Korea (2015)
10. Greengard, S.: The Internet of Things. MIT Press, Cambridge (2015)
11. Jannach, D., Zanker, M., Felfernig, A., Friedrich, G.: Recommender Systems - An Introduction. Cambridge University Press, Cambridge (2010)
12. Konstan, J., Miller, B., Maltz, D., Herlocker, J., Gordon, L., Riedl, J.: GroupLens: applying collaborative filtering to Usenet news full text. Commun. ACM **40**(3), 77–87 (1997)
13. Kremers, M., Van Dissel, H.: Enterprise resource planning: ERP system migrations. Commun. ACM **43**(4), 53–56 (2000)
14. Maglogiannis, I., Ioannou, C., Tsanakas, P.: Fall detection and activity identification using wearable and hand-held devices. Integr. Comput.-Aided Eng. **23**(2), 161–172 (2016)
15. McGrath, M.J., Scanaill, C.N.: Wellness, fitness, and lifestyle sensing applications. In: McGrath, M.J., Scanaill, C.N. (eds.) Sensor Technologies, pp. 217–248. Apress, Berkeley (2013). https://doi.org/10.1007/978-1-4302-6014-1_10
16. Menychtas, A., Doukas, C., Tsanakas, P., Maglogiannis, I.: A versatile architecture for building IoT quantified-self applications. In: 2017 IEEE 30th International Symposium on Computer-Based Medical Systems (CBMS), pp. 500–505. IEEE (2017)
17. Menychtas, A., Tsanakas, P., Maglogiannis, I.: Automated integration of wireless biosignal collection devices for patient-centred decision-making in point-of-care systems. Healthc. Technol. Lett. **3**(1), 34–40 (2016)
18. Miorandi, D., Sicari, S., DePellegrini, F., Chlamtac, I.: Internet of Things: vision, applications and research challenges. Ad Hoc Netw. **10**, 1497–1516 (2012)
19. Munson, S.A., Consolvo, S.: Exploring goal-setting, rewards, self-monitoring, and sharing to motivate physical activity. In: 2012 6th International Conference on Pervasive Computing Technologies for Healthcare (PervasiveHealth), pp. 25–32. IEEE (2012)
20. Panagopoulos, C., Malli, F., Menychtas, A., Smyrli, E.-P., Georgountzou, A., Daniil, Z., Gourgoulianis, K.I., Tsanakas, P., Maglogiannis, I.: Utilizing a homecare platform for remote monitoring of patients with idiopathic pulmonary fibrosis. In: Vlamos, P. (ed.) GeNeDis 2016. AEMB, vol. 989, pp. 177–187. Springer, Cham (2017). https://doi.org/10.1007/978-3-319-57348-9_15
21. Pattaraintakorn, P., Zaverucha, G.M., Cercone, N.: Web based health recommender system using rough sets, survival analysis and rule-based expert systems. In: An, A., Stefanowski, J., Ramanna, S., Butz, C.J., Pedrycz, W., Wang, G. (eds.) RSFD-GrC 2007. LNCS (LNAI), vol. 4482, pp. 491–499. Springer, Heidelberg (2007). https://doi.org/10.1007/978-3-540-72530-5_59
22. Pazzani, M., Billsus, D.: Learning and revising user profiles: the identification of interesting web sites. Mach. Learn. **27**, 313–331 (1997)
23. Swan, M.: Sensor mania! the Internet of Things, wearable computing, objective metrics, and the quantified self 2.0. J. Sens. Actuator Netw. **1**(3), 217–253 (2012)
24. Calero Valdez, A., Ziefle, M., Verbert, K., Felfernig, A., Holzinger, A.: Recommender systems for health informatics: state-of-the-art and future perspectives. In: Holzinger, A. (ed.) Machine Learning for Health Informatics. LNCS (LNAI), vol. 9605, pp. 391–414. Springer, Cham (2016). https://doi.org/10.1007/978-3-319-50478-0_20
25. Want, R.: An introduction to RFID technology. IEEE Pervasive Comput. **5**(1), 25–33 (2006)

26. Wei, J.: How wearables intersect with the cloud and the Internet of Things: considerations for the developers of wearables. IEEE Consum. Electron. Mag. **3**(3), 53–56 (2014)
27. Wiesner, M., Pfeifer, D.: Adapting recommender systems to the requirements of personal health record systems. In: Proceedings of the 1st ACM International Health Informatics Symposium, pp. 410–414. ACM (2010)
28. Wiesner, M., Pfeifer, D.: Health recommender systems: concepts, requirements, technical basics and challenges. Int. J. Environ. Res. Pub. Health **11**(3), 2580–2607 (2014)
29. Yao, L., Sheng, Q., Ngu, A., Li, X.: Things of interest recommendation by leveraging heterogeneous relations in the Internet of Things. ACM Trans. Internet Technol. **16**(9), 1–25 (2016)

A Smart-Home IoT Infrastructure for the Support of Independent Living of Older Adults

Stefanos Stavrotheodoros(✉), Nikolaos Kaklanis, Konstantinos Votis,
and Dimitrios Tzovaras

Information Technologies Institute, Centre for Research and Technology Hellas,
Thessaloniki, Greece
{stavrotheodoros,nkak,kvotis,tzovaras}@iti.gr

Abstract. Although the healthcare sector has been hugely benefited from the advantages made in the Information and Communication Technology (ICT) domain in the recent years, the emerging technology breakthrough of the Internet-of-Things (IoT), in which all devices and services are collaborating while reducing human intervention, promises new solutions that will enable users to have a more home-centric healthcare, and a sustainable active and healthy ageing. This paper is proposing a smart-home IoT infrastructure for the support and extension of the independent living of older adults in their living environments that responds also to real needs of caregivers and public authorities. The proposed infrastructure seamlessly utilizes health and monitoring devices for the provision of a safe environment for an elderly, the mitigation of frailty and the preservation of quality of life and autonomy. It also provides a mechanism for easy setup and testing of the installed equipment and a decision support system that offers advanced data analytics and visual analytics mechanisms to the formal and informal caregivers of the elderly for the efficient monitoring of their health and activity status.

Keywords: Telemedicine · Internet of Things · Elderly monitoring

1 Introduction

Most of the countries are encountering a shift in the distribution of their population towards older ages, caused by rising life expectancy, declining birth rates, or a combination of both.

Although the current health caring model is hospital-centric, it is expected to gradually be transformed to a more hospital-home-balanced by 2020 [1], and eventually to home-centric. Ageing in place does not only reflects the preferences of the elderly who wish to stay in their own homes as they age [2], yet in addition of the policymakers, who are attracted by the possibility of keeping the health care expenditures within the bounds of economic possibility [3].

The effort made in this health caring model transformation is primarily based on the use Ambient Assisted Living (AAL) solutions. Typically, AAL refers to the use of ICT,

L. Iliadis et al. (Eds.): AIAI 2018, IFIP AICT 520, pp. 238–249, 2018.
https://doi.org/10.1007/978-3-319-92016-0_22

assistive devices and smart home technologies in a person's daily living to enable individuals living in their place in a convenient and safe manner. It ensures greater autonomy and provides supportive home environments by means of integrating sensors, actuators, smart interfaces, and artificial intelligence [4].

IoT emerged as one of the major communication advantages in recent years and is defined as the ability of everyday life objects to connect and communicate with each other [5]. These devices, objects or things are identifiable, readable, recognizable and even controllable via the Internet. With the use of IoT, AAL systems are enhanced and able to consist of medical sensors, wireless sensors, computer hardware, computer networks, software applications, and databases, which can be interconnected to exchange data and provide services in an Ambient Assisted environment [6].

One of the main problems with the IoT is that it is so vast and such a broad concept that there is no proposed, uniform architecture. In order for the idea of IoT to work, it must consist of an assortment of the sensors, network, communications and computing technologies, amongst others [7]. Creating an IoT health system that will ensure the monitoring and independent living of an elderly at his home has many challenges that must be faced. An efficient topology must be selected, and devices produced to different specification and using different communication protocols must be integrated. All vital private information such as personal healthcare information must also be protected by providing confidentiality, integrity, authentication and authorization.

Although several IoT platforms have been developed to support cognitively impaired individuals, a major challenge is to provide a solution that combines efficiently health and behavioural monitoring, thus addressing a large variety of daily needs of the elderly.

This paper presents a smart-home IoT infrastructure for the support of independent living of the elderly developed in the context of the ACTIVAGE H2020 EU project. Specifically, the architecture developed for the Greek deployment site, where a large-scale pilot will take place in three different regions with 500 beneficiaries, is presented. The proposed architecture includes a wireless sensor network consisted of devices and sensors of different communication protocols and provides tools for easy installation of the equipment by the personnel. The platform aggregates information gathered by sensors and health devices and integrates them to support the delivery of telehealth services. The collected data are stored in cloud infrastructure and can be accessed only by authorized informal and formal caregivers for monitoring of the health and activity status of the elderly.

The rest of the paper is structured as follows: Sect. 2 describes several solutions that have been implemented for monitoring and supporting the independent living of elderly people, whereas Sect. 3 describes the architecture and the layers of the proposed solution along with an in-detail analysis of all used devices/sensors and protocols. Finally, Sect. 4 concludes the paper.

2 Related Work

The technological advances in microelectromechanical systems have made available efficient, low cost, low power miniature devices for use in remote monitoring applications. Several platforms have been implemented in order to monitor and support the independent living of elderly adults. For example, the IN LIFE system [8] is a cloud-based platform that provides AAL support to cognitively impaired elderly people, through numerous provided tools and services. The MyLife project [9] supports independence for older people with reduced cognitive function by giving them access to simple and intuitive services that adapt to their individual needs and wishes. Although both platforms, meet several needs posed by cognitive decline, they do not utilize the capabilities provided by the IoT infrastructure. On the other hand, numerous solutions adopt the IoT paradigm for the indoor support of elderly people and mainly focus on human activity recognition (HAR) and health monitoring.

The goal of the human activity recognition is to recognize common human activities in real life settings by extracting knowledge from the data acquired by smart sensors [10].

There are HAR solutions that utilize sensors that are placed in various locations within a smart home, acting as non-intrusive monitoring devices for identifying human behaviors. In particular, Kasteren et al. [11] designed a system for recognizing various living activities in a smart home deploying door sensors, pressure-sensitive mats, float sensor, and temperature sensor. For the TAFETA project [12], a home-based automated system has been implemented that monitors the health and well-being of an elderly while remaining unobtrusive by using various types of intelligent sensors in the elderly's home. Chen et al. [13] designed a system for recognizing complex living activities in a smart home deploying contact, motion, tilt and pressure sensors, while Zhang et al. [14] also describe a similar system named "Smarter and Safer Home" that deploys sensors in homes, acting as non-intrusive monitoring devices for human behavior of elderly people. The aggregated data of the aforementioned systems are used in order to identify "abnormal" situations.

Other HAR solutions provide activity-monitoring functionalities by using wearable devices for indoor localization. Komai et al. [15] describe an activity monitoring system that utilizes a wearable BLE beacon device for indoor localization. Popleteev [16] presented an activity tracking and indoor positioning system with a wearable magnet and similarly, Belmonte-Fernández et al. [17] by using a Smart-watch wearable device that acquires the Wi-Fi strength signals of surrounding installed Wireless Access Points. Finally, [18] Santos et al., has proposed an RFID based M-health care system using IoT based connected devices, that identifies the position of an m-health related item (e.g. elderly) carrying an RFID tag.

Regarding the health monitoring, its goal is to allow an individual to closely monitor his/her vital signs, provide feedback for maintaining an optimal health status and create alerts when vital measurements are below or over a predefined threshold [19].

Several health-monitoring systems utilize devices that are placed in the living environment of the elderly and are used by him/her periodically during the day for measuring vital signs. Specifically, the system presented by [20] utilizes an electronic blood pressure device that transmits the measured data (i.e., pulse wave) to the data processing center, from where they are accessible in real-time by a doctor. In a similar way, Cao and Liu [21] developed an IoT system that measures saturation peripheral oxygen and pulse rate, and transmits them to a cloud-side server.

Other solutions use wearable bio-signal sensors that monitor human vital signs continuously. Menychtas et al. [22] introduced a mechanism for uniform biosignals collection from wearables and biosignal sensors, and decision support modules for patient monitoring. In [23] a holistic solution for communication and management of Bluetooth biosignal sensors and activity trackers promoting mHealth and self-care is proposed. A glucose monitoring system based on an implantable unit that utilizes Bluetooth low energy, to transmit the measured glucose data to patients' mobile phone or PDA is presented by Ali et al. [24]. Pinto et al. [25] demonstrated a platform for monitoring and registering patients' vital information as well as providing mechanisms to trigger alarms in emergency situations by using a wristband equipped with numerous sensors.

The infrastructure proposed in this paper supports the efficient monitoring of the elderly through a combination of heterogeneous devices that provide both human behavior monitoring and measurement of vital signs of the elderly in his/her living environment in a non-intrusive way. It also supports a mechanism that enables the easy installation and testing of the equipment. The collected data are securely forwarded to a cloud infrastructure offering also decision support functionalities to the formal and informal caregivers of the elderly through advanced data analytics and visual analytics.

3   Proposed Solution

Before describing the proposed solution, it is essential to present the end-users of the platform and their needs:

- **Assisted person:** Elderly people, from 65 year and above, with chronic health problems or with frailty due to physical, cognitive or emotional problems, who need formal or informal support when staying at home or in their daily living environment for safety and security.
- **Informal caregiver:** responsible for providing support on a daily basis to a relative that suffers from a chronic condition and cannot live alone and yet be safe. The service will allow him/her to monitor the relative remotely and respond immediately and effectively in case of an emergency.
- **Formal caregiver:** responsible for providing systematic daily assistant at home or at a daycare center. The service will allow the formal caregiver to coordinate different care recipients at the same time more efficiently as well as respond to different emergency cases faster.

In order to meet the needs of the aforementioned user groups, an IoT infrastructure was designed and implemented, as it is depicted in Fig. 1, which enables devices with sensing, processing and communication capabilities to be connected to the Internet. It is an extension of the three-layered architecture proposed by [26] where each layer is equivalent to the most basic features of an IoT-based platform: data collection, transmission, and analysis [27]. The installed devices are connected to the Internet through a gateway, forming a Machine-to-Machine (M2M) network.

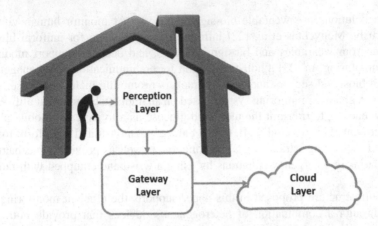

Fig. 1. The adopted three-layered system architecture

A lab-based pilot was used as a reference site to test the proposed infrastructure. Specifically, the smart home of CERTH/ITI was used for living lab testing, providing a fully controllable environment similar to the real cases. The assessment was based on gathering data from different sensors, in which CERTH/ITI employees and a limited number of elderly performed activities of daily living in standardized scenarios. Based on the aforementioned lab-based pilot, the proposed solution produced promising preliminary feedback and results.

3.1   The Perception Layer

The first layer that is named *Perception Layer* (Fig. 2) is responsible for cognizing and collecting information of devices for a user and integrating them into the next layers. It includes a number of heterogeneous, wireless sensors and health devices that create a Wireless Sensor Network (WSN) and a central node is in charge of gathering the sensed data. The central node that is referred as an *Aggregation Point* in this paper is part of the second layer and is described in detail in the following section. The used devices are using common communication protocols that are featured by low power consumption, short-range communication, and lightweight protocol stack.

The selection of the devices and protocols was made after an in detail examination of the necessities and requirements of the user groups. In particular, these are the protocols used by the selected devices:

- Bluetooth standard [28]
- Z-Wave [29]
- ZigBee [30]
- RF (869.2-869.25 MHz)

All devices are battery operated. Consequently, the sensor placement is not constrained by the availability of a nearby power socket, enabling this way an easy installation phase.

Perception Layer

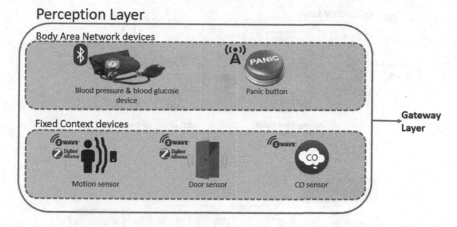

Fig. 2. The *Perception Layer* that contains all integrated devices

According to [26], the devices in the *Perception Layer* can be summarized in two main categories: (1) Body Area Network (BAN) devices, which are on-body devices usually for obtaining user health/activity status, and (2) fixed context devices that are generally installed in the home. In a manner corresponding to this categorization, these are the devices used in the implemented system:

- Body Area Network (BAN) devices (transmit on demand)
  - **Wearable panic button:** for emergency cases, a panic button is utilized. It is a small, wearable device, which the elderly has on him. Its activation results in the device automatically transmitting an emergency alarm notification to the carers of the elderly.
  - **Health device for vital signs:** this device is able to measure the vital signs of the elderly, such as the blood pressure and pulses or the blood glucose levels

- Fixed context devices (transmit data on an event basis or as periodic reports)
  - **Passive InfraRed (PIR) sensors:** by installing Passive Infrared (PIR) sensors in each room, it is possible to track the presence and motion of an elderly in the home and trace occupancy habits.
  - **Magnetic contact sensors:** the central entrance of the home is equipped with a magnetic contact sensor that transmits a signal that indicates the binary state of "open" or "closed".
  - **Sensor for measuring hazardous levels of CO:** one of the most common symptoms that patients with early stages of Alzheimer's or dementia have is the frequent and progressive memory loss [31]. Forgetting to turn off one of the devices that are usually located in the kitchen may turn hazardous for the elderly. By installing this sensor, it is able to determine if there are dangerous levels of CO in the home.

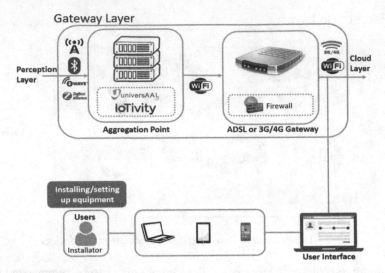

Fig. 3. The *Gateway Layer* that is responsible for the aggregation of the sensed data

3.2 The Gateway Layer

The second tier is the *Gateway layer* (Fig. 3), which receives all sensor data and measurements of the perception layer and then transmits them to the third layer. For this layer, a smart device named *Aggregation Point* is used that undertakes the data aggregator role in the home environment and enables the communication/connection between all installed devices/sensors. It is equipped with a variety of transceiver modules that enable the communication with the devices through the aforementioned protocols, and it features an IoT platform that is responsible for their integration and orchestration. The supported IoT platforms are:

- **universAAL** [32], which is an open source platform that enables seamless interoperability of devices, services and applications on an unprecedented scale.
- **IoTivity** [33], which is an open source software framework enabling seamless device-to-device connectivity.

All data collected by the end-devices are forwarded to the Internet, and specifically to the *Cloud Layer* described in the next section. This is accomplished through an ADSL router or a mobile router (3G/4G) in cases of homes that do not have an ADSL connection.

The communication protocol used for the transmission of the sensed data to the next layer is the message queuing telemetry transport (MQTT) connectivity protocol and its selection was based on the work produced by Campo et al. [34]. Its simplicity and the fact that it does not need high CPU and memory usage make this protocol ideal for the interconnection between the *Gateway Layer* and the *Cloud Layer*. Moreover, it supports an extensive variety of different devices and mobile platforms, and it provides TSL/SSL security at transport layer [35].

Additionally, a mechanism for easy setup and testing of the installed equipment in the smart home by the installer is provided through a web-based application supported by each *Aggregation Point*. In particular, the aforementioned web-based application supports the configuration of the *Aggregation Point* for the communication with the *Cloud Layer* and provides forms for describing and registering the devices/sensors. It communicates with the IoT platform installed on the *Aggregation Point* via RESTful services exposed for identifying the communication protocol to be used, and handling the pairing and the communication with the devices. The following main functionalities are supported by this application:

- **Device registration** for adding and describing a new sensor/health device.
- **Device removal** for removing a sensor/health device from the smart home ecosystem
- **Device discovery** by querying the registered devices, along with details regarding their capabilities.
- **Device update** for updating information related to a device, e.g. change device password.

3.3   The Cloud Layer

The third layer is the *Cloud Layer* (Fig. 4) that incorporates a cloud-based software architecture that collects the information gathered from the sensors installed in each home and provides the two following functionalities: (1) storing collected information and (2) analyzing this information and providing a decision support mechanism through advanced data analytics & visual analytics to the end-users.

For example, the motion sensors are stored in the various rooms of the elderly home and automatically recognize the traceability of each home space. The information transmitted is properly analyzed in order to automatically recognize user habits within a home (e.g. how often he/she visits the bathroom, when he/she visits the kitchen, and for how long, etc.). Recognizing the habits of the elderly contributes to the automatic detection of risk-bearing situations (e.g. the elderly has not visited the bathroom during the day) as well as changes in habits that may be related to health problems (e.g. while the elderly used to be in the kitchen for one hour every noon to prepare his/her daily meal, this custom has changed).

Moreover, the door opening and closing detector that is placed in the central entrance of each home automatically identifies the entrance/exit of the elderly from the house. This information, combined with the information provided by the home-based motion detectors, is properly analysed to identify the user's habits (e.g., how often he/she exits the house, for how long, etc.) and consequently contribute to the automatic detection of risk situations (e.g. the elderly has not exited home for a long time) as well as changes in habits (for example, a change in the number of the weekly exits and the duration).

The special panic button, which the elderly always has on him, can be used in an emergency case (e.g. fall, severe dizziness, sickness, etc.). At the click of the panic button, the person (s) indicated by the elderly (e.g. relatives, health personnel, etc.) is informed in order to contact with him/her and take appropriate action for help provision.

Similarly, an alarm notification will be created in case the blood pressure or blood glucose levels indicate abnormal vital signs.

Regarding the security of the accumulated data, anonymization and encryption techniques are applied. Data anonymization preserves privacy by eliminating identifiability from the dataset, i.e., the link between sensitive information and people, while encryption protects the confidentiality of the data and prevents unauthorized third parties or threat actors from accessing them. Finally, further research is currently made in order to make the platform compliant with the new General Data Protection Regulation (GDPR) [36], which will come into force on May 2018.

The data accumulated is accessible to two different types of users, for whom the following applications have been implemented:

- Application for helping carers (both formal and informal) monitor the health status/activity of the corresponding elderly through advanced data analytics.
- Application for offering monitoring and decision support to the administrator of the infrastructure through advanced data analytics.

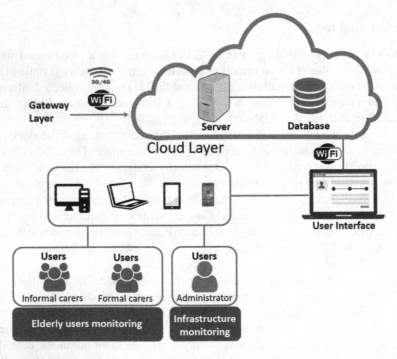

Fig. 4. The *Cloud Layer* that is responsible for the storing of the information collected from all sites

4   Conclusion

There is a major researching movement that explores various ICT arrangements in order to enhance healthcare provision by mobilizing the potential of IoT. In this paper, we exhibited a smart-home IoT infrastructure created for monitoring the health and activity status of elderly individuals in their living environments. For supporting the independent living of older adults in their living environments and providing perceived safety, a set of heterogeneous sensors, able to provide behavioural and environmental condition information, was utilized in addition to health devices, used for vital sign measurement. The installation and the efficient set up of these devices are feasible through a web-based application implemented for the corresponding personnel. All the aggregated data are collected in a transparent way by the IoT infrastructure deployed in the home and stored securely in a cloud-based infrastructure, where they analysed. The outcome of the analysis is advanced data analytics & visual analytics presented to the formal and informal caregivers, thus providing them with a decision support mechanism.

The platform will be additionally tested and evaluated through large-scale pilots that will take place in three different regions of Greece, in the context of the ACTIVAGE project. In these pilots, the platform will be deployed in 500 homes and it will provide activity and health status monitoring of elderly people living autonomously in real life scenarios. Inputs from these pilot sites will enable the further evaluation and refinement of the platform.

Acknowledgement. This work is supported by the EU funded project ACTIVAGE (H2020-732679).

References

1. Koop, C.E., Mosher, R., Kun, L., Geiling, J., Grigg, E., Long, S., Macedonia, C., Merrell, R., Satava, R., Rosen, J.: Future delivery of health care: cybercare. IEEE Eng. Med. Biol. Mag. **27**(6), 29–38 (2008)
2. Wiles, J.L.: Home as a new site of health care consumption. In: Andrews, G., Phillips, D.R. (eds.) Aging in Place. Routledge, London (2005)
3. Grabowski, D.: The cost-effectiveness of long-term care services: review and synthesis of the most recent evidence. Med. Care Res. Rev. **63**(1), 3–28 (2006)
4. Sixsmith, A., Mueller, S., Lull, F., Klein, M., Bierhoff, I., Deleaney, S., Byrne, P., Sproll, S., Savage, R., Avatangelou, E.: A user-driven approach to developing ambient assisted living systems for older people: the SOPRANO project. In: Soar, J., Swidell, R., Tsang, P. (eds.) Intelligent Technologies for Bridging the Grey Digital Divide. IGI Global, Hershey (2010)
5. Dohr, A., Modre-Opsrian, R., Drobics, M., Hayn, D., Schreier, G.: The Internet of Things for ambient assisted living. In: Proceedings of the Seventh International Conference on Information Technology: New Generations, pp. 804–809. IEEE Press (2010)
6. Memon, M., Rahr Wagner, S., Pederson Fischer, C., Aysha Beevi, F.H., Overgaard Hansen, F.: Ambient assisted living healthcare frameworks, platforms, standards, and quality attributes. Sensors **14**, 4312–4341 (2014)
7. Gigli, M., Koo, S.: Internet of Things, services and applications categorization. Adv. Internet Things **1**, 27–31 (2011)

8. Stavrotheodoros, S., Kaklanis, N., Tzovaras, D.: A personalized cloud-based platform for AAL support to cognitively impaired elderly people. In: Maglaveras, N., Chouvarda, I., de Carvalho, P. (eds.) Precision Medicine Powered by pHealth and Connected Health. IP, vol. 66, pp. 87–91. Springer, Singapore (2018). https://doi.org/10.1007/978-981-10-7419-6_15

9. MyLife project. http://www.mylife-project.org. Accessed 19 Mar 2018

10. Kim, E., Helal, S., Cook, D.: Human activity recognition and pattern discovery. IEEE Pervasive Comput. 9(1), 48–53 (2010)

11. Van Kasteren, T., Englebienne, G., Krose, B.J.: An activity monitoring system for elderly care using generative and discriminative models. Personal Ubiquit. Comput. 14(6), 489–498 (2010)

12. Arcelus, A., Jones, M.H., Goubran, R., Knoefel, F.: Integration of smart home technologies in a health monitoring system for the elderly. In: Proceedings of Advanced Information Networking and Applications Workshops 2007, pp. 820–825 (2007)

13. Chen, L., Nugent, C.D., Wang, H.: A knowledge-driven approach to activity recognition in smart homes. IEEE Trans. Knowl. Data Eng. 24(6), 961–974 (2012)

14. Zhang, Q., Su, Y., Yu, P.: Assisting an elderly with early dementia using wireless sensors data in smarter safer home. In: Liu, K., Gulliver, S.R., Li, W., Yu, C. (eds.) ICISO 2014. IAICT, vol. 426, pp. 398–404. Springer, Heidelberg (2014). https://doi.org/10.1007/978-3-642-55355-4_41

15. Komai, K., Fujimoto, M., Arakawa, Y., Suwa, H., Kashimoto, Y., Yasumoto, K.: Beacon-based multi-person activity monitoring system for day care center. In: 2016 IEEE International Conference on Pervasive Computing and Communication Workshops (PerCom Workshops), pp. 1–6 (2016)

16. Popleteev, A.: Activity tracking and indoor positioning with a wearable magnet. In: Proceedings of the 2015 ACM International Joint Conference on Pervasive and Ubiquitous Computing and Proceedings of the 2015 ACM International Symposium on Wearable Computers, pp. 253–256 (2015)

17. Belmonte-Fernández, Ó., Puertas-Cabedo, A., Torres-Sospedra, J., Montoliu-Colás, R., Trilles-Oliver, S.: An indoor positioning system based on wearables for ambient-assisted living. Sensors 17(1), 36 (2016)

18. Santos, A., Macedo, J., Costa, A., Nicolau, M.J.: Internet of Things and smart objects for M-health monitoring and control. Procedia Technol. 16, 1351–1360 (2014)

19. Yap, J.H., Jeong, D.U.: Design and implementation of ubiquitous ECG monitoring system by using android tablet. In: Han, Y.H., Park, D.S., Jia, W., Yeo, S.S. (eds.) Ubiquitous Information Technologies and Applications. Lecture Notes in Electrical Engineering, vol. 214, pp. 269–277. Springer, Berlin (2013). https://doi.org/10.1007/978-94-007-5857-5_29

20. Wang, J., Sun, S., Zhang, K., Zhang, L., Xing, B., Gao, Z.: Smart blood pressure monitoring system based on Internet of Things. In: CHI 2013 (2013)

21. Cao, G., Liu, J.: An IoT application: health care system with android devices. In: Gervasi, O., Murgante, B., Misra, S., Rocha, A.M.A.C., Torre, C., Taniar, D., Apduhan, B.O., Stankova, E., Wang, S. (eds.) ICCSA 2016. LNCS, vol. 9786, pp. 563–571. Springer, Cham (2016). https://doi.org/10.1007/978-3-319-42085-1_46

22. Menychtas, A., Tsanakas, P., Maglogiannis, I.: Automated integration of wireless biosignal collection devices for patient-centred decision-making in point-of-care systems. Healthc. Technol. Lett. 3(1), 34–40 (2016)

23. Menychtas, A., Papadimatos, D., Tsanakas, P., Maglogiannis, I.: On the integration of wearable sensors in IoT enabled mHealth and quantified-self applications. In: Auer, M.E., Tsiatsos, T. (eds.) IMCL 2017. AISC, vol. 725, pp. 77–88. Springer, Cham (2018). https://doi.org/10.1007/978-3-319-75175-7_9

24. Ali, M., Albasha, L., Al-Nashash, H.: A bluetooth low energy implantable glucose monitoring system. In: 2011 41st European Microwave Conference (EuMC). IEEE, pp. 1265–1268 (2011)
25. Pinto, S., Cabral, J., Gomes, T.: We-care: an IoT-based health care system for elderly people. In: 2017 IEEE International Conference on Industrial Technology (2017)
26. Azimi, I., Rahmani, A.M., Liljeberg, P., Tenhunen, H.: Internet of things for remote elderly monitoring: a study from user-centered perspective. J. Ambient Intell. Humaniz. Comput. 8(2), 273–289 (2017)
27. Touati, F., Tabish, R.: u-Healthcare system: state-of-the-art review and challenges. J. Med. Syst. 37(3), 1–20 (2013)
28. Bluetooth Standard. https://www.bluetooth.com/. Accessed 19 Mar 2018
29. ZWave Alliance. http://www.z-wave.com. Accessed 19 Mar 2018
30. ZigBee Alliance. http://www.zigbee.org/. Accessed 19 Mar 2018
31. Small, G.W.: What we need to know about age related memory loss. BMJ 324, 1502–1505 (2002)
32. Hanke, S., Mayer, C., Hoeftberger, O., Boos, H., Wichert, R., Tazari, M.-R., Wolf, P., Furfari, F.: universAAL - an open and consolidated AAL platform. In: Wichert, R., Eberhard, B. (eds.) Ambient Assisted Living. Advanced Technologies and Societal Change, vol. 63, pp. 127–140. Springer, Heidelberg (2011). https://doi.org/10.1007/978-3-642-18167-2_10
33. Subash, A.: IoTivity – connecting things in IoT. In: TIZEN Developer Summit, pp. 1–48 (2015)
34. Campo, A.D., Gambi, E., Montanini, L., Perla, D., Raffaeli, L., Spisante, S.: MQTT in AAL systems for home monitoring of people with dementia. In: Proceedings of the 27th Annual IEEE International Symposium on Personal, Indoor and Mobile Radio Communications (PIMRC), pp. 1–6 (2016)
35. Asim, M.: A survey on application layer protocols for Internet of Things (IoT). Int. J. Adv. Res. Comput. Sci. 8(3), 996–1000 (2017)
36. General Data Protection Regulation (GDPR). https://www.eugdpr.org/. Accessed 19 Mar 2018

A Generic Approach for Capturing Reliability in Medical Cyber-Physical Systems

Argyro Mavrogiorgou[✉], Athanasios Kiourtis, and Dimosthenis Kyriazis

Department of Digital Systems, University of Piraeus, Piraeus, Greece
{margy,kiourtis,dimos}@unipi.gr

Abstract. Cyber-physical systems (CPSs) are slowly emerging to dominate our world through their tight integration between the computational and physical components. While the reliability evaluation of physical systems is well-studied, the one referring to CPSs is difficult due to the fact that software systems do not degrade, as they follow a well-defined failure model like in physical systems. Henceforth, a great attention has been given to tackle the challenge of reliability in CPSs, especially in the field of Medical CPSs (MCPSs) that are being considered as a powerful candidate for healthcare applications. This paper proposes a generic approach for effectively measuring reliability in MCPSs, taking into consideration the multiple MCPSs' applications that exist. The proposed approach captures the MCPS's reliability by initially modelling its components, accompanied with the selection of the evaluation environment, which is finally being followed by the failure analysis, and the reliability estimation, which are necessary for deciding whether a MCPS is considered as reliable or not.

Keywords: Cyber-physical systems · Medical cyber-physical systems
Reliability

1 Introduction

Cyber-Physical Systems (CPSs) are attracting a lot of attention in recent years and are being considered as an emerging key research area, where according to [1], CPS market is globally expected to drive growth through 2027, whilst it is listed as the number one research priority by the US President's Council of Advisors on Science and Technology [2]. A CPS is able to combine computation and communication capabilities with the physical world, meaning that it can control the physical world as well as the connections between objects. Therefore, a CPS is a concept that seeks to converge with the cyber world composed of various physical systems [3], while using a distributed software that implements smart algorithms in order to control these entities. CPSs are able to add smart mechanisms to fully automate manufacturing processes, manage and enhance the operations and safety of environments and infrastructures, enhance energy consumption in smart buildings, or improve healthcare for patients, among others [4, 5].

However, the development of such complex systems that are composed of many distributed and heterogeneous components interacting in various ways and capabilities,

L. Iliadis et al. (Eds.): AIAI 2018, IFIP AICT 520, pp. 250–262, 2018.
https://doi.org/10.1007/978-3-319-92016-0_23

is extremely difficult [4]. CPSs, compared to purely computational or purely physical systems, exhibit quite a number of challenges, as the connection between the computational and the physical entities is far from smooth. Due to device proliferation and large-scale connectivity, a variety of functionalities are now feasible in CPSs. Connectivity however, also means that CPSs function in unreliable open environments, where due to the fact that the software gets further coupled with hardware and users, reliability evaluation becomes a significant challenge [6]. Henceforth, a great attention has been given in particular to tackle this challenge, confronting system reliability as a fundamental requirement of CPSs.

This requirement becomes extremely important to the healthcare domain [7], where CPSs are being considered as a powerful candidate for healthcare applications including in-hospital and in-home patient care [8]. In fact, a separate class of CPSs, namely Medical Cyber Physical Systems (MCPSs) are recognized in the literature [9, 10], as interconnected, intelligent systems of medical devices that support a holistic treatment of a patient. For example, in the context of a hospital, the ones that were previously used as stand-alone medical devices are now being designed with embedded software, and integrated with network interfaces [11, 12]. These network interfaces are used to communicate with other devices during patient treatments as well as monitoring, and healthcare systems [13]. Hence, MCPSs constitute a technological chance for new applications in healthcare assuring more advanced care and treatment of patients.

However, the development of a systematic reliability analysis of CPSs, especially in the healthcare domain, has not received an adequate consideration. To address this challenge, in this paper a generic approach is proposed that can be used to effectively measure the reliability in MCPSs. This approach captures a general MCPS's reliability following four (4) sequential steps. Initially, the modelling of the MCPS's components takes place, whilst afterwards, the selection of the evaluation environment occurs, followed by the failure analysis, and the reliability estimation that are necessary for finally deciding whether the MCPS is being considered as reliable or not.

The rest of this paper is organized as follows. Section 2 describes the study of the state of the art regarding MCPSs and their applications, while the challenges of the MCPSs are being analysed, citing a more detailed view of the reliability challenge. Section 3 describes the proposed approach for measuring reliability in MCPSs, while Sect. 4 is addressing the future challenges, analyzing our conclusions and plans.

2 Related Work

2.1 Medical CPS

The term "Cyber-Physical System" was created a few years ago. The concept had existed for several decades, as the Computer Science and Engineering community has been dealing with it by calling CPSs as "real-time computing systems" or "embedded computing systems" [14]. However, the last few years, those terms have been replaced by the official name of "Cyber-Physical Systems", suggesting that these systems provide the people with much more properties and functionalities. In particular, the definition from Cyber-Physical Systems Week [15] refers to the CPSs as "complex engineering systems that rely on the integration of physical, computation, and communication processes to function". In more details, CPSs refer to the integration of computation with physical processes (i.e. they are about intersection, not the union of the physical and the cyber [16, 17]). In that case, embedded computers and networks monitor and/or control the physical processes based upon local and remote computational models, usually with feedback loops, where physical processes affect computations and vice versa [18–20]. In other words, CPSs are specialized computing systems that interact with control or management objects, integrating computing, communication, and data storage with real world's objects and physical processes, in a real-time, safe, secure, as well as efficient manner [21, 22].

CPSs are being applied in many domains [17, 23, 24], however those in the healthcare domain in particular, are among the most remarkable ones. More specifically, in this domain a separate class of CPSs exists, namely Medical Cyber Physical Systems (MCPSs) [10, 17], that are being considered as interconnected, intelligent systems of medical devices that support a holistic treatment of a patient. The inherent feature of MCPSs is a conjunction of embedded software control of networked medical devices with complex safety that always have to match the needs of the patients [25]. Hence, MCPSs are context-aware, life-critical systems with patient safety as the main concern, demanding rigorous processes for validation to guarantee user requirement compliance and specification-oriented correctness [26]. For that reason, medical devices and systems must be dynamically reconfigured, distributed, and interact with patients and caregivers in complex environments. For example, devices such as infusion pumps for sedation, ventilators and oxygen delivery systems for respiration support, as well as a variety of sensors for monitoring patients' conditions are used in many operating rooms. Often, these devices must be assembled into a new system configuration to match specific patient or procedural needs. The challenge is to develop systems and control methodologies for designing and operating these systems that are certifiable, safe, secure, and reliable [27].

Consequently, CPSs' research is revealing numerous opportunities and challenges in the healthcare domain, aiming to transform the delivery of healthcare by enabling smart medical treatments and services [28]. Some examples of these include intelligent operating rooms and hospitals, image-guided surgery and therapy, fluid flow control for medicine and biological assays, in-home sensors for detecting changing health conditions, new operating systems for making personalized medical devices interoperable, and the development of physical and neural prostheses [28, 29]. Other opportunities of utilizing CPSs in healthcare include the introduction of coordinated interoperation of autonomous and adaptive devices, as well as new concepts for managing and operating medical physical systems using computation and control, miniaturized implantable smart devices, body area networks, programmable materials, and new fabrication approaches [30].

2.2   Applications of Medical CPS

The research on CPSs in healthcare is still in its early stages. Although many CPSs' architectures have been proposed in the literature, the number of CPSs' architectures proposed for healthcare applications is very low. However, various research efforts have been conducted on developing CPSs for healthcare applications, based on integrating sensor and cyber infrastructures, and focusing mainly in the areas of the patients' daily living, monitoring, as well as medication intake.

Concerning the patients' daily living applications and their medication intake, the authors in [31] proposed the Ambient-Intelligence Compliant Objects (AICOs) that exist in a virtual layer overlaid by ordinary household objects integrated by various multi-modal and unobtrusive wireless sensors, so as to represent one or more activities of a person. In the same concept, the authors in [32] presented the Wireless Identification and Sensing Platform (WISP) that utilizes the enhanced passive Radio Frequency Identification (RFID) tags with sensors so as to facilitate the data communication from sensor to receiver. The authors in [33] proposed the iCabiNET, a system that utilizes smart RFID packaging. Being capable of recording the removal of a pill by breaking an electric flow into the RFID circuit, using either residential network at home or smart appliances. In the same notion, the authors in [34] presented the iPackage, an intelligent packaging prototype that consists of remote medication intake and vital signs monitoring. More-over, in [35] the LiveNet is presented, which is a real-time distributed mobile platform for monitoring the activities of Parkinson's disease and epilepsy patients. What is more, the authors in [36] proposed a system that detects fall by using an accelerometer on the head level and identify the fall via an algorithm. Finally, the authors in [37] proposed the HipGuard, which is a posture analysis application used for detecting the posture for the recovery period of eight to twelve weeks after hip replacement surgery, by integrating seven sensors positioned in specific locations near surgery.

Concerning the patients' monitoring, the authors in [38] proposed the MobiHealth, a system that gathers data from the wearable sensor devices that the patients carry all day, collecting audio and video signals to provide early response in case of accidents. Furthermore, in [39] the CyPhyS+ system is presented, a comprehensive, low-cost and standards' compliant CPS, based on the concept of Internet of Things (IoT) for remote health monitoring of elderly, while in [25] a dependable MCPS for telecare of pregnant women at home has been presented. Moreover, the authors in [40] presented the Mobile ECG system that uses smart phones as base station for electrocardiography (ECG) measurement and analysis, forwarding the received data to the medical professionals. The authors in [41] presented the CodeBlue, a platform that consists of biomedical sensors (e.g. pulse oximeter, motion sensor), aiming to manage the communication among these devices. Finally, in the same concept, the authors in [42] proposed the AlarmNet, a wireless biosensor network system prototype, consisting of heart rate, pulse rate, oxygen saturation, and ECG system, that is able to monitor all the patients' meas-urements, and provide a graphical user interface to assist healthcare professionals to monitor the vital signs of their patients.

2.3 Reliability in Medical CPS

Due to the importance of MCPSs' applications and the complexity of their development process, huge research efforts have been started on different CPSs' challenges [4, 30, 43]. However, a great attention has been given in particular to the reliability challenge, confronting system reliability as a fundamental requirement of MCPS. More particularly, reliability is a measure of the ability that the system operates as expected under predefined conditions for a predefined duration of time. As systems are composed of a number of components, reliability of systems is expressed through the aggregation of the reliability of each of their components [6]. Reliability may be measured in different ways depending on the particular situation [44, 45], and can be estimated using either a qualitative or a quantitative method. To accurately describe quantitatively the concept of reliability it is essential to define the notions of fault, failure and error, as all of them are highly related to the concept of reliability [20]. However, some systems' reliability cannot be estimated quantitatively due to various reasons (e.g. lack of failure data), and therefore qualitative methods may be applicable.

Reliability has been recognized as a critical requirement for CPSs. In [17] it is pointed out that CPSs will not be deployed into mission critical applications as traffic control, automotive safety, and healthcare without improved reliability. An unreliable system may lead to disruption of service, financial cost and even loss of human life [46–48]. For that reason, the demand for reliability in CPSs, and especially in MCPSs, has constantly been increased. If demands for reliability are not addressed effectively, further deployment of MCPSs will be slowed down in applications [17, 18]. Therefore, the reliability analysis for MCPSs is very challenging, and for that reason a lot of effort has been put into the research area in order to cope with this challenge. More particularly, in [49] a hybrid method that uses fault-tolerant structures with formal verification is proposed. The presented architecture supports the design of reliable CPSs. Another example of such efforts is presented in [50] that describes a service-oriented CPS with a service-oriented architecture and a mobile Internet device [6]. What is more, the authors in [51] developed a reliability model where Markov models are constructed for each component, in order to estimate the reliability of an Integrated Modular Avionics (IMA) system. In the same concept, in [52] a Markov Imbedded System (MIS) is used in order to model dependence between components in a smart power grid. Additionally, in [53] a phased-mission system model, which consists of Markov models for individual components and a binary decision diagram is proposed, so as to analyze the reliability of a fuel management system in an aircraft. Furthermore, the authors in [54] developed a reliability framework through a weighted reliability metric, using individual components' reliabilities and the performance metric of the CPSs considering their services, cyber security, resilience, elasticity, as well as vulnerability. Moreover, the authors in [55] presented the Failure Analysis and Reliability Estimation (FARE), a data-driven approach for reliability evaluation using historical data, accelerated life testing data, and real-world data.

Therefore, it becomes clear that the reliability of CPSs has received great attention in different applications. However, all of the aforementioned researches, do not highlight the complete reliability of the existing systems, which is crucial for any CPS in the healthcare domain. Moreover, most of these approaches are giving specific solutions to problems of a particular domain, arising the need of a holistic approach. Especially in MCPSs a little work has been done, even though this field seems to be of extremely importance, taking into consideration that the MCPSs are expected to be safe and reliable even in changing environments and unforeseen conditions [56]. For that reason, in this paper an approach is being presented that constitutes a generic approach for effectively measuring the reliability in MCPSs. More specifically, this approach provides a set of methods and metrics on failure analysis, as well as reliability estimation for capturing MCPSs' reliability. Therefore, the proposed approach includes a more general and accurate representation of MCPSs' reliability, measuring various metrics for estimating systems' reliability, as well as offering a holistic system representation that covers the different MCPSs' applications that exist. It is worth mentioning that the proposed approach is extensible for accommodating new reliability measurement techniques and metrics. It does not only provide a retrospect evaluation and estimation of the MCPSs' system reliability using past data, but also provides a mechanism for continuous monitoring and evaluation of MCPSs' reliability for runtime enhancement.

3 Proposed Approach

Our approach proposes a generic way for effectively measuring the reliability in MCPSs. More specifically, the proposed approach consists of four (4) different stages: (i) the CPS modelling, (ii) the evaluation environment, (iii) the failure analysis, and (iv) the reliability estimation, as depicted in Fig. 1.

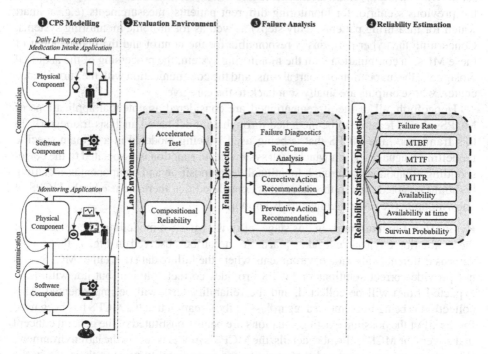

Fig. 1. Proposed approach architecture

CPS Modelling. In this stage of the proposed approach, the modelling of the MCPS's components takes place, using a specific domain modelling language [57] to capture the component-component interactions, whilst taking into consideration the different applications that the MCPSs may be implemented. In more details, the specific MCPS whose reliability is going to be examined, may have been used either for daily living applications, or for patients' monitoring, or for medication intake of patients. As depicted in Fig. 1, the MCPS always consists of the physical or hardware components (i.e. physical part), the cyber or software components (i.e. cyber part), and the communication between them. However, each one of them is differentiating according to the three (3) aforementioned situations of usage of the MCPS.

Regarding the patients' daily living applications and their medication intake, as for the physical part, in both situations this is comprised of a set of networked diverse medical devices (MDs) including biomedical sensors and actuators. The latter are used either for monitoring different patients' measurements (e.g. a smart watch for measuring patients' daily steps) or for capturing whether a patient has taken her medication or not (e.g. an electronic monitoring device for measuring medication adherence). Regarding the cyber part, this is responsible for the control and the management of these MDs, the processing of the acquired biosignals, as well as the invocation of the smart alarms that go back to the patient herself.

Regarding the patients' monitoring, as for the physical part, this is comprised of a set of MDs including biomedical sensors and actuators. The latter are being used, as in the previous scenario, for monitoring different patients' measurements (e.g. a smart watch for measuring patients' daily steps) as well as for in-home monitoring systems. Concerning the cyber part, this is responsible for the control and the management of these MDs, in combination with the monitoring system, the processing of the acquired biosignals, the invocation of smart alarms, and the communication with the surveillance center, whose outputs are finally sent back to the caregiver.

Henceforth, all of the aforementioned are considered as potential applications of MCPSs, being feasible to be modelled through a model-based analysis framework. In this framework, the MCPS that is being used is being modeled in a domain specific modelling language [57] in which each system-level function is associated to the corresponding component(s) through functional decomposition and component association. It should be noted, that in this stage, it is considered that there are used only MCPS of known nature (i.e. their architecture is known).

Evaluation Environment. In this stage, after the MCPS's modelling, the selection of the evaluation environment takes place. As it can be observed in Fig. 1, there exist various different evaluation environments where the failure data (i.e. either MCPS does not provide correct solutions or MCPS provides correct solution, but not within the expected time) will be collected, and the reliability tests will be implemented. This collection is being implemented regardless of the situation that the MCPS has been used for, as all of the possible existing situations are being constituted of the general concept that covers the MCPSs. In more details, the MCPS's model is sent to the lab environment, as medical systems need to be properly tested for reliability prior to their use in the medical operations. To this end, two (2) different types of tests may occur in the lab environment. In the first case, accelerated tests [58] can be applied based on a life test that simulates the actual running environment. More specifically, these tests include the Highly Accelerated Life Test (HALT) in a normal pace, which is similar to the stress test that creates a situation such that failure is more likely to happen. It is a method based on physics of failure, an approach for reliability assessment based on modelling and simulation that relies on understanding the physical processes contributing to the appearance of the failures [59]. However, in some cases the accelerated tests are not applicable in a lab environment, thus the second type of test can be applied. This type, is being based upon the components' reliability data (i.e. compositional reliability) that can be used to construct the whole MCPS's reliability. Although there are many ways to do the compositional reliability [60], it should be noted that these estimates are not often indicative or accurate for representing the whole system reliability, mainly due to the communication failure that is often not easy to be incorporated in these models [61].

Failure Analysis. After the selection of the most suitable case for the lab environment in order to perform the evaluation, the failure analysis stage occurs, which includes the failure detection and diagnostics, along with domain knowledge and heuristics. In general, the operation of a CPS can be divided into three (3) possible scenarios: (i) the CPS provides the correct solution, within the expected time, (ii) the CPS does not provide correct solution (i.e. incorrect solution or no solution at all), and (iii) the CPS provides the correct solution, but not within the expected time. The last two cases are considered as system-level failure cases of a CPS and are being taken into consideration in our proposed approach. In more details, regarding the failure detection, this can be used as a proxy to a system's failure (e.g. an out of range measurement), whilst it might be induced by the external environment, a human mistake or an internal system fault [62, 63].

As for the failure diagnostics, these are responsible for processing the detected failure data using [64]:

(i) the root cause analysis that is used to classify the failure type, analyze its nature and mechanism,
(ii) the corrective action recommendation that is used to correct the current failure and avoid future recurrence of the same type of failure,
(iii) the preventive action recommendation that is used to prevent occurrence of a certain potential failure before it happens.

Reliability Estimation. In the final stage of the proposed approach, after ingesting the failure detection and diagnostics data, the estimation of the MCPS's reliability takes place. More particularly, as mentioned in Sect. 2.3, reliability can be estimated using either a qualitative or a quantitative method. In our approach, we primarily examined and used quantitative methods for MCPSs' reliability estimation, implementing some commonly used reliability metrics [55]:

- *Failure Rate*: It is defined as the total number of failures within an item population, divided by the total time expended by that population, during a particular measurement interval under stated conditions.
- *Mean Time Between Failures (MTBF)*: It is the mean expected time between system failures, in terms of the predicted elapsed time between inherent failures of a system during operation.

- *Mean Time To Failure (MTTF)*: It is sometimes used instead of MTBF in cases where a system is replaced after a failure.
- *Mean Time To Repair (MTTR)*: It is the mean time required to repair a failed component or device.
- *Availability* or *Mission Capable Rate*: It is the proportion of time that a system is in a functioning condition.
- *Power-on hours (POH)*: It is the length of time (in hours), during which electrical power is applied to a device.
- *Availability at time*: It is the probability that the system is able to function on a specific pre-defined time.
- *Survival Probability*: It is the probability that the system does not fail in a time interval (0; t].

Consequently, in order to calculate the reliability of the chosen MCPS in terms of whether it is considered as reliable or not, a pre-defined threshold level is being set for each different reliability metric. Afterwards, the results of each metric are being aggregated, calculating the average value of the pre-defined metrics, and finally deciding whether the MCPS is considered as reliable or not.

4   Conclusions

In this paper, we have raised the importance of addressing reliability of CPSs, by deeply studying the challenging topic of MCPSs' reliability. We have considered all the possible existing applications of MCPSs whose architecture is known in advance, and proposed a generic approach for effectively capturing the reliability metrics of MCPSs so as to calculate the degree of the MCPSs' reliability. In this approach four (4) sequential steps were implemented, beginning from the modelling of the MCPS's components, followed by the selection of the evaluation environment, the failure analysis, and finally, the reliability estimation.

Currently, we are working on the evaluation of the developed approach, by testing it with multiple existing MCPSs in the lab environment. Our future work includes the development of a mechanism that does not require prior knowledge of the used MCPS's architecture. Furthermore, one of our main goals is to extend the existing approach by including more metrics concerning the failure analysis, as well as the reliability estimation. Finally, we are willing to implement a visualization module providing the final results of the approach, enabling the users to observe the reliability results of each MCPS.

Acknowledgements. The authors would like to acknowledge the financial support from the "Hellenic Foundation for Research & Innovations (HFRI)".

References

1. Cyber-physical systems market globally expected to drive growth through 2027. http://www.findmarketresearch.org/2018/02/cyber-physical-systems-market-globally-expected-to-drive-growth-through-2027/
2. Wang, J., Abid, H., Lee, S., Shu, L., Xia, F.: A secured health care application architecture for cyber-physical systems. Control Eng. Appl. Inform. 13(3), 101–108 (2011)
3. Seo, A., Jeong, J., Kim, Y.: Cyber physical systems for user reliability measurements in a sharing economy environment. Sensors 17(8), 1868 (2017)
4. Mohamed, N., Al-Jaroodi, J., Lazarova-Molnar, S., Jawhar, I.: Middleware to support cyber-physical systems. In: 2016 IEEE 35th International Performance Computing and Communications Conference (IPCCC), pp. 1–3. IEEE, December 2016
5. Al-Jaroodi, J., et al.: Software engineering issues for cyber-physical systems. In: IEEE SMARTCOMP (2016)
6. Lazarova-Molnar, S., Shaker, H.R., Mohamed, N.: Reliability of cyber physical systems with focus on building management systems. In: 2016 IEEE 35th International Performance Computing and Communications Conference (IPCCC), pp. 1–6. IEEE, December 2016
7. FDA approves world's smallest pacemaker that attaches directly to heart. http://www.foxnews.com/health/2016/04/07/fda-approves-worldssmallest-pacemaker-that-attaches-directly-to-heart.html
8. Milenkovi´c, A., Otto, C., Jovanov, E.: Wireless sensor networks for personal health monitoring: issues and an implementation. Comput. Commun. 29(13–14), 2521–2533 (2006)
9. Lee, I., Sokolsky, O.: Medical cyber physical systems. In: 2010 47th ACM/IEEE Design Automation Conference (DAC), pp. 743–748. IEEE, June 2010
10. Lee, I., Sokolsky, O., et al.: Challenges and research directions in medical cyber-physical systems. Proc. IEEE 100(1), 75–90 (2012)
11. King, A.L., Feng, L., Sokolsky, O., Lee, I.: Assuring the safety of on-demand medical cyber-physical systems. In: 2013 IEEE 1st International Conference on Cyber-Physical Systems, Networks, and Applications (CPSNA), pp. 1–6. IEEE, August 2013
12. Sokolsky, O., Lee, I., Heimdahl, M.: Challenges in the regulatory approval of medical cyber-physical systems. In: Proceedings of the Ninth ACM International Conference on Embedded Software, pp. 227–232. ACM, October 2011
13. Grispos, G., Glisson, W.B., Choo, K.K.R.: Medical cyber-physical systems development: a forensics-driven approach. In: 2017 IEEE/ACM International Conference on Connected Health: Applications, Systems and Engineering Technologies (CHASE), pp. 108–113. IEEE, July 2017
14. Kim, K.H.: Challenges and future directions of cyber-physical system software. In: 2010 IEEE 34th Annual Computer Software and Applications Conference (COMPSAC), pp. 10–13. IEEE, July 2010
15. Cyber-physical systems week. http://www.cpsweek.org/
16. Lee, E.A., Seshia, S.A.: Introduction to Embedded Systems: A Cyber-physical Systems Approach. MIT Press (2016)
17. Lee, E.A.: Cyber physical systems: design challenges. In: 2008 11th IEEE International Symposium on Object Oriented Real-Time Distributed Computing (ISORC), pp. 363–369). IEEE, May 2008
18. C. S. Group: Cyber-physical systems executive summary. CPS Summit (2008)
19. Cyber-physical systems. http://cyberphysicalsystems.org/
20. Lee, E.A.: Computing foundations and practice for cyber-physical systems: a preliminary report. Technical report, University of California, Berkeley, UCB/EECS-2007-72

21. Rajkumar, R.: A cyber–physical future. Proc. IEEE **100**, 1309–1312 (2012). (Special centennial issue)
22. Skorobogatjko, A., Romanovs, A., Kunicina, N.: State of the art in the healthcare cyber-physical systems. Inf. Technol. Manag. Sci. **17**(1), 126–131 (2014)
23. NIST: Strategic R&D opportunities for 21st century cyber-physical systems. In: Foundations for Innovation in Cyber-Physical Systems Workshop, US (2012)
24. Nannapaneni, S., Mahadevan, S., Pradhan, S., Dubey, A.: Towards reliability-based decision making in cyber-physical systems. In: 2016 IEEE International Conference on Smart Computing (SMARTCOMP), pp. 1–6. IEEE, May 2016
25. Pawlak, A., Jezewski, J., Horoba, K.: Dependable medical cyber-physical system for home telecare of high-risk pregnancy. Ada User **36**(4), 254 (2015)
26. Silva, L.C., Almeida, H.O., Perkusich, A., Perkusich, M.: A model-based approach to support validation of medical cyber-physical systems. Sensors **15**(11), 27625–27670 (2015)
27. National Aeronautics Research and Development Plan. https://obamawhitehouse.archives.gov/sites/default/files/microsites/ostp/aero-rdplan-2010.pdf
28. Cyber-physical systems: enabling a smart and connective world. http://www.nsf.gov/news/special_reports/cyber-physical/
29. Al-Mhiqani, M.N., et al.: Cyber-security incidents: a review cases in cyber-physical systems. Int. J. Adv. Comput. Sci. Appl. **9**(1), 499–508 (2018)
30. Haque, S.A., Aziz, S.M., Rahman, M.: Review of cyber-physical system in healthcare. Int. J. Distrib. Sens. Netw. **10**(4), 217415 (2014)
31. Lu, C.H., Fu, L.C.: Robust location-aware activity recognition using wireless sensor network in an attentive home. IEEE Trans. Autom. Sci. Eng. **6**(4), 598–609 (2009)
32. Philipose, M., Smith, J.R., Jiang, B., Mamishev, A., Roy, S., Sundara-Rajan, K.: Battery-free wireless identification and sensing. IEEE Pervasive Comput. **4**(1), 37–45 (2005)
33. Lopez-Nores, M., Pazos-Arias, J.J., Garcia-Duque, J., Blanco-Fernandez, Y.: Monitoring medicine intake in the networked home: the iCabiNET solution. In: 2008 Second International Conference on Pervasive Computing Technologies for Healthcare. PervasiveHealth 2008, pp. 116–117. IEEE, January 2008
34. Pang, Z., Chen, Q., Zheng, L.: A pervasive and preventive healthcare solution for medication noncompliance and daily monitoring. In: 2009 2nd International Symposium on Applied Sciences in Biomedical and Communication Technologies, ISABEL 2009, pp. 1–6. IEEE, November 2009
35. Sung, M., Marci, C., Pentland, A.: Wearable feedback systems for rehabilitation. J. Neuroeng. Rehabil. **2**(1), 17 (2005)
36. Wang, C.C., Chiang, C.Y., Lin, P.Y., Chou, Y.C., Kuo, I.T., Huang, C.N., Chan, C.T.: Development of a fall detecting system for the elderly residents. In: 2008 The 2nd International Conference on Bioinformatics and Biomedical Engineering. ICBBE 2008, pp. 1359–1362. IEEE, May 2008
37. Iso-Ketola, P., Karinsalo, T., Vanhala, J.: HipGuard: a wearable measurement system for patients recovering from a hip operation. In: 2008 Second International Conference on Pervasive Computing Technologies for Healthcare. PervasiveHealth 2008, pp. 196–199. IEEE, January 2008
38. Konstantas, D., Herzog, R.: Continuous monitoring of vital constants for mobile users: the MobiHealth approach. In: 2003 Proceedings of the 25th Annual International Conference of the IEEE Engineering in Medicine and Biology Society, vol. 4, pp. 3728–3731. IEEE, September 2003

39. Dagale, H., et al.: Cyphys+: A reliable and managed cyber-physical system for old-age home healthcare over a 6lowpan using wearable motes. In: 2015 IEEE International Conference on Services Computing (SCC). IEEE (2015)
40. Kailanto, H., Hyvarinen, E., Hyttinen, J.: Mobile ECG measurement and analysis system using mobile phone as the base station. In: 2008 Second International Conference on Pervasive Computing Technologies for Healthcare. PervasiveHealth 2008, pp. 12–14. IEEE, January 2008
41. Shnayder, V., Chen, B.R., Lorincz, K., Fulford-Jones, T.R., Welsh, M.: Sensor networks for medical care (2005)
42. Wood, A.D., et al.: Context-aware wireless sensor networks for assisted living and residential monitoring. IEEE Netw. **22**(4) (2008)
43. Key design drivers and quality attributes. http://www.informit.com/articles/article.aspx?p=2756464&seqNum=3
44. Thomas, M.O., Rad, B.B.: Reliability evaluation metrics for internet of things, car tracking system: a review, In: I.J. Information Technology and Computer Science, Modern Education and Computer Science (MECS) (2017)
45. Rausand, M., Høyland, A.: System Reliability Theory: Models, Statistical Methods, and Applications, 2nd edn. Wiley, Hoboken (2003)
46. Wu, L.L.: Improving system reliability for cyber-physical systems. Technical reports (2011). http://hdl.handle.net/10022/AC:P:13134
47. Baheti, R., Gill, H.: Cyber-physical systems. Impact Control Technol. **12**, 161–166 (2011)
48. Voas, J., Chillarege, R.: Reliability of embedded and cyber-physical systems. IEEE Secur. Priv. **8**(5), 12–13 (2012)
49. Sha, L., Meseguer, J.: Design of complex cyber physical systems with formalized architectural patterns. In: Wirsing, M., Banâtre, J.-P., Hölzl, M., Rauschmayer, A. (eds.) Software-Intensive Systems and New Computing Paradigms. LNCS, vol. 5380, pp. 92–100. Springer, Heidelberg (2008). https://doi.org/10.1007/978-3-540-89437-7_5
50. La, H.J., Kim, S.D.: A service-based approach to designing cyber physical systems. In: 2010 IEEE/ACIS 9th International Conference on Computer and Information Science (ICIS), pp. 895–900. IEEE, August 2010
51. Wu, Z., Huang, N., Zheng, X., Li, X.: Cyber-physical avionics systems and its reliability evaluation. In: 2014 IEEE 4th Annual International Conference on Cyber Technology in Automation, Control, and Intelligent Systems (CYBER), pp. 429–433. IEEE, June 2014
52. Marashi, K., Sarvestani, S.S.: Towards comprehensive modeling of reliability for smart grids: requirements and challenges. In: 2014 IEEE 15th International Symposium on High-Assurance Systems Engineering (HASE), pp. 105–112. IEEE, January 2014
53. Sun, X., Huang, N., Wang, B., Zhou, J.: Reliability of cyber physical systems assessment of the aircraft fuel management system. In: 2014 IEEE 4th Annual International Conference on Cyber Technology in Automation, Control, and Intelligent Systems (CYBER), pp. 424–428. IEEE, June 2014
54. Li, Z., Kang, R.: Strategy for reliability testing and evaluation of cyber physical systems. In: 2015 IEEE International Conference on Industrial Engineering and Engineering Management (IEEM), pp. 1001–1006. IEEE, December 2015
55. Wu, L., Kaiser, G.: FARE: a framework for benchmarking reliability of cyber-physical systems. In: IEEE Conference on Systems Applications and Technology Conference (LISAT), pp. 1–6 (2013)
56. N. H. C. Software and S. C. Group: High-confidence medical devices: Cyber-physical systems for 21st century health care. Technical report. http://www.nitrd.gov/about/meddevice-final1-web.pdf

57. Pradhan, S.M., Dubey, A., Gokhale, A., Lehofer, M.: Chariot: a domain specific language for extensible cyber-physical systems. In: Proceedings of the Workshop on Domain-Specific Modeling, pp. 9–16. ACM, October 2015

58. Meeker, W.Q., Escobar, L.A.: Statistical Methods for Reliability Data. Wiley, Hoboken (2014)

59. Matic, Z., Sruk, V.: The physics-of-failure approach in reliability engineering. In: 2008 30th International Conference on Information Technology Interfaces. ITI 2008, pp. 745–750. IEEE, June 2008

60. Glaß, M., Yu, H., Reimann, F., Teich, J.: Cross-level compositional reliability analysis for embedded systems. In: Ortmeier, F., Daniel, P. (eds.) SAFECOMP 2012. LNCS, vol. 7612, pp. 111–124. Springer, Heidelberg (2012). https://doi.org/10.1007/978-3-642-33678-2_10

61. He, W., Liu, X., Zheng, L., Yang, H.: Reliability calculus: a theoretical framework to analyze communication reliability. In: 2010 IEEE 30th International Conference on Distributed Computing Systems (ICDCS), pp. 159–168. IEEE, June 2010

62. American Society for Quality. http://asq.org/learn-about-quality/process-analysis-tools/overview/fmea.html

63. Phan-Ba, M.D.N.: A literature review of failure detection. Doctoral dissertation, University of British Columbia (Vancouver) (2015)

64. Croskerry, P.: Diagnostic failure: a cognitive and affective approach (2005)

Advancing Quantified-Self Applications Utilizing Visual Data Analytics and the Internet of Things

Dimitris Chousiadas[1], Andreas Menychtas[2], Panayiotis Tsanakas[3],
and Ilias Maglogiannis[2(✉)]

[1] National Technical University of Athens, 15773 Athens, Greece
dim.chousiadas@gmail.com
[2] Department of Digital Systems, University of Piraeus, 18532 Piraeus, Greece
{amenychtas, imaglo}@unipi.gr
[3] Greek Research and Technology Network (GRNET), 11523 Athens, Greece
tsanakas@grnet.gr, panag@cs.ntua.gr

Abstract. The exponential growth of the number and variety of IoT devices and applications for personal use, as well as the improvement of their quality and performance, facilitates the realization of intelligent eHealth concepts. Nowadays, it is easier than ever for individuals to monitor themselves, quantify and log their everyday activities in order to gain insights about their body performance and receive recommendations and incentives to improve it. Of course, in order for such systems to live up to the promise, given the treasure trove of data that is collected, machine learning techniques need to be integrated in the processing and analysis of the data. This systematic and automated quantification, logging and analysis of personal data, using IoT and AI technologies, has given birth to the phenomenon of Quantified-Self. This work proposes a prototype decentralized Quantified-Self application, built on top of a dedicated IoT gateway, that aggregates and analyses data from multiple sources, such as biosignal sensors and wearables, and performs analytics and visualization on it.

Keywords: Quantified-Self · Internet of Things · Visual data analytics
Personal informatics · Sensors · Activity tracking · eHealth · Containers

1 Introduction

The technological developments of the last decade contributed to an abundance of commercially available and affordable biomedical sensors, activity trackers and wearables. Moreover, these sensors come with specially developed smartphone applications, which enable the users to collect data about themselves, in a systematic and automated manner, and have access to reports and analyses, providing insights and valuable feedback.

The types of data that is collected in the context of Quantified-Self are virtually countless, including but not limited to: health, physical activity, nutrition, psychological and mental state or environment [26]. For each of these categories, several applications exist that focus on the collection and analysis of relevant data, all of them aiming at

© IFIP International Federation for Information Processing 2018
Published by Springer International Publishing AG 2018. All Rights Reserved
L. Iliadis et al. (Eds.): AIAI 2018, IFIP AICT 520, pp. 263–274, 2018.
https://doi.org/10.1007/978-3-319-92016-0_24

highlighting the individual characteristics of the user's lifestyle, identifying his or her strong and weak points and triggering desirable behavior change. Machine learning and big data are technologies that are applied in this area to facilitate that analysis of the data and the creation of personalized knowledge for users and medical experts [8].

According to research, the mere monitoring and logging of values, such as body weight, is effective in itself, by making the user conscious of its importance and in turn, leading to lifestyle changes [17]. The tracking of values over time, additionally, produces insights regarding the user's progress, highlighting the direct relation between their efforts and the results (e.g. systematically going to the gym leads to a decrease of body fat percentage [20]). State-of-the-art solutions include mobile applications for GPS tracking of cardio activities, websites for tracking body weight, fat percentage and bone mass using connected body scales, mobile apps for blood pressure monitoring, apps with integrated activity tracking [24].

Research has shown, however, that over 50% of people using similar applications have given up on them after a few months [11]. Some of the reasons include absence of a holistic approach to data collection and analysis, and lack of customization capabilities [19]. The constant emergence of new applications and corresponding wearable devices, usually incompatible with the previous ones, hardens the adoption of a vendor-free solution like the one proposed in this work. Furthermore, there exist privacy concerns in current Quantified-Self applications, since, typically, the collected data is permanently stored in the cloud, giving ownership and, thus, control of it to the application provider. The greater the sensitivity of the data, the greater the risk for the user, in case of data loss, data manipulation or hacker attacks. Moreover, a lot of providers, in order to maintain the free-of-charge status of their Quantified-Self services, sell the data to third parties (e.g. for advertising or marketing purposes) [13].

The proposed Quantified-Self approach aims to provide the technical and functional background to support data collection from multiple sources, in the context of health and activity tracking, the analysis of that data and the visualization of the results, while taking into consideration the aforementioned shortcomings of the state-of-the-art applications. On the one hand, it allows the user to combine on the same platform several devices, resolving the compatibility issues by exploiting the advancements of Bluetooth communication technologies, and particularly of BLE [15]. On the other hand, being built on top of the innovative software stack of AGILE [1] and deployed on a Raspberry Pi, instead of the typical hybrid deployment in smartphone and cloud, it gives ownership of the data over to the user.

The rest of the paper is structured as follows: Sect. 2 describes the related work in the area of Quantified-Self while Sect. 3 presents the proposed solution and the implementation of the system. The resulting application, with the data analysis and visualization features is presented in Sect. 4. Finally, Sect. 5 discusses the advancements of this approach compared to other approaches, concludes this work and highlights the future plans.

2   Related Work

A Quantified-Self application, such as the one presented here, aims at, not simply quantifying and gathering data, but also exploiting data analysis methodologies and tools to give feedback to the user and promote behavior change. Bentley et al. [3] have studied the ways such change can occur, particularly in the context of health and wellbeing, highlighting the importance of the general (environmental and personal) context of the user's life, a conclusion that has also been reached by Choe et al. [6], who have shown that not tracking context and triggers leads to decreased chances to improve outcomes. This necessitates a holistic approach to data collection, in order to capture and quantify the whole spectrum of this context while in parallel, given the multifaceted nature of the user's everyday life, sophisticated data mining techniques need to be used, in order to uncover hidden, meaningful patterns in it. F. Bentley's et al. research, moreover, explores how users perceive and react to recommendations about behavior change, suggesting that the use of natural language, instead of charts or numbers, can sometimes be more effective.

With regards to the ways IoT data can be harvested, Chen et al. [5] have presented an overview of the various data mining techniques, applied in the context of IoT. What distinguishes IoT systems, concerning data mining, is the requirement for real-time data processing, as well as processing at the edge of the network (Edge Analytics). As an example, such requirements exist in telemonitoring systems, such as the ones presented by Panagopoulos et al. [23] and Aguilar et al. [2], where doctors need to monitor patients and receive notifications in real time. Strongly connected with the above is the research of Li et al. [14], which investigates the potential IoT applications in a more general context than that of health and medical care. More concretely, through the lens of fog computing the researchers highlight the ways Smart Living can be advanced, in various aspects of everyday life (work, entertainment, energy consumption and, naturally, health) through the quantification and analysis of data.

Regarding the specific sensors that are used, as well as the architecture of the sensor network and the flow of collected data, the works of Kor et al. [12] and De Silva et al. [7] make obvious the relevance and applicability of the Internet of Things and Quantified-Self concepts in healthcare and mHealth. Finally, Weinberg et al. [27] have examined the privacy concerns that accompany the transition from Web 2.0 to Internet of Things. Conflicts of interests between users and organizations have elevated data ownership to a crucial issue. In the context of IoT, where data is generated automatically and continually, the question of who owns it is, indeed, of paramount importance.

3   System Architecture

The Quantified-Self concept is targeting data acquisition on aspects of a person's daily life in terms of inputs (e.g. food consumed, quality of surrounding air), states (e.g. mood, arousal, blood oxygen levels), and performance (mental and physical activities) through a modern, health centric, social and mobile enabled, communication platform that resides in the gateway (in terms of collecting and visualizing data).

However, the ecosystem of biosignal sensors and activity trackers is very diverse from both business and technical perspectives. The vendors have also different business and market strategies, and in many cases these strategies are reflected in the devices themselves in technical and operational level. The open source designs for such devices that can be used for producing or communicating with them are uncommon. The hardware and firmware of the majority of the devices is proprietary and closed source, hence establishing communication with the device as a third-party required guidance from the vendors either by providing access to the communication protocols or through libraries/APIs. Therefore, what is usually happening today, is that the users are obliged to use each wearable and sensor with different, companion applications, which store the date to independent systems.

The unique characteristic of the proposed approach is that the Quantified-Self application is deployed on top of an IoT Gateway [18], which eliminates the need for additional applications or hardware. Wearable activity trackers and medical sensors automatically communicate with the gateway whenever within range, and offload the most recent data. However, for the wearables that the manufacturers provide only API libraries for Android and iOS, or specific applications for synchronizing the data with manufacturers' cloud platforms, neither of which is compatible with the proposed setup. In these cases, the activity data offloading is achieved via Internet and the public APIs of the cloud platform.

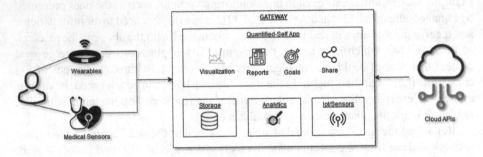

Fig. 1. Quantified-Self concept

Figure 1 presents the general architecture for the proposed Quantified-Self application. Each user connects the various activity tracking devices and biosignals sensors (such as oximeters, blood pressure monitors or glucometers), to monitor their daily physical activity and physical condition. The user is able to visualize and manage the locally stored data and create reports. In parallel, the data are processed and analyzed on the gateway, with personalized recommendations being sent to the users, encouraging them to reach their physical activity goals. In order to address the requirements for modularity and extensibility, the architectural model of the application is based on containers. More specifically, four main containers are deployed on the gateway to provide the required functionality of the application: (a) *IoT/Sensors* for managing the communication with the various sensors and acquiring the biosignal measurements, (b) *Storage* for storing the data locally, (c) *Analytics* for the periodic and ad-hoc analysis of the data in order to create valuable knowledge for the users' health condition and activity and finally (d) *the Quantified-Self Web Application* which coordinates the previous containers and provides a UI with modern reporting and data visualization functionality.

All components of the application (the core application, database and Shimmer) run on a Raspberry Pi, on top of the AGILE Software Stack [18], on a Linux based operating system. The container-based deployment approach of AGILE was adopted, ensuring the virtual isolation of the components from each other and providing the required flexibility for the maintenance and extension of the system with additional features.

3.1 IoT Sensors Integration

The AGILE IoT Gateway software stack is a flexible architecture built for single board computers running independently or on the edge of the network. By providing developers ready, short distance networking abilities, such as Bluetooth or Zigbee, it allows acquisition from local sensors, view and local storing of data. For the integration of the Quantified-Self biosignal sensors and activity trackers, the respective components of AGILE were used. Using the harmonized REST API, the integration of any sensor is simplified in the cases where specific commands or operational workflows are required, custom device drivers are implemented. This approach follows a registration/publish/subscribe device model. Each device needs to be registered before use and the application can subscribe to the sensor data endpoints in order for published data to be streamed to the user. This model works well with BLE devices, which use GATT notifications [4] to stream data to the host.

3.2 Data Management

Attempting to combine on the same platform data from different medical devices, such as oximeters, glucometers, smart scales and blood pressure monitors, introduces significant complexities regarding the storage and manipulation of that data. Integrating, furthermore, data from the cloud APIs of Fitbit [9] and GoogleFit [10], only increases these complexities. The homogeneous and consistent manipulation of the collected data, however, is a necessary prerequisite for any meaningful processing to take place in the system. To this end, the tools developed by the open-source project Open mHealth [22] proved particularly useful. These tools include, a collection of schemata that define the structure of health data. Specifically, these schemata standardize the representation of health data following the syntactic rules of JSON, i.e. key-value pairs, defining the keys to be used for all types of health data. For the purposes of the proposed Quantified-Self application this standardization facilitates the easy and smooth integration of the data, regardless of the source, and simplifies the architectural choices for the database and the REST API. In the case of the medical sensors that communicate with the gateway through BLE, the conversion of the data to JSON objects that comply with the Open mHealth rules takes place during that communication.

3.3 Data Analytics

The amount of the activity and medical data that is collected gives ample opportunity for the analysis of that data and the discovery of patterns in it, providing valuable feedback to the user. The analytics component is based on the python tools of Scikit-learn [25], Matplotlib [16] and Numpy [21] which have been deployed on a specific container configured to communicate with the database and the web application. Scikit-learn, specifically, is a well-known machine-learning library for Python, featuring classification, regression and clustering algorithms, including the k-means algorithm that was extensively used in the proposed application. Numpy is numerical library for Python that provides, primarily, support for multi-dimensional arrays and matrices, designed to interoperate with Scikit-learn. The data visualization was realized utilizing Matplotlib, which is a plotting library for Python, along with the drawing capabilities of the JavaScript programming language.

Since all data are stored locally, the data analytics component periodically, or upon user's request, processes the activity and biosignal data in order to create reports and aggregated information to be presented in the web app. In the current implementation data clustering and correlation techniques have been used, and the results are also exploited to provide motivational messages to the users. Regarding the clustering techniques, data cleaning and pre-processing was necessary. This included removing the outliers from the datasets, normalizing the measurements values, as well as adding potential missing values, either by replacing them with the mean value of the dataset or by filling in the respective values from the nearest data vector in the Euclidean space. Once the data cleaning was done, the data was aggregated, in most cases by day, and the k-means algorithm was applied on that aggregated data.

3.4 Quantified-Self Web Application

The user interacts with the system through a web application, which is also hosted on the IoT Gateway and is only accessible through the local home network and does not expose itself or the user's data to public networks or the Internet. Through the application, the users are able to manage the various IoT sensors (e.g. register and initialize them) and the stored data by communicating with the respective components of the system. The web application also visualizes the user's activity data, collected both from local sensors (if available) and the APIs of GoogleFit and/or Fitbit. The activity consists of the number of steps taken each day, the duration of physical activity every day, as well as the calories burned. Examples of such visualizations are shown in Figs. 2 and 3, where the user can see the number the steps taken during the last 7 days or the average duration of the user's physical activity for each day of week for the last year.

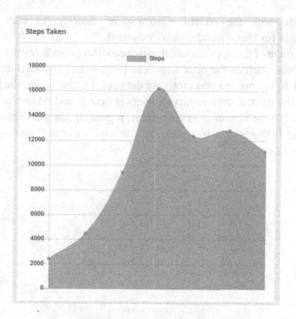

Fig. 2. Number of steps taken the last 7 days

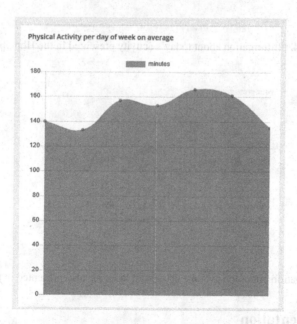

Fig. 3. Duration of physical activity on average per day of week

Another category of data is the biosignals, namely heart rate, blood pressure, oxygen saturation, glucose levels and body weight. These are collected through specific sensors that communicate with the AGILE Gateway or directly, as user input. Similar visualization exists for that second category as well.

On the home page of the application, the user can find general results of the statistical analysis of the data, such as the ones shown in Figs. 4 and 5. Based on these, relevant messages appear to encourage and motivate the user. Furthermore, the system informs the user of how the overall community of users is doing, and he or she compares to it. Finally, there is also the option of setting goals, regarding the performance of the user. Ultimately, these features aim to maximize the user's commitment and bring about improved performance.

Today's Report

You have taken 11110 steps today!
You have reached your daily goal! Congrats!

You have burned 1262 kcal today!
You have 1238 more to burn!

You've been active for 158 minutes today!
You have reached your daily goal! Congrats!

Fig. 4. Information about today's activity presented in the Homepage

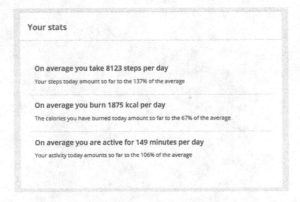

Your stats

On average you take 8123 steps per day
Your steps today amount so far to the 137% of the average

On average you burn 1875 kcal per day
The calories you have burned today amount so far to the 67% of the average

On average you are active for 149 minutes per day
Your activity today amounts so far to the 106% of the average

Fig. 5. Information about the average activity of the user, also presented in the Homepage

4   Experimentation

The proposed Quantified-Self application was provided to real users in order to assess the visual data analytics functionality. The biosignals data were analyzed using well-known k-means algorithm. As an example of this, in particular, the heartbeat and oxygen saturation data have been clustered in three clusters. Specifically, each data point represents the average heartbeat and oxygen saturation measurements in a specific day and the choice of three clusters corresponds to the intuition that, for any given user, there are days with good measurements (green cluster), days with medium measurements (red cluster) or days with bad measurements (blue measurements). Furthermore, using the elbow method, the choice of three clusters was shown to be close to optimal, and it was, thus, selected due to its to intuitive interpretation. Once the clustering has been made, each day can be assigned to one cluster, informing, thus, the user, of the quality of his/ her measurements that day. The results of the clustering can be presented to the user with a pie chart, as in Fig. 6 with the percentage of the user's measurements in each cluster.

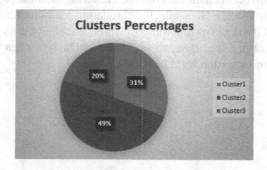

Fig. 6. Percentage of measurements in the 3 clusters (Color figure online)

Another example of how clustering can provide useful insights to the user is presented in Fig. 7. Specifically, each day of week is broken down in the percentages of the measurements of that day that belong to each one of the 3 clusters.

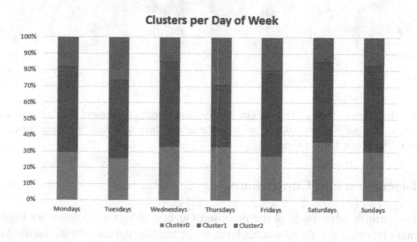

Fig. 7. Clusters per day of week

Moreover, a visualization is also included in the web application in order to provide valuable information to the user presenting the results of the clustering analysis as a time series. Concretely, to each one of the, say, last 30 days, a cluster 1 to 3 is assigned, with cluster 1 representing good measurements, cluster 2 medium measurements and cluster 3 bad measurements. It is possible to see, then, how the clustering changes or, in other words, how the quality of the user's measurements changes between days. In Fig. 8 the visualization of such an analysis can be seen. Specifically, the blue columns represent the cluster values for each day in the last month, whereas the orange ones present the delta of these values, namely, how small or big the change is between days. In this way, significant changes, i.e. anomalies can be traced.

Along with the clustering, the application computes the correlation between the two datasets, using the Pearson Correlation Coefficient, in order to indicate the strength of the linear relationship between the data (for the clustering example presented above, the coefficient is equal to -0.22). Generally, the correlation coefficient can be calculated for any combination of the data types in the application, enabling the user to receive feedback in the form of natural language phrases, such as: "On days when you run more than 20 min, your oxygen saturation level increases".

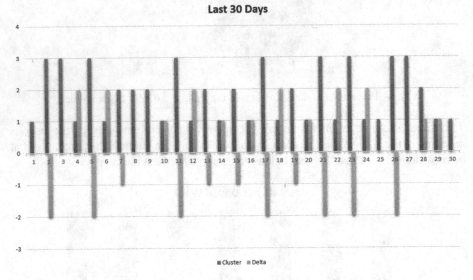

Fig. 8. Time series of the clusters of last 30 days: the blue bars represent the cluster to which each one of the last 30 days belongs, whereas the orange bars represent the change of clusters between days (Color figure online)

5   Discussion and Conclusions

The competitive advantages of the proposed Quantified-Self application are twofold. The main innovation, on the business level, is the fact that the data remain on the user's gateway, while data processing and analytics are provided locally. On the technical level, the infrastructure of the AGILE Gateway supports communication with and integration of several devices on the same platform. These two, combined, bring several benefits for the end-user, as well as for the developers' community. Furthermore, the visualization that the application employs provide valuable feedback to the user. The combination of different charts, shapes, coloring and phrasing of the results aim at enabling the users to intuitively understand and interpret their behavior and performance.

The application proposes a fully automated solution that requires minor engagement of the user, making it suitable for people unfamiliar with technology. What further makes the solution user-friendly and advances its ease-of-use is the fact that the underlying IoT gateway can be built using affordable, commodity hardware. Moreover, the native support for modularity, extensibility and high customization, without the need to speed effort across the different layers and components of the gateway, is one of the most important benefits for the Quantified-Self application allowing for its continuous evolution and adaptation following the users' growing requirements and the new technological solutions and trends in the domain.

The application will be further extended by employing more sophisticated gamification techniques to advance the goal setting and data sharing features, as well as additional machine learning methods, like classification or regression, which would be used to predict value for the user, such as future body weight. Furthermore, there is also room for the integration of more interactive and informative visualization tools, which would build on top of the existing ones.

Acknowledgements. Dr. A. Menychtas acknowledges the Greek State Scholarship Foundation (IKY). This research was implemented with a Scholarship from IKY and was funded from the action "Reinforcement of postdoctoral researchers" of the programme "Development of Human Resources, Education and Lifelong Learning", with priority axes 6, 8, 9 and it was co-financed by the European Social Fund-ESF and the Greek State.

References

1. AGILE-IOT, H2020 EU Research Project. http://agile-iot.eu
2. Aguilar, K.M., Campbell, R.S., Fiester, A., Simpson, R.L., Hertel, C.: Bringing care home: how telemonitoring can expand population health management beyond the hospital. Nurs. Adm. Q. **38**(2), 166–172 (2014)
3. Bentley, F., Tollmar, K., Stephenson, P., Levy, L., Jones, B., Robertson, S., Price, E., Catrambone, R., Wilson, J.: Health Mashups: presenting statistical patterns between wellbeing data and context in natural language to promote behavior change. ACM Trans. Comput.-Hum. Interact. (TOCHI) **20**(5), 30 (2013)
4. Bluetooth GATT specifications. https://www.bluetooth.com/specifications/gatt
5. Chen, F., Deng, P., Wan, J., Zhang, D., Vasilakos, A.V., Rong, X.: Data mining for the internet of things: literature review and challenges. Int. J. Distrib. Sens. Netw. **11**(8), 431047 (2015)
6. Choe, E.K., Lee, N.B., Lee, B., Pratt, W., Kientz, J.A.: Understanding quantified-selfers' practices in collecting and exploring personal data. In: Proceedings of the 32nd Annual ACM Conference on Human Factors in Computing Systems, pp. 1143–1152. ACM (2014)
7. De Silva, A.H.T.E., Sampath, W.H.P., Sameera, N.H.L., Amarasinghe, Y.W.R., Mitani, A.: Development of a wearable tele-monitoring system with IoT for bio-medical applications. In: 2016 IEEE 5th Global Conference on Consumer Electronics, pp. 1–2. IEEE, October 2016

8. Fawcett, T.: Mining the quantified self: personal knowledge discovery as a challenge for data science. Big Data 3(4), 249–266 (2015)
9. Fitbit. https://www.fitbit.com/eu/home
10. GoogleFit. https://www.google.com/fit/
11. Ledger, D., McCaffrey, D.: Endeavour Partners Report: Inside Wearables: How the Science of Human Behavior Change Offers the Secret to Long-term Engagement (2016)
12. Kor, A.L., Yanovsky, M., Pattinson, C., Kharchenko, V.: SMART-ITEM: ioT-enabled smart living. In: Future Technologies Conference (FTC), pp. 739–749. IEEE (2016)
13. Leibenger, D., Möllers, F., Petrlic, A., Petrlic, R., Sorge, C.: Privacy challenges in the quantified self movement–an EU perspective. In: Proceedings on Privacy Enhancing Technologies, pp. 315–334 (2016)
14. Li, J., Jin, J., Yuan, D., Palaniswami, M., Moessner, K.: EHOPES: data-centered Fog platform for smart living. In: 2015 International Telecommunication Networks and Applications Conference (ITNAC), pp. 308–313. IEEE (2015)
15. Mackensen, E., Lai, M., Wendt, T.M.: Bluetooth low energy (BLE) based wireless sensors. In: Sensors, 2012 IEEE, pp. 1–4. IEEE (2012)
16. Matplotlib: Plotting library for the Python. https://matplotlib.org/
17. McGrath, M.J., Scanaill, C.N.: Wellness, fitness, and lifestyle sensing applications. In: Sensor Technologies, pp. 217–248. Apress, Berkeley (2013)
18. Menychtas, A., Doukas, C., Tsanakas, P., Maglogiannis, I.: A versatile architecture for building IoT quantified-self applications. In: IEEE 30th International Symposium on Computer-Based Medical Systems (CBMS), pp. 500–505. IEEE (2017)
19. Menychtas, A., Tsanakas, P., Maglogiannis, I.: Automated integration of wireless biosignal collection devices for patient-centred decision-making in point-of-care systems. Healthc. Technol. Lett. 3(1), 34 (2016)
20. Munson, S.A., Consolvo, S.: Exploring goal-setting, rewards, self-monitoring, and sharing to motivate physical activity. In: 6th International Conference on Pervasive Computing Technologies for Healthcare (PervasiveHealth), pp. 25–32. IEEE (2012)
21. Numpy: Package for scientific computing with Python. http://www.numpy.org/
22. Open mHealth. http://www.openmhealth.org/
23. Panagopoulos, C., et al.: Utilizing a homecare platform for remote monitoring of patients with idiopathic pulmonary fibrosis. In: Vlamos, P. (ed.) GeNeDis 2016. AEMB, vol. 989, pp. 177–187. Springer, Cham (2017). https://doi.org/10.1007/978-3-319-57348-9_15
24. Pcmag.com: The best fitness trackers of 2017. http://www.pcmag.com/article2/0,2817, 2404445,00.asp
25. Scikit-learn: Machine learning in Python. http://scikit-learn.org/stable/
26. Swan, M.: The quantified self: fundamental disruption in big data science and biological discovery. Big Data 1(2), 85–99 (2013)
27. Weinberg, B.D., Milne, G.R., Andonova, Y.G., Hajjat, F.M.: Internet of things: convenience vs. privacy and secrecy. Bus. Horiz. 58(6), 615–624 (2015)

Author Index

Printed in the United States
By Bookmasters